Education and Social Stratification in South Korea

Education and Social Stratification in South Korea

Shin ARITA

University of Tokyo Press

First English edition is published on February 2020
by University of Tokyo Press.
Copyright © 2020 by Shin Arita

All rights reserved. This book, or parts thereof, may not be reproduced in any form or by any means, electronic or mechanical, including photocopying, recording or any information storage and retrieval system now known or to be invented, without written permission from University of Tokyo Press

University of Tokyo Press
4-5-29 Komaba, Meguro-ku, Tokyo 153-0041, Japan
Website: http://www.utp.or.jp/

Printed in Japan
ISBN978-4-13-057201-9

Table of Contents

Preface to the English Edition ... v

Introduction. Framing the Issues 1

PART I: THEORY, STRUCTURE, AND INSTITUTIONS

Chapter 1. Theoretical Considerations 15
   I. Functionalist Theories: Techno-Functionalism, Industrial Society Theory, and Human Capital Theory ... 16
   II. Screening Theory ... 18
   III. Conflict Theory ... 21
   IV. The Consequences of Educational Expansion ... 24
   Conclusion ... 28

Chapter 2. Social Stratification and Industrialization 31
   I. Social Stratification and Mobility in Traditional Society ... 31
   II. Industrialization and Change in the Employment Structure ... 35
   III. Occupational Hierarchy and Change ... 41
   IV. The Structure of Occupational Prestige in South Korea ... 50
   Conclusion ... 58

Chapter 3. School Education and the Selection System 61
   I. The School System in South Korea ... 61
   II. Secondary and Higher Education Policies and Their Influence on Selection Systems ... 66
   III. The Social Issues of Supplementary Study ... 84
   Conclusion ... 90

PART II. ECONOMIC REWARDS, OCCUPATIONAL STATUS, AND SOCIAL MOBILITY

Chapter 4. The Monetary Benefits of Academic Credentials 95
   I. Fluctuations in Average Wage Gaps ... 96
   II. Analysis of Wage Gaps by Estimation of the Wage Function ... 103
   III. Private Rate of Return on Investment in Higher Education ... 112
   IV. Time-Series Analysis on Demand for Advancing to Higher Education ... 117
   Conclusion ... 124

Chapter 5. Academic Credentials and Occupation Acquired............................ 127
    I. Occupational Opportunity and Academic Credentials: The Macro Statistical View ... 128
    II. New College Graduate Employment Processes and How They Changed ... 139
    III. The "Higher Occupational Status" Effect: Comparative Analysis of High School Student Job Preferences ... 169
    Conclusion ... 183

Chapter 6. Academic Achievement, Social Class Origin, and Social Mobility 187
    I. Structure and Classification of South Korean Social Classes ... 189
    II. Effects of Social Class Origin and Academic Credential on Socioeconomic Status ... 194
    III. Effect of Social Class Origin on Educational Achievement ... 201
    IV. Educational Achievement and Intergenerational Social Mobility ... 215
    V. Characteristics and Mobility of the Old Middle Class: Achievement of Socioeconomic Status without Advanced Education ... 222
    Conclusion ... 233

Chapter 7. Images and Impact of the Academic Credential Society 237
    I. Review of Images of the Academic Credential Society ... 237
    II. Perceptions of Academic Meritocracy and the Issue of Distribution ... 243
    III. Diagnosis of the Education System in South Korea ... 247

References ... 253

Index ... 271

About the Author
Shin ARITA, is professor at the Institute of Social Science, the University of Tokyo. He majored in sociology as an undergraduate and earned his Ph.D. in area studies from the University of Tokyo. He also studied at Seoul National University and served as visiting scholar at Stanford University. He has expanded his research from Korean studies into comparative sociology, and his current interests include the labor market, education, and social stratification in East Asian countries. He has recently launched the SARI (Sociological Analysis of Reward Inequality) project to explore why and how reward inequalities are legitimized from the sociological perspective by conducting a comparative survey in Japan, South Korea, and the United States. Some of his recent publications are: *Sociology of Reward Inequality Based on Employment Positions: A Comparison of Non-standard Employment and Social Stratification in Japan and Korea* (in Japanese, University of Tokyo Press, 2016); "Inequality in Educational Returns in Japan" (with Yoshimichi Sato), in Fabrizio Bernardi and Gabriele Ballarino (eds.), *Education, Occupation and Social Origin: A Comparative Analysis of the Transmission of Socio-Economic Inequalities* (Elgar, 2016); "Educational Expansion and Labor Market Entry of New Graduates in Korea and Japan," in Hyunjoon Park and Kyung-keun Kim (eds.), *Korean Education in Changing Economic and Demographic Contexts* (Springer, 2014). Through these publications, as well as the original Japanese edition of this book, *Kankoku no kyoiku to shakai kaiso* (Education and Social Stratification in South Korea; University of Tokyo Press, 2006), he was awarded several academic prizes including the JSPS (Japan Society for the Promotion of Science) prize, the Award for the Promotion of Studies on Developing Countries, and EHESS/Fondation France-Japon Best Paper Award.

Preface to the English Edition

The people of the Republic of Korea (South Korea) are remarkable for the intensity of their desire for education. In order to be able to obtain high scores on college entrance examinations in the future, even elementary school students take extra study classes until late at night. Whole families are known to emigrate abroad to assure their children will acquire proficiency in English. Many South Korean parents channel all their resources into their children's education.

Why do South Koreans have such a strong desire for educational attainment? This book explores the advantages of acquiring academic credentials and people's perceptions of them to answer this question. Based on analysis of a wide spectrum of documentary and statistical data, the study explains the drive to acquire advanced education from the perspective of the social structure of South Korea.

This study attributes the intensity of people's drive to achieve academic superiority to the optimistic social perceptions of the status achievement obtainable through education. At least until the 1990s, the time frame examined in this book, it was widely accepted in South Korea that anyone could attain a distinguished academic pedigree as long as they made sufficient effort and had sufficient ability, and that academic credentials could largely determine a person's socioeconomic status.

This book focuses on the two factors that contribute to forming such optimistic social perceptions and that fuel the strong ambitions for educational achievement that pervade South Korean society. The first is the large gap in social prestige between white- and blue-collar workers; South Korean students focus their occupational preferences on the white-collar jobs they believe have more social prestige. Furthermore, because there is a large gap in remuneration among companies in South Korea, it is generally taken for granted that achieving more advanced educational attainment than competing candidates is required in order to obtain the preferred white-collar job at a large corporation. Given such occupational preferences and the structure of competition, the "socioeconomic-status-determining effect of academic credentials" ("academic credentials effect," for short) will be sustained at a high level, making the competition for higher academic credentials increasingly intense.

The second factor is that a distinct notion of the fair distribution of educational opportunity and a unique set of educational policies based on that notion of fairness are in place in South Korea. South Koreans believe that educational opportunity is the passport to promotion to higher socioeconomic positions. For this reason, they are extremely sensitive about how evenly such opportunities are distributed.

In this social environment, the South Korean government has enforced quite distinctive and drastic measures in implementing its policies on equal opportunity in education. Specifically, it has pursued a formal and thoroughgoing policy of equal access to education at the elementary and lower secondary levels, and has taken measures to level the quality and standards of education offered by high schools. For the college entrance examinations, the government requires the use of multiple-choice tests, which are believed to provide "objective judgment" of student abilities. On the basis of applicants' scores on these tests, it distributes students to institutions of higher education, from the top-ranking universities that are believed to be the gateways to high socioeconomic positions to the lower-ranking institutions. This was long considered to be the "fair" method of selection. The government's efforts to establish such an open and fair selection system has the secondary effect of persuading people to take part in the competition, thereby further increasing the number of participants.

The social characteristics of South Korea described above are much different from those of Japan, which is also known for the intensity of the competition around its entrance examinations and is used as reference for comparison in this book. Regarding the selection system, Japanese high schools are broadly differentiated by level of academic performance required, and the high school entrance examinations serve as a means of measuring performance, allowing some idea of what paths are open to each student after high school. In other words, prior to confronting the college entrance examinations, through the process of undergoing high school entrance examinations and the socialization they experience in high school itself, Japanese students' aspirations are gradually shaped to become more realistic. (Nakamura 2003)

The structure of occupational preferences, too, is also quite different between the two countries. In Japanese society, a solid tradition of craftsmanship and preference for manual labor occupations has been sustained to a certain degree, whereas the majority of South Korean students prefer white-collar work, as described in chapter 5. This difference is another reason the aspiration for educational achievement in South Korean society is much more intense than that in Japanese society.

This book describes South Korean society in the 1990s and before. Since then, South Korea has experienced drastic change in its societal and economic conditions, including the turmoil caused by the Asian monetary crisis.[1] As a result, while trust in the benefits of academic credentials has not changed, people have come to suspect that the competition for academic credentials and higher socioeconomic positions is becoming more advantageous to individuals from the wealthier strata of society. The optimistic social perception that anyone could attain a distinguished academic pedigree by sheer effort and ability has become a thing of the past. The fact that differences in the level of wealth now clearly determine one's success in both academic achievement and employment is wryly expressed in the phrases popular among young people these days, "Were you born with a silver spoon in your mouth?" or "Were you born with a wooden spoon in your mouth?"[2] The optimism of the past is clearly fading.

Discontent with the present situation has led to strong criticism of members of the upper classes for using their personal influence to secure academic credentials and jobs for their children. In fact, in 2016, it was revealed that Choi Soon-sil, a friend of then president Park Geun-hye, had used her position to have her daughter admitted to a prestigious university in Seoul. The popular indignation at such favoritism became part of the movement later launched against Park that ultimately forced her to resign.

Although current expectations in South Korea of being able to climb the social ladder with academic credentials are much more rigid than the optimistic aspirations that prevailed during the period described in this volume, the findings of this book are still essential to understand education and society in South Korea today. The methods for distributing educational opportunity considered desirable by the social consensus in the 1970s and 1980s formed the premise behind the "ideal" that later emerged in South Korean society. Even today that ideal is the point upon which people base their criticism of the current situation and determine the direction for the educational system. I believe that observing the principles South Koreans have regarding equal distribution of educational opportunity and fairness of selection systems explored in this volume will give the reader a much deeper understanding of Korean society and its perceptions of education.

One conclusion that may be drawn from this study is that South Korea has been relying too much on the principle of equal distribution of educational opportunity as a means for overcoming social and economic inequity. While sustaining the

---

[1] The issues of status attainment through education and inequity among the social classes since the monetary crisis are an important theme that deserves a whole book in itself. That task must be left for the future, leaving this book to present analysis of data from the 1990s and before.
[2] The original wordings in Korean are "a golden spoon" and "a dirt spoon," respectively.

tension of its rivalry with the North Korean regime, South Korea has found it nearly impossible to implement the pseudo-socialistic policy of redistribution of social resources. "Equal opportunity in education" was a relatively easy-to-implement anti-inequality policy—perhaps the only anti-inequality policy—the free nation could pursue. As a result, in addition to the transmission of knowledge and technology, the South Korean educational system was burdened with the social function of ensuring "fairness" in the selection of students for admission to schools. To fulfill this, educational institutions—particularly high schools—had to take extreme measures, sometimes at the expense of their original purpose in society. By comprehensively discussing these issues, this book offers useful suggestions about how emerging nations can build educational institutions and selection systems to respond to rising popular aspirations toward academic attainment.

This book is a translated and revised version of the text of *Kankoku no kyōiku to shakai kaisō: "Gakureki shakai" e no jisshōteki apurōchi* (Education and Social Stratification in South Korea: An Empirical Approach to the "Academic Credential Society"), published by the University of Tokyo Press in 2006. I am deeply pleased to be able to share the results of my research with English readers. I would like to thank Dr. Cho Shinil at La Roche College in the United States for his original draft of the translation, the Center for Intercultural Communication, particularly Lynne E. Riggs and Takechi Manabu, for supporting its further editing and polishing for publication, and Goto Kensuke, the University of Tokyo Press for managing the whole process of publishing this book.

One of the features of sociological research in Japan is, I believe, its sensitivity and detailed attention to the social contexts and institutional conditions of the society it is studying. This is the research environment in which I have pursued my investigation of Korean society. I hope this book will contribute to readers' deeper understanding of East Asian societies with both the similarities and the subtle differences in their social contexts and institutional conditions.

Acknowledgement
The translation and publication of this book is supported by Grant-in-Aid for Publication of Scientific Research Results (18HP5177) from the Japan Society for the Promotion of Science, the grant for publication of English books from the University of Tokyo, and the Core University Program for Korean Studies (AKS-2014-OLU-2250002) from the Ministry of Education of the Republic of Korea and Korean Studies Promotion Service of the Academy of Korean Studies.

INTRODUCTION

Framing the Issues

Education occupies a unique status in South Korea, and every aspect of society is influenced by the characteristically Korean phenomena of education deriving from that unique status. Explaining how education is integrated into South Korean society may therefore be considered the key to understanding that society.

Intense Aspirations toward Educational Achievement
The zeal with which people strive to attain higher levels of education is one of the most remarkable features of education in South Korean society (Seth 2002; Sorensen 1994). Aspirations toward academic achievement in comparison to standard of living have been extraordinarily high from the time the country regained its independence in 1945 to the present day.[1] The rapid expansion of education in South Korea was made possible because parents who wished their children to receive a high level of education were willing to shoulder educational costs on behalf of a government that remained fiscally weak (Umakoshi 1981). Unlike governments in many other developing countries, South Korea's government was not very concerned about the issue of improving the nation's level of education.

Aspirations toward educational achievement were already high in the last quarter of the twentieth century, which is the main period of analysis in this book. A 1996 survey of middle and high school students showed that 14.2 percent of middle school students planned to attend junior college (short-term vocational institutions of higher education), and 65.6 percent intended to enter a four-year college. Furthermore, 16.7 percent wished to go on to graduate school. This means that nearly 96 percent of middle school students wanted to advance to higher education (Korean National Statistical Office 1999). The survey also showed that 95.3

---

[1] Korea was colonized by Japan from 1910 to 1945.

percent of high school students wished to pursue higher education, indicating that the era of universal aspiration to higher education had already arrived in the 1990s in South Korea.

The high level of educational ambition reflects more than the wishes of the students themselves. One of the characteristics of Korean society was that parents were actively engaged in the education of their children, and they were willing to make tremendous sacrifices to support their children's efforts. The frenzy surrounding after-school private tutoring, referred to as "shadow education" (Bray 1999), which was one of largest social issues in South Korea for many years, is one indication of their fervor. Parents who wanted their offspring admitted to prestigious universities were willing to go to extraordinary lengths to give their children even a small competitive advantage in preparing for the college entrance examinations. According to a survey conducted by the Korea Consumer Agency in 1997, Koreans spent close to 12 trillion won (equivalent to approximately 13 billion US dollars at that time) on supplementary private tutoring (Korea Consumer Agency 1997: 3). This amount is equivalent to approximately 10 percent or more of the government budget, and is the same as the amount spent on public education in the general government account. Another survey conducted in 2017 reported that the total amount spent on private tutoring for elementary, middle, and high school students had increased to 19 trillion won (approximately 17 billion US dollars), although the number of students had fallen by more than 30 percent (Korean National Statistical Office 2018).

In addition to the financial burdens it entailed, this single-minded focus on educational attainment also gave rise to various societal problems. The ferocity of the competition around Korea's college entrance examinations, fueled by the zeal of both students and parents to gain entrance to the most prestigious schools, became widely known. Survey data revealed that one out of four high school students who went to cram school received therapy for stress and symptoms of depression (Korea Consumer Agency 1997: 205). In fact, the intense pressure to excel academically was widely seen as a cause of youth suicide, especially among students who were severely discouraged by their scores on the College Scholastic Aptitude Test conducted by the government each autumn.

The appetite for educational achievement among South Koreans affected social phenomena that might seem unrelated to education. One example was population migration: parents' desire to improve their children's educational opportunities caused many to move to cities where the educational environment is believed to be better. This is one reason, it is believed, for the high population density of Seoul, especially in certain school districts. Korea's birthrate, which is one of the lowest in the world, is another issue that correlates with educational ambition. In order to obtain a high-level education with the limited funds they can devote to it, families conclude it is better to have fewer children and invest more per child. Such decisions within each household have accelerated the decline of South Korea's birthrate.

The Korean aspiration toward educational achievement, which is quite distinct from that found in other nations, can be characterized by three qualities. First, it is very intense. The financial and other resources that the average consumer of education invests or is willing to invest are apparently greater in South Korea than in other countries. The ratio of total private expenditures for education to GDP reached 2.96 percent in 1998, which was much higher than the US ratio of 1.61 percent, the 1.17 percent spent in Japan, and the 1.11 percent spent on average in the OECD countries (TRI-KITA 2002: 14).[2] The ratio for non-monetary costs of education in South Korea is similar. For example, the amount of time spent by Korean elementary, middle school, and especially high school students on preparing for the college entrance examination is much greater than in other countries. A survey of elementary and middle school students (ages 7 to 15) conducted in South Korea, Japan, and the United States shows that South Korea has the highest ratio of students who study two hours or more every day after school (63.6 percent), which is significantly larger than the U.S. (41.4 percent) and Japan (23.2 percent) (Youth Affairs Administration, Management and Coordination Agency 1996: 23–24). This intense educational ambition is characterized not only by the extraordinary motivation of the students, but also by the willingness to devote substantially more monetary and non-monetary resources to academic achievement.

Second, the high level of educational ambition is very persistent. As shown in chapter 4, neither the strong demand for advancement of education nor the cost of implementing educational achievement in South Korea are decreasing because demand for higher education is increasing as household income level (i.e., the ability to pay the cost of higher education) increases. The following observation accurately sums up this tendency: "When we observe historical experience in South Korea, passion for education once ignited does not easily subside" (Lee Jong-Gak 2000: 23).

Third, the high level of academic aspiration is universal; it can be observed in all strata of Korean society. In fact, previous studies clearly show that not only middle-class parents, but also farming and working-class parents had very high expectations for the education of their children during the process of industrialization (Bae Jong-Geun and Lee Mi-Na 1988; Korean Educational Development Institute 1993). According to the aforementioned survey of three countries, depend-

---

[2] The ratio began to fall in the late 2000s due to increased public spending on education and the shrinking of the student population.

ing on their academic background, income, and occupation, parents in Japan and the United States have very different expectations regarding whether their children will complete a four-year or higher degree. However, there is no significant difference in South Korea (Youth Affairs Administration, Management and Coordination Agency 1996: 126).

Optimistic Images of the Benefits and Opportunities of Education
Why are aspirations toward educational achievement so intense in South Korea? The standard answers to this question, from a historical and cultural point of view, often refer to the influence of Confucianism, along with strong respect for the literary arts and the traditional higher civil-service examination system,[3] but the more popular explanations from a social-science perspective cite the socioeconomic benefits and advantages obtained by education. That is, academic credentials correlate to significant differences in wages and occupational position. The higher the level of education received, the greater the income and the higher the position that can be attained. The benefits and advantages are the main driving force behind the zeal for educational achievement.[4]

The "education" that South Koreans want to attain, it should be noted, is seen as unfolding from start to finish within the public education system. They have little interest in educational activities outside the system (Choi Bong-Young 2000: 55). As this suggests, the strong drive for educational accomplishment may not arise from enthusiasm for learning, but rather the desire to obtain the academic credentials provided by public education (Kim Yong-Suk 1986). Underlying that drive is the goal of raising one's socioeconomic position and obtaining the rewards to be enjoyed from such academic credentials.

In fact, the belief that academic credentials will significantly affect the socioeconomic position a person will eventually attain (Sorensen 1994: 28) is broadly shared across Korean society. Kim Bu-Tae points out, based on the results of attitudinal surveys, "Members of our society believe academic credentials and other badges of social value are attained through the effort and ability of the individual," and "they firmly believe in the performance-based system based on the premise that those who put forth diligent effort in the arena of school education will perform well in their studies, and that superior academic performance will bring the person social success" (Kim Bu-Tae 1995: 242).

---

[3] Even the report by the Korean Educational Development Institute (1993), which comprehensively discusses the issue of South Korea's "education fever," states that the "view of education as the key to success and fame," as shaped by the Confucian reverence for literary arts and the traditional higher civil-service examination system, is a factor behind the "education fever" in society today.

[4] For discussion of the causes of "education fever" in South Korean society, see Park Nam-Gi (1994).

This belief in academic achievement as a basis for social status is also shared by the lower-income strata of society. Based on fieldwork conducted among the rural poor, Bae Sook-Hee observes, "They believe that they are poor because they are not educated. Therefore, they believe that the way to escape poverty is to attain education, and they display tremendous enthusiasm for their children's education" (Bae Sook-Hee 1991: 128). What Kim Mee-Ran called "the widespread belief in meritocracy" is precisely the growing belief that advancement in society is based on academic performance (Kim Mee-Ran 2000: 3).

The results of past surveys verify that this is the image South Koreans have of their society. In 2004, a research group (which included this author) conducted the "2004 Korean National Survey on Occupation." The survey of members of the adult male and female population throughout South Korea showed that 63.5 percent of total respondents (903 people) think that "graduating from a prestigious university is essential to obtaining a high social rank and income"; that figure is much higher than the 40.0 percent for Japan (2003 Social Stratification Survey Research Committee 2004a: 48; 2004b: 63).

The South Korean Social Science Research Council reported that over half of the subject group of nearly 2,000 male and female adults it surveyed in 1995 felt that distribution of or access to income or property, law enforcement, employment opportunity, and female remuneration was "unfair." Only about 10 percent of respondents responded that they felt it was "fair." However, more than 40 percent answered that access to educational opportunity was fair, exceeding the proportion of respondents who felt it was "unfair" (Park Jong-Min 1997: 155). This suggests that, although Koreans have a keen awareness of existing socioeconomic disparities and inequities, they do not criticize their level of access to educational opportunities as strongly. This corroborates Kim Bu-Tae's observation of South Koreans' widely shared image of the availability of performance-based educational opportunities.[5]

The generally accepted perception that educational achievement largely determines a person's socioeconomic position and that the distribution of educational opportunities is generally fair also leads people to have a positive view of opportunities for intergenerational social mobility. According to the Social Statistics Survey (1994) conducted among male and female adults by the National Statisti-

---

[5] However, this perception of fairness began to change with the financial crisis that occurred in 1997 and its harsh effects on South Korean society. Criticism of the gaps in educational opportunity between lower-income and higher-income families has gradually been rising. In fact, according to the aforementioned 2004 Korean National Survey on Occupations, only 28.7 percent agree with the statement, "The opportunity to receive higher education is available to everyone regardless of differences in wealth." Although this book mainly studies South Korean society before the financial crisis, further detailed discussion of such changes in social images is needed.

cal Office of Korea, 60.3 percent of respondents agreed that "there is a good possibility that the social position of children will be higher than that of their parents in South Korean society today." Only 7.6 percent answered "the possibility is small."[6] The proportion of respondents agreeing on the possibility of *intra*-generational social mobility decreased significantly from the 1980s to 1990s, but the ratio of those agreeing about the possibility of *inter*-generational mobility remained high. It is interesting to note that the responses showed no correspondence to the academic background and area of residence of the subjects. These results imply that optimistic acceptance of the possibility of intergenerational upward mobility through education is widely shared across all levels of Korean society.[7]

The Validity of Positive Perceptions and Previous Research
The question we must ask, however, is whether popularly held positive images of the benefits of education and distribution of educational opportunities accurately reflect reality. If they do, South Korea might be recognized as an ideal society in which opportunities for upward social mobility are open to everyone. If that were the case, even if the highly competitive approach to education has triggered various societal problems, they would be accepted as the social costs of maintaining the system of fair distribution of opportunity.

Of course, it is possible that such an ideal does not prevail in reality. If social perceptions do not accurately reflect the reality of South Korean society, then they become a mere ideology that conceals the actual inequalities in society. Does attainment of academic credentials have a significant effect in climbing the socioeconomic ladder? Is it possible to achieve higher social status through academic credentials in South Korea because different societal classes have equal opportunity to access education? If that is true, what are the conditions that make it possible?

To answer these questions, we need to analyze the distribution of the social resources, such as educational and occupational opportunities, that underlie educational aspirations. Analysis of the distribution of educational opportunity, the effect of academic credentials on wages and promotion, and opportunities to gain social status and social mobility through academic credentials can play a significant role in understanding people's intense drive toward educational achievement and revealing the functions of education in South Korean society.

However, few studies have been made from that broad perspective. Of course,

---

[6] Both quotations are from "Social Indicators in Korea," National Statistical Office of Korea (1996).
[7] Needless to say, most people in South Korean society recognize that the power and wealth of a portion of the rich and privileged classes tend to be passed on to their children, and that it is not only the principle of merit that determines the distribution of wealth and achievement.

empirical research has been conducted on particular topics, as they are core subjects of sociology, economy, and the sociology of education. Since prior studies on individual subjects will be referred to in the following chapters, here we only list them briefly. Regarding economic research on educational background and its relationship to wages and job opportunity, pioneering work was done by Park Se-Il (Park Se-Il 1984) and other authors, including Jeong Jin-Hwa (1996), and Jeong Jin-Ho et al. (2004). Cha Jong-Chun and Chang Sang-Soo also conducted empirical studies on education and social mobility in South Korea (Cha Jong-Chun 1992; 1997; 2002; Chang Sang-Soo 2001). In addition, Kim Young-Hwa and other sociologists of education have conducted research on disparities in educational opportunity among the social classes and disparate opportunities for achieving status through education (see, for example, Kim Young-Hwa 2000).

As mentioned above, many of these previous studies are limited to considering rather specific topics, and there is little research that comprehensively examines the role of education in the attainment of socioeconomic status and social mobility by focusing on the unique context of South Korean society. The majority of such studies have been conducted by South Korean scholars in their home country, and they often lack a clear comparative point of view from which to identify the particular characteristics of South Korean society.[8]

Several studies on the relationship between the desire for educational achievement and the social structure have been conducted from a broad perspective. These include a study by the Korean Educational Development Institute (1993), which was the first comprehensive study to directly address the subject of "education fever"; one by Kim Bu-Tae (1995) examining various aspects of the academic credential society in relation to the characteristics of South Korea's system of dependent state-monopoly capitalism; and a study by Kim Mee-Ran (2000) revealing the structure of the academic meritocratic society of South Korea. However, these educational research studies tend to fall short in their empirical analysis of the effect of academic credentials on socioeconomic position in South Korea from the perspective of the social sciences.[9] Other valuable studies are Kim Dong-Chun (2000), which explains "education fever" in terms of the political and economic order, the social structure, and the ruling system; and Seth (2002), which is the first English

---

[8] However, excellent empirical studies on South Korean education and society from a comparative perspective have been published since the 2000s (Park Hyunjoon 2003; Sandefur and Park Hyunjoon 2007; Byon Soo-yong and Kim Kyung-keun 2010; Park Hyunjoon 2013, Park Hyunjoon and Kim Kyung-keun 2014).

[9] In addition, although Oh Mahn-Seug et al. (2000), Oh Ook-Wahn (2000), Lee Jong-Gak (2003), and other researchers have been conducting research on "education fever" in South Korea, they tend to approach the issue from educational or historical and cultural points of view, and thus do not empirically examine it in relation to socioeconomic structure.

book to comprehensively address "education fever" in South Korea. In terms of empirical validation of their arguments, however, they suffer the same limitations as the other studies. Furthermore, the study of "education fever" in South Korea has generally been discussed from a static point of view; very little research looks dynamically at how educational aspirations and what elicits them have changed over time, such as the effects of the rapid expansion of the educational system in South Korea on people's academic ambitions.

Research Objectives and Research Questions
Considering the social conditions in South Korea and the trends in research described above, the purpose of this book should be defined as follows: to examine, through international and time-series comparisons, the widespread perceptions that the effect of academic credentials on socioeconomic status is great, that educational opportunities are equitably distributed, and that intergenerational social mobility is easy to achieve, and to determine whether these perceptions reflect the reality of South Korean society in the last quarter of the twentieth century. In addition, based on that examination, this book will also attempt to reveal the social factors underlying people's desire for educational achievement and the role education plays in the distribution of resources in South Korean society.

In order to achieve these purposes, what issues should be examined? Noting that aspirations toward educational achievement in South Korea can be characterized as intense, persistent, and universal, this book must discuss the following three corresponding issues.

First, are the socioeconomic benefits acquired by education great enough to explain the intensity of academic ambition? Are academic credentials worth the high cost of acquiring them? To elucidate this issue, we will analyze the effect of academic credentials on socioeconomic rewards and status in South Korean society as compared to other societies.

However, there is more to consider. We must also explore how South Koreans perceive the effects of academic credentials on their socioeconomic status and what truly motivates them to pursue educational attainment. Quite a bit of previous research has been done on this subject, but very few studies discuss the significance of those effects for South Koreans. While noting the unique aspects of occupational prestige in Korea, we will understand how the objective effects of academic credentials on socioeconomic status are converted into subjective motivations for academic achievement from Korean people's point of view.

Second, regarding the persistence of people's educational ambitions, we must examine how the effects of academic credentials on socioeconomic status have shifted. Here, we need to determine how the rapid expansion of education prompted by people's enthusiasm for educational achievement has affected the socioeconomic advantages afforded by academic credentials. As discussed in chapter 1, the theory of equilibrium suggests that expansion of education would reduce the advantages of academic credentials, in turn dampening people's motivation toward educational achievement. An empirical study examining how the expansion of education has changed the advantages of academic credentials in South Korea, and comparing the results with theoretical projections, should therefore shed significant light on the correlation between academic credentials and socioeconomic status in South Korea.

Third, concerning the degree of universality, we need to study the disparities in educational opportunity and attainment of socioeconomic status that prevail among social classes. Are there really no disparities from one level to another in the acquisition of academic credentials? Is it possible that anyone, regardless of their social-class origin,[10] can obtain high socioeconomic status once having acquired "high" academic credentials? Based on the results of empirical analysis, this book will reveal, from a broad perspective, the relationship between opportunities for upward social mobility and educational achievement in South Korean society.

Considerations for Analysis

A number of considerations guide the analysis of these issues. First, the assessment and analysis of academic credentials needs to focus not only on differences in vertical stages (whether a person has completed high school, university, graduate school, etc.), but also horizontally, on the "school pedigree" among institutions at the same level. The level of education and the academic credentials that are the primary determinant of socioeconomic position are not necessarily preordained, but may vary according to the social and educational background conditions. That being the case, we must first attempt to determine at which stage of the educational system and in what respects differences in people's educational careers become significant in determining their socioeconomic status.

Second, overly simplistic application of quantitative methods and frameworks that ignore specific contexts should be avoided. As the above issues are subjects relatively suited to quantitative analysis, this study mainly applies the statistical method to social-survey data.[11] Regarding the issues of education and social mobility, various quantitative methods have been developed in close connection with the analytical framework. Using those methods, once a data set for a particular society

---

[10] In this book, the author uses the term of "social-class origin" in a broad sense to include differences in both parental occupation and educational background.
[11] This book, of course, applies non-quantitative techniques as required for supplementary purposes, depending upon the issue.

is obtained, it is possible to generate analytical outcomes very easily. If those methods are applied mechanically, however, without considering the unique context of the society under study, there is a risk of obtaining outcomes that do not reflect reality. To avoid that risk, the assumptions of each method are checked as required and variables and categories are chosen carefully to refine the quantitative analysis. Adequate knowledge of the context and background of the subject of analysis is crucial to interpret the outcomes properly.

Third, this book focuses on how people perceive the realities of the social structure and what meaning they attach to those realities based on their own point of view. To better understand South Korean society, it is necessary in order to bridge the gap between analysis of the objective aspects of social structure (such as the effect of academic credentials on socioeconomic status) and subjective issues such as people's aspirations for academic achievement. In a sense, people's "subjective and stratified world of meanings" (Hara and Seiyama 2005: 163), which is taken for granted even by South Korean researchers, should be examined in order to bridge the gap. It is hoped that attention to the above considerations will ensure the most productive quantitative study of Korea possible.

This book consists of two parts, one comprising three chapters describing the background and context of academic credentials and the social structure in Korea, and the other presenting three chapters of empirical analysis on specific issues forming the backdrop of Korea's academic credential society. Chapter 1 discusses why and how individual academic credentials are connected to socioeconomic status and rewards, and reviews previous theoretical research on the topic. It also compares the projections set out by each theory as to the consequences of educational expansion, and then attempts to refine the analytical tasks for this book.[12]

Chapter 2 discusses the social structure of South Korea during its rapid industrialization, in particular describing in detail the changes in societal class structure. This chapter also carefully examines the characteristics of occupational prestige in South Korea and how they have changed in order to reveal the objective and subjective inequities within the division of labor in South Korean society.

Chapter 3 looks at how the South Korean educational system, particularly the school system and the selection system for secondary and higher education, has changed to reflect the education policies of successive government regimes. We also consider how the characteristics of the school system and selection system have shaped the nature of academic credentials and affected the distribution of educational opportunity and the state of entrance examination competition.

---

[12] Readers wishing to read about education and society in South Korea immediately can skip this theoretical chapter and come back to it as needed.

Figure 1. Framework for Analyzing Education, Status Achievement, and Social Mobility

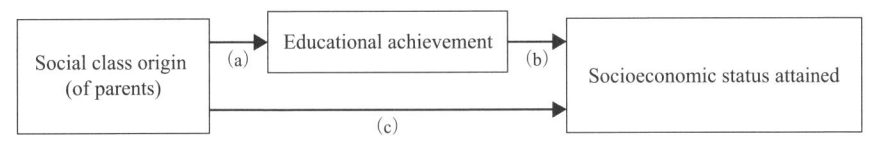

```
┌─────────────────┐       ┌─────────────────────────┐
│ Social class    │  (a)  │ Educational achievement │  (b)   ┌──────────────────────────┐
│ origin          │──────▶│                         │───────▶│ Socioeconomic status     │
│ (of parents)    │       └─────────────────────────┘        │ attained                 │
└─────────────────┘───────────────────(c)───────────────────▶└──────────────────────────┘
```

Part II presents empirical analyses of the relationship between education and achievement of socioeconomic status or social mobility in South Korea. Chapters 4 and 5 analyze the relationship between academic credentials and the social status attained, which is depicted by arrow b in figure 1. Chapter 4 also takes up the issue of the monetary benefits for those who obtain a university or college degree in South Korea, conducting an empirical analysis of the wage structure. In addition, it discusses how the rapid increase in college graduates in the 1980s altered those benefits and affected people's demand for higher education over time.

Chapter 5 examines the relationship between acquired educational credentials and occupation, with the latter greatly affecting the position of an individual in the social hierarchy as well as his or her income. In this chapter, we consider what effect a college degree has in raising an individual's occupational status, observing the various practices that affect new graduates in their job hunting and their selection of employment. Furthermore, in order to understand how the effect of educational achievement on occupational status benefits people, we compare the occupational aspirations of high school students in South Korea with those of Japanese students.

Based on the results of the analyses conducted in the previous chapters, chapter 6 considers the interrelation of social class origin, educational achievement, and attained social status. Here, we study the disparity in educational opportunities by social status origin (arrow a in figure 1), the direct effect of social status origin on attained social status that is not mediated by educational achievement (arrow c in figure 1), and the "possibility of attaining a social status that requires no higher educational achievement" in the self-employment sector. The discussion of changes in the openness of social mobility through education is based on an integration of the results of all these findings.

The final chapter reviews the subjects proposed in the introduction to discover the nature of South Koreans' intense drive for achievement in education. We also discuss the social function of education, particularly that demanded of the school education system, and reveal the structure of South Korean society.

While the direct subject of this book is a consideration of the relationship between education and socioeconomic status in society, it also reflects the author's commitment to elucidating the structure of South Korean society through a focus on education. As will be demonstrated in detail, various institutions of South Korean society are premised upon strong expectations of and optimism toward upward social mobility through education, and it is upon that unique basis that the issue of distribution of social resources is "solved."[13] In other words, education is uniquely embedded into South Korean society. The book empirically reveals not only the relationship between education and socioeconomic status, but also people's attitudes regarding the desirable relationship between the two and the policies that the South Korean government has been implementing in order to shape that relationship.

---

[13] In this sense, this book discusses how a society in the throes of industrialization using a state-led economic development strategy under a free economic system has attempted to utilize the education system to "solve" the distribution issue, how successful the attempt has been, and what impact the attempt has had on society and the educational system.

PART I

Theory, Structure, and Institutions

CHAPTER 1

Theoretical Considerations

In a society where industrialization has advanced to a certain degree, there is a more or less positive correlation between people's level of education and their socioeconomic status. What factors are behind this correlation? Why can people who have completed more education earn more and increase their status in society?

A system in which rewards are differentiated by level of education acts as a motivation to achieve higher levels of education. If people can gain greater rewards by attaining an advanced degree or attending an institution of greater prestige, their academic ambitions will increase, collectively fueling the expansion of education in society. However, the expansion of education may change the level of reward received by having attained an advanced degree, and consequently drive people's academic ambitions. What impact does the resultant expansion of education have on socioeconomic status and people's aspirations toward educational achievement? As we will observe below, different theories may have opposite predictions about that impact depending upon how the relationship between academic credentials and socioeconomic status is viewed.

This chapter examines major theoretical perspectives regarding the correlation between people's level of education and socioeconomic rewards; the objective is to reveal how the consequences of educational expansion are predicted differently depending on the theoretical perspective. In so doing, I attempt to construct a sound theoretical foundation for conducting an empirical analysis of the relationship between academic credentials and socioeconomic status as well as changes in that relationship in South Korean society.

I. FUNCTIONALIST THEORIES: TECHNO-FUNCTIONALISM, INDUSTRIAL SOCIETY THEORY, AND HUMAN CAPITAL THEORY

The theories examined in this chapter vary markedly in their explanations of how differences in ability and attribution correspond to differences in educational background, and what determines socioeconomic rewards. The various forms of functionalist theory provide answers that are relatively close to what would be considered common knowledge regarding these two points.

Functionalist Theories in Sociology

Davis and Moore attributed differences in socioeconomic rewards according to position in the social structure to two factors: first, the functional importance of a given position in society; and second, the training and talent required to carry out the duties of that position (Davis and Moore 1945: 243). The existence of this kind of mechanism in a society in which socioeconomic rewards are variable motivates people to seek higher positions and perform the duties of their position. This mechanism allows for the efficient distribution of human resources—that is, the assignment of the right person to the right job throughout society—thereby making the efficient management of society possible.

According to the Davis-Moore theory, any position in the social structure requires certain skills and abilities. Education being a training process enabling people to improve the abilities and skills required to perform work, the more education they receive, the more important positions they can attain at higher levels of skill and ability (Davis and Moore 1945: 244). Needless to say, since the rewards for such positions are greater in order to compensate for the longer-term training, according to this theory, there is a positive correlation between level of education and socioeconomic rewards.

The supposition that education nurtures skills and abilities required to perform work—and that individuals in society receive compensation according to their skills and abilities—often appears as a dominant theme in industrial society theory. In an industrial society where technological innovations are made every day, the skill levels required for work are continuously rising, and this leads to emphasis on acquisition of ever-higher levels of skill; i.e., completion of more advanced education in order to obtain better positions (Clark 1962; Kerr et al. 1960).

Industrial society theorists assume that the education system in an industrial society is completely different from the traditional education system of previous times, and offers training that is useful for enhancing the productivity of the industrial labor force (Kerr et al. 1960). They also generally expect that people will obtain greater rewards from working in the more industrialized sectors of society that require higher levels of skill. Thus, it is assumed that the positive correlation between educational level and socioeconomic status will grow stronger with the advance of industrialization.

It is further assumed that such changes accompanying industrialization tend to increase opportunities for social mobility. Industrial society theory considers that, in accordance with the demand for greater efficiency in society that accompanies the development of industrialization, people are singled out and their status in society is determined not by such attributes as class affiliation or family origin, but by their own individual achievements (Kerr et al. 1960; Lipset and Bendix 1959, etc.). Since individual achievement is substantially affected by modern school education, this creates more opportunities for social mobility through education. According to these theorists, the necessity for maximum utilization of human resources in the industrialization process leads to a marked expansion of educational opportunities, and at the same time to the implementation of educational reforms aimed at distribution of educational opportunity based on the principle of merit. Quantitative and qualitative changes in the distribution of educational opportunity not only increase but also equalize opportunities for social mobility through education (Erikson and Goldthorpe 1992: 5–6).

Human Capital Theory

While the above theories are mainly in the field of sociology, human capital theory presents the same explanation for the relationship between level of education and wages as treated in the field of economics. It extends neoclassical economic theory to the subject of education by viewing educational advancement as "investment in human capital" (Becker 1964; Schultz 1963; Mincer 1974).

Similar to the functionalist theories, the fundamental premise of human capital theory is that school education is capable of increasing individual productivity through acquisition of knowledge and skill (Becker 1964: 40–42). In other words, it presumes that a person with a better educational background will be a more productive asset to economic activity. Human capital theory, within the paradigm of neoclassical economics, also presumes complete information in the labor market. For this reason, it is assumed, an employer can easily comprehend a worker's potential productivity at the time of employment, and will pay according to the marginal productivity of the person hired. On these assumptions, people with a better educational background will be able to sustain higher labor productivity utilizing the ability they have acquired, which in turn assures them a higher wage level.

Based upon these assumptions, acquiring education is understood as a sort of investment in oneself. The individual thus exchanges payment of various expenses (including foregone earnings resulting from attending school instead of working) for monetary advantages to be accrued in the future by attaining the capacity for increased productivity through advanced education. Furthermore, human capital theory holds that each individual decides whether to advance to the next level of education by comparing the cost against the expected increase in future income at current values (Becker 1964: chap. 2).[1]

The logic used by human capital theory to explain the relationship between academic credentials and wages is similar to that of the functionalist theory in sociology, but there is a fundamental difference. In classical functionalist theory the differences in rewards corresponding to level of education are assumed to appear due to social structural factors, whereas in human capital theory—or the neoclassical economics upon which it is based—the differences in rewards are the result of the employer's pursuit of economic efficiency.

II. Screening Theory

The various functionalist theories reviewed above emphasize the function of education in improving labor productivity and regard an individual's education level as the level of their ability enhanced by education. However, there are other, quite different views that are critical of such functionalism. Screening theory is one.

Screening Theory Assumptions

Screening theory[2] (Arrow 1973; Spence 1973; 1974; Stiglitz 1975) considers that a person's level of education correctly reflects their ability, and therefore regards the distribution of rewards according to level of education as based on the principle of merit, as do the other theories of functionalism. However, when it comes to the effect of education on ability, screening theory adopts the opposite interpretation.

Screening theory holds that education does not always improve a person's productivity, or that it contributes nothing to productivity. So why, according to screening theory, do people with higher academic credentials receive higher wages? One of the reasons is that, compared to the functionalist theories discussed in the previous section, screening theory makes completely different assumptions about information on the labor market. Contrary to neoclassical economics, screening theory assumes the incompleteness (asymmetry) of information on the labor market. In other words, it is very costly to obtain accurate information about a job applicant's potential productivity. Under the circumstances, in the hiring process, employers rely on some other kind of indicator to make up for the lack of information about productivity.

---

[1] In obtaining an education, in addition to the aspect of investment, there is also an aspect of consumption where one's objective is learning itself. However, many advocates of human capital theory do not regard the latter as a direct subject of analysis.

[2] This includes signaling theory, which focuses on the function of signaling from the job seeker's side.

A leading advocate of screening theory, Kenneth J. Arrow, assumes that, even when information about the job applicant's productivity is difficult to obtain, an employer can examine the academic credentials of a job applicant at no cost; furthermore, the distribution of productivity of people with or without college diplomas is known as general information or through previous experience. In this manner, an employer uses the information about whether an applicant has a college diploma as an indicator in making decisions about hiring and pay (Arrow 1973: 194–95). Needless to say, decisions based on such indicators may be considered the "rational" approach under circumstances where information is incomplete.[3]

Why can one's academic credentials be an indicator of productivity and the ability to perform an assigned job? Screening theory points out the affinity between abilities required for achievement in education and performance of a job. In order to earn a higher level of education, one must have a sufficiently high academic performance to pass entrance examinations and perform well on coursework examinations. That ability would include effort and perseverance in studying, as well as intelligence. Such attributes are considered to have a strong correlation with the ability to perform a job. Thus, an employer would conclude that an applicant with a more advanced level of education has a greater capacity to perform a job, and as a result, the applicant would be accorded higher pay and/or higher occupational status.

In this way, screening theory, on the assumptions of incomplete information and a positive correlation between the ability to perform well in study and in work, explains the relationship between level of education and rewards in a manner that is completely different from functionalist theories. According to screening theory, people with better academic credentials obtain higher wages or status not because their education is believed to support an increase in productivity, but because their higher potential ability, which is necessary to obtain better educational credentials, indicates that they will be able to perform a job well. In short, screening theory emphasizes the importance of the screening function that filters out people based on measurement through various tests rather than on the function of accumulating human capital.

Thurow's Job Competition Model

Lester C. Thurow proposed the "job competition model," regarded as an integration of the aforementioned screening theory with internal labor market theory, as a

---

[3] According to Spence, even if the education offered is not particularly useful in providing the knowledge and skill required for performing a job, an individual may be motivated to advance to higher education. In a situation where an employer decides to hire someone based on level of education as an indicator of ability, demonstrating a higher ability than others by receiving a higher level of education (signaling) is rational behavior for a job seeker (Spence 1973; 1974).

challenge to the predominant wage-competition model. In orthodox neoclassical economics, the wage-competition model regards the labor market as an arena of competition in which job seekers vie for wages acceptable to themselves. On the contrary, Thurow argues, "marginal products reside in the job and not in the man," and "the individual's earnings depend upon the job he acquires and not directly upon his own personal characteristics" (Thurow 1975: 77). He assumes that jobs have a definite structure in which wages are fixed regardless of what worker occupies the position.

Such assumptions are closely linked with another important aspect of Thurow's model; namely, assumptions about acquiring the ability to perform a job. Thurow posits that "most cognitive job skills are not acquired before a worker enters the labor market, but after he has found employment through on-the-job training programs" (Thurow 1975: 76). Therefore, the labor market can be described as a "training (opportunity) market" in which workers are distributed to various gateways to training. Thurow further considers that in general, workers are first employed in entry-level jobs, which provide the initial stage of training; after receiving sufficient on-the-job training, they are promoted internally. Thus, according to Thurow's model, workers compete to obtain job opportunities that will afford the greatest amount of training and earn them the highest income.

For employers, the most rational decision for increasing profit is to hire workers who need less training for a job to yield marginal products with the least investment in the costs of training. With the assumption of incomplete asymmetric information in the labor market, Thurow argues that the educational attainment of workers functions as a good indicator of their potential training costs, because "the ability to absorb one type of training probably indicates something about the ability to absorb another type of training" (Thurow 1975: 88).

Such an argument is clearly based upon assumptions similar to those in screening theory regarding the function of education.[4] Academic credentials are used as a measure of trainability or the training cost, and persons with a higher educational background may receive more training and get jobs that pay higher wages.

As observed above, the point at which functionalist and screening theories diverge in their different explanations for the relationship between educational background and socioeconomic status is whether the completeness of information in the labor market is accepted or not. However, screening theory assumes that employers can obtain adequate information on the distribution of productivity of each of the groups with different educational levels by relying on general information

---

[4] However, Thurow does not deny that people in an education curriculum are learning how to be trained.

and past experience, even though it admits that they cannot acquire full information on workers' expected productivity.

Moreover, according to screening theory, the substantive effect of academic credentials on socioeconomic rewards does not originate in the absolute level of education achieved, but rather in the relative level of education, since the level of one's potential ability in comparison with others is the most important. If relative level of education is an important factor in determining socioeconomic rewards, then, as we will see later, the competition for obtaining higher academic credentials than others becomes endless.

Screening theory assumes that the educational system can properly distinguish the potential abilities of students that are closely related to ability to perform a job. Although such assumptions are often introduced to simplify the model, there are no theoretical grounds to guarantee it unconditionally. Rather, whether an employer may use information on academic credentials as a substitute for proven ability largely depends on the actual conditions of the education and selection systems in a society. It also depends on the extent to which people trust the reliability of the education and selection systems.

III. Conflict Theory

The above theories view systems that distribute rewards according to educational level in a positive light, as the reward distribution is based on the merit principle. However, others reject the meritocratic character of such systems, asserting that differences in rewards are established in order for ruling groups to maintain their vested interests. These critics do not believe that a person's educational level reflects their ability to perform a job. How, then, do they explain the relationship between level of education and socioeconomic rewards?

Neo-Weberian and Neo-Marxist Theories

Unlike the functional theorists, who see society as being harmonious, Randall Collins, who is regarded as a neo-Weberian, views society as an arena of conflict over wealth and power among status groups. He asserts that organizations stress academic credentials in hiring not because such credentials indicate the level of knowledge and skill, but rather because they indicate the degree of socialization into the culture of the governing status group (Collins 1971; 1979).

According to Collins, the core activity of schools is not the teaching of knowledge and skills, but rather the inculcation, inside and outside the classroom, in the culture of a certain status group (Collins 1971: 1010). An employer sets academic credentials as the screening criteria in such a way as to identify the extent to which a person has acquired the elite culture, or the attitude of respecting that elite culture. Thus, Collins believes that the higher the academic credentials, the more closely connected a person becomes to higher socioeconomic status, as academic credentials are utilized as a measure of socialization into the mores of the elite culture.[5]

The functionalist explanation for a positive correlation between education and socioeconomic status has been criticized not only by neo-Weberians, but also by neo-Marxists. Bowles and Gintis condemn the assumptions of human capital theory. They assert that the distribution of social status according to academic credentials is based on false meritocracy, and that it directly contributes to reproduction of the unequal social division of labor (Bowles 1971; Bowles and Gintis 1975; 1976).

Bowles and Gintis consider that in a capitalist society the vested interests of the governing capitalist class are significantly projected on the educational system, and that their purpose is to smoothly reproduce the existing hierarchical division of labor. In schools attended by many children of the working class, education is said to focus primarily on rote memorization and teaching students to carry out their assigned tasks obediently. Schools attended by middle-class children, by contrast, will offer education focusing on creativity as appropriate to office jobs in the future; furthermore, they accord the most creative education to children of the capitalist class. Thus, in this view, the educational system is instrumental in teaching children to acquire the personality required to perform future jobs similar to their parents', in accordance with their social class of origin (Bowles 1971).

Furthermore, teachers' differential treatment of students according to social-class origin affects not only students' personality, but also their academic records, ultimately reproducing disparities in educational achievement. In sum, Bowles and Gintis assert that the different levels of educational achievement are not the result of differing levels of intellectual ability, but rather of different social-class origins. Thus, the relationship between level of education and socioeconomic rewards is not mediated by the academic performance of the individual, but rather arises from one's parents' social class or from the values or personality attributes that correspond to that class (Bowles and Gintis 1976: chap. 4). They assert that the positive appraisal of social-status achievement by merit—i.e., that ability and effort determine educational achievement, which then affects socioeconomic status—is just an ideology that conceals the perpetuation of an unequal class structure.

---

[5] Collins admits that "employers tend to have quite imprecise conceptions of the skill requirements of most jobs" (Collins 1971: 1007), based on the hypothesis of "bounded rationality" proposed by March and Simon (1958).

Inequality Perpetuating Education
As described above, these conflict theories do not view the relationship between level of education and socioeconomic rewards as reflecting a just relationship based on merit, but assert that it functions as a core device for maintaining inequality among status groups or classes of society.

However, even if one does not assert, as in neo-Marxism, the strong teleological assumption of an educational system that directly reflects the vested interests of the ruling class, it is highly possible that social inequality is being reproduced through education. Although the aforementioned theories of industrial society optimistically anticipate that merit-based opportunities for social mobility through education will increase, even in an industrial society there is the possibility that educational achievement will be significantly affected by social-class origin due to economic and cultural factors.

Considering the realities of South Korean society, economic disparities in family of origin can be the source of disparity in ability to pay the costs of education, in turn also possibly determining the level of education achieved. The neoclassical economics model assumes that educational expenses—or funds to be invested on education—may be easily procured through the capital market even when funds in hand are lacking. However, in South Korean society, such assumptions about potential sources for procurement of funds are unfounded. It is undeniable that a family's ability to pay for the education of its children can be decisive in the level of education those children achieve.

In South Korea, moreover, the cost of supplementary study, including cram school classes and private tutoring in preparation for entrance examinations, is very high. As will be demonstrated in chapter 3, the gap in the ability to pay for such supplementary study has been criticized as bringing about inequality in educational opportunity. If supplementary study does in fact significantly improve academic performance, as is widely believed in South Korea, the impact of parents' economic status on educational achievement will be all the greater.

However, the influence of family origin on educational achievement does not come only from economic factors. Cultural factors, too, can be significant, as Pierre Bourdieu suggests in his cultural reproduction theory concerning the influence of non-economic factors on education.

Bourdieu points out the importance of inheritance of cultural capital in the family as a factor leading to the reproduction of social classes. Cultural capital is defined as the cultural resources from which a person may benefit in the future, embodied in such pursuits as hobbies, personal cultivation, and manners, or in concrete form such as books and paintings. The volume of cultural capital is very different from one class to another, and is passed on from one generation to the next in a similar manner to economic capital. Thus, families of higher social class will transfer greater amounts of cultural capital to their progeny.

Disparities in cultural capital have a significant influence on status achievement, and school education plays an important role in that process. In the realm of school education, "orthodox" or "proper" culture is more valued than popular culture, and it has greater affinity with the cultural capital accumulated in families of the upper classes. Those who are closest to the upper classes, therefore, possess the greatest quantity of cultural capital that is most highly valued by school education, allowing them to occupy the most advantageous positions in actual educational achievement. Cultural capital accumulated in families is thus converted into academic credentials, and those credentials in turn make attainment of socioeconomic status possible (Bourdieu 1979a; 1979b). According to this argument, the education system plays a role in "approving" inherited cultural capital, contributing thereby to the reproduction of the social class structure.

Many other studies have been conducted on the mechanisms by which social classes are reproduced through cultural factors, including Basil Bernstein's linguistic code theory (Bernstein 1990). According to these theories, even when selection based on merit is carried out formally with "fair" procedures, there will be major disparities in educational achievement depending on class origin, disparities that in turn reinforce class structure.

Taking these arguments into consideration, when we analyze the effect of academic credentials in South Korean society, we need to focus not only on the two variables—educational achievement and socioeconomic status of individuals—but we should also closely examine the effect of class origin on both variables in order to study how differential distribution of socioeconomic rewards based on level of education relates to the reproduction of social inequities. The effect of social-class origin on educational achievement depends on a society's class structure and its education system. For this reason, chapters 2 and 3 of this book will examine the South Korean social-class structure and education system in detail.

IV. THE CONSEQUENCES OF EDUCATIONAL EXPANSION

This section considers aspects of change in the relationship between level of education on the one hand and socioeconomic rewards on the other. If educational opportunities at a certain level are expanded in a context where acquiring academic credentials brings socioeconomic benefits, how does this change the way academic credentials affect socioeconomic rewards? This question is critical because any change in the effect of academic credentials following the expansion of education would affect aspirations in society to advance to the next stage of education.

As we shall see, depending upon the theoretical point of view, assessments of such changes sometimes arrive at opposite predictions of the consequences of educational expansion. In this section, we closely consider the consequences of educational expansion as seen in each theory, particularly focusing on the differences in theoretical assumptions.

Predictions Based on the Wage Competition Model
Regarding the effect of an increasing number of college graduates on wage differences based on education, Thurow contrasts the consequences predicted by the "wage competition model" based on orthodox neoclassical economics with those predicted by the "job competition model" he himself proposes. If the wage competition model is used as a basis, the increase in the number of college graduates lowers the wages of college graduates (Thurow 1975: 119). The increase in supply brings the supply curve down, and consequently the wages of college graduates fall. At the same time, wages of high school graduates remain the same or even increase.[6]

If this occurs, the economic returns from a college education will be diminished. According to the general model of decision-making about advancing to higher education, a decrease in the benefits of pursuing higher education will discourage such ambitions in that society. Thus, in the wage competition model of neoclassical economics, since the market mechanism readily acts to achieve equilibrium both in the labor market and the market of higher education opportunity, academic credentials are not seen as driving the limitless desire to advance to ever-higher levels of education.[7]

However, such predictions are established upon several strong assumptions of neoclassical economics. They assume that the demand and supply of the workforce is matched separately according to skill level (i.e., level of academic credentials) in addition to assuming that information in the labor market is complete. Moreover, the above theories do not take into account differences in occupation, because they do not regard them as an essential factor in wage differences.

Predictions Based on the Job Competition Model
In contrast to the above wage competition model, the "job competition model" proposed by Thurow predicts the result of an increased number of college graduates in a different way. As confirmed above, Thurow's job competition model has the unique characteristic of recognizing that educational level acts as a proxy for potential ability to be trained at a lower cost, and assumes a firm structure of jobs whose wages are fixed regardless of what worker occupies the position. In this

---
[6] The decrease in the number of workers who are new high school graduates raises their wages, because there are fewer of them in the workforce.
[7] From the viewpoint of the techno-functionalist theory proposed by scholars such as Davis and Moore, a very similar consequence is predicted (Davis and Moore 1945: 248).

model, labor productivity and wages cannot be considered without an actual "job" in which one is engaged; wages are paid not for workers' inherent productivity, but for the job they are assigned.

In discussing how the increase in college-graduate workers due to exogenous factors changes the average wage of college- and high-school-graduate workers, Thurow proposes a situation where "education is the only background characteristic" and "all college workers are preferred to all high-school workers" (Thurow 1975: 115). Under these circumstances, since training college graduates is assumed to cost less than training high school graduates, employers allocate the relatively high-wage jobs among those previously given to high school graduates to college graduates, whose numbers have increased, by raising the academic credential requirements. However, those jobs pay lower wages compared to those previously taken by college graduates, which in turn lowers the average wage of college graduates. The overall consequences of this prediction are the same as for the wage competition model.

However, the prediction of the average wages for high school graduates are different from that predicted by the wage competition model. Of all the jobs that high school graduates previously obtained, the relatively high-wage ones have been taken by college graduates, so the average wages of high school graduates become lower. The change in economic returns of a college education is determined by whether the decrease in average wages of college graduates is greater than that of high school graduates, or vice versa. The extent of decrease in average wages cannot be unequivocally decided because it depends on several factors, including the distribution of jobs with certain wages. Nevertheless, Thurow concludes that, in many cases, the disparity between the average wages of college graduates and of high school graduates is maintained, and in some cases, it even increases (Thurow 1975: 189–90).

According to Thurow's model as described above, increasing the number of college graduates does not necessarily reduce the economic advantages of going on to higher education. Moreover, if we apply Thurow's model, it is how high one's education level is compared with others, rather than the absolute level of education, that plays an important role in determining economic rewards. Therefore, "as the supply of more highly educated labor increases, individuals find that they must improve their own educational qualifications simply to defend their current income position" (Thurow 1975: 96). Thurow suggests that once education expands, people want to achieve higher levels of education than they did previously, which may cause excessive investment in education by society.

Dore's "Diploma Disease" Hypothesis
Ronald Dore's hypothesis of "diploma disease" is close to the prediction made by

Thurow, in the sense that it does not see education expansion as reducing people's aspirations toward educational achievement, but rather as inducing the inflation of academic credentials and making competition for acquiring academic credentials more intense. Dore analyzed several societies, including Japan's, and concluded that educational organizations have a stronger screening function in late-developing countries. When an employer decides to hire from among many applicants, he suggested, the workers with the highest academic credentials are likely to be chosen on the assumption that people with higher academic credentials have greater ability and perseverance, even if the job does not actually require such a high level of education. As in screening theory, the value of academic credentials is in relative differences of level, rather than on an absolute level, and the educational background of job seekers is indefinitely inflated by the interaction between (potential) job seekers who attempt to acquire higher academic credentials and employers who raise the threshold of academic requirements as the overall academic credentials of job seekers are enhanced (Dore 1976).

The particularly important premise supporting Dore's assertion is the dual economic structure in a late-developing country; i.e., the large gap in wages between the traditional sector and the modern sector. The later the country's development, the greater the gap between the traditional and modern sectors and the larger the disparity in wages between those sectors. And since, in the case of many developing countries, the modern sector is typically composed of government-run and state-owned enterprises, the relationship between occupation and educational standards is clearly prescribed, so there is a strong tendency for educational attainment to be used as a criterion for hiring. Thus, in cases where there is a significant wage gap between the modern sector and the traditional sector, everyone is eager to obtain the higher academic credentials that are perceived as a "visa" to modern-sector employment (Dore 1976: 2–3). This is the late-development effect asserted by Dore.

These arguments by Dore are close to Thurow's job competition model, in that Dore argues that wages are not directly determined by the workers' productivity but by what jobs they perform, assuming the existence of a firm structure of jobs whose wages are fixed. If we apply Thurow's model to the dual structure presented by Dore, the distribution of jobs whose wages are fixed would have a dual peak with a large wage gap in between. When the number of college graduates increases rapidly under these circumstances, the additional college graduates will take over the job opportunities in the modern sector that high school graduates had previously taken; as a result, the high school graduates are pushed back into the traditional sector. When that occurs, the average wage of high school graduates is predicted to decrease more sharply than the average wage of college graduates, further intensifying aspirations toward higher education. Through these processes, expansion of education intensifies competition for educational attainment.

As summarized above, if we rely on theories that put more weight on the screening function of school education than on the function of accumulating human capital, an increase in the number of individuals with higher academic credentials not only lowers their own average wages, but also those of people with relatively less-advanced academic credentials. This is the greatest point of difference from predictions based on orthodox neoclassical economics. For this reason, the expansion of education may not reduce economic incentives for going on to higher education.[8]

CONCLUSION

Why do people with higher academic credentials attain higher socioeconomic rewards? The explanation offered by the functionalist theories is that school education has the effect of improving students' productivity; those with a higher level of education have the higher levels of skill and knowledge that are required for performing a job, and may demonstrate higher productivity. The screening theory, by contrast, holds that because, in the absence of complete information, employers assume that people with higher educational attainments will have higher potential abilities, they distribute jobs and monetary rewards based on workers' educational level. Nevertheless, both theories agree that the distribution of rewards based on educational level is fair according to the merit principle. Conflict theory, by contrast, understands that rewards systems that are differentiated according to educational attainment are shaped by the dynamic relationships among status groups in society and class-based vested interests, and therefore cannot be considered fair.

Differences among these theories also appear in their predictions of the way the expansion of educational opportunities affects socioeconomic rewards derived from educational attainment. The functionalist theories assert that expansion of education diminishes the effect of academic attainment on rewards, and even reduces the drive to pursue schooling to a higher level, leading to equilibrium in demand and supply on the market of educational opportunity. Screening theory and Thurow's job competition model, however, do not support the notion that expansion of education reduces the effect of academic attainment, which leaves the possibility that competition for educational advancement could continue intensifying indefinitely.

---

[8] It is difficult to draw clear conclusions about the consequences of educational expansion based on conflict theory. However, the conflict theorists who consider the correlation between academic credentials and socioeconomic position a means of reproducing a hierarchical class structure would not make the optimistic assertion that expansion of education reduces inequalities among different academic credentials.

How did education and socioeconomic rewards become so closely tied together in South Korean society, and how has that relationship affected people's aspirations toward educational achievement? In examining these issues in the following chapters, the theoretical observations about the impact of expanding educational opportunities discussed above will carry great significance. By empirically investigating how the rapid expansion of education affects the relationship between academic credentials and socioeconomic rewards, and by comparing the results with the theoretical predictions, we can reveal the essence of the relationship between the two in South Korean society.[9]

For this purpose, we should consider the extent to which the various theories' assumptions about educational systems or the labor market are appropriate when applied to the realities of South Korean society. If a theory can properly explain the change in the effects of academic credentials after the expansion of education, the assumptions that theory is based on would be more suitable to the realities of South Korea. Is it an absolute level of educational achievement that determines socioeconomic rewards, or is it a relative standard? Does ability or productivity determine rewards, or is it the job itself? The following chapters will examine the appropriateness of these theoretical hypotheses for exploring how the education and selection systems in South Korean society influence the effect of academic credentials on socioeconomic rewards.

---

[9] There seems to be only Park Se-Il's works (1982; 1983), which entails rigorous previous research on the longitudinal changes in the relationship between academic credentials and socioeconomic rewards during the rapid expansion of education in South Korea.

CHAPTER 2

Social Stratification and Industrialization

The relationship between academic credentials and later-achieved social status, or that between social class of origin and level of education achieved, is greatly influenced by the structures of inequality in a country. Here, as background for the analysis of the relationship in part II of the book, we examine the characteristics of social stratification in South Korea and how they changed during the period of rapid industrialization after 1945.[1] To that end, the topic of analysis focuses mainly on individuals' occupations. In an industrialized society, after all, a person's social status is largely determined by occupation, and in fact, most empirical studies on social stratification try to understand social status by focusing on individuals' occupations.

I. SOCIAL STRATIFICATION AND MOBILITY IN TRADITIONAL SOCIETY

The social stratification structure in the Joseon era (1392–1897) more or less overlapped with the traditional social class (or status) system, which comprised three major classes: *yangban* (aristocrats), *sangmin* (commoners), and *cheonmin* (the underclass). Although the *cheonmin* were distinguished from others under the law, the *yangban* class—the governing class at that time—"was not established by law, but was a relative and subjective status, which, while it had formed through social custom, was defined by very clear criteria" (Miyajima 1995: 20). Miyajima points out that the aristocrat class was made up of those whose ancestors passed the Korean civil-service examinations, or who had a famous scholar among their ancestors and had a clear genealogical relationship with the person, as well as those

---

[1] Japan's colonization of Korea began in 1910, and Korea's sovereignty was restored in 1945, an event which is known as "the Liberation" from colonization by Japan.

who maintained an aristocratic lifestyle, faithfully performed memorial services to their ancestors, and pursued study for self-cultivation, all of which are criteria rooted in the subjective judgments of community members.[2]

Officially, the civil-service examinations were open to the common people, but in actuality, due to financial and other reasons, most applicants were limited to members of the aristocratic class; members of the commoner class seldom moved into the *yangban* class via success in the examinations. However, the fact that performance-based distribution of social status based on scores on the written examinations had become established even in premodern Korean society paved the way for easy acceptance, in later times, of the idea of status distribution according to the written examination scores.

The common people (*sangmin*) included farmers, merchants, and artisans. The Joseon dynasty, backed by Confucianism and in particular Neo-Confucianism (Cheng-Zhu school), set a high value on developing agriculture but disdained commerce and industry. Consequently, there was no significant development in commerce and industry until the late Joseon dynasty. At the same time, discrimination against commerce and industry was strong, and artisans and merchants were considered to be lower than farmers in social status, even though they all belonged to the same commoner class (Shin Yong-Ha 1991; Yoshida 1998; Ito 2001).

Some point out that traditional Korean society was distinguished from those of Japan and China in that the former "had a relatively rigid social hierarchy, and the principle of the social order centering on the *yangban* penetrated throughout society on the level of daily life" (Suenari 1987: 45). However, even if that principle of the social order was more pervasive in society and consequently the social hierarchy was more rigid than in Japan and other countries—or because it was more rigid—mobility within the Korean class hierarchy was much greater. Of course, this was because social status in Joseon times was not determined only by law. Commoners appear to have expended great effort to move into the *yangban* class by, for example, compiling new "genealogies" and purchasing social status and government posts at that time. In fact, Shikata (1938=1976), Lee Joon-Gu (1993), and others who have used family registry records of the time to identify changes in the class composition of various local societies, have pointed out the significant increase in the *yangban* class and the decrease in the *cheonmin* class. Their arguments are based on the increase in the number of people who held positions that were deemed specific to the *yangban* class. Others, however, have pointed out that not all of those who had such job positions necessarily belonged to the *yangban*

---

[2] However, many *yangban* were landlords in terms of economic class, and exercised considerable economic power.

class (Song Jun-Ho 1987). Nevertheless, through the process of what Miyajima (1995) called "yangbanization," many people who did not belong to the *yangban* class made great effort to raise their status by obtaining *yangban*-level posts. In the late Joseon Dynasty, there was a general recognition that changing social class was not at all impossible. The fact that many commoners of those times attempted to enhance their social status by accepting the culture of the governing class is particularly important in understanding why people of all social strata in South Korean society today are so highly motivated to increase their social standing.

Landlord System Expansion and Differentiation of the Peasantry
With the trend toward increasing exports of grain following the opening of Korea in 1876, and the incursion of Japanese landlords into Korea after the first Sino-Japanese War (1894–95), Korean agriculture gradually came to be dominated by the landlord-tenant system which led to major economic disparities between landlords and tenant farmers. The abolition of the traditional class system during the Gabo Reforms beginning in 1894 heightened the importance of owning farmland as a criterion of social class.

Expansion of the landlord system accelerated under Japanese colonization. The Land Survey Project that began immediately after the 1910 Japan–Korea Annexation Treaty shows that many small farmers who had maintained stable operations were reduced to tenant status because the property rights or occupancy rights the peasants had effectively held until then were often not recognized.

Many farmers, impoverished by the massive shipping of rice to Japan and the expansion of the landlord system under colonial rule, had no choice but to leave the villages where they had been born and raised. Modern industries in Korea, however, had not yet reached the point where they could absorb the labor surplus resulting from the break-up of the farming class. Compared to the Joseon period, when most people had been engaged in agriculture, industrialization advanced somewhat during the colonial period, and Korean industrial capitalists did emerge. But because industry did not yet occupy a substantial proportion of the Korean economy, many farmers moved out of the Korean peninsula to seek jobs in Japan and Manchuria.[3]

During the colonial period, as bureaucratic institutions were put in place, various job opportunities in the public sector became available. However, since important government positions were naturally monopolized by Japanese, Koreans

---

[3] In particular, from the first half of 1930s to the first half of 1940s, the policy of making Korea a "supply base" expanded the industrial sector to a certain degree, and the number of workers in industry increased. However, industrialization during this period was basically capitalintensive, and did not have the capacity to sufficiently absorb surplus employment.

who could not obtain adequate educational credentials served only as low-level officials (Kim Chae-Yoon 1980: 101).

South Korean Society Immediately after the End of Colonial Rule
Not long after the defeat of Japan in 1945, the Korean Peninsula was divided into North Korea and South Korea, with the northern part occupied by the Soviet Union and the southern part by the United States. Major changes took place in South Korean society as a result of subsequent agricultural land reforms and the outbreak of the Korean War.

Among those social changes, the effect of the agricultural land reform was very large. The land reform began when the U.S. occupation distributed the farmland owned by the Japanese during the colonial period. Finally, after many complications, two years after the establishment of the Republic of Korea, in 1950, the land reform law was implemented to distribute farmland owned by non-cultivating landlords and privately owned land exceeding 3 *jeongbo* (7.4 acres) to actual cultivators. However, some landlords got around the change in ownership by establishing a foundation or using another person's name (Park Jin-Do 1987). Nevertheless, while land cultivated by independent farmers (in contrast with land cultivated by tenant farmers) comprised only 35 percent of all farmland at the end of 1945, it increased to 88.2 percent by April 1950 (Korea Rural Economic Institute 1989: 89–90). The agricultural land reform paved the way for the emergence of many independent farmers, and economic disparities in agricultural communities were indisputably reduced (Kuramochi 1994).

Furthermore, in the period immediately after 1945, social mobility in South Korea increased significantly with the repatriation of people from Japan and Manchuria and the influx of people "crossing to the South" as a result of the north-south division, eventually amounting to a total of more than two million people. The outbreak of the Korean War in June 1950 resulted in more than two million lives lost, including those of civilians, and the shifting front lines displaced many people. Amid these dramatic social events, large numbers of people settled in the cities; at the same time, the traditional societal structures that remained in rural areas were also weakened to some extent. The increase in social mobility, together with the weakening of the traditional social hierarchy prompted by the external factors described above, set the stage for the general heightening of popular aspirations toward upward mobility.

Although the urban population represented over 20 percent of the total in the 1950s, the economic underpinnings of the non-agricultural sector were still weak. Among the industrial facilities established during the colonial period, many of the large-scale plants were located in what became North Korea; those located in the South had been significantly damaged in the war. There were small businesses in the tertiary sector at that time, but most of them were tiny enterprises engaged in low-productivity and low-income activities. For this reason, although the ratio of the urban population increased significantly compared to the colonial period, there was no industry that was able to absorb the labor force in urban areas. As a result, in the 1950s, the unemployment rate in South Korea was very high, reaching nearly 20 percent. At that time, the per-capita GNP was less than 100 dollars. Although hardly imaginable nowadays, South Korea was then among the poorest countries in the world.

II. Industrialization and Change in Employment Structure

The Park Chung-Hee regime, established by military coup in 1961, announced the "Five-Year Economic Development Project" the following year and implemented a series of aggressive economic development measures. Since then, South Korea's industrialization has steadily advanced. Many books and articles have dealt with the economic policies and the process of growth in this period (Hattori ed. 1987; Watanabe 1985; Amsden 1989; Wade 1990), so the details need not be repeated in this book. Suffice it to note the following four characteristics that closely relate to the discussion here.

First, the speed of industrialization was exceptionally rapid, when compared to anywhere else in the world. Growth often exceeded 10 percent, and the per-capita GNP, which was less than 100 dollars in 1960, exceeded 10,000 dollars in the mid-1990s. Such compressed rapid industrialization was made possible by taking advantage of "late development" through technology transfer from advanced industrialized countries (Watanabe 1985; Amsden 1989). Second, the industrialization process made the manufacturing industry, with its very large employment capacity, the leading sector. At the beginning of the first Five-Year Economic Development Project, the "import-substitution industrialization strategy" was adopted in order to achieve autarky, but after 1964, the state pursued an aggressive policy of "export-oriented industrialization" in order to foster the export industry (Westphal 1978; Kimiya 1994). Under that strategy, by mobilizing the cheap and abundant labor supply that was its sole resource at that time, the country enhanced the global competitiveness of its products and achieved export expansion, mainly through labor-intensive industry. Through these efforts, the light industries, such as textiles, showed marked growth in the 1960s, and among the heavy and chemical industries, relatively labor-intensive industries like electronics and shipbuilding became the key industries that led the South Korean economy from the 1970s onward. During the process of changing the economic structure, there was considerable labor mobility among industrial sectors.

Third, although the government drew up the blueprint for economic development and attempted to implement it through various industrial policies, most of the actual economic activity was carried out by the private sector following government directives. The large, often family-owned conglomerates (chaebols) that achieved remarkable growth during that period operated their businesses by collaborating with the government's development projects and reaping various benefits selectively provided by the government. In that process, collusive relations between the government and the chaebols were formed. This is the reason the South Korean economy was often described as "crony capitalism," and the monopoly and oligopoly of the chaebols were often the target of social criticism (Kang 2002).

Fourth, the South Korean government strictly controlled and suppressed the labor movement during the economic development period. The economic strategy was to expand exports by taking advantage of low-priced, labor-intensive products. Until real democratization got underway in the late 1980s, therefore, the South Korean government was unsympathetic to the rights of workers and blocked any efforts they made to organize. As a result, the living standard of workers— whose numbers increased dramatically, particularly in the manufacturing sector, during the economic development period—remained at a relatively low level, and their working conditions were also very poor.

Outside researchers have often evaluated South Korea's economic development process, along with those of Japan and Taiwan, as an example of having achieved rapid economic development and relatively equal income distribution at the same time (World Bank 1993). However, the great disparity between the rich, who have accumulated their wealth through collusive relationships with the government, and the poor, who are unable to enjoy the benefits of economic development, has always been considered within South Korea itself to be a major problem.

Changes in the Working Population by Industry and Occupation
South Korea's rapid industrialization from the 1960s transformed the structure of its society. Let us look first at changes in the working population (including the employed and self-employed) by industry and occupation using the census data collected every five years in South Korea.

Figure 2–1 shows that in 1960—which was before full-scale economic development began—nearly 70 percent of the working population was employed in the primary industries (agriculture, forestry, and fisheries). The proportion of the population working in the secondary industries (mining, manufacturing, and construction) was less than 10 percent.[4] After the 1960s, however, the population working

---

[4] Although in Korea the construction business is considered a tertiary industry, we included it as a secondary industry in keeping with international standards.

Figure 2–1. Working Population by Industry

	1960	1966	1970	1975	1980	1985	1990	1995
Agriculture, forestry, and fisheries	66.2	57.2	50.9	49.0	37.8	31.1	20.9	15.9
Mining	0.7	1.1	1.0	0.7	0.7	0.7	0.4	0.2
Manufacturing	6.9	12.0	14.3	17.4	22.1	23.0	27.6	23.8
Construction	1.8	2.4	4.6	3.8	5.2	6.6	7.1	8.6
Electricity, gas, and water supply	0.2	0.3	0.3	0.3	0.3	0.4	0.4	0.5
Wholesale, retail, restaurants, and accommodation	8.5	10.5	12.6	13.4	16.2	17.2	19.4	22.9
Transportation, storage, and telecommunications	2.1	2.1	3.3	3.4	4.3	5.2	5.2	5.3
Social and private services	13.6	14.3	13.0	12.0	13.3	15.9	19.0	22.8
Total	100.0	100.0	100.0	100.0	100.0	100.0	100.0	100.0

Source: Based on the "Report on Population and Housing Census" (Korean National Statistical Office).

in the primary industries rapidly decreased,[5] falling to nearly 10 percent in the 1990s. Although not shown in the figure, as the population by industry rapidly changed, the urban population also increased in a short time period, rising from 28.0 percent in 1960 to 78.5 percent in 1995. Society thus made the transition from an agricultural to an industrial society in an exceptionally short time, outpacing even Japan, which is also known for its rapid industrialization.

The rapid outflow of workers from the primary industries was absorbed by urban industry through intra- and intergenerational mobility. Figure 2–1 indicates that the capacity of secondary industry—the manufacturing sector in particular—to absorb labor was very large, as South Korea accomplished its economic growth mainly through labor-intensive manufacturing. The population working in manufacturing reached 27.6 percent in 1990, a ratio similar to the level in Japan at its highest around 1970.

The percentage of the population working in the tertiary industries also increased greatly; in particular, the proportion of workers in wholesale and retail services and the hospitality and food-service industries was remarkable. However,

---

[5] The absolute number of people engaged in agriculture, forestry, and fisheries began falling in the second half of the 1970s.

38 | Part I   Theory, Structure, and Institutions

Figure 2–2.   Working Population by Occupation   (%)

Year	Professional and technical workers	Administrative and managerial workers	Clerical workers	Sales workers	Service workers	Agricultural, forestry and fisheries workers	Manufacturing (production) and related workers, transport equipment operators, and laborers	Total
1960	2.4	1.3	2.7	8.3	6.1	65.9	13.3	100.0
1966	2.8	0.9	4.3	10.7	5.4	56.8	19.2	100.0
1970	3.2	1.0	5.9	10.2	6.7	51.1	21.8	100.0
1975	3.3	0.8	6.7	10.5	6.5	49.2	23.0	100.0
1980	4.6	1.1	9.5	12.1	7.1	37.6	28.1	100.0
1985	6.1	1.3	12.2	12.6	7.8	30.9	29.1	100.0
1990	7.5	2.1	15.4	14.0	8.8	20.7	31.6	100.0
1995	10.5	4.3	14.5	15.8	11.8	16.1	27.0	100.0

Source: "Report on Population and Housing Census" (Korean National Statistical Office).
Note: The values of the year 1995 are cited from Hong Doo-Seung et al. (1999: 47).

what is important is that the characteristics of the tertiary industries themselves changed markedly. Although prior to economic growth, in 1960, the tertiary industries consisted mostly of small retailers and enterprises engaged in low-productivity activities, their capital and financial stability increased with the advance of economic growth.

Next, let us look at changes in the composition of the working population by occupation. Figure 2–2, showing figures based upon population census data, shows the shifts in population in the major occupational categories. Since the classification of occupations in South Korea changed significantly in 1992, it is difficult to make comparisons around that time. Nevertheless, this table presents the data based on the old classification used until 1992, referring to Hong Doo-Seung et al. (1999), which reported on a re-calculation of the ratios of the working population by occupation in 1995, using a 2-percent sample of the population.

Studying the table, we notice on one hand that the ratio of agricultural, forestry, and fisheries workers decreases rapidly. On the other hand, the occupations with the greatest expansion are manufacturing-related. The ratio of workers in manufacturing-related occupations increased steadily from 13.3 percent in 1960 to 31.6 percent in 1990 due to rapid growth in the manufacturing industries. At the same time, the proportion of professionals and technicians, managers, and clerks also increased; the total ratio of these occupations jumped from 6.4 percent in 1960 to

Figure 2-3. Social Class Classification by Hong Doo-Seung

Level of control of social resources	Sector		
	Corporate and government	Self-employed	Agriculture
Upper	Upper middle class	Upper class	—
Middle	New middle class	Old middle class	Independent farmer
Lower	Working class	Urban lower class	Rural lower class

Source: Hong Doo-Seung (1983a: 179).

25.0 percent in 1990. The rise in those engaged in these occupations was presumably due to the advancing level of technology and the increased specialization and organization of the economy during the industrialization process.[6] The figure for those engaged in sales also consistently increased, although its growth was not as large compared to those mentioned above. This tendency reflected the pronounced growth of the distribution industry due to the substantial increase of the urban population and level of national consumption.

Changes in the Class Structure

The shifts in the composition of the working population by industry and occupation described above correspond to changes in the class structure of society. We can examine this using the class scheme provided by Hong Doo-Seung.

Hong argues that when distinguishing the classes of South Korean society, one should attach importance not only to the possession/non-possession of means of production, but also to degrees of possession and level of control of other social resources.[7] At the same time, he emphasizes that each different sector—the corporate and government sector, the self-employed sector, and the agricultural sector—connects directly to different classes, and establishes the matrix shown in figure 2–3 that ranks the sectors by level of control of social resources. Although the upper level of the agricultural sector would normally be occupied by the landlord class, it is blank because South Korea did not have large-scale landlords after the postwar agricultural land reforms. The "upper class" (capitalist class), which is the upper layer in the self-employed sector, is extremely small; hence it was excluded

---

[6] The increased number of professionals may be attributed in part to the marked increase in "education-related professionals" with the explosive expansion of education to be discussed in chapter 3.
[7] The class scheme provided by Hong is close to neo-Weberian schemes.

Figure 2–4. Social Class Composition Based on Hong Doo-Seung Classification (%)

Year	Upper middle class	New middle class	Old middle class	Working class	Urban lower class	Independent farmer class	Rural lower class	Total
1960	0.9	6.6	13.0	8.9	6.6	40.0	24.0	100.0
1970	1.3	14.2	14.8	16.9	8.0	28.0	16.7	100.0
1975	1.2	15.7	14.5	19.9	7.5	28.2	12.9	100.0
1980	1.8	17.7	20.8	22.6	5.9	23.2	8.1	100.0
1990	1.9	26.1	19.3	31.3	4.2	13.0	4.9	(100.0)
1995	3.6	25.5	22.2	27.7	8.2	12.1	0.6	100.0

Source: Hong Doo-Seung, et al. (1999: 141).
Note: The data for the year 1995 are based on reanalysis of a 2 percent sample of the *General Survey on Population and Housing*. The total for the year 1990 is 101.0 percent, indicating there is a possible 1 percent difference in the data entry for the year.

from the empirical study, leaving the seven classes shown in figure 2–3 for actual analysis.

Looking at the relationships between these classes and minor occupational categories, Hong defines the upper middle class as consisting primarily of high-ranking managers (such as large company department heads or higher, and presidents of small to medium-sized companies) and high-ranking professionals (such as doctors, lawyers, and professors), and the new middle class as consisting of management-level workers and professionals not included in the upper middle class, clerical workers, and some sales and service workers. The working class consists of factory workers and some sales and service workers. In the self-employed sector, the urban lower class corresponds to low-income, financially unstable sales and service workers, including peddlers and domestic service personnel. The rural lower class in the agricultural sector consists of tenant farmers and farm laborers.

Figure 2–4 shows the ratio of each class in the population and fluctuations based on census data, classified according to the above scheme. Over the last 30 years or so, the independent farmer class and the rural lower class have rapidly decreased while the working class increased considerably. This working class, however, started to decrease in the 1990s, a tendency stemming from the transition from manufacturing to service industries in the 1990s. The figures for the new middle class show how it steadily expanded until the 1980s; the decrease during the first half of the 1990s was not as large as for the one seen in the working class.

Of particular interest is the trend shown by the old middle class; i.e., the urban self-employed class. As exemplified by the growth of the large chaebol conglomerates, economic activity became increasingly organized in the course of South

Korea's industrialization. Even so, the urban self-employed class steadily increased into the 1990s, showing no tendency to decline as predicted by classic Marxist theory. Considering that this class occupies a significant proportion of South Korean society, it will be the subject of vigorous analysis in this book.

III. Occupational Hierarchy and Change

In this section, we use the outcome of previously conducted surveys in order to discuss the disparities in rewards and attitudes among occupations and how they changed during the rapid industrialization process. Whereas the previous section dealt with quantitative changes in working population by occupation, this section clarifies qualitative changes in an attempt to determine how they were connected to changes in social stratification.

Occupation and Social Class in the 1960s
Referring to the outcome of the first full-scale study[8] on South Korean social stratification conducted by Lee Sang-Beck and Kim Chae-Yoon in 1962, let us look at the occupational hierarchy prior to rapid industrialization.

The Lee Sang-Beck and Kim Chae-Yoon (1966) study reports on distribution by age, income, educational level, and social status identification for six occupational categories: professionals, managerial personnel, clerks, sales, skilled workers, and unskilled workers. Figure 2–5 shows the distribution of individual income by occupation. Calculation of mean income for each occupational category based on the distribution indicates that the highest income is for managerial personnel (15,900 won), followed by professionals (12,700 won), clerical workers (7,800 won), salespeople (6,900 won), skilled workers (4,500 won), and unskilled workers (3,700 won). The mean incomes for managerial personnel and professionals are three to four times higher than for unskilled workers, and there are large income differences among the occupations. The mean income of clerical workers is about two times higher than that of unskilled workers; their income is quite high, considering that a relatively large number of them are young.

By comparison, the mean income of skilled workers is not particularly high, at more or less the same level as that of unskilled workers. This may be attributed to the fact that demand for skilled workers in South Korean society at a time when industrialization was still in the developing stage was not that great. On the other hand, the income of sales workers is much higher than that of skilled and unskilled workers. However, income for salespeople varies widely: two-thirds earn "less

---

[8] The sample of this "survey on social stratification and mobility" consisted of 675 male householders living in Seoul, Daegu, and Jeonju. It did not include people engaged in agriculture.

Figure 2–5. Income Distribution by Occupation (1962 Survey) (%)

(won)	Less than 2,000	2,000–4,000	4,000–6,000	6,000–8,000	8,000–10,000	10,000–15,000	15,000–20,000	20,000–30,000	More than 30,000
Professional	0.0	0.0	9.6	23.1	21.2	28.8	5.8	3.8	7.7
Managerial	1.4	7.1	8.6	12.9	4.3	31.4	8.6	11.4	14.3
Clerical	6.7	5.6	38.2	27.0	9.0	4.5	2.23	4.5	2.2
Sales	10.8	29.2	24.9	10.8	1.6	11.4	7.6	3.2	0.5
Skilled	8.9	40.0	31.1	13.3	2.2	4.4	0.0	0.0	0.0
Unskilled	18.5	54.3	16.0	3.7	2.5	4.9	0.0	0.0	0.0

Source: Lee Sang-Beck and Kim Chae-Yoon (1966: 102).

than 6,000 won" while about 20 percent earn "10,000 won and more." Such a large variance in income is a characteristic of the sales occupation.

The income disparities among sales workers may be due to differences in employment status or the scale of the business. For example, a retailer with a fixed shop of a certain scale earns an income as high as a professional or manager while a small, self-employed worker like a peddler or salesperson earns an income as low as a skilled or unskilled worker.

When we examine differences in level of education, we notice that educational level differs widely by occupational category. The ratio of workers with an education of high school and above is 100 percent for professionals, 82.6 percent for managerial personnel, and 60.6 percent for clerical workers. These are extremely high figures considering the proportion of those who were educated through high school and above in South Korean society at that time. The ratio for sales workers is relatively high at 40.2 percent, but only 12.0 percent for skilled workers and 12.2 percent for in unskilled workers. Considering these findings, we may conclude that in the South Korean society of the early 1960s, the educational level of an individual was already a key factor in obtaining employment opportunities and, further, in determining his or her income.

Examining people's perceptions of their social status identification by occupation (figure 2–6), we observe high figures for professionals and managerial personnel who consider themselves as belonging to the upper and middle classes. A total of 86.6 percent of professionals and 87.4 percent of managerial personnel perceive themselves as belonging to the middle and upper classes, followed by 56.6 percent of clerical workers and 45.7 percent of sales workers. What is notable

Figure 2–6. Status Identification by Occupation (1962 Survey) (%)

	Lower-lower	Lower-upper	Lower-middle	Upper-middle	Upper	Total
Professional	0.0	13.5	48.1	30.8	7.7	100.0
Managerial	4.2	8.3	45.8	34.7	6.9	100.0
Clerical	11.1	32.2	41.1	14.4	1.1	100.0
Sales	19.4	34.9	37.1	8.1	0.5	100.0
Skilled	31.1	37.8	26.7	4.4	0.0	100.0
Unskilled	39.5	33.7	24.4	2.3	0.0	100.0
Total	20.6	29.1	35.5	12.5	2.4	100.0

Source: Lee Sang-Beck and Kim Chae-Yoon (1966: 103).

here is the relatively small variance of status identification among sales workers, compared to that of income.

As confirmed by figure 2–5, some sales workers have incomes higher than the mean incomes of professionals and managerial personnel. The ratio of sales personnel with an income of 10,000 won (22.7 percent) was higher than that of clerical workers (13.4 percent). However, in the distribution of perceptions of social status (see figure 2–6), the upper figures for sales personnel are very low: the total of those who answered "upper middle" or "upper" is only 8.6 percent, a value far lower than those seen for managerial personnel (total 41.6 percent) and professionals (total 8.5 percent), but also lower than for clerical workers (total 15.5 percent). These results suggest that perceptions of social status are affected not only by income but to a great extent by non-economic factors such as the prestige of particular occupations.

Fluctuations in Wage and Income Differences among Occupations

How did the status of people in various occupations change with the advance of industrialization? To examine this issue, we may turn to the raw data of the Survey on Inequality and Equity (hereafter, 1990 Equity Survey). This study was a nationwide survey of the distribution of social resources and people's perceptions about equality and fairness (valid sample: 1,974). The reliability of the data was very high, as great care had been taken in the design and implementation of the survey.[9]

---

[9] This survey was conducted by the Korean Social Science Research Council in 1990. For details of the survey, see Hwang Il-Chung (1992). I would like to thank one of the council members for his kind cooperation in allowing us to analyze the raw data for this survey.

44 | Part I   Theory, Structure, and Institutions

Figure 2–7. Average Monthly Income by Occupation (1990 Survey) (thousand won)

	Professional	Administrative and managerial	Clerical	Sales	Service	Manufacturing-related	Agricultural, forestry and fisheries	Total
Average	915	1318	688	868	790	585	385	666
Standard deviation	516	853	355	636	549	265	326	513
Number of cases	93	72	203	295	102	359	417	1,541

Source: Compiled by the author based on 1990 Equity Survey data.

Based on the survey data, figure 2–7 shows the average monthly individual income (men only and excluding unpaid family workers) by major occupational category. The highest average income was for administrative and managerial personnel (1,318 thousand won), followed by professionals (915 thousand won). Although a rigorous comparison is difficult to make because the occupational categories are not exactly the same as those in figure 2–5, it is interesting to note that the income of workers in sales, services, and manufacturing is very high compared with those shown in the figure based on the Lee Sang-Beck et al. survey conducted in 1962. Among urban occupations, the lowest income of manufacturing workers is nearly half the highest income of administrative and management personnel; the income gap seems to have become smaller compared to the survey in 1962. The average income of sales workers (868 thousand won) and service workers (790 thousand won) is much greater than the average income of clerical workers (688 thousand won). The standard deviation figures for the income of sales and service workers are large relative to average income figures, indicating that there is a great internal income gap within each occupation. Nevertheless, we should note that the average income disparity among occupations did shrink significantly.

The tendency toward a narrowing of the disparity in economic rewards for various occupations is also confirmed by the data of the Wage Structure Surveys conducted annually by the Korean Ministry of Labor. These are sample surveys of employees at firms of 10 or more employees. Figure 2–8 shows the relative average income for each occupation, assuming the overall average wage for each year is 100, during the period when the occupational categories were unchanged (1974–92). As illustrated by this graph, the wages of administrative and managerial employees were 3.59 times that of manufacturing workers' wages in 1975, but this number gradually shrank to 2.16 times in 1992. In addition, the average wages of professionals and clerical workers showed a relative decrease. The same ten-

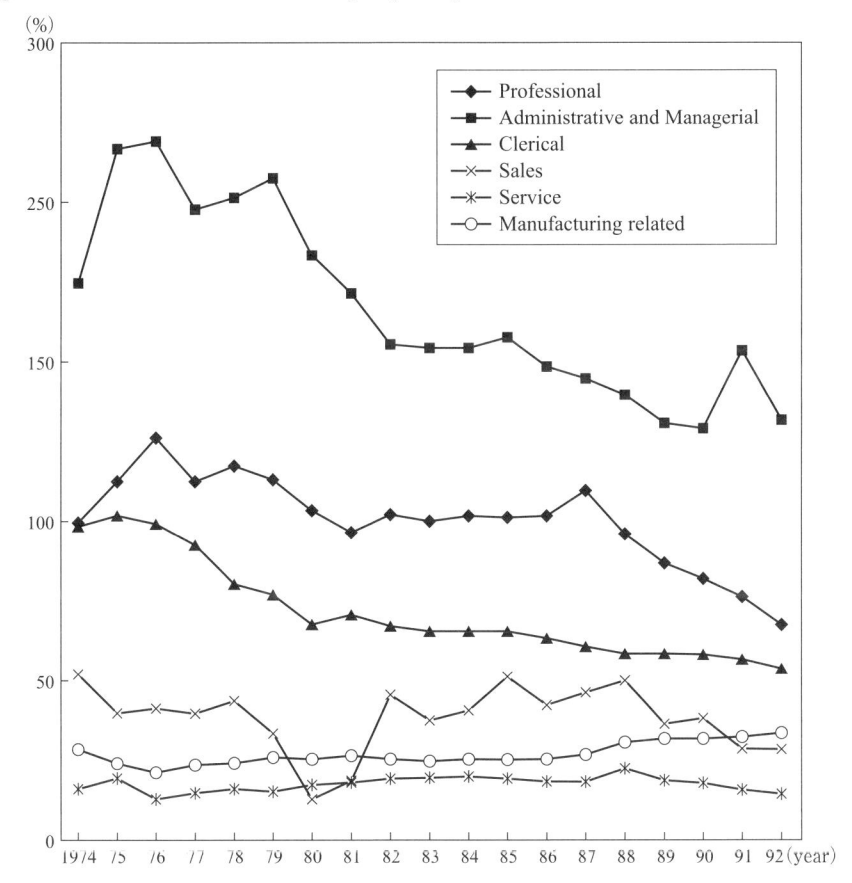

Chapter 2 Social Stratification and Industrialization | 45

Figure 2–8. Fluctuations in Relative Wages by Occupation

(%)

- ◆ Professional
- ■ Administrative and Managerial
- ▲ Clerical
- ✕ Sales
- ✶ Service
- ○ Manufacturing related

Source: Compiled from annual editions of "Report on Wage Structure Survey" (Korean Ministry of Labor).

dency was observed for the wage gaps among other occupations.[10] From these survey results, too, we may conclude that the wage gaps among occupations in South Korea grew markedly smaller during its period of rapid industrialization.

What factors caused these changes in the wage structure? The first point to note is the change in the relationship between supply and demand in the labor force. As the economy grew and labor-intensive industry rapidly emerged, South Korea passed through the Lewis turning point in the 1970s, and thereafter the relation-

---

[10] In figure 2–8, the variation of wages for sales workers is large due to a small sample size (less than 1 percent of the total). This is because the majority of sales workers were self-employed or employees of small shops and were not included in the survey samples.

ship of supply and demand in the labor force changed: unskilled labor went from being in unlimited supply to being in limited supply (Watanabe 1982: 135–42). The expansion of employment occurring in the process of industrialization and the close relationship between supply and demand in the unskilled labor force accompanying that process presumably brought about the relative increase in the wages of unskilled laborers, gradually shrinking the wage disparities among occupations.[11]

A second factor contributing to the reduction in wage disparities was the considerable increase in wages of manufacturing workers following the intensification of labor-management disputes in the wake of the democratization movement starting in 1987. Prior to democratization, the South Korean government strictly limited the activities of organized labor, such as a group struggle for higher wages, and thus there seem to have been many cases where the wages of workers (manufacturing workers in particular) were set lower than the equilibrium level determined by the relationship between supply and demand. The labor movement that intensified from the second half of the 1980s led to the elimination of such political and institutional limitations on wages.[12]

In addition, the increasing number of college graduates may have led to a decrease in wages for white-collar workers, resulting in a reduction in wage differences among occupations. We will return to this issue in chapter 4.

Changes in Socioeconomic Status of the Urban Self-Employed

The relative wages of employed sales, service, and manufacturing workers, then, were increasing. But were the incomes of urban self-employed workers engaging in these occupations also increasing? The data from the 1990 Equity Survey gives the mean incomes of these three occupations by employment status. For sales workers, the employed (employees) had an average income of 625 thousand won, while for the self-employed (including employers) the average was 894 thousand won; for service workers, the average income was 434 thousand won for the employed and 968 thousand won for the self-employed; and for manufacturing workers, average income for the employed was 543 thousand won and 766 thousand won for the self-employed. This means that the average income difference between the employed and the self-employed amounted to between 223 thousand

---

[11] However, the progress of globalization and the increasing number of immigrant workers did not increase the wages of unskilled workers in South Korea as much as the Lewis model anticipated.

[12] However, the wages of manufacturing workers in this period might not have increased without certain underlying factors, including the lack of skilled and unskilled workers and the resultant formation of the internal labor market around large corporations (Jung Ee-Hwan 1992; Yokota 1994).

and 534 thousand won. The average income of self-employed workers in sales and service is much higher than for clerical workers, and about the same or somewhat more than for professionals.

Until the first half of the 1980s, similar to other developing countries, the urban self-employed of South Korea were in the "urban informal sector,"[13] and their low productivity and income were often emphasized. For example, Bae Moo-Gi assumed in his study published in the early 1980s that self-employed workers and small companies in urban areas with less than 10 employees were the "urban traditional sector"; he states, "Although workers in the urban traditional sector include high-income professionals, such as practicing doctors and lawyers, and small-scale commerce and manufacturing earning relatively high profits, they are few in number; the majority of the sector consists of workers who have a low level of income, unstable employment, and poor working conditions" (Bae Moo-Gi 1982: 573).

Koo Hagen and Hong Doo-Seung conducted a survey of Seoul residents in 1976 to compare the income of the different classes of society based on their categorization. The survey results illustrated the rather wide disparity in average monthly incomes: of the capitalist class (182,050 won), the new middle class (142,240 won), the petite bourgeoisie class (120,480 won), the working class (75,100 won), and the marginal class (47,380 won). (Koo Hagen and Hong Doo-Seung 1980: 620). The marginal class, which made up more than 10 percent of the whole sample, mainly consisted of the self-employed in the urban informal sector, including peddlers and stallholders; their mean income was much lower than the workers stably employed by corporations and other organizations. Even though the petite bourgeoisie class does not include the small-scale self-employed with low productivity, the mean income of the petite bourgeoisie class was less than that of the new middle class, which consisted of professionals, administrators, and clerical workers. At least in the 1970s, Bae Moo-Gi's view that the urban self-employed in South Korea were close to the urban informal sector, at least with respect to income, was persuasive.[14]

By comparing the income of the urban self-employed between 1976 and 1990, we can observe that their economic status improved dramatically. In 1990, the income of self-employed workers in sales, service, and manufacturing was about the same as or higher than the average income of professionals and clerical workers,

---

[13] According to Torado (1969) and Fields (1975), the urban informal sector has low barriers to entry and extremely low marginal labor productivity; the workers in this sector are regarded as a kind of "pseudo-unemployed."

[14] The 1962 survey indicated that the income of sales workers that included many self-employed workers was more or less the same as that of unskilled workers, except for a small portion of high-income workers, implying that the most of them were in the urban informal sector.

who had long earned relatively high incomes in South Korean society. Of course, not all self-employed persons earned such a high income,[15] and there were many who worked in unstable environments because of the small scale of their businesses. Nevertheless, we may say that economic growth during that period markedly increased their income and raised the living standards of the urban self-employed in general.

The incomes of workers in the agricultural, forestry, and fishery industries were very low. As many farmers are more or less food self-sufficient, the actual living standard could be somewhat higher than the cash revenue level. Compared with other occupations, however, their income was much lower. The income gap has contributed to the rapid population outflow from the agricultural sector in Korea.

Level of Education and Status Identification

Lastly, let us compare level of education and status identification for workers in different occupations. Based on the outcomes of previous analyses, we would expect workers in sales, service, and manufacturing-related jobs to identify with a different social level according to whether they were self-employed or employed. For this reason, we separate those working in the sales, service, and manufacturing-related sectors into those who are self-employed and those who work for an employer. This creates two categories: "employees in sales, service, and manufacturing-related work" and "self-employed in sales, service, and manufacturing-related work"—for analysis.[16]

Referring to the data from the 1990 Equity Survey, we compare the distribution of level of education for workers in each occupation. The level of education of professionals, administrative/management employees, and clerical workers is indeed very high. The survey shows that 97.9 percent of professionals, 94.4 percent of administrative/management employees, and 89.7 percent of clerical workers have completed high school or higher education; this number is 61.8 percent for those self-employed in sales, service, and manufacturing-related work and 52.1 percent for employees in sales, services, and manufacturing related work, and 27.9 percent for workers in agriculture, forestry and fisheries. The differences in the level of education of employees and the self-employed in sales, service, and manufacturing work are relatively small; however, there is a large income gap between those who own the means of production and those who do not.

---

[15] In fact, the income variation among the self-employed is very large. The standard deviation of monthly income is 660 thousand won for self-employed sales workers, 578 thousand won for self-employed service workers, and 382 thousand won for self-employed manufacturing workers.

[16] The monthly average income of the former is 539 thousand won; that of the latter is 885 thousand won.

Figure 2–9. Status Identification by Occupation (1990 Survey) (%)

	1 (Lowest)	2	3	4 (Middle)	5	6	7 (Highest)
Professional	0.0	4.3	25.5	53.2	14.9	2.1	0.0
Administrative and managerial	2.8	2.8	29.2	41.7	20.8	2.8	0.0
Clerical	4.4	6.9	37.3	42.6	8.8	0.0	0.0
Self-employed in sales, service and manufacturing	7.6	17.2	37.7	31.0	5.7	0.5	0.2
Employees in sales, service and manufacturing	14.9	29.3	33.8	20.0	2.0	0.0	0.0
Agricultural, forestry and fisheries	22.5	26.2	24.3	25.1	1.9	0.0	0.0
Total	12.2	19.6	32.0	30.2	5.5	0.4	0.1

Source: Compiled by the author based on 1990 Equity Survey data.

Figure 2–9 shows South Korean status identification by occupation based on responses to the question, "If the strata of society are numbered from 1 to 7, lowest to highest, where do you think you belong?" Considering the categories of 4 and the adjacent 3 and 5 as the middle level, we found that approximately 90 percent of professionals, administrative/managerial personnel, and clerical workers identify themselves with the middle level. We also found that 74.4 percent of the self-employed in sales, service, and manufacturing think of themselves as occupying the middle level. The share of employees in sales, service, and manufacturing and agricultural/forestry/fishery workers identifying with the middle level, at 55.8 percent and 51.3 percent respectively, are not much different from the percentage that selected categories 1 and 2 (the lower level). Judging from these figures, we may conclude that, as far as sales, service, and manufacturing workers are concerned, not only with regard to their income but also their subjective status identification, there are significant differences between those who work for an employer and the self-employed. At the same time, the distribution of status identification for the self-employed in sales, service, and manufacturing is much lower on the 1-to-7 scale than for professionals and clerical workers. Since the income of the self-employed in sales, service, and manufacturing is about the same or even higher than that of professionals and clerical workers, their perception of being in a lower social level is noteworthy. That perception can be considered to stem from the unstable nature of urban self-employment and the low prestige of these occupations, as described in the next section.

IV. THE STRUCTURE OF OCCUPATIONAL PRESTIGE IN SOUTH KOREA

In our societies, people's occupations determine their status in the structure of society through differences in economic rewards as well as in the prestige associated with a given occupation. Occupational prestige means, in the narrow sense, the esteem derived by being engaged in the occupation, the respect of others, and the social influence originating in that respect. However, in many cases, it means the overall evaluation of the social status of an occupation includes not only prestige, but also income and power (Treiman 1977; Okamoto 1993). Inasmuch as occupational prestige—the unequal evaluation of occupations—can influence the direction of career choice (Naoi and Suzuki 1977: 152–53), in order to analyze and understand aspirations toward educational achievement or upward social mobility through education in South Korea, we need to establish a firm understanding of the structure of occupational prestige in South Korean society.

As pointed out in the first section of this chapter, the Confucianist view of occupations, in which intellectual work is highly valued while commerce and industry are less valued, was prevalent in traditional Korean society. How did this view of occupations and the structure of occupational prestige change in the course of Korea's rapid manufacturing-centered industrialization?

Occupational Prestige Structure Prior to Industrialization

Lee Man-Gap (1957) conducted the earliest research on the structure of occupational prestige in South Korea. The usefulness of his research is somewhat limited, however, because it targeted only high school students in cities. The 1962 survey conducted by Lee Sang-Beck and Kim Chae-Yoon (see figures 2–5 and 2–6) targeting adults in general, while coming somewhat later, has the strength of having been based on a larger sample. The discussion herein of the occupational prestige structure in South Korean society prior to full-scale industrialization is based on the Lee, et al. survey.

The survey asked the participants to rank the social status of 32 typical occupations on a five-point scale. Figure 2–10 is the average score of each of the 32 occupations calculated by converting the five-point scale to a 0-to-100-point scale.

First, we can observe from figure 2–10 that there are significant differences in the scores by occupation. Lee and Kim also made this observation by comparing occupational prestige in South Korea with that of the United States, the United Kingdom, and Japan. Through their comparison, they concluded that in Korean society (and British society) "discrimination on the basis of occupation is particularly strong" (Lee Sang-Beck and Kim Chae-Yoon 1966: 45).

Observing the ranking of occupational prestige in figure 2–10, we notice that the top ranks are professionals, followed by administrative and managerial em-

Figure 2–10. Occupational Prestige Scores (1962 Survey)

	Occupation	Score
1	University professor	85
2	Medical doctor	75
3	Attorney	72
4	Politician	68
5	Engineer	66
6	Military officer (field officer)	60
7	Section chief of government office	57
8	Corporate section chief	55
9	Pastor/priest	54
10	Independent farmer	52
11	Elementary school teacher	51
12	Newspaper reporter	51
13	Corporate employee	37
14	Railroad station employee	32
15	Retail shop owner	32
16	Subcontractor	30
17	Policeman	27
18	Tenant farmer	25
19	Driver	24
20	Miner	21
21	Fisherman	19
22	Carpenter	18
23	Craftsman	17
24	Secondhand dealer	17
25	Shop clerk	16
26	Barber	16
27	Field publicity agent	15
28	Cook	13
29	Peddler	11
30	Real estate agent	9
31	Bicycle-drawn cart porter	8
32	Waiter	6

Source: Lee Sang-Beck and Kim Chae-Yoon (1966: 43).

ployees and clerical workers. By contrast, the scores for service, sales, and manufacturing workers are quite low. There is a large gap between the prestige score of a newspaper reporter, ranked 12 (51 points), and that of a corporate employee, ranked 13 (37 points); this can be seen as the divide between the "highly prestigious occupation group" and the rest. The occupations belonging to the highly prestigious group are mostly professionals, administrators, and clerical workers. Therefore, we may conclude that there is a substantial gap in occupational prestige between them and the group encompassing sales, service, and manufacturing workers on the other. Furthermore, the order of occupational prestige more or less coincides with the distribution of income by occupation shown in figure 2–5.

Detailed study of individual scores for occupational prestige, moreover, reveals some interesting characteristics. First, we notice that "independent farmer" scores high (52 points), placing it in the aforementioned "highly prestigious occupation group." The score for "tenant farmer"—who is not the owner of the land farmed—is somewhat higher than for most of the service, sales, and manufacturing occupations. We attribute these high scores for farmers to the nature of South Korean society at that time, in which the overall income levels were low; the availability of sufficient food is the key criterion that determines people's standard of living.

It should be pointed out that the scores for the urban self-employed overall were remarkably low. Even though owners of retail shops, subcontractors, and secondhand dealers have scores slightly higher than employees in the service, sales, and manufacturing sectors, their scores were quite low compared to those of clerical workers and independent farmers. We attribute these findings to the instability and low productivity of the urban self-employed at that time.

As suggested by Lee and Kim, the aforementioned structure of occupational prestige in South Korea may reflect not only the actual incomes and levels of living standards, but also the Confucian work ethic of traditional society (Lee and Kim 1966: 43). The traditional high occupational value accorded to intellectual work as contrasted with the lower value placed on commercial and industrial occupations may have contributed to the low scores for the sales, service, and manufacturing-related occupations.[17]

---

[17] Based on outcomes of the prestige survey conducted in 1967, Kim Kyong-Dong (1970 [1992]) also discussed the influence of traditional occupation values on the occupational prestige structure. However, although the *jung-in* class, including professionals and bureaucrats, was ranked one step lower than the *yangban* class in traditional society, this survey reported that professionals, including doctors and engineers, enjoyed high prestige, indicating that the occupational prestige structure in the 1960s did not completely reflect traditional occupation values.

Figure 2–11. Occupational Prestige Scores (1990 Survey)

	Occupation	Score	Standard Deviation
1	Judge	93.0	16.0
2	University or college professor	89.2	17.3
3	Military officer	82.3	23.9
4	Government office bureau chief	79.5	19.7
5	Large corporation department chief	72.3	18.5
6	Pharmacist	70.2	19.8
7	Newspaper reporter	67.7	20.7
8	Middle school teacher	62.7	18.7
9	Bank section chief	62.6	18.8
10	Electronics shop owner	61.0	21.3
11	Small/medium-sized company section chief	59.8	17.6
12	Supermarket owner	44.9	20.9
13	Restaurant owner	43.4	19.9
14	District office worker	41.1	17.7
15	Traffic policeman	39.4	20.3
16	Factory team leader	36.1	20.0
17	Independent farmer	35.9	25.6
18	Laundry shop owner	33.4	20.1
19	Chief cook	31.4	21.9
20	Taxi driver	29.3	19.1
21	Barber	25.9	19.5
22	Department store clerk	23.8	18.6
23	Carpenter	23.0	22.4
24	Factory worker	17.3	20.2
25	Sewing machine operator	16.5	19.1
26	Miner	14.4	20.0
27	Apartment security staff	14.1	17.8
28	Peddler	11.0	17.9
29	Maid	9.9	16.7
30	Unskilled worker	8.5	17.4

Source: Compiled by the author based on 1990 Equity Survey data.

Structure of Occupational Prestige after Industrialization

How did the structure of occupational prestige presented above change or remain the same during South Korea's rapid industrialization? To discuss this issue, we again return to the raw data from the 1990 Equity Survey, while comparing South Korea with Japan, which has an occupational structure similar to South Korea's.

In the 1990 Equity Survey, 30 occupations are evaluated on a five-point scale. Figure 2–11 converts the average five-point scale evaluation to one with scores ranging from 0 to 100, and lists the mean scores and standard deviations for the occupations in descending order of the former.

While the mean prestige scores of occupations range from 93.0 points for a judge to 8.5 points for an unskilled worker, the standard deviations are not much different among occupations. Regarding the characteristics of occupational prestige in Japan, Naoi and Suzuki observed, based on the results of the National Survey of Social Stratification and Social Mobility (SSM)[18] in 1975, that "there was little variation in evaluations regarding middle-ranking occupations, whereas variation in evaluation of occupations in the upper and lower ranks is pronounced" (Naoi and Suzuki 1977: 127–28). In South Korea, this tendency is not observed, although individual examination by occupation shows that there are larger standard deviations for independent farmers and military officers. The wide variation in evaluations for independent farmers is a consequence of the lower scores given by farmers themselves and the higher scores given by non-farmers expressing their longing for rural life (Hong Doo-Seung 1992: 155). We may surmise that the wide variation in evaluations for military officers is the result of differing perceptions of political leaders with a military background who exercised power during the authoritarian regime.

Next, in order to grasp the characteristics of the structure of occupational prestige in South Korea in 1990, let us compare it with the occupational prestige scores in Japan obtained by the SSM survey in 1995. For 16 occupations that are common to the surveys of both countries, a regression equation estimated between the South Korean prestige score (Y) and the Japanese prestige score (X) (Tsuzuki ed. 1998) is as follows (values in parentheses are the standard errors):[19]

$$Y = -49.214 + 1.656X$$
$$(8.127) \quad (0.138)$$

---

[18] The "National Survey of Social Stratification and Social Mobility" (SSM survey) is conducted every 10 years since 1955; its objective is to understand the Japanese social stratification structure and opportunities for social mobility. The latest was conducted in 2015.

[19] In order to control the number of occupation samples, if an occupation title belongs to a subcategory of another title (e.g., "landed farmer" and "farmer") they are regarded as one occupation in this analysis.

$R^2 = 0.911$

The square root of the determination coefficient (0.911) is 0.954, which is the coefficient of correlation between Japanese and South Korean scores of occupational prestige. Considering the comparative studies among various countries conducted so far, this correlation coefficient is very high (Inkeles and Rossi 1956; Treiman 1977, etc.). Therefore, as far as rank order is concerned, we may conclude that the structure of occupational prestige in South Korea is not particularly different from Japan's.

Even if the rank order is similar, there are still large differences in the absolute level of the prestige score. The regression analysis estimated the regression coefficient of X to be 1.656, which means that the disparity in prestige scores among occupations in South Korea is 1.7 times larger than that in Japan. As figure 2–11 indicates, the large score disparity in South Korea may be attributed to the markedly low scores for non-white-collar occupations.

Following the three-groups (high, middle, low) approach of Naoi and Suzuki (1977) by combining "highest" and "quite high" to mean "high," and "lowest" and "quite low" to mean "low," let us further compare the distribution of occupation evaluations in Japan and South Korea. Needless to say, these disparities in prestige scores among occupations are the result of the choices of categories from lowest to highest in the evaluation of occupations by survey respondents. In South Korea, out of the 30 occupations, 10 (33.3 percent) are mostly rated as "high" in prestige; 4 (13.3 percent) are mostly rated as "middle"; and 16 (53.3 percent) are mostly rated as "low." In Japan's 1995 SSM survey, by contrast, among 56 occupations, 18 (32.1 percent) are mostly rated as "high," and the remaining 38 (67.9 percent) are mostly rated as "middle," with none mostly rated as "low." The SSM survey conducted in 1975 also showed a similar distribution; there were only a few occupations with peaks at "low." We can conclude that there are larger gaps in prestige among occupations in South Korea, and evaluation of occupations tends to be strongly polarized between "high" and "low."

Continuity in Prestige Rankings

When we look at the list of occupational prestige scores, we notice that there is a very large gap between "11. Small/medium-sized company section chief" and "12. Supermarket owner." In the three-group evaluation described above, the highly prestigious group ranging from "1. Judge" to "11. Small/medium-sized company section chief" has more than 40 percent of the "high" responses, whereas "12. Supermarket owner" and below have at most 10 percent of the "high" responses and more "low" responses. The latter group can be divided into two sub-groups: the average prestige group of "12. Supermarket owner" to "15. Traffic policeman," where "middle" predominates, and the low-prestige group in which "16. Factory team leader," and below where "low" predominates.

What is important is the fact that the groups based on the prestige evaluations clearly correspond to the occupational categories based on occupational types and employment status. The highly prestigious group consists of white-collar jobs including professionals, administrative/management employees, and clerical workers. Occupations in the 12th rank and below generally consist of the other jobs (including shop-floor clerical work). The subdivision of this group reveals a clear differentiation between the middle prestige group and the low prestige group. The former includes self-employed sales and service workers and shop-floor clerical workers, while the latter comprises employee positions in sales, service, and manufacturing work (including laundry shop owner and independent farmer).

From the above, we may conclude that the fundamental ranking of occupational prestige has not changed much since Lee Sang-Beck conducted the survey in 1962, even after South Korea achieved industrialization. As confirmed in the previous section, while the wage and income gaps between occupations were substantially reduced with rapid industrialization, the disparities in occupational prestige rankings have remained, and perhaps have even expanded. Compared with the survey in 1962, although the prestige scores of some professional and managerial occupations have increased significantly, the prestige scores of sales, service, and manufacturing employees generally increased by only a few points, staying in the lower ranks. In particular, the consistently low evaluations of the occupations of factory worker and sewing-machine operator, which contributed to the manufacturing-industry-led rapid economic growth, showed very little change before and after industrialization. Based on the outcome of surveys conducted in 1967 and 1978, Kim Kyong-Dong revealed that people's evaluation of the social status of occupations does not have any correlation with evaluations of their contribution to economic development (Kim Kyong-Dong 1979=1992). The conclusions of the above discussion agree with that observation.

However, when we examine the prestige scores of individual occupations in detail, we find there are occupations for which the relative rank in the occupational prestige structure noticeably changed, reflecting fluctuations in economic rewards. Among them, the rank of "independent farmer" (landed farmer) is remarkable. Although the prestige score was 52 in 1962, ranking in the "highly prestigious occupation" along with some professional workers, the score for this occupation fell to 35.9 in 1990, similar to the scores for those in sales and service. This change in relative rank is presumably due to the elimination of absolute poverty and the development of secondary and tertiary industries.

In addition, among the occupational sectors that underwent a significant change in economic status in the process of industrialization we can cite the urban self-employed. As mentioned in section III (p. 47), prior to full-scale industrialization, the urban self-employed tended to consist of persons engaged in low-productivity activities, and their income was very low. During economic growth, however, their average income increased to levels similar to those of professionals and clerical workers. Even so, their occupational prestige did not increase to match the level of their economic rewards. In the occupational prestige score for 1990, the urban self-employed (except for "laundry shop owner" at 33.4 points) were in the middle prestige group; for example, "supermarket owner" stood at 44.9 points and "restaurant owner" at 43.4 points. Nevertheless, there was a large gap in occupational prestige between the urban self-employed and many white-collar workers. Based on this data, we may conclude that the occupational prestige structure in South Korea does not change as a reflection of economic rewards and other factors, but rather exhibits continuity with historical and cultural influences.

Evaluator Effects on Occupational Prestige Evaluations
Do all members of South Korean society share the same perceptions of occupational prestige ranking? Or is the ranking different for each social subgroup? To answer these questions, we examine the influence of gender, age, level of education, and occupation on evaluations of occupational prestige. First, we obtain the different sets of occupational prestige scores for the 30 occupations within each subgroup for the evaluator attributes shown in figure 2–12. Then, for each attribute variable, we calculate the correlation coefficients of the obtained prestige scores for all possible combinations of two subgroups with the variable. Figure 2–12 shows the highest, mean, and lowest values of the correlation coefficients of the occupational prestige scores between the subgroups. As shown in this figure, the correlation coefficients of the occupational prestige scores for subgroups of each attribute variable are very high; even the lowest value is at least 0.98. Thus, the effect of the evaluator attributes on their evaluations of occupational prestige is negligible in terms of correlation.

Even when we use the three-level occupational classification of "high," "middle," and "low" to compare the distribution of occupational evaluations, there is no large difference in the distribution among the categories of evaluator attributes. Likewise, evaluator occupations do not make much difference. In other words, there is essentially no tendency to evaluate one's own occupation very highly or very poorly except in limited cases such as the aforementioned "independent farmer." In this regard, we may conclude that the occupational prestige structure in South Korea exhibits considerable consistency.

Given this rigid structure of occupational prestige, many non-white-collar workers, including those in sales, service, and manufacturing, evaluate their own occupations negatively. According to the 1990 Equity Survey, 83.9 percent of

58 | Part I   Theory, Structure, and Institutions

Figure 2–12. Evaluator Attribute Variable, Category, and Correlation Coefficients of Occupational Prestige Scores

Variable	Category	Correlation Coefficient		
Gender	Male	0.998		
	Female			
Age	20s	Average		0.996
	30s	Highest		0.999
	40s	(30s × 40s)		
	50s	Lowest		0.990
	60s and older	(20s × 60s and older)		
Level of education	Uneducated	Mean		0.994
	Elementary school	Highest		0.999
	Middle school	(High school × junior college)		
	High school	Lowest		0.984
	Junior college	(Uneducated × four-year college and above)		
	Four-year college and above			
Occupation	Professional	Mean		0.994
	Managerial	Highest		0.998
	Clerical	(Sales × manufacturing)		
	Sales	Lowest		0.985
	Service	(Managerial × agricultural, etc.)		
	Manufacturing			
	Agricultural, Forestry and Fisheries			

Source: Compiled by the author based on "1990 Equity Survey" data.

manufacturing workers themselves rated "plant worker" as "low"; this ratio is more or less the same as the 88.5 percent of evaluators other than manufacturing workers who gave a "low" rating. A similar tendency is also observed for sales and service workers; in South Korea, many workers—chiefly in non-white-collar jobs—evaluate their own occupations negatively, even after rapid industrialization. The wide disparities and the rigid ranking of occupational prestige can be considered factors that contribute to people's dissatisfaction with the social status of their own occupation and motivate them to seek a higher-ranked occupation.

CONCLUSION

Since the end of the Joseon Dynasty, Korean society has passed through a dramatic process that has included colonization, division into North and South after the

Liberation, the Korean War, agricultural land reforms, and the industrialization that followed. The rapid changes of this period have transformed its traditional social structure, including the way the society is stratified. The hierarchical strictures of traditional rural society have been substantially eased during this era of dramatic change, paving the way for rapidly growing social mobility. The relaxation of the traditional social structure and increased social mobility became the critical background motivating people from all levels of society to participate in the competition for social-status achievement.

The changes in the social structure that accompanied industrialization were especially conspicuous. The decrease of the farming population and the increase in white- and blue-collar employment by corporations and other organizations are phenomena generally observed not only in South Korea, but other industrializing countries as well; however, the industrialization of South Korea was far more rapid and compressed than most other countries (Chang Kyung-Sup 2010), bringing about much more drastic change in the occupational structure. The urban social classes in South Korea were formed by these dramatic changes, and their members are the first generation to achieve their present status through inter- and intra-generational mobility (Hsiao 1999). On the whole, rapid change in the industrial structure has provided South Koreans with many opportunities for social mobility.

The socioeconomic status of workers of all occupations has also changed substantially in the process of industrialization. There was a very large wage gap between white-collar and blue-collar workers prior to full-scale industrialization. That gap has narrowed since the 1970s, partially because of the disappearance of unskilled surplus laborers. Another reason for the narrowing of the gap is the fact that the urban self-employed are no longer engaged in small, low-productivity businesses that made them part of the "informal sector," but came to earn, on average, a decent income during the period of rapid economic growth.

Despite major changes in wage and income structure among occupations, the occupational prestige structure has not changed much. Reflecting traditional values, there have been wide disparities in the prestige of occupations in society throughout history. Even after industrialization, there was essentially no change in the structure of occupational prestige (the only noticeable decline being among independent farmers) and the ranking of occupations. Compared to the changes that took place in economic rewards among occupations, the occupational prestige structure of South Korea exhibits a steady continuity. The society has still been under the influence of traditional values, and the wide disparities in occupational prestige have been perpetuated by those members of society who are affected by traditional values. Since the structure of occupational prestige is extremely rigid and stable in South Korean society, even after rapid industrialization, many non-white-collar workers evaluate their own occupational status negatively. People's dissatisfaction with the status of their occupation drives their desire to move up the occupational status ladder.

CHAPTER 3

School Education and the Selection System

After the end of World War II, both Japan and Korea were guided by the United States in implementing single-tracked education based on the 6–3–3–4 system, so at first glance, their educational systems seem very similar. In detail and content, however, the South Korean education system is distinctive, and relies on a completely different selection system.[1] The current system is the result of several stages of vigorous government intervention in policies regarding secondary and higher education from the late 1960s onward, to be explained in detail in this chapter.

The specifics of the education and academic selection systems define the value of the academic credentials and determine their impact on socioeconomic status. The nature of these systems may also have an influence on people's aspirations toward educational attainment and social-status achievement through education.

I. The School System in South Korea

Before we discuss the characteristics of South Korean education and selection systems, let us take a brief look at the school system and the changes in it up to around 2000.[2] As mentioned above, the South Korean school system is based on the "6–3–3–4 system," illustrated in figure 3–1. Although the Korean constitution

---

[1] I use the term "[academic] selection system" to describe how and at what age the society separates students in order to provide them presumably "better" educational opportunities according to their intellectual ability and potential. Therefore, it is shaped by the school system and institutions for school admission.

[2] I do not refer to changes in the school system after the 2000s, because this book focuses on South Korean education and society in the second half of the twentieth century. For details about the current South Korean school system and education, see Korean Educational Development Institute (2017), Park Hyunjoon (2013), and Kim Young-Chun (2016).

Figure 3–1. South Korean School System

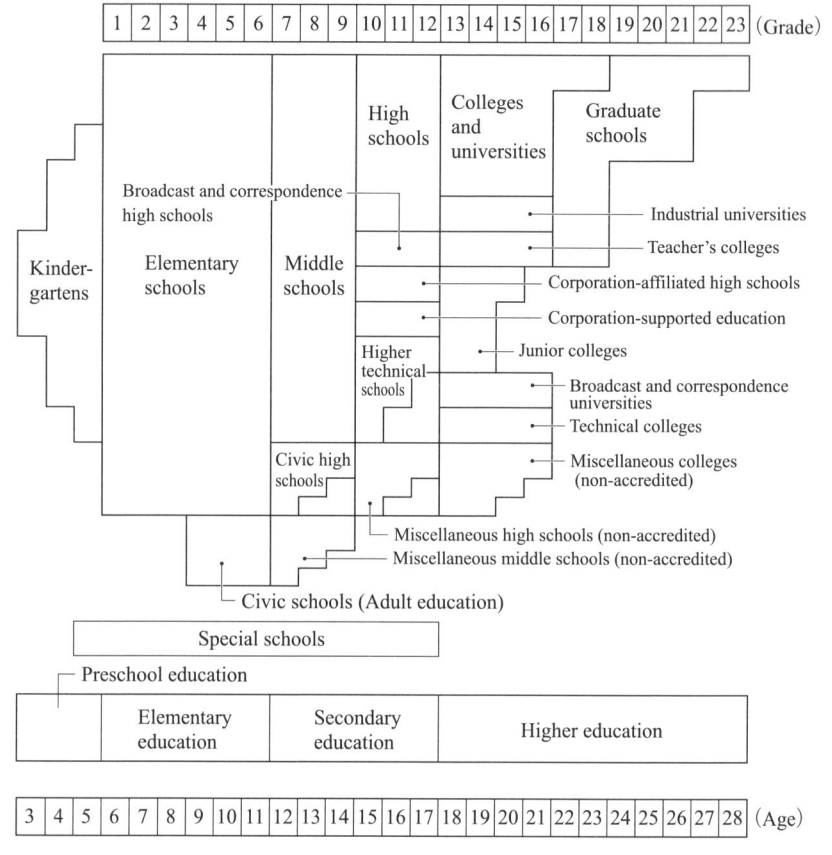

| 1 | 2 | 3 | 4 | 5 | 6 | 7 | 8 | 9 | 10 | 11 | 12 | 13 | 14 | 15 | 16 | 17 | 18 | 19 | 20 | 21 | 22 | 23 | (Grade) |

- Kindergartens
- Elementary schools
- Middle schools
- High schools
- Broadcast and correspondence high schools
- Colleges and universities
- Graduate schools
- Industrial universities
- Teacher's colleges
- Corporation-affiliated high schools
- Corporation-supported education
- Higher technical schools
- Junior colleges
- Broadcast and correspondence universities
- Technical colleges
- Civic high schools
- Miscellaneous colleges (non-accredited)
- Miscellaneous high schools (non-accredited)
- Miscellaneous middle schools (non-accredited)
- Civic schools (Adult education)
- Special schools
- Preschool education
- Elementary education
- Secondary education
- Higher education

| 3 | 4 | 5 | 6 | 7 | 8 | 9 | 10 | 11 | 12 | 13 | 14 | 15 | 16 | 17 | 18 | 19 | 20 | 21 | 22 | 23 | 24 | 25 | 26 | 27 | 28 | (Age) |

Source: *Statistical Yearbook of Education*, Korean Ministry of Education (2000: 23).
Note: English translation of school types is revised from the original version.

calls for compulsory education to be provided "free of charge" to all citizens, due to fiscal limitations, that ideal was only realized at the elementary school level when the constitution was established in 1948. The government gradually began to implement free education in middle schools (lower secondary schools) in the 1980s, and finally in 2004 was able to make compulsory education through the third year of middle school available free of charge nationwide.

Primary Education

Korean elementary schools, which are divided into six grades, are mostly public. Unlike Japan, there are no elementary schools that are part of private school systems extending through college that allow students to get on an "escalator" to higher affiliated schools.

Under the Education Law (1949) established under the Korean constitution (1948), elementary schools were defined as compulsory education, and all educational expenses including enrollment fees and tuition were to be covered by public funding. In reality, however, the fiscal state of the Republic of Korea government at that time was too weak to secure adequate school facilities and teachers to accommodate all children of school age as well as implement compulsory education. During the first and the second decades after the Liberation (1945), the parents of students paid for most of the expenses of maintaining elementary schools. Construction costs for adding new classrooms, as well as running costs and teacher benefit payments, were covered through Parent-Teacher Association (PTA) fees (Korea Education Ten-Year History Compilation Committee 1959: 117).

Despite these circumstances, the number of schoolchildren attending elementary school rapidly increased immediately after 1945, and in the late 1950s, the enrollment rate exceeded 90 percent (Korean Ministry of Education 1958: 51–52).[3] South Korea, in other words, had already achieved a rate of elementary school enrollment close to that of advanced countries, even though GNP per-capita income was still less than 100 dollars US at the time. The rapid expansion of elementary schools was made possible by the peoples' passion for education simultaneously supporting the government's efforts to institute compulsory education.

Secondary Education

The pattern of educational expansion with the beneficiaries paying the costs extended to South Korea's secondary education as well. Although early on the government adopted the policy of making middle school education available free of charge, the policy only began being partially implemented on islands and remote areas in 1985. Even at the end of the 1970s, parents in South Korea continued to pay over 70 percent of the running costs of public middle schools (Yun Jeong-Il 1985: 93).

For this reason, the financial burden on households when children entered middle school became extremely high. In 1965, less than half of the middle-school-age population was attending school (figure 3–2). After that time, however, the rate of middle school attendance rapidly increased to reach 95.1 percent in 1980; in 1985, only 20 years after 1965, it reached 100 percent. Even prior to the full implementation of compulsory education with the government covering educational expenses, a near-perfect school attendance rate had been attained. Considering the very low support for the costs of the middle school education from public coffers, such

---

[3] Abe (1972: 115).

64 | Part I Theory, Structure, and Institutions

Figure 3–2. School Attendance Rate by Stage of Education

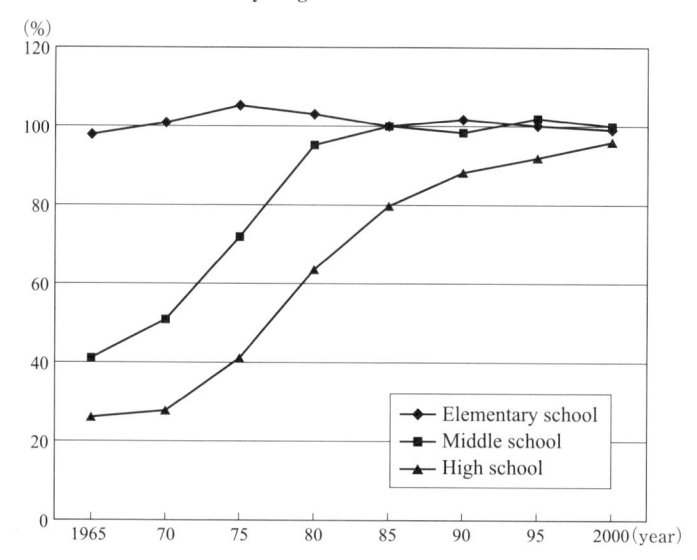

Source: Compiled by the author based on Korean Educational Development Institute (1997b) and "Social Indicators in Korea" (Korean National Statistical Office).
Note: School attendance rate is calculated by the ratio of the actual number of students registered to the school age population. Thus, it is possible that the rate exceeds 100 percent as students registered may be outside school age.

a rapid expansion may be attributed to the fact that per-capita income rose during this period, increasing the ability of households to afford such expenses.

In Korea, high schools—the upper secondary phase of education—are divided into two groups: academic high schools intended to prepare students to advance to higher education, and vocational high schools for students who plan to enter the workforce directly or proceed to (vocational) junior college, which will be explained below. During the Park Chung-Hee regime (1961–79), which pursued economic development based on the manufacturing industry, there was a strong emphasis on expansion of vocational high schools, and in some years the number of vocational high school students was greater than that of the academic high schools. However, as students' desire for higher education increased, the number of applicants to academic high schools, which were more advantageous to those wishing to advance to higher education, rose as well; the number of students enrolled in academic high schools has comprised over 60 percent of the total number of high school students since the latter half of 1980s.

In addition to these high schools, in South Korea, there are some special professional (*teuksu mokjeok*) high schools. The purpose of these elite special professional high schools is to nurture gifted students' talents at an early age through high-level education in small classes for professional fields such as science, foreign languages, arts, and physical education.[4] Many of these special professional high schools—science high schools in particular—were established during the Chun Doo-Hwan regime (1980–88), which made promoting science and engineering its top priority in an effort to address the lack of early or gifted education caused by the policy of leveling academic high schools in the 1970s (see pp. 68ff).[5]

During the 1970s and 1980s, upper secondary education, too, naturally expanded greatly. While the rate of continuation to high school was relatively low from the 1960s to the early 1970s, it increased rapidly from the late 1970s onward, and over 95 percent of the school-age population attended high school in 2000 (figure 3–2). This rapid expansion of high school education was possible because the burden of school expenses was largely borne by the students and their families.

Higher Education

For higher education in South Korea, there are junior colleges (*jeonmun daehak*) and four-year (or six-year) colleges. The junior colleges, established in 1979 by consolidating former junior colleges (*chogeup daehak*) and vocational schools (*jeonmun hakkyo*), are two- to three-year vocational education institutions to train mid-level professionals and technicians for industry. Therefore, the junior colleges have a strong orientation to teaching practical occupational skills.

By contrast, the colleges are generally institutions of higher education that offer four-year academic courses of study, except some schools and departments such as schools of medicine and dentistry, which have six-year courses of study. In addition, teachers colleges for training elementary school teachers, which were originally two-year institutions, expanded to four-year programs in 1980.

Figures 3–3 and 3–4 (p. 74) show the number of students enrolled in higher education and the rate of advancement of high school graduates to higher education, respectively. As will be explained in more detail below, because the govern-

---

[4] There are far fewer special professional high schools than academic high schools. Considering that the number of students admitted to the special professional high schools is very limited, entrance to such schools is very exclusive. In addition, a new type of private high school which exercises a large degree of freedom in selecting applicants and in programming curricula have been established since the 2000s.

[5] However, when students apply for entrance to college, the academic records of the special professional schools, which are based on relative scores used within the school, are used without adjustment for inter-school differences, which could be to their disadvantage, so some students prefer to attend an academic high school. Such measures were based on the government policy of "making no differences in formal educational opportunities as much as possible until advancing to college."

ment had long strictly controlled and supervised the quota of students admitted to higher education, the number of students directly reflects the government's policy at the time. However, from the time the strict college-entrance controls were instituted, demand for advancement to higher education in South Korea was always greater than the government quotas. Although the increased number of students enrolled in higher education was a direct consequence of the government's quota policy, the increase was made possible because the beneficiaries were willing to pay the costs, considering the fact that private universities, which account for a substantial part of higher education in South Korea, rely on the tuition paid by enrolled students for their operating costs (Yun Jeong-Il 1985; Kim Nam-Sun 1992). Therefore, we may conclude that the expansion of higher education was also achieved through financial investment by the beneficiaries.

As described above, particularly on the financial side, the rapid expansion of the educational system in South Korea following the Liberation (1945) was made possible not so much at the initiative of the government, but through the support of students and their parents. Nevertheless, that did not mean the South Korean educational system was built without government control. On the contrary, exercising strong authoritarian powers, the South Korean government has forcefully intervened in the administration and regulation of the overall school education system, including private schools. In the next section, we will discuss government intervention in student quotas and methods of selection.

II. SECONDARY AND HIGHER EDUCATION POLICIES AND THEIR INFLUENCE ON SELECTION SYSTEMS

Since the 1960s, the South Korean government has followed a rather unusual policy for its secondary and higher education systems; this, along with the proactive intervention of government, has led to the development of a quite idiosyncratic selection system. South Korea's selection system is characterized by being college-entrance centered, government-controlled, and highly unified. These features emerged in the late 1960s, and were maintained into the 2000s with only minor modifications.[6]

---

[6] However, the selection system has gradually changed. For example, the right to determine the quotas of students entering universities has been partially transferred to the universities since the 2000s. In addition, the South Korean government has conducted neo-liberal educational reforms since the 2000s (Park Hyunjoon 2013).

Secondary Education and Its Selection Systems

Of the policies on secondary education adopted since the 1960s, two had a major role in shaping the selection system: the decision to allow entrance to middle schools without examinations, and the measures taken to "level" the academic high schools (i.e., to even out the caliber of students attending the academic high schools). We will discuss these two policies in detail below, including their background and consequences.

Middle School Admissions without Entrance Exams
Since middle schools in South Korea were not initially part of compulsory education, until the end of the 1960s, applicants could choose any school within their school district. Consequently, popular middle schools, even the public ones, set entrance examinations and selected students by their scores on the examinations.[7] From the 1950s, as elementary education expanded, the number of students who wanted to go to middle school also increased. However, many of the newly built middle schools lacked adequate financial resources and were unable to accommodate the increased number of students. Thus, between the newly established schools and the older established schools with a solid financial foundation, there were large gaps in the conditions for education, such as school facilities, teacher quality, and the number of students who went on to attend top-ranking high schools. Students who wanted to take advantage of the best middle schools in order to gain entrance to good high schools and colleges flocked to select older established middle schools, intensifying the entrance-examination competition (Abe 1971).

The intense competition to enter middle schools became the cause of various social ills. Impediments to the physical and mental growth of students due to the emphasis on rote memorization in elementary education, such as an increase in nearsighted students, became the topic of much public discussion. In the 1960s, the middle school entrance examination system sparked considerable turmoil. In one case, a group of parents contesting the official answers to exam questions conducted fierce demonstrations, and in another case a lawsuit was filed over the officially announced exam answers.[8]

---

[7] See Korean Education 30 Years History Compilation Committee (1980), Seoul City Board of Education (1981), etc., for information about the selection of applicants to middle schools from the 1950s to the 1960s.

[8] In the lawsuit over the answers in an entrance examination, after the applicants won the case and were admitted to the prestigious middle school they sought to enter, some wealthy families took advantage of the situation and used their personal connections with members of the National Assembly to have their children enter the school together with the winners of the suit. The scandal was later exposed amid great public outcry.

Under these circumstances, the Korean Federation of Teachers' Associations prepared and proposed a plan to abolish middle school entrance examinations completely.[9] In 1968, in order to reduce the competition for entry to middle school, the Ministry of Education announced a new policy under which the middle school entrance examinations were abolished and all students were allowed to enter middle school, being allocated to schools in their districts by lottery. In addition, in order to eliminate the notion of "best schools" among students preparing for entrance examinations, the government abolished some of the prestigious old established schools. The no-entrance-examination policy for middle schools applied to private schools as well as public schools. Under this policy, private schools were not allowed to exercise their own discretion in admissions, and students were not permitted to choose which school they would attend.[10]

The no-entrance-exam middle-school admission policy, implemented in Seoul in 1969 and in nine other major cities in 1970, was expanded nationwide in 1971, completely eliminating competitive entrance examinations at the middle school level.

The Academic High School "Leveling" Measure

As the no-entrance-exam middle school policy was implemented, the number of students entering middle schools increased, in turn intensifying the competition for entrance to high schools and triggering similar issues all over again. At that time, since middle school students could apply to any high school in their residential city or prefecture (*do*), and high schools could screen students by their own admissions standards, including achievement tests, as had been the case for middle schools previously, the competition to gain entrance to the best high schools grew fierce.

The Council on Reform of the Entrance Examination System, organized in 1972 as an advisory committee to the Ministry of Education, pointed out the educational problems related to the intense competition for top-ranked academic high schools, including: impediments to healthy physical and mental development of students caused by the heavy burden of study, increased tension and anxiety among students due to the obsession with entrance examinations, overemphasis on rote memorization in middle school education, an increase in self-centered and competitive attitudes, and widening regional disparities in schools and educational

---

[9] "Middle School Entrance Examination Improvement Proposal: Middle School No Examination Selection System," Middle School Entrance Examination Research Committee, Korean Federation of Teachers' Associations (April 26, 1968).
[10] Measures were taken to implement exceptions in the case of some schools run by religious organizations (Abe 1971: 53).

levels. The council also listed the socioeconomic issues, including the negative impact of heavy spending on supplementary educational activities (see section III of this chapter, p. 84ff) on household budgets and the national economy, excessive parental involvement in education and social disturbances caused by entrance examination-related issues, increased distrust in school education due to the spread of supplementary educational activities, rising problems relating to private tutors and preparatory schools (*hagwon*), and the spread of cliques and factions judging people by the schools they attended (Suhr Myong-Won 1973).[11]

In order to take action against the extremely competitive high school entrance examination situation and the accompanying problems described above, in 1973, the Ministry of Education announced its "measure for leveling academic high schools." Following a proposal by the Council on Reform of the Entrance Examination System, it was an extremely radical measure abolishing the admission procedures for individual academic high schools. All prospective students for academic high schools in a particular district were to be selected and assigned to schools in the district by lottery.

The leveling measures were of the same type as the no-entrance-exam policy for middle schools that had been implemented since 1969. They were similar to the joint selection system for Tokyo metropolitan high schools that was implemented in the 1970s, but in South Korea they were very thorough: students were not allowed to select a school group, but were automatically assigned to the school group in their residential area; and not only public high schools, but also private academic high schools were included as targets of the leveling policy.[12] Students who wanted to go to an academic high school had no choice as to what school they would attend.

The measures for leveling academic high schools began in Seoul in 1974 and extended to 21 middle- to large-sized cities in South Korea; the basic idea continues to be implemented today.[13] Academic high schools in small cities and rural areas were excluded from the measures. The leveling measures in cities achieved their purpose in ending the high-pressure competition for high school entrance examinations, because almost all of the "best schools" prior to the implementation were in the middle- to large-sized cities.

---

[11] Yun Jeong-Il, et al. (1991: 42).
[12] Art high schools and some high schools run by religious organizations were exempt from these measures. The special professional high schools such as science high schools established later were also exempt.
[13] These measures were subsequently cancelled in several middle-sized cities where significant adverse effects from the leveling measures emerged because of the very small number of academic high schools.

Intent of the Policy on Equal Opportunity in Secondary Education
The reforms made to the admission system for secondary schools were aimed at resolving the intensely competitive entrance examinations, which had become a serious social issue. There appeared to be other purposes behind the reforms, however. The reforms of the secondary-school admission system may have been as thoroughgoing as they were for the following reasons.

First, we can argue that the abolition of entrance exams for middle schools must have been implemented with the plan to extend compulsory education to middle school in mind. Korea's neighbors Japan and Taiwan had already made the lower stage of secondary education—i.e., middle schools—part of compulsory education, and it was a much-sought objective of the South Korean government as well. At the time, the government lacked the fiscal leeway to provide the education that was a prerequisite for establishing compulsory education free of charge. The no-entrance-exam policy for middle schools could be introduced as a first step toward that goal, ensuring that all citizens would have an equal opportunity to obtain a middle school education (Umakoshi 1981: 63).

The academic high school leveling policy was likewise implemented in response to changes in the role of upper secondary education. The Council on Reform of the Entrance Examination System that proposed this reform included many who objected to leveling the academic high schools. In their view, high school education should be based on the principles of merit and competition. They viewed the competitive nature of high school entrance examinations in a positive light, arguing that "human beings are engaged in competition from the time they are born, and competition for good intent is an unavoidable part of life." They were also concerned that leveling would bring about a decline in overall scholastic ability. Their opposition, however, was overruled by the proponents of the leveling policy, who argued from the extremely idealistic view that "high schools should be institutions of upper secondary education that respect human values, where all can gather in one place to acquire general knowledge regardless of disparities of wealth, birth, and ability." The latter view prevailed, and legislation for the leveling measures was enacted and implemented (Min Kwan-Sik 1975: 75–76). Figure 3–2 shown above shows how the high school attendance rate rapidly increased from the mid-1970s. This increase was a result of the gradually increased enrollment quotas for high schools that reflected the changing role of high school education in South Korea.

Another plausible reason for the South Korean government's strong support for the universalization of secondary education was its need to cultivate manpower for economic development. The early 1970s, when the academic high school leveling measures were being implemented, was also a time when many two-year vocational schools (the predecessors of the junior colleges) for training middle-echelon technicians were first established. South Korea was in the midst of a shift from light industry to heavy industry, so behind the policy for making secondary education more egalitarian and open was the intent to raise the overall level of education and institute technical education at the secondary and the higher levels of education in order to develop workers with higher-level skills.

Third, the radical reforms to secondary education were regarded as the government's attempt to diminish inequality in the distribution of social resources. Under the banner of "first growth, then distribution," the government considered economic development its top priority, and did not institute adequate policies to solve the distribution problem. Under these circumstances, the best the Park regime could do at the time was to achieve pro forma equalization of educational opportunity by instituting reforms to the secondary school system that would promote equal distribution of opportunity at minimal cost and without conflicting with the top priority of economic development. Considering that there was a certain amount of enthusiasm for upward mobility through education in South Korea at that time, these egalitarian policies for secondary education were quite significant as a means of distributing social resources.

Although competition to gain entrance to a few prestigious middle schools and high schools was intense, in fact only a limited sector of society had been able to afford the educational cost of participating in the competition before the abolition. These policies seemed to have appeal as eliminating the privileged opportunities to advance to the "best middle schools" and "best high schools" that had once been the exclusive realm of the wealthy (and that could ultimately lead to entrance into prestigious universities or to higher socioeconomic status) and opening up the opportunities for educational achievement to members of every social class. The very intent of solving the problem of inequality of status and rewards among the social classes by correcting the educational opportunity gap was what gave the reforms to the secondary education system, especially high school education, their quite radical nature.

The changes in secondary education policy implemented from the end of the 1960s to the early 1970s, including the policy barring entrance exams for middle school, the leveling of the academic high schools, and the expanded enrollment quotas of secondary schools, altered the selection system of South Korea drastically. With these measures, selectivity at the secondary education level became far less significant. We may conclude that this formal equalization of educational opportunity reduced inequality in educational opportunity as far as secondary education is concerned.

Government Control of Higher Education

After the Liberation, South Korea's higher education expanded more rapidly than its elementary and secondary education. Higher education opportunities in colonial Korea had been very limited, consisting solely of Keijo (Seoul) Imperial University, the only institution accredited to grant advanced degrees.[14] After 1945, however, numerous new universities and colleges (assume both hereafter), some of which had been college-level "vocational schools" in the colonial period, were established, and the number of enrolled students rapidly increased. Although there were only around 8,000 students in higher education in 1945, the number had increased to more than 100,000 by 1960.[15] The U.S. military administration and the Rhee Syngman regime supported the expansion of higher education mainly led by private universities, and did not intervene in any particular way. In 1955, the Ministry of Education issued the "College Establishment Standards" to impose some restrictions on newly established universities; however, the standards were substantially relaxed in 1958, and did not do much to dampen the expansion of higher education (Umakoshi 1981: 147). Until the early 1960s, although the Ministry of Education had set the enrollment quotas for each institution, in fact private universities accepted many more students for financial reasons.[16]

The exceedingly rapid expansion of higher education was to be the source of various social issues, the most critical of which was that efforts to improve quality could not keep pace. Some private universities, managed like business corporations, admitted far more than the maximum enrollment without sufficient facilities or teaching staff. Many were institutions of higher education in name only. Since South Korea's industry was still in the process of growing, the rapid expansion of higher education was not based on actual demand in the labor market. This imbalance meant that employment conditions for college graduates were extremely poor, and unemployment among college graduates rose to massive proportions. The presence of so many unemployed college graduates itself stirred social unrest, and at the same time, provoked strong criticism of the unbridled expansion of higher education.

The Park Chung-Hee regime, which came into power by military coup in 1961, began to exercise a forceful intervention policy in higher education. Making eco-

---

[14] Additionally, there were several post-secondary "vocational schools."
[15] *Statistical Yearbook of Education* 1963, Korean Ministry of Education. The rapid expansion of higher education occurred due to several factors: College students were exempted from military service during the Korean War; new high school graduates who were unable to find jobs because of the job shortage advanced to colleges; and landlords afraid of losing land due to agricultural land reforms established higher-education institutions in order to avoid having their agricultural land confiscated by making it corporate property (Umakoshi 1981).
[16] Taking 1962 as an example, enrolled students in colleges increased to about 175 percent of the full quota on average (*Statistical Yearbook of Education* 1963, Korean Ministry of Education).

nomic development its top priority, the government aimed to improve the efficiency and quality of higher education so as to better contribute to that objective through the implementation of various institutional reforms. The most important of these was that the state would control the maximum enrollments of the colleges and supervise the college entrance examinations.

Enrollment Quotas
Strict governmental control under the Park regime over the number of students to be admitted to colleges altered the higher education admission system from its foundations. In order to rein in the quantitative expansion of higher education as much as possible, in 1965 the Park regime sought to cope with the aforementioned social issues by issuing a presidential decree on college student quotas. The quotas of students at all colleges, including private colleges, were to be determined by presidential decree, and the State Council would have to approve any change in the quotas.[17] At the same time, the government strictly enforced the decree. Each college was required to submit a list of the students it wished to accept to the Ministry of Education and receive its stamp of approval prior to sending out letters of acceptance to the students; if they did not, the government could render some of the acceptances void. (Song Kwang-Yong 1989: 21).

Thus legal quotas were established to control the number of students at all colleges in the country. However, the content of the policy on enrollment quotas in fact changed quite a bit from one time to another, and that caused considerable fluctuation in the number of students finishing higher education.

As the governmental controls on enrollment quotas were instituted to deal with the social issues brought about by the rapid expansion of higher education from the Liberation in 1945 to the early 1960s, the tone of the enrollment quota policy initially tended to be restrictive. As shown in figure 3–3, although the absolute number of college students in the 1960s was increasing, the rate of increase was significantly smaller in comparison to the 1950s. It was even smaller than the increase in the number of high school graduates; thus, as shown in figure 3–4, the rate of new high school graduates advancing to higher education appeared to be shrinking.

The purpose of higher education policy from the 1970s onward was not only to

---

[17] Prior to that time, although the Park Chung-Hee regime attempted, through the "Standards for Maintenance and Improvement of Schools" (1961), etc., to control the quotas of college students in response to manpower demand from the labor market, those measures were not sufficiently effective. At the time of the 1965 decree, although the private colleges objected strongly, the government succeeded in enforcing the enrollment quota measures, probably because the Park Chung-Hee regime had a firm grip on political power.

74 | Part I   Theory, Structure, and Institutions

Figure 3–3. Student Enrollment in Higher Education

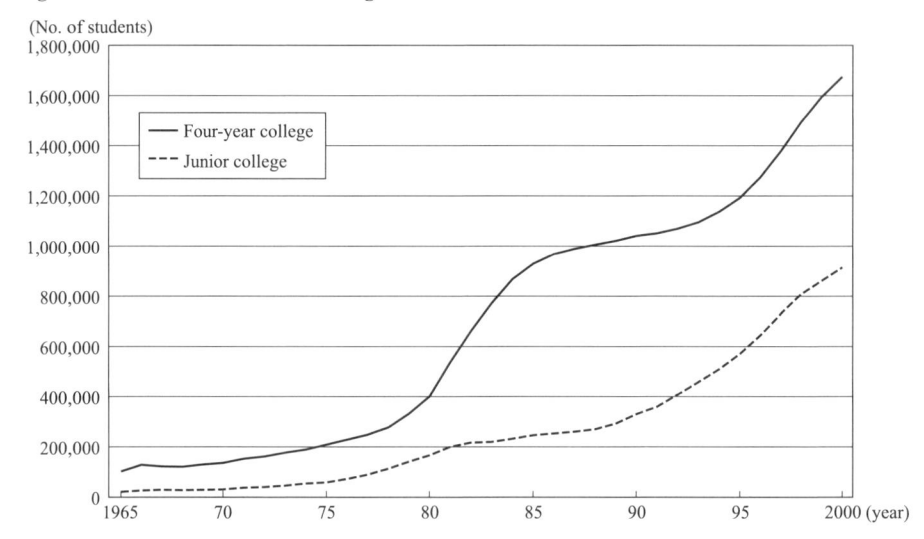

(No. of students)

Source: Compiled by the author based on *Statistical Yearbook of Education* (Korean Ministry of Education).

Figure 3–4. Rate of Direct Advancement to Higher Education among High School Graduates (%)

Year	Academic high school	Vocational high school	Total
1965	38.6	14.9	28.9
1970	40.2	9.6	26.9
1975	41.5	8.8	25.8
1980	39.2	11.4	27.2
1985	53.8	13.3	36.4
1990	47.2	8.3	33.2
1995	72.8	19.2	51.4
2000	83.9	42.0	68.0

Source: Compiled by the author based on *Statistical Yearbook of Education* (Korean Ministry of Education).

control the quantity of students; the government also set a high value on the link between educational policy and economic development policy. While the third (1972–76) and fourth (1977–81) five-year economic plans aimed to develop the heavy and chemical industries, nurturing technical expertise through institutions of higher education to support such industrial growth was a major challenge.

Thus, from the early 1970s, selective increases in the quotas of students advancing to higher education were made, especially in the sciences and engineering. The quotas for social sciences and humanities majors remained restricted as before.

The most important aspect of policy on higher education in the 1970s was the active promotion of the establishment of "vocational schools" (*jeonmun hakkyo*) offering vocational education to nurture middle-echelon professionals and technicians for industry. From 1970, when the government approved their establishment, the vocational schools—two- or three-year institutions of higher education—proliferated rapidly; the student quotas for vocational schools stood at about 70 to 80 percent of the quotas for four-year colleges by the end of the decade. The basis of policy on student quotas for higher education in the 1970s was to respond to the gradually increasing demand for advancement to higher education by increasing the quotas for students in vocational schools offering practical training while continuing to limit the number of students entering four-year colleges, with the exception of science and engineering majors (Yun Jeong-Il 1991: 259–61).

Contrary to the situation in the early 1960s, the extremely rapid expansion of the South Korean economy in the 1970s meant that the lack of a college-educated workforce became a serious issue. Calls from industry to expand the student quotas intensified, and finally, around 1978, the education ministry decided to increase the quotas for students in higher education overall. However, what brought about the most significant change in the policy on quotas for higher education was the change in government regimes. As will be explained in the next section, in 1980 the Chun Doo-Hwan regime came to power by military coup, and its lack of legitimacy was a critical issue. The new government sought to soften the negative national sentiment directed at it by substantially increasing the quotas for students entering higher education, thereby mitigating the competition surrounding college entrance examinations.

For the same purpose, the Chun Doo-Hwan regime altered the method for regulating the number of students in higher education from "admissions quotas" to "graduation quotas"; this controlled the number of students graduating from college, rather than those entering, and allowed for additional admissions. Starting in 1981, the government approved additional admissions, pushing the quotas for four-year college graduates up by 30 percent and those for junior college graduates up by 15 percent.[18] This "graduation quota" system was originally to be made workable by forcing students with low academic performance to drop out, ultimately allowing only the number of students within the graduation quota to graduate. However, these extremely strict parameters drew criticism from both inside

---

[18] In 1979, vocational schools and other two-year colleges were combined to become "junior colleges" (*jeonmun daehak*).

and outside the colleges, and within a few years they were no longer being enforced. In the mid-1980s, the government took action to allow almost all students admitted to graduate, and to readmit those previously expelled (Yun Jeong-Il 1991: 261–64).[19]

Under these policies, the number of students advancing to higher education in South Korea began increasing rapidly around 1980. Over the four-year period from 1977 to 1981, the number of students advancing to junior colleges increased from 48,924 to 106,316, and the number advancing to four-year universities nearly tripled, rising from 60,338 to 179,935.

After this period, the number of students advancing to higher education remained steady up to the end of the 1980s. However, in the early 1990s, the number began to increase again with the advent of the Kim Young-Sam administration. In addition, the number of new high school graduates peaked at 761,922 in 1990, and decreased thereafter due to the decreasing population of this age group. Therefore, for new high school graduates in the 1990s, the decline in the population of their age group, as well as the actual increase in enrollment quotas, meant that they had greater opportunities to advance to higher education.

College Entrance Examinations
In addition to controlling enrollment quotas, after the 1960s the government also started intervening in the process of college admissions. Governmental control of the college entrance examinations was intended to combat the qualitative decline of higher education institutions. As described above, during the period from immediately after the Liberation in 1945 to the 1960s, many private universities, thinking only of increasing tuition revenues, were not selective enough in their admissions, accepting many students who were underprepared for study at the higher education level (Umakoshi 1981: 204).

Although the government had previously attempted to control the admission of students advancing to higher education, it had failed because of the strong objections of private colleges. Its plans were not realized until 1969, when governmental control over private colleges had been sufficiently leveraged through enforcement of the policy on student admission quotas. If established a system whereby applicants to all colleges, including national and public as well as private institutions, became obligated to take a national qualification examination called the "Preliminary College Entrance Examination" (PCEE). Applicants who passed the qualification examination were eligible to take a secondary entrance examination offered by each college (Umakoshi 1981: 204–05).

---

[19] In 1988, the graduation quota system was abolished, and the admissions quota system was reinstated.

In the early days after the system went into effect, the threshold for passing the qualification examination was set to be 150 percent of the total quota of students admitted to individual colleges, but it was increased to 180 percent in 1972 and 200 percent in 1974. Nevertheless, according to the figures published annually by the Korean Ministry of Education in its *Statistical Yearbook of Education*, the overall passing rate was approximately 50 percent, which implies that the Preliminary College Entrance Examination functioned well as a screening device in the admission system. In 1979, students advancing to junior colleges also became obligated to take the PCEE. Thus, the same national examination was imposed on almost all applicants to higher education, including private universities, which made the selection in advancing to higher education far more unified.

Later, the Preliminary College Entrance Examination was no longer used for the preliminary selection of applicants qualified for higher education. Renamed the "Scholastic Ability Test for College Entrance" in 1982 and then the "College Scholastic Ability Test" from 1994 to the present, it became a universal first-stage college entrance examination comparable to Japan's National Center Test for college admissions. The score on the test was used only as one factor determining admission by individual colleges. However, during this period, the second-stage entrance examinations (subject-specific written examinations) offered by each college were abolished following complaints that "the second-stage examinations of some hard-to-enter universities are so difficult that the preparation required imposes an excessive burden on applicants." Consequently, applicants were selected by referring to their score on the Scholastic Ability Test for College Entrance or the College Scholastic Ability Test, their high-school grade records, and tests conducted by individual colleges, including an additional essay test, interview, and practical subject test scores. Therefore, as it had previously, the unified academic achievement test provided by the government played an important role in gaining admission to higher education.

College-Entrance-Centered, Goverment-Controlled, Unified
As we can see from the above discussion, government policy on secondary education and on higher education were moving in completely different directions.

The Policy on Secondary and Higher Education and Its Consequences
Regarding secondary education, efficiency received little consideration, as all efforts were focused on achieving a formal egalitarianism. The primary policy of the government was to reduce, to the greatest extent possible, qualitative differences in the educational opportunities students were receiving through the completion of their secondary education. At the same time, secondary education opportunities were rapidly expanding. What was happening was that selectivity at both the

lower and upper stages of secondary education was significantly lowered.

By contrast, when it came to higher education—a factor that can determine the technological level of a country, and one requiring much greater expenditures than secondary education—efficiency of education was thoroughly pursued, and the issues of formal egalitarianism in educational opportunity were given little attention. The government determined its student quotas for higher education not by student demand, but by the demand of industry for human resources; it required applicants to take achievement examinations to assess their "scholastic ability." The differences in level of achievement among colleges were accepted without hesitation. Thus, the selectivity of advancement to college remained high; with no meaningful selection process held at lower levels, the selection system in South Korea became heavily college-entrance-centered.

From the Park regime onward, extremely rigorous goverment supervision and control became the norm in the South Korean selection systems at the higher education level as well as at the secondary school level. The state enforced very strict controls over the number of students to be admitted to colleges, private institutions included, and individual institutions had little room for admitting students at their own discretion until the 2000s, when the admission system became open. This state control is an important characteristic of the South Korean educational selection system.

Furthermore, the single framework of selection from national to private colleges, and including not only four-year universities but also the (vocational) junior colleges, characterizes this government-controlled selection system. Given this framework, applicants to the institutions of higher education with widely differing purposes and curriculums are required to take the same examination and go through the same selection procedure. If we follow Hopper's definition of the degree of "centralization and standardization in educational selection" as a rubric for categorizing education systems, South Korea would be recognized as a system with an extremely high degree of centralization and standardization (Hopper 1968).

Turner (1960) pointed to the "folk norms" of upward social mobility between the two countries to explain the difference between the school systems of the United Kingdom and the United States. If we follow his typology, the selection system of South Korea delays decisive selection and separation as much as possible in order to avoid a situation where only some participants may gain an advantage, making it closer to the "contest mobility" type of system found in the United States. With this selection system, however, the decisive effect of selection is small even at the higher education stage in the United States, whereas in South Korea the selection process is very decisive at the stage when students advance to higher education. Moreover, centralization and standardization of selection is extremely weak in the United States, while South Korea imposes strong governmental control in order to achieve standardized education and selection processes. Strong control made it possible for the South Korean government to realize its policies of granting no advantages or disadvantages because of disparity in educational conditions up to the stage of advancement to college.

The Impact of a Unified Selection System
The distinctive selection processes of South Korea's education system as described above exert a significant influence on the nature of academic credentials in South Korean society and on the competition surrounding their acquisition.

For one thing, selectivity at the secondary education stage was substantially reduced, while the decisive selection process was focused on the college-entrance stage, so the competition for entrance to college became very intense. This was not the simple quantitative effect of the increased number of high school graduates eligible to advance to higher education due to the expansion of secondary education. By abolishing and weakening selectivity at the middle and high school entrance stage, decisive student selectivity was postponed until the college entry stage. This did not at all lessen the aspirations of secondary school students toward academic achievement, and raised their overall desire to enter higher education.[20] Kim Young-Hwa et al. observe as follows:

> After implementing the policy of no entrance examinations for middle school in 1969 and the policy leveling high schools in 1974, we do not have educational selectivity in our country in the true sense of the word except for the college entrance examinations. . . . Therefore, opportunities for students to obtain a realistic assessment of their abilities are postponed to the stage of entering higher education. Even students who might have given up on going to college if there had been selectivity prior to that stage never let go of their desire to go to college. (Korean Educational Development Institute 1993: 102)

The increasing number of students aspiring to higher education as a result of such quantitative and qualitative factors caused the college entrance examinations in the second half of the 1970s to become extremely competitive, and many students were left to fail. This was the natural consequence of the discrepancy between the egalitarian-oriented secondary education policies and the efficiency-oriented higher education policies.

Second, leveling the academic high schools allowed students of a wide variety of academic abilities to attend high school. In order to further promote "equal opportunity" in secondary education, however, the Ministry of Education an-

---

[20] We will discuss this issue in detail in chapter 4 through time-series analysis of the number of applicants to universities.

nounced a policy banning class formation based on academic performance.[21] As a result, there were large gaps in scholastic ability among students in a single classroom, which caused great difficulties in actual teaching. This policy significantly lowered the ability of the academic high schools to perform their original function, which was to prepare students to advance to higher education.

Third, and most importantly, these features of the South Korean selection system exert an important influence on the nature of academic credentials. From the perspective of screening theory (see chapter 1, pp. 18–19), the reduced selectivity at the secondary education level caused little essential difference in academic credentials prior to the stage of higher education. In other words, for those who completed high school after the reform of secondary education—i.e., those born after the late 1950s—higher education academic credentials are the only "significant" ones.

Governmental control over the college entrance examinations also had significant impact on the value of higher education credentials. From that same screening-theory perspective, the Preliminary College Entrance Examination conducted after 1969 essentially gave the endorsement of the state to the academic abilities of students admitted to colleges. The unified examination guaranteed that all freshmen had a certain level of academic ability, regardless of which college they entered. That change further enhanced the value of the college diploma as proof of academic ability.

As described earlier, applicants to all institutions of higher education, including junior colleges, were required to take the unified test in 1979; the entrance examinations conducted by individual institutions were abolished with the transformation of the PCEE to the Scholastic Ability Test for College Entrance in the early 1980s. This caused greater importance to be placed on unified test scores in the selection of applicants for higher education (i.e., the establishment of the unitary selection system), and institutions gradually came to be ranked according to scores on the unified examination needed for admission. Although four-year colleges and junior colleges were established for very different educational functions, as this ranking developed among them, junior colleges for vocational training became recognized as one rank "lower" than four-year institutions because applicants to junior colleges were admitted with lower unified test scores.[22] Furthermore, dis-

---

[21] In June 1978, the Ministry of Education adopted a policy of allowing classes to be formed on the basis of academic performance for certain specified courses (Inaba 1993: 89–90). In actual practice, however, the schools often faced difficult situations due to complaints from the parents of students who were assigned to lower-ranking classes.

[22] It seems that such negative evaluations were internalized even by students attending junior colleges. Kim Mee-Ran (2000) conducted a survey of four-year-college and junior-college students in Seoul, asking, "Which students are better, [four-year] college students or junior-col-

parities appeared in the degree of difficulty of getting into four-year colleges in Seoul as opposed to other areas.

What is notable here is the highly visible indicator—i.e., scores on the unified examination—used to show the difficulty of gaining entrance to college. The establishment of the unitary selection system, where all applicants to higher education were sorted according to scores on a unified scholastic achievement test, heightened the visibility of the ranking of institutions of higher education, and consequently created a situation in which the institution from which one graduated became overwhelmingly important.

In addition, the rapid expansion of higher education around 1980 exacerbated the "rank differences" between universities in Seoul and those in regional areas. The increase in the number of students admitted to four-year colleges at that time, which was about three times greater than before, can largely be attributed to the expansion of the student quotas themselves, and to the establishment of new universities and colleges. It should be noted that at that time the government seldom approved the establishment of a new university or college in Seoul and its suburbs; it did not increase the student quota for institutions there, either, because overpopulation of the city was a serious social problem. Therefore, the rapid expansion of four-year colleges was observed mainly in regional institutions (or regional campuses of institutions with a main campus in Seoul). The expansion of higher education under such institutional restrictions made opportunities to advance to colleges in Seoul even rarer, so that whether a college was in Seoul or not became an even more prominent determiner in the hierarchy of higher educational institutions.[23]

The Influence of Enrollment Quota Policy Changes
Of the distinctively South Korean policies, the quotas imposed on acceptance of students at each stage of education also influenced the nature of academic credentials. As described above, secondary and higher education expanded remarkably after the Liberation, and the speed of expansion—for higher education in particu-

lege students?" in each of the following areas: "common sense," "professional knowledge," "expressiveness," "positiveness," "responsibility," "cooperativity," "courtesy," and "patience." According to this survey, both college students and junior college students had a tendency to say that college students were better than junior college students in the areas of common sense, professional knowledge, and self-expression.

[23] The expansion of secondary education and increase in household income, which enhanced people's overall financial ability to bear the cost of college entrance, also raised the discriminative capacity of college graduate credentials. The increased number of participants competing to advance to higher education meant an increased number of students were subject to the "filtering out" system at that stage, and inevitably heightened the reliability of the college entrance examinations to do that filtering.

82 | Part I   Theory, Structure, and Institutions

Figure 3–5.   Education Level of Population by Birth Cohort (Year 2000 Census)   (%)

Birth Year	Age in 2000	Elementary school	Middle school	High school	Junior college	Four-year college	Graduate school	Uneducated
Male								
1976–80	20–24	0.2	1.6	29.3	27.1	41.0	0.5	0.1
1971–75	25–29	0.5	2.7	42.6	19.5	30.0	4.5	0.2
1966–70	30–34	0.9	3.8	46.3	15.4	28.4	4.9	0.3
1961–65	35–39	2.9	7.7	44.9	12.6	26.2	5.3	0.4
1956–60	40–44	6.0	14.3	45.0	9.8	19.1	5.2	0.6
1951–55	45–49	11.3	19.4	42.5	6.3	14.7	4.7	1.0
1946–50	50–54	17.0	22.0	37.6	4.6	13.4	3.6	1.8
1941–45	55–59	24.3	22.6	30.4	3.7	12.4	2.9	3.7
1936–40	60–64	31.4	19.3	25.2	3.4	11.5	2.3	6.9
1931–35	65–69	36.0	16.0	19.9	3.5	10.6	1.7	12.3
–1930	70–	36.5	12.3	9.7	2.8	5.7	0.9	32.1
Female								
1976–80	20–24	0.2	1.3	35.9	28.3	33.0	1.1	0.1
1971–75	25–29	0.4	2.1	51.1	19.8	23.4	3.0	0.2
1966–70	30–34	1.2	5.4	57.8	13.3	19.8	2.4	0.3
1961–65	35–39	4.5	14.9	54.4	8.8	15.3	1.7	0.4
1956–60	40–44	11.5	25.1	46.9	5.3	8.9	1.3	0.9
1951–55	45–49	22.9	29.4	34.8	3.4	6.6	0.9	1.9
1946–50	50–54	35.9	26.7	24.3	2.4	5.2	0.6	4.9
1941–45	55–59	46.8	19.7	15.2	1.5	3.5	0.3	13.0
1936–40	60–64	49.3	13.0	9.5	0.9	2.0	0.2	25.2
1931–35	65–69	43.3	8.1	6.4	0.6	1.0	0.1	40.5
–1930	70–	25.8	3.0	2.7	0.4	0.4	0.0	67.6

Source: Compiled by the author based on the "Report on Population and Housing Census" for the year 2000 (Korean National Statistical Office).
Note: Includes those in school and withdrawn.

lar—fluctuated widely, reflecting the changes made to student quota policies. The breadth of educational opportunities that were open to each birth cohort, therefore, differed considerably. Figure 3–5 shows the distribution of educational level by birth cohort. This figure shows the higher education completion ratio by males and females, and in particular, the percentage of completion of four-year college degrees (including those attending school and those who withdrew), revealing large differences between the cohorts. There was no significant difference in the ratios for four-year colleges and above for the 1941–45, 1946–50, and 1951–55 birth cohorts; these were less than 20 percent for males, and a few percent for females.

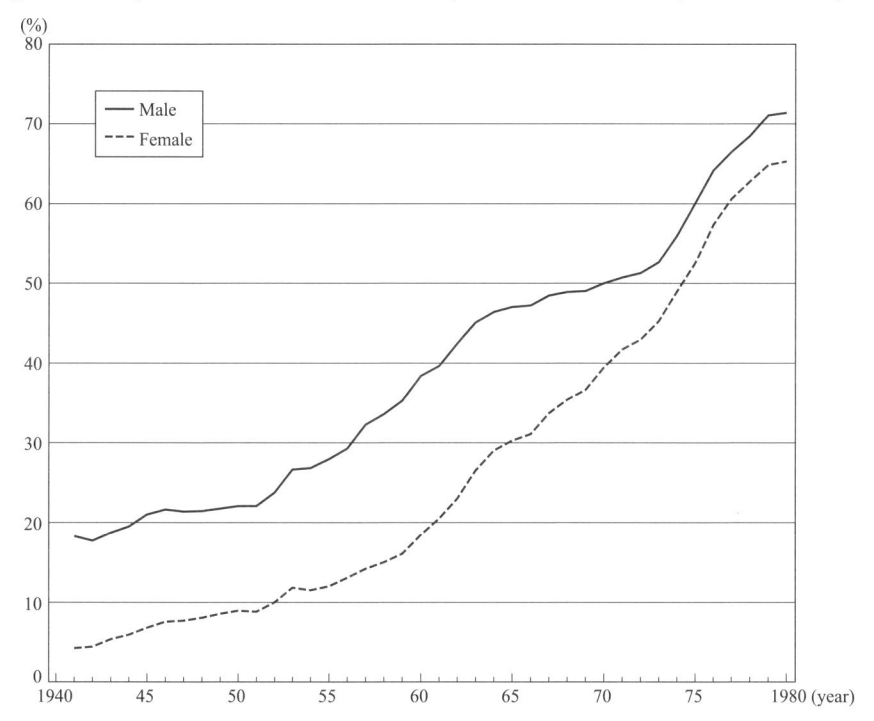

Figure 3–6. Higher Education Enrollment Ratios by One-Year Birth Cohort (Year 2000 Census)

Source: Compiled by the author based on the "Report on Population and Housing Census" for the year 2000 (Korean National Statistical Office).

However, for the 1956–60 birth cohort who became old enough to advance to higher education when student quotas were partially expanded, the ratio rose to 24.3 percent for males and 10.2 percent for females. The figures then quickly increased to 30–40 percent for males and 10–30 or greater for females for the 1961–65 birth cohort, and the following cohort, the members of which became old enough to advance to higher education after student quotas were being expanded dramatically.

The ratio of enrollment in higher education (including junior colleges) by one-year birth cohort clearly indicates the differences in educational opportunities depending on year of birth. Figure 3–6 shows that the ratio of students advancing to higher education had increased gradually for birth cohorts before the early 1950s, then rapidly increased for the 1952 and the 1953 birth cohorts. After that, there was an even larger increase for the late 1950s to the early 1960s birth cohorts. As a result, within the five-year gap between the 1958 birth cohort and the 1963 birth cohort (33.7 percent of males and 14.9 percent of females; 45.0 percent of males and 26.4 percent of females, respectively), there was a 10-point difference in the proportion of students who advanced to higher education. What triggered this rapid increase in enrollment ratios was the change in the higher education student quota policy described in this chapter.[24]

The disparities in educational level among different birth cohorts caused by the government student quota policies might mean that the social and economic advantages accruing from academic credentials differed from one generation to the next. In particular, the substantial increase in quotas for students advancing to higher education around 1980 significantly altered the distribution of the educational level of people entering the labor force; this would, in turn, significantly influence the labor market. The rapid expansion of higher education at that time provides us with an ideal case for empirical examination of the consequences of educational expansion discussed in chapter 1 (see chapter 1, p. 24). This issue will be investigated in the following chapters.

III. THE SOCIAL ISSUES OF SUPPLEMENTARY STUDY

The policy of leveling the academic high schools and the consequent decline of their function as preparatory schools for advancement to higher education had an important effect on the competition for entry into institutions of higher education, which had become very intense due to the increased number of high school graduates. Students determined to gain access to college, but lacking trust in the education offered at regular high schools, rushed to take after-school classes (supplementary study) with a private tutor or at a preparatory school, causing the competition to enter higher education to shift into competition for access to supplementary study.

The Chun Doo-Hwan regime, which had come to power by a military-led coup d'état in December 1979 and established itself following the bloody suppression of democracy movement protests (the Gwangju Uprising) in May 1980, enforced a drastic policy that completely prohibited supplementary study, which by that time had become a major social issue. In this section, we will examine the supplementary study issue in detail, exploring the logic that led the government to intervene to such a degree in the private educational activity of attending after-school

---

[24] However, we may say that the change in the rate of enrollment in higher education per birth cohort was gradual relative to the change in the student quotas entering higher education. Because South Korean men are obligated to perform military service, there were many cases where students did not enter higher education immediately after graduating from high school, but did so several years later. Such variance in the age of first-year students in higher education would be a factor of smoothing the shift in the enrollment rates by birth cohort.

classes and determining how the competition in advancement to institutions of higher education changed as a result. In so doing, we attempt to understand how South Koreans perceived fairness in educational opportunity and what the government did in the endeavor to secure it.

The Advent of the After-School Study Issue
The policy of leveling the academic high schools made it difficult to teach in an efficient manner, and this led many students to take after-school classes to prepare for the entrance examinations to higher education. In large cities such as Seoul, 43.9 percent of academic high school students, and about 23.2 percent of vocational high school students, were taking after-school classes as of 1980 (Korean Educational Development Institute 1981). As shown in figure 3–4, at that time, the ratio of high school students advancing to higher education immediately after graduation was close to 40 percent for academic high schools and over 10 percent for vocational high schools. Therefore, many of the high school students who were planning to take college entrance examinations had been taking after-school classes.

In the years leading up to the ban on supplementary study, the media had carried numerous articles describing the fierce competition for after-school study services, particularly among members of the wealthy class. A documentary in the May 1979 issue of *Shin Dong-A* reported that tutors who could produce good results were called "special A-grade tutors." They offered 90-minute one-on-one lectures twice a week for a monthly fee of 200,000 to 250,000 won (approximately 400 to 500 US dollars at that time). This was a huge amount—equivalent to the average monthly income of a salaried worker. Nevertheless, since many parents of middle school and high school students hoped to hire such tutors, some parents even made reservations for their services years in advance (Cho Gang-Hwan 1979). Furthermore, in the following year (1980), the situation became more serious: the demand for hiring one of the special A-grade tutors increased by between 50 and 100 percent from the previous year, and just an introduction to one of the best-regarded tutors required a fee of about 1 million won (approximately 2,000 US dollars) (*Dong-A Ilbo*, February 14, 1980).

Of course, only some wealthy families could afford such costly after-school tutoring, but it was not so rare that a family of more modest means would manage to come up with the money to obtain supplementary help in preparing their children for the college entrance examinations. The January 1978 article of the *Monthly Joong-Ang* reported the case of student K, who was in his third year of high school. His family, living in the Seoul suburbs, consisted of his father, incapacitated by illness; his mother, an itinerant seller of cosmetics; his sister, who was a factory worker; and his brother. They had a very tight family budget with a monthly income of about 70,000 won. Even so, following his sister's advice, student K and his middle-school second-year brother began taking after-school classes. The father's medicine cost 15,000 to 20,000 won and the after-school classes fees were 15,000 won, which, when subtracted from the family's annual income, left little for the family of five to subsist on. Nevertheless, K's sister declared, "We cannot cut the cost of the medicine, but we can't cut my brothers' after-school study fees, either" (Chun Taek-Won 1978: 272).

Judging from newspaper and magazine accounts, near the end of the 1970s there was a prevailing fear among parents and students that taking high school classes alone was not sufficient to get into prestigious colleges in South Korea.[25] Parents were aware of the wide disparity in teaching skills and performance among after-school tutors. Those who were sensitive to the tutors' skills and performance were willing to pay more, and the market mechanism kicked in, driving up the fees of some outstanding private tutors.

As the competition for after-school classes intensified, it became the target of social criticism. From the end of the 1970s, newspaper and magazine articles recorded the realities of "after-school-class hell" (*gwawoe jiok*) and "the malaise that will ruin the nation" (*mangguk byeong*). While the distrust of schools and the widespread participation in after-school classes were naturally regarded as indicative of the decline in the public education system, newspapers and magazines also emphasized the excessive financial burden imposed on households by the fees for after-school tutoring. Although parents and their children freely chose to take after-school classes, parents who wanted their children to attain higher education had no choice but to shoulder the substantial financial burden of after-school classes because of the strong belief in their effectiveness and the aforementioned distrust of public education.

Another potential issue that emerged in the rush to attend after-school classes was the gap in access to supplementary education across the social classes. Unequal educational opportunities between the children of rich families who were able to afford the after-school study fees and the children of other families could result in unfairly disparate opportunities to advance to higher education. At a panel discussion on the issue of after-school classes held by the editorial department of *Shin Dong-A*, Associate Professor Kim In-Whoe of Yonsei University expressed the following opinion:

> As the cost of after-school study continually goes up, it seems that only a few students can take special after-school classes and attain access to good schools. For 30 years after the

---

[25] Teachers in active service even began to offer private after-school tutoring, resulting in a vicious cycle in which both teachers and students began to neglect regular school classes.

Liberation in 1945, our country has been a society where mobility across the social classes through education is very active, more so than in any other country. If after-school tuition costs continue to increase and the competition becomes more intense while the quotas of students admitted to prestigious universities remain fixed, there will be no more mobility across the social classes. Once a society is solidified like this, there will be discord among the classes, fueling great frustration among youth who cannot afford after-school classes and, in turn, stirring unrest in society. (Editorial Department, *Shin Dong-A* 1980: 320)

The professor's criticism is based on the assumption that after-school classes—especially high quality tutoring—have an unquestionably positive effect on academic achievement. On that point, he seemed to have little doubt.[26]

As Professor Kim indicates in his editorial, the expectation of widespread equal opportunity for social mobility though education was very strong in South Korean society at that time. The fact that high-priced after-school classes had become such a major social issue, requiring some corrective measures from the viewpoint of social fairness, was a reflection of people's high expectations of social mobility through education.

Some government officials also criticized the situation, remarking that, from the standpoint of the national economy, the frenzied rush toward after-school study was a waste of people's spending on education. Government officials involved in policy planning had the idea that the spending on after-school classes, which was costing the entire society a huge amount, was not a productive investment from the viewpoint of the national economy; if possible, those monies should be used to develop public education, which was suffering from the insufficient allocation of funds (Han Jun-Sang 1990).

The 7.30 Education Reform Measure

The Chun Doo-Hwan regime came to power by coup d'état, established martial law, and violently suppressed the Gwangju Uprising. This cost it popularity and legitimacy in the eyes of the nation. The government, aiming to win popular support by tackling a matter of pressing importance to society, seized on the issue of after-school supplementary study. The "Special Committee for National Security Measures" (hereafter the Committee for National Security), established in May 1980 as the president's advisory committee (a body which, under martial law, actually possessed full administrative and legislative powers), announced it would make solving the urgent issue of after-school classes its task for national administration. Chun Doo-Hwan instructed the Committee for National Security's subcommittee on education and public information to plan and implement a solution.

---

[26] Empirical analysis on the actual effects of after-school classes on student achievement was not conducted until the 2000s (e.g., Kim Kyung-keun 2014; Byun Soo-yong 2014).

On July 30, 1980, the "program for normalizing education and resolving the overheated problem of after-school classes," which came to be known as "the 7.30 Education Reform Plan," was announced. The reform plan aimed to mitigate the competition for entrance to higher education by significantly increasing the quotas for students entering individual institutions and by expanding opportunities for entering higher education through the introduction of a graduate quota system.[27] Also, by placing greater weight on high school grade records in admissions to higher education and by abolishing the entrance examinations administered by individual colleges, it aimed to reduce time spent on after-school classes so that high school students could concentrate their energies on their regular schoolwork.

The most important point of the plan was that it prohibited enrolled school students from taking any after-school classes.[28] This plan, enforced from August 1, completely banned all out-of-school supplemental learning.[29] In order to implement the prohibition, the government created measures for enforcement of the law and established an office where violations could be reported; strict penalties were imposed. Any schoolteacher found to be involved in after-school teaching was immediately fired. Students who took an after-school class were expelled from school. The parents of a student who took after-school classes, if they were civil servants, would be dismissed; otherwise, their employers were expected to fire them.

Although the 7.30 education reform was so radical that it was called "the education coup," it did not address the structural problems surrounding the intense competition for admission to college. It did include several measures, such as expanded admissions quotas, abolition of individual college entrance examinations, and giving greater weight to high-school grade records in college admissions; however, unlike the middle school and high school reforms, none of the 7.30 reforms changed the fundamental structure of the higher-education selection system.

In fact, in the process of planning the 7.30 education reforms, the leveling of higher education had been studied at the request of the military authorities, who

---

[27] The rapid increase in the number of students advancing to higher education described on p. 75 is the result of this reform.

[28] The year following the ban on after-school classes, the government established an "education tax" in order to secure a budget for expanding public education. With this tax, it achieved its goal of turning people's spending on supplementary education fees into an investment in public education.

[29] Preparatory schools for high school graduates who had failed the college entrance examinations were exempted; tutoring in music and art and instruction in hobby activities were permitted by pre-registration. After that, some temporary mitigating measures, including approval for make-up classes for students with poor academic performance, were implemented, although the basic principle of prohibiting after-school classes was maintained (Yun Jeong-Il, et al. 1996).

considered solving the issue of after-school classes a top priority. Much like the leveling of the academic high schools, the plan for equalizing higher education would have been to collectively select applicants by region and major, and then to use a lottery system to allocate the selected applicants to individual institutions in order to eliminate discrepancies among the institutions, thus using structural means to reduce the intense competition surrounding entrance examinations (Jung Tae-Soo 1991: 51). However, Ministry of Education officials and educators strongly objected to the idea, asserting, among other reasons, that it would undermine the quality of higher education, and in the end it was not implemented. Thus, neither the ranking structure nor the selection system for applicants to higher education institutions were significantly altered; on the contrary, abolishing the individual institution entrance examinations actually strengthened the ranking structure. As described above, the unitary standards encompassed by the unified test (the Scholastic Ability Test for College Entrance/College Scholastic Ability Test) and high-school grade records were used in selecting applicants, which made the discrepancies between colleges in terms of difficulty of entry much more visible.

Furthermore, it should be noted that the education reform plan made no mention of the leveling policy applied to the academic high schools, even though it was often cited as the major factor exacerbating the issue of after-school classes. This may be attributed to the fact that many officials in the Ministry of Education who participated in planning the education reforms were reluctant to reject the outcomes of past government policies. For this reason, no change was made in the tendency of the South Korean education system to focus on college admissions, and the inability of the academic high schools to prepare students for higher education was also left unaddressed.

Thus, even though after-school classes were prohibited, the incentive for engaging in supplementary study remained strong, and as a result, some after-school classes continued to operate in secret despite the risks involved. Those offering such classes charged higher fees as a hedge against the risks, and only a few wealthy families were able to afford them.[30]

The 7.30 education reform measures implemented in 1980 thus turned out to be an extension of the existing selection policy. They sought to level the field for all participants in the competition for educational achievement as much as possible until graduation from high school. They were intended to achieve unified selection based on students' scholastic ability at the time they were ready to enter college.

---

[30] Later, as South Korea achieved greater democratization, the ban on after-school classes was strongly criticized as an infringement on freedom of education. From the end of the 1980s, the strictures on after-school classes were gradually mitigated. In 2000, the Constitutional Court of Korea decided that the ban on after-school classes was indeed unconstitutional and infringed on the right to pursue education freely, and the measures were abolished completely.

Prohibiting after-school classes may have further promoted the formal equalization of educational opportunity and ensured greater fairness in the competition for entrance to higher education. After all, the reform did not significantly alter the structure of college entrance competition; rather, it aimed at a fairer, purer competition.

In addition, the fact that the government attempted to ensure fairness in the competition for college entrance, even to the point of infringing on individuals' freedom to pursue education, implied official recognition of the importance of participating in the competition and of the value of the "prize" to be gained by winning. These government-created circumstances surrounding academic competition resulted in the widespread permeation of the academic credential society—one where socioeconomic status could be achieved only if higher academic credentials were acquired—and a consequent increase in the number of participants in the college entrance competition.

Conclusion

As observed in this chapter, the South Korean government has vigorously controlled and supervised the country's educational system since the 1960s. The targets of control ranged from the school system in its entirety to the student quotas for institutions, admissions standards, and even to after-school classes taken at cram schools or under private tutors. The government control and supervision extended equally to the national and public schools and private schools. Such thorough regulation of the educational system was possible because South Korea's state power was extremely strong and because education was seen as having a highly public character. As the government's intervention in the educational system was very thorough, education in South Korea has directly reflected the government's unique educational policies.

This thoroughness is also the reason for the selection system being college-entrance-centered, government-controlled, and unified. Since the Park Chung-Hee regime, South Korea has been enforcing strongly egalitarian policies in secondary education in order to achieve the formal equalization of educational opportunity to the greatest extent possible. Higher education, by contrast, aimed for efficiency of education in tandem with economic development; at the same time, the government became directly involved in the selection process. Government policies on education were enforced not only at national and public schools, but equally at private schools. The differing vectors of policies for secondary and higher education caused selection to be focused more strongly on the college-entrance stage than in other countries.

The selection system thus shaped by government policies is thought to have resulted in broader participation in the competition for admission to college, because the decreased selectivity in secondary education did nothing to reduce students' desire to pursue higher education at the stage prior to taking the college entrance examinations. Given these features of the South Korean selection system, the competition surrounding the college entrance examinations became fiercer and fiercer. This likely contributed to the prevailing view that the level of a person's educational achievement is determined purely by effort and ability.

The government's effort to ensure fairness in college admissions by eliminating disparities in educational opportunity outside of the public education system have also contributed to the spread of the belief that educational achievement is evidence of a person's effort and ability. The South Korean government took the step of completely banning after-school classes, even restricting people's right to the free pursuit of education, in order to eliminate disparities in educational opportunity caused by the unequal economic conditions among students' families. The government seemed keen to avoid any deviation from the perception that everyone had equal access to upward social mobility through education, regardless of family origin.

Kim Mee-Ran points out that the perception of unequal distribution of educational opportunities improved significantly between 1980 and 1981, when the 7.30 Education Reforms were implemented, and she attributes this to the reforms having expanded opportunities for higher education (Kim Mee-Ran 2000: 66–68). However, if this was indeed achieved, not only the expanded quotas, but also the government's efforts to level competition by prohibiting after-school classes, contributed substantially to this improvement.

The changes in the selection system and the accompanying changes in the competition for entering higher education in turn greatly altered the characteristics of the academic credentials created by the selection system. Most importantly, the effects of all these changes have substantially enhanced the availability of academic credentials in the labor market as an indication of applicants' level of ability. In other words, through strong governmental control of the selection of students advancing to higher education, implementation of the unified examinations, and increased participation in the competition surrounding college entrance examinations, the capacity of the entrance examinations to distinguish differences in students' scholastic abilities in a unified manner rapidly improved. The availability of information on individual abilities as reflected by academic credentials also greatly increased. We believe that the enhanced availability of academic credentials and the government's efforts to maintain fair competition had the effect of justifying the use of the academic credentials as proxy for applicants' abilities in the labor market. Therefore, as long as the examinations for advancing to higher education are believed to appropriately delineate the applicants' intellectual ability, which is also important for job performance, these changes would cause the relationship between academic credentials and socioeconomic status to become stronger and stronger.

This chapter also reveals that, given that the quotas of students enrolled are under the firm government control, the number of graduates at each educational level fluctuates considerably in South Korea. In particular, the fact that the number of graduates tripled within only a few years in the 1980s was notable. Taking into account the observations in this chapter, the next three chapters will examine empirically how qualitative and quantitative changes to South Korea's education and selection systems influenced the socioeconomic advantages accruing from academic credentials, and how they affected the equal distribution of educational opportunity.

PART II

Economic Rewards, Occupational Status, and Social Mobility

CHAPTER 4

The Monetary Benefits of Academic Credentials

Most of the economic explanations of the intense enthusiasm for education in South Korea assume the perspective of human capital theory, which applies neo-classical economics to the field of education. According to this perspective, the individual's choice to advance to a higher level of education has been understood as "investment" in oneself, pursuing the monetary advantages to be obtained. Indeed, the wage gap between persons with different academic credentials—particularly between high school graduates and college graduates—was large until at least the 1980s. This is the reason that "monetary benefit" is given in many explanations for the rise in popular aspirations for higher education.

However, even if we rely on this perspective, we need first to investigate the impact of the expanded college admissions quotas described in chapter 3 on the wage gap between university and high school graduates in the 1980s. According to the labor-market model of neo-classical economics discussed in chapter 1, an increase in the supply of college graduates acts to lower their wages, which in turn reduces the monetary advantages of a college education. On the other hand, as illustrated in Thurow's job competition model, it can be argued that, contrary to neo-classical economics, a rapid increase in the supply of college graduates does not necessarily alter wages, and the advantage of going to college may not decrease. Depending on how we understand the mechanisms determining wages and job opportunities in the labor market, the influence of the increased number of new college graduates on wages will be predicted in quite different ways.

Our first task, then, is to investigate how the rapid increase of college graduates in the 1980s impacted the labor market and changed the relationship between academic credentials and wages. Further, we should ask what feedback effect the increase had on people's aspirations for educational attainment. Seeking answers of these questions will provide us with the keys to understand the persistence of intense educational ambitions, and furthermore, the nature of the relationship between academic credentials and economic rewards in the South Korean labor market.

This chapter uses statistical data on wages to analyze the effect of higher education on economic rewards and how they changed. We focus on the impact of higher education because of the highly "college-entrance-centered" nature of the South Korean selection system and because popular aspirations for academic achievement are more or less equivalent to the ambition to go to university. This chapter examines wage gaps for employed persons only; the relationship between income and academic credentials of the self-employed will be taken up in chapter 6. This chapter also presents a time-series analysis of people's aspirations for advancement to higher education in order to understand the feedback effect of changes in the monetary benefits on such ambitions.

I. Fluctuations in Average Wage Gaps

In the early 1980s, Park Se-Il conducted a series of pioneering studies on the relationship between education and the labor market in South Korea (Park Se-Il 1982; 1983; 1984). To explore the factors leading to the wage disparities between different levels of education, he considers market factors based on screening theory and the monopsonistic discrimination model, but also recognizes the importance of the historical and institutional factors unique to South Korea, important among which is the period of colonial rule by Japan (Park Se-Il 1983: 34–35). One factor is the effect of "divide and rule" logic that pervaded the Korean labor market under colonial rule. People who had high-level academic credentials and worked as managers and administrators of government agencies or at Japanese companies earned much higher wages than workers who had low-level academic credentials and engaged in low-skilled manual jobs.

What is notable for this study is that the wage system created under the conditions of colonial governance continued in the Korean government and government-affiliated corporations without major modification even after the Liberation in 1945. At that time, the college-graduate labor force was relatively limited and the private companies that had grown large on the wave of industrial development were unable to hire college graduates unless they offered wages as high or even higher than those offered to graduates in the public sector. That meant that private companies, too, succeeded to the conventional wage system characterized by large disparities by level of education. This is the crux of Park's colonial-inheritance hypothesis explaining the prevalence of the large wage disparities by level of education in South Korea (Park Se-Il 1983: 34–35).

Following Dore's argument (see pp. 26–27), Park Se-Il further attributes the large wage gap among different academic credentials to South Korea's late industrialization. South Korea did not develop modern industrial technology from traditional indigenous technology but imported it from advanced countries and disseminated it through institutions of higher education. Academic credentials, which were assumed to be a measure of the ability to digest and apply modern technology, had significant meaning in the South Korean labor market (Park Se-Il 1983: 35–36).[1]

There are a number of other arguments that recognize the effect of non-economic factors on the wage gap among different academic credentials. For example, while analyzing the rate of return on investment in education, Kong Eun-Bae et al. state "The cultural and institutional influences of better treatment of people with higher academic credentials results in college graduates earning relatively higher wages than high school graduates, regardless of actual labor productivity" (Kong Eun-Bae et al. 1994: 173). Sorensen also points out that Confucian values act as a factor producing a large wage gap between the more educated and less educated (Sorensen 1994).

However, if the South Korean wage structure has a large gap among different academic credentials due only to such institutional factors, it would be stable and the economic incentive for educational achievement would not change easily even if educational composition of new entrants to the labor force should rapidly change. Could this interpretation be accurate?

Average Wages and Fluctuation

First, let us examine the average wage ratios among different levels of schooling, which can be interpreted as the economic benefits of education, and how they fluctuated. Figure 4–1 shows the ratios of the average wages (male) of junior college and four-year college graduates to the average wage of high school graduates based on the annual *Report on the Wage Structure Survey* issued by the Korean Ministry of Labor.[2] While this survey has been conducted since 1968, there were

---

[1] Although Park further analyzed changes in the wage structure caused by the increase in college graduates, the period of analysis of his studies did not go beyond 1981, after which the rapid increase of college graduates occurred. There are some other studies on wage disparities according to level of education in the 1980s and 1990s, such as Jang Soo-Myung (2002), Choi Young-Sup (2003), Kim Gwang-Jo (1995), and Jeong Jing-Ho et al. (2004), but most of them do not consider sufficiently the fluctuations in the wage gap between college graduates and high school graduates. Therefore, our analysis of changes in the wage structure in the 1980s and the first half of the 1990s and the feedback effect of such changes on educational aspiration has significant meaning in understanding the economic basis of educational ambitions among South Koreans.

[2] All wage data we use in this section are from the *Report on the Wage Structure Survey*. The wage amount we use as the analysis subject in this chapter is the total sum of a monthly basic

Figure 4-1. Wage Ratios of Junior College/Four-Year College Graduates to High School Graduates

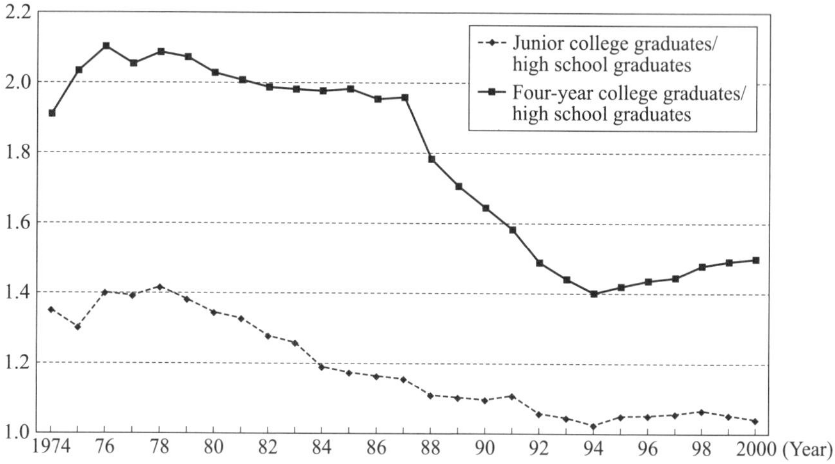

Source: Compiled from the annual reports of the Wage Structure Survey (Korean Ministry of Labor).

some format deficiencies and inconsistencies in the educational categories in the early reports. For this reason, this analysis focuses directly on data from 1974. We limit our analysis to the period until 2000, around when there was significant change in the structure of labor market due to the severe economic crisis. Moreover, because the size of the sample for females is relatively small due to the low rate of labor participation of females during the period under study and a completely different analysis is required for female workers owing to the unique employment patterns of women in South Korea, here we focus on the male samples.

Figure 4-1 indicates the large wage gaps between high school graduates and four-year college graduates (upper line) and between high school graduates and junior college graduates (lower line) until the early 1980s. In particular, average wages for four-year college graduates were about two times that of high school graduates.

From the late 1980s to the mid-1990s, however, there was a rapid shrinkage of the wage ratios, and in the last few years up to 2000 the gap shrank to between 1.4 and 1.5. The wage ratio for junior college graduates to high school graduates shrank from the early 1980s, and the average wage of junior college graduates is only a few percent higher than that of high school graduates in the second half of the 1990s. The ratios for both remained steady after the mid-1990s, showing little change.

---

salary, a monthly overtime compensation, and a monthly average of annual bonus. This survey includes graduate school graduates as the four-year college graduates. However, prior to 1990, because the number is negligible, we simply ignore it.

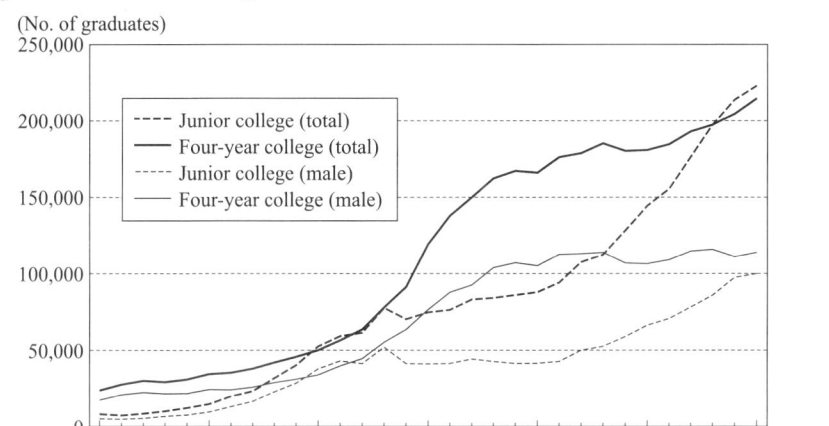

Figure 4–2. Number of College Graduates

(No. of graduates)

- - - - Junior college (total)
——— Four-year college (total)
- - - - Junior college (male)
——— Four-year college (male)

Source: Compiled from the annual reports of the Wage Structure Survey (Korean Ministry of Labor).

The trend in the wage ratios of college graduates to high school graduates appears to correlate with the change in the number of students newly graduated from colleges. As discussed in chapter 3, South Korea amended its college admissions quota policy around 1980, increasing the number of entrants to higher education. Figure 4–2 charts the number of students newly graduated from colleges by year 1970 to 2000. From this figure, we observe that the number of junior college graduates increases rapidly from around 1980 and the number of four-year college graduates increases rapidly from the mid-1980s. In the case of male students, four-year college graduates totally approximately 20,000 to 30,000 in the 1970s, steeply increased to 100,000 and then leveled off at around 110,000. The change pattern, "Stable at a high level → Rapid decrease → Stable at a low level" of the wage ratio of four-year college graduates to high school graduates corresponds to that of the number of newly graduated students from four-year colleges, "Stable at a low level (1970s) → Rapid increase (1980s) → Stable at a high level (1990s)" with a time lag of several years. Similarly, the gradual decrease of the wage ratio of junior college graduates to high school graduates from the 1980s onwards corresponds to the increasing tendency of the number of newly graduated students from junior colleges.

We calculated the coefficient of correlation between the relative ratio of the number of new college graduates to the number of new high school graduates not advancing to higher education in the same year (the ratio obtained by dividing the former by the latter), and the ratio of average wages between college graduates and high school graduates for the period from 1975 to 1997. For four-year college graduates, it is −0.961 with a five-year time lag, indicating that their wage level has a strong negative correlation to the relative ratio of the number of college graduates to high school graduates. For junior college graduates, the coefficient of correlation with a five-year time lag is −0.848, which also indicates the negative correlation is strong although not as strong as for four-year college graduates. Therefore, we conclude that the South Korean wage structure is quite sensitive to the change in educational composition of new entrants to the labor force.

The Wage Gap by Age Group
The aforementioned average wages for college graduates and their ratios to high school graduates have been treated as indices that represent the monetary benefits of achieving higher education in South Korea. However, these values are rough indices because they are simple average wages by level of education for various kinds of workers who have various attributes, and therefore further analysis controlling the attributes of workers is necessary.

First, we focus on the age of workers. The general tendency observed is that, as workers get older, they may generally earn higher wages. When we take this tendency into consideration, there is a possibility that the increase of new college graduates and the consequent decrease in high school graduates shift the age distribution of college graduate workers to the younger side (= the relatively lower wage side) as well as that of high school graduate workers to the older side (= the relatively higher wage side), which results in lowering the ratio of average wages of college graduates to high school graduates even if there are no changes in the relationship between academic credentials and wage levels.

In order to control this age effect, let us examine changes in the wage ratios among academic credentials that are calculated assuming there was no change in the age distribution of each worker group of academic credentials (i.e., the counterfactual trend of wage ratios) at the time of comparison shown in figure 4–3. This figure reveals that the wage ratio of four-year college graduates to high school graduates (the values in parenthesis) became substantially lower in the late 1980s to the early 1990s but hardly changed in the early 1980s. The wage ratio of junior college graduates to high school graduates exhibits a similar tendency.[3]

The above data acquired by controlling age distribution allows us to attribute the actual changes in wage ratios to those caused by changes in the age distribution of high school graduates and college graduates, and pure changes in the wage

---

[3] Although another opportunity is needed to discuss the impact in detail, there is considerable change in the wage gap among different academic credentials since the late 1990s, when the economic crisis greatly affected South Korea, due to factors other than the change in the educational composition of the labor force.

Figure 4–3. Wage Ratios of High School and College Graduates (Based on Age Distribution in 1980)

	1980	1985	1990	1995	2000
High school graduate	0.994	0.927	0.920	0.929	0.893
Junior college graduate	1.266	1.170	1.099	1.044	1.019
	(1.341)	(1.262)	(1.194)	(1.124)	(1.141)
Four-year college graduate	1.910	1.873	1.658	1.446	1.451
	(2.023)	(2.020)	(1.801)	(1.556)	(1.625)

Source: Compiled from the annual reports of the Wage Structure Survey (Korean Ministry of Labor).
Note: Upper row and lower row (in parentheses) are relative wage when average wage of all workers and average wage of high school graduates are set at 1.0, respectively.

difference between college and high school graduates. For example, from 1980 to 1995, the actual wage ratio of four-year college graduates to high school graduates decreases from 2.023 to 1.420 (figure 4–1). The portion that can be attributed to the changes purely in the wage ratio between four-year college and high school graduates within the total decrease (0.603) is the decrease in the wage ratios without change in the age distribution, 0.467 (= 2.023 – 1.556). This corresponds to 77.4 percent of the total reduction, and the remaining 22.6 percent should be attributed to change in the age composition of college and high school graduates and the interaction between these two factors. Judging from these facts, although the change in the age distribution of groups with and without higher education partially explains the actual change in the wage ratio between the two groups, the substantial change in the wage gaps explains the majority of the actual changes in the wage ratio between them.

Next, let us examine the fluctuations in the wage ratios for each academic credential group to the average wages of all workers controlling the changes in the age composition, referring to figure 4–3 (the values outside parentheses). Even in the case when change in age distribution is controlled, we observe that the relative wages of junior college graduates decreased from the early 1980s and that of four-year college graduates decreased from the late 1980s. The relative wages of high school graduates to workers as a whole, however, did not change significantly from the 1980s, particularly from the late 1980s to the early 1990s when the number of college graduates increased rapidly.

This tendency is quite different from what is predicted according to Thurow's job competition model. As noted in chapter 1, Thurow's model, which assumes the existence of a definite structure of jobs to which different fixed wages are connected, expects that an increase in the number of college graduate workers pushes

102 | Part II Economic Rewards, Occupational Status, and Social Mobility

Figure 4–4. Wage Ratios of College to High School Graduates by Age Group

	Year	\multicolumn{9}{c}{Age}
		20–24	25–29	30–34	35–39	40–44	45–49	50–54	55–59	60–
Junior college/High school graduates	1980	1.139	1.193	1.184	1.201	1.182	1.357	1.344	1.487	1.598
	1985	1.115	1.077	1.172	1.217	1.205	1.200	1.335	1.384	1.071
	1990	0.952	1.006	1.102	1.185	1.268	1.275	1.204	1.418	1.308
	1995	0.953	0.994	1.044	1.113	1.201	1.146	1.206	1.304	1.427
	2000	0.945	0.959	1.024	1.095	1.187	1.293	1.284	1.318	1.317
Four-year college/High school graduate	1980	1.687	1.530	1.570	1.806	1.884	1.986	1.894	1.979	1.964
	1985	1.492	1.482	1.593	1.764	1.845	1.973	1.961	2.265	1.752
	1990	1.312	1.265	1.412	1.629	1.758	1.875	2.023	2.175	2.315
	1995	1.030	1.075	1.221	1.371	1.513	1.638	1.933	2.124	2.400
	2000	0.996	1.101	1.280	1.428	1.536	1.683	1.844	2.380	2.433

Source: Compiled from the annual reports of the Wage Structure Survey (Korean Ministry of Labor).

high school graduate workers into jobs with lower wages. Consequently, it predicts that not only the average wages of college graduate workers, but also those of high school graduate workers will decrease. However, since the late 1980s, the relative wages of high school graduate workers did not noticeably decrease, which indicates that Thurow's model does not adequately explain the changes in the wage structure.

Finally, we observe the changes in the wage gaps by age group. Figure 4–4 shows the wage ratios of junior college and four-year college graduates to high school graduates by age group. According to this table, a decrease in the wage ratio of four-year college graduates to high school graduates from the late 1980s to the early 1990s is particularly noticeable in the younger age groups. It shows the significant decrease in the wage gaps for those younger than 40 in the late 1980s and in the wage gaps for those younger than 50 in the early 1990s, while the wage gaps for those older than 50 did not change much.

The age groups that experienced the decrease in the wage gap of the 1980s and later are the cohorts (and their adjacent cohorts) that enjoyed the rapid expansion of higher education thanks to the change in policies on student quotas. South Korean adult males are obligated to perform around two years (previously three years) of military service in their 20s, and many male students of four-year colleges fulfill their military duties by taking off school when they are in their third or fourth year. For this reason, male graduates of four-year colleges are usually in their late twenties or older when they enter the labor market. Considering that factor, we may conclude that the wage gap between the four-year college graduates and high school graduates after the late 1980s was reduced because of the lower wages of the increased number of college graduates when they newly entered the labor market, and even after that, their wages (and the wages of adjacent cohort college graduates) did not increase as rapidly compared to high school graduates. This change in the wage structure would be close to the wage equilibrium mechanism of the labor market based on the supply-and-demand relationship assumed by neo-classical economics.[4]

II. Analysis of Wage Gaps by Estimation of the Wage Function

In this section, in order to analyze in detail changes in the wage structure from the 1980s to the early 1990s, we analyze the raw data of the Wage Structure Survey to estimate the wage function and the effect of education on wages. The data we use for this analysis is 10 percent random samples of raw data acquired in 1980, 1985, 1990, and 1995 from the Wage Structure Surveys.[5]

Estimation of the Wage Function

Estimations of the wage function for analyzing the monetary benefits of achieving education often use the Mincerian function (Mincer 1974: 84), as follows:

$\ln E_t = \ln E_0 + rs + \beta_1 t + \beta_2 t^2$

(where s is number of years of education, t is years of experience in the labor market, and E_t is earning capacity after t years, or wages)

The analysis for estimating the wage function in this section also uses this equation with some modifications. The equation includes the first order term ($\beta_1 t$) and the second order term ($\beta_2 t^2$) of years of experience, which can capture a tendency to gradual decline of the wage-increase range with more years of experience. In the following analysis, we use the respondent's age minus the standard age for completing each educational stage to calculate the number of years of experience in the labor market.

The Mincer's wage function assumes that, regardless of educational stage, a one-year increase of education has the same degree of effect on wages. However,

---

[4] It is possible that the then Chun Doo-Hwan regime wage negotiation guidance policy to reduce the wage gap among different educational credentials was a factor in the changes in wages.
[5] The sample sizes for males are sufficiently large: 18,029 in 1980, 19,456 in 1985, 34,602 in 1990, and 28,992 in 1995. We would like to thank Professor Phang Ha-Nam of Kookmin University for his kind cooperation for the analysis of the raw data.

this assumption is not appropriate when analyzing in detail the wage-increase effect of various stages of education and its fluctuations. Thus, in the following analysis, in order to separately explore the increase effect, we use dummy variables corresponding to various educational stages instead of years of education. We set this equation as the baseline model (Model 1) and add the occupational and other dummy variables to this model as necessary. In this section, because of various problems including insufficient size of the sample, we limit the target of analysis (regretfully, for the reasons mentioned above) to male employees.

Figure 4–5 shows the results of the estimation based on Model 1, and Model 2 which adds occupational dummy variables to Model 1 from the years 1980, 1985, 1990, and 1995. However, because of revision in the Korean Standard Classification of Occupations in 1992, it is impossible to compare occupations with those of previous years, so we did not make an estimation based on Model 2 for the 1995 samples.

From the estimated coefficients of the dummy variables for Model 1, we can obtain the degree of wage disparity among the different academic credentials and their fluctuations by controlling for years of experience. Because the dependent variable of the regression analysis is the natural logarithmic value of wages, the actual wage ratio for each educational stage to high school graduates as reference category controlling for years of experience is a natural exponential value of the estimated coefficient of the dummy variable. The estimated actual wage ratio of four-year college graduates to high school graduates is about twofold: 1.99 in 1980, and 1.97 in 1985 and then is substantially lower: 1.60 in 1990 and 1.52 in 1995. The wage ratio of junior college graduates to high school graduates also shows a tendency to decrease: 1.34 in 1980 to 1.27 in 1985, and to 1.13 in 1990 and 1995. These figures agree with our findings obtained in the previous section. However, they reveal that the shrinkage of the wage gap between four-year college graduates and high school graduates progressed more rapidly in the late 1980s than in the early 1990s.

Next, we examine the degree of wage disparity and its fluctuations among young people for which the analysis in the previous section revealed a significant reduction after the expansion of higher education. Figure 4–6 shows the result of the estimation based on the same models as those in figure 4–5 for samples in their 20s to early 30s, which include many college graduates newly entering the labor market. This figure reveals that wage gaps between junior college graduates and high school graduates and between four-year college graduates and high school graduates noticeably decreased, similar to the case for subjects of all ages.

However, comparing the estimated coefficients of dummy variables in Model 1 for junior college graduates and four-year college graduates with those of figure 4–5, we find that although there is hardly any difference in the 1980s, the esti-

Figure 4–5. Estimation of Wage Function (All ages)

	1980		1985		1990		1995
	Model 1	Model 2	Model 1	Model 2	Model 1	Model 2	Model 1
Constant	11.469***	11.429***	11.952***	11.917***	12.706***	12.748***	13.240***
Years of experience	.072***	.069***	.080***	.076***	.067***	.060***	.078***
(Years of experience)^2(×100)	−.118***	−.113***	−.132***	−.129***	−.114***	−.101***	−.137***
Education (ref. high school graduate)							
Elementary school graduate	−.477***	−.387***	−.421***	−.328***	−.325***	−.266***	−.217***
Middle school graduate	−.323***	−.245***	−.295***	−.219***	−.257***	−.206***	−.204***
Junior college graduate	.294***	.175***	.235***	.097***	.123***	.064***	.124***
Four-year college graduate	.687***	.527***	.677***	.499***	.473***	.361***	.416***
Occupation (ref. Manufacturing)							
Professional		.221***		.300***		.072***	
Management		.414***		.418***		.293***	
Clerk		.162***		.154***		.090***	
Sales		−.146**		.038		−.075*	
Service		−.233***		−.155***		−.325***	
Agriculture, forestry and fisheries		−.237*		.091		−.195***	
R^2	.531	.559	.531	.564	.326	.366	.421
N	18,029		19,456		34,602		28,992

Source: Compiled from a 10 percent sample of the annual data for pertinent years of the Wage Structure Survey.
Notes: * $p < .05$, ** $p < .01$, *** $p < .001$.

mated coefficients for four-year college graduates and junior college graduates decreased further for the younger ages than those for all ages in the 1990s. This implies that reduction of the wage gap between college graduates and high school graduates is larger for younger age brackets. In fact, the actual wage ratio calculated from these estimated values is 1.08 times between junior college graduates and high school graduates of younger ages in 1995, whereas the gap is 1.40

106 | Part II   Economic Rewards, Occupational Status, and Social Mobility

Figure 4–6. Wage Function Estimates (Age 20–34)

	1980		1985		1990		1995
	Model 1	Model 2	Model 1	Model 2	Model 1	Model 2	Model 1
Constant	11.496***	11.452***	11.900***	11.866**	12.636***	12.641***	13.178***
Years of experience	.067***	.064***	.087***	.083***	0.086***	0.085***	.099***
(Years of experience)^2 (×100)	−.079***	−.070***	−.136***	−.125***	−.207***	−.205***	−.238***
Education (ref. High school graduate)							
Elementary school graduate	−.504***	−.438***	−.465***	−.406***	−.437***	−.414***	−.302***
Middle school graduate	−.328***	−.264***	−.308***	−.251***	−.255***	−.242***	−.178***
Junior college graduate	.297***	.208***	.233***	.109***	.098***	.074***	.074***
Four-year college graduate	.679***	.561***	.650***	.507***	.415***	.376***	.333***
Occupation (ref. Manufacturing)							
Professional		.202***		.261***		.032***	
Management		.402***		.416***		.191***	
Clerical		.158***		.150***		.049***	
Sales		−.076		.036		−.140***	
Service		−.163***		−.077***		−.185***	
Agriculture, forestry and fisheries		−.150		.083		−.053	
R^2	.443	.464	.448	.447	.248	.257	.333
N	10,748		11,371		18,063		14,011

Source: Compiled from a 10 percent sample of the annual data for pertinent years of the Wage Structure Survey.
Notes: * $p < .05$, ** $p < .01$, *** $p < .001$.

between four-year college graduates and high school graduates for that year, indicating that the gap for younger ages is even smaller than that for all ages. This result confirms the fact that the reduction of the wage gap between college graduates and high school graduates at this period is particularly significant in young college graduates who newly entered the labor market.

Wage Disparities by Occupation

When we discuss the trend in wage disparities in the 1980s and after, we also need to consider the changes in wages among different occupations. In South Korea, the labor movement had been intense since the June 29 Declaration of Democratization and Reform in 1987, primarily led by manufacturing workers placed in harsh working environments. One of the objectives of the movement was improvement of working conditions, including raised wage levels. In fact, the industrial dispute at that time helped to raise manufacturing workers' wages.

The reduction of wage disparities among college graduates and high school graduates could be attributed to the reduction of the wage gap between manufacturing and other occupations. Because there are far more high school graduates than four-year college and junior college graduates working in the manufacturing sector, the rapid increase in manufacturing workers' wages and consequent reduction of the occupational wage disparity could appear as a decrease in the wage ratio of college graduates to high school graduates. In fact, as shown in figure 4–1, the wage ratio of college graduates to high school graduates began to rapidly decrease in 1987 after democratization was established and labor-management disputes in industry intensified.

In order to control the wage gap reduction between manufacturing and other occupations, we add dummy variables for occupations to Model 1 to create Model 2 as shown in figures 4–5 and 4–6. From the results of this estimation, we see that the estimated coefficients of four-year college graduates noticeably decrease in the late 1980s and the estimated coefficients of junior college graduates significantly decrease in the 1980s both for all ages and for younger ages even after controlling the wage gaps among occupations. From the above results, we observe that even if we control the reduction of the wage gap between manufacturing and other occupations during the time period, the gap between four-year college graduates and high school graduates rapidly decreases in the late 1980s while the gap between junior college and high school graduates rapidly decreases in the 1980s. In other words, the decrease in the wage gap between college and high school graduates in the late 1980s was not caused solely by decrease in the wage disparity between manufacturing and other occupations triggered by the labor movement, but is substantially the result of a straightforward decrease in the wage gap between college graduates and high school graduates.[6]

Nevertheless, the estimated coefficients of the dummy variable for each occupation in Model 2 show a marked decrease in the wage gap among occupations in the late 1980s. The estimated coefficients for each occupation using manufactur-

---

[6] In fact, in the second half of the 1980s, even among white-collar workers including professionals and clerical workers, the wage gap between college graduates and high school graduates tended to decrease.

ing workers as reference category, especially white-collar professions including professional, managerial, and clerical workers, hardly change in the early 1980s; even with workers with the same number of years of schooling and years of experience, by becoming a professional one would be able to expect a wage increase of 20 to 30 percent, and clerical workers would be able to expect a wage increase of 10 percent or more.

However, all of the estimated coefficients substantially decreased in the late 1980s. The decrease of the estimated coefficients of dummy variables for younger professional and clerical workers was even more significant, nearing zero in 1990. This means that among workers with the same educational qualifications and years of experience, there was essentially no increased-wage effect from becoming a professional or clerical worker, compared with a manufacturing worker. While the wages of manufacturing workers were politically controlled during the economic development stage, as the policy suppressing the labor movement weakened, wage gaps with other occupations, in particular with white-collar occupations, have largely diminished.

In sum, although the wage ratio between college graduates and high school graduates decreased partially because of the reduction in the wage gaps among different occupations, the large part of the drop in the wage ratio can be attributed to the straightforward reduction in wage disparities in each occupation between college and high school graduates. A more realistic interpretation would be that intense labor-management disputes triggered overall reform of the wage system, and in the transition, the wage gaps between college and high school graduates were also reduced as the increased number of college graduates newly entered the labor market.[7]

Change in Determination Coefficients and Corporate Size Effect

Estimation of the wage function using raw data samples from the Wage Structure Survey may help us reveal another important aspect of the wage structure that the analysis of aggregate data was unable to adequately treat, namely, issues related to wage variance. This can be approached by focusing on the determination coefficients of regression models.

Let us briefly examine the fluctuations in the determination coefficients of the regression models shown in figures 4–5 and 4–6. The coefficient of determination

---

[7] As for the increase of the wage of the manufacturing workers in this period, there are arguments that point out the effects of the short supply of the unskilled labor and the accompanied formation of the internal labor market in large corporations (Jung Ee-Hwan 1992; Yokota 1994). If they are true, the wage increase of manufacturing workers and the wage gap reduction among different educational credentials are not separate phenomena but caused by the same factor of supply and demand of labor.

of the regression model is an index of how much of the variance in the dependent variable (wage level in this case) may be explained by the independent variables, and the index takes a value between 0 and 1 depending on the explanatory strength of the independent variables. The estimation of Model 1 in figure 4–5 finds that the coefficient of determination is about 0.531 in 1980 and 1985 and decreased considerably to 0.326 in 1990. Based on these, the determination coefficients indicate that approximately 53 percent of dispersion of the logged wage levels is explained by years of experience and educational background in 1980 and 1985 while their explanatory strength drops to 33 percent in 1990. Although the data in 1995 somewhat increases the coefficient to 0.421, it is smaller than those in 1980 and 1985.

For younger generations, too, the determination coefficient noticeably declines: the independent variables explain 44 and 45 percent of dispersion in 1980 and 1985 respectively, but only 25 percent in 1990. As described above, the decreasing wage gap between college and high school graduates in the late 1980s also appears as the decreasing explanatory strength of the two variables of experience year and the educational background for the dispersion of wage levels. Is there any variable that comes to explain the variance of the wage level in place of these variables?

Here we focus on the effect of corporate size. Because manufacturing workers employed by large companies led the intense labor movement in the late 1980s, some researchers point out that the wage gaps among different company sizes increased during the period (Nam Ki-Gon 1999).

Model 3 in figure 4–7 adds the firm size variable to Model 1 shown in figure 4–5 for all ages and figure 4–6 for younger ages.[8] Although this newly added firm size variable has a positive significant effect for the 1985 data, the determination coefficient increases only from 0.531 in Model 1 to 0.557 in Model 3 for all the generations and from 0.448 to 0.478 for the younger generation. Therefore, the increases of the coefficient of determination are not so large. By contrast, the 1990 data show that the determination coefficient largely increases from 0.326 in Model 1 to 0.486 in Model 3 for all the generations after adding the firm size variable. The younger generation shows an even greater increase from 0.248 to 0.442, which makes the determination coefficient comparable to that of the 1985 data.[9]

---

[8] There are six categories for the variable of firm size for which the respondents work, and the number of employees for the categories are: 10–29, 30–99, 100–299, 300–499, 500–999, and 1000 or more. Because the logarithmic values of each lower limit of each category are at an almost equal interval, we assigned natural numbers from 1 to 6 to the categories and used it as firm size variable.

[9] In all cases, increases of the determination coefficients are significant at a 0.1% level.

Figure 4–7. Wage Function Estimates Including Firm Size Variable

	1985 Model 3		1990 Model 3	
	All ages	Age 20–34	All ages	Age 20–34
Constant	11.697***	11.665***	12.396***	12.363***
Years of experience	.078***	.087***	.062***	.078***
(Year of experience)^2 (×100)	−.128***	−.140***	−.101***	−.002***
Education (ref. High school graduate)				
Elementary school graduate	−.397***	−.417***	−.284***	−.314***
Middle school graduate	−.271***	−.2770***	−.225***	−.178***
Junior college graduate	.247***	.240***	.168***	.140***
Four-year college graduate	.675***	.642***	.460***	.391***
Firm size	.050***	.045***	.087***	.080***
R^2	.557	.478	.486	.442

Source: Compiled from a 10 percent sample of the annual data for pertinent years of the Wage Structure Survey.
Notes: *$p < .05$, **$p < .01$, ***$p < .001$.
The numbers of samples are the same as in figures 4–5 and 4–6.

The estimated coefficient of the firm size variable also increases, indicating that the wage gaps among companies were expanding in this period.

From the above analysis, we may conclude that changes in the wage structure in the late 1980s were a process where the overall wage determination of educational qualifications and years of experience decrease while the firm size comes to have strong effects on the wage level. Such transitions are more distinct in the younger generations.

Firm Size Effect by Educational Level

What relationship does increase in corporate-size effect have on the rapid increase of college graduates or the shrinking wage gap between college and high school graduates in the same period? To investigate this question, let us analyze the fluctuations in the wage structure during the period in greater detail by separately estimating wage function by the educational level of respondents.

First, we divided the wage survey data in 1985 and 1990 based on the educational level of respondents, and separately conducted a regression analysis of wages using only years of experience and its square as independent variables for groups of high school, junior college, and four-year college graduates. The regression model is denoted Model 1′ because it is equivalent to the model that excludes the dummy variables on education from Model 1 in figures 4–5 and 4–6. Although we omit the figure showing detailed results, the coefficient of determination decreases from 1985 to 1990 in all educational groups.[10] The younger generation (ages 20 to 34) also shows a similar tendency: the dispersion of wage levels that cannot be explained by years of experience increases for both high school graduates and college graduates during this period.

Second, let us examine the explanatory power of corporate size by educational group by comparing the determination coefficients of the regression analysis of Model 1' with those of Model 3', which added firm size to Model 1'.[11] From the 1985 data, the increases of the determination coefficients from Model 1' to Model 3' are not so large for all groups of high school graduates (0.363 → 0.412), junior college graduates (0.380 → 0.433), and four-year college graduates (0.464 → 0.480). The same tendency can be applied to the younger generations, and in particular, the increment for young four-year college graduates is quite small (0.322 → 0.339). Therefore, we may conclude that the explanatory power of firm size was not that large in 1985.[12]

By contrast, from the 1990 data, the determination coefficient for all ages greatly increase when the firm size variable is added in all educational groups: high school graduates (0.217 → 0.413), junior college graduates (0.291 → 0.424), and four-year college graduates (0.368 → 0.466). This tendency is particularly large in the younger generation: high school graduates (0.156 → 0.420), junior college graduates (0.257 → 0.395), and even four-year college graduates (0.190 → 0.339), indicating that the explanatory power of firm size on wages becomes large especially in the younger generations among four-year college graduates.

Let us evaluate wage gap due to firm size for the younger generations in detail. If we calculate the wage ratio of large companies (1000 or more employees) to small companies (10–29 employees) using the estimated coefficients of Model 3', the ratio turns out to be 1.32 for high school graduates in 1985, which means that one's wages working for a large company will be 32 percent greater than if working for a small company. By contrasts, in 1990, this ratio increases to 1.51 (i.e., the wage increases by 51 percent). Such an increase of firm size effect is also observed for four-year college graduates: the wage ratio between the two different firm sizes is 1.17 in 1985 and increases to 1.40 in 1990.[13]

From the late 1980s onward, expansion of the wage gap due to firm size has of-

---

[10] There is not much difference in the estimated residual variance among different groups by level of education.
[11] This Model 3' corresponds to Model 3 shown in figure 4–7.
[12] Because the sample sizes are large to a certain extent, in all cases, increases of the determination coefficients are significant at a 0.1% level. The same may be applied to the data of 1990.
[13] For junior college graduates, although the wage premium increases from 29 to 38 percent, the increase is relatively small compared to that for college graduates.

ten been understood in relation to the labor-management disputes that frequently took place in that period. Nam Ki-Gon, for example, hypothetically states, "institutional factors, i.e., the labor movement centering around the large corporations from the late-1980s onward and the resultant threat-effect of the labor unions, secured increases in the wages of workers of large corporations relative to others, resulting in the wage gap due to firm size" (Nam Ki-Gon 1999: 187).

However, if the labor movement involving manufacturing employees is the primary factor in expanding the wage gap due to firm size, we presume that college graduates, whose numbers are fewer among manufacturing employees, would not have such a large increase of wage gap due to firm size. Nevertheless, our analysis in this section reveals that an increase in the wage gap due to firm size is observed not only among high school graduates, many of whom work in manufacturing jobs, but also among college graduates, and even in four-year college graduates, who primarily work in white-collar jobs.

In the case of four-year college graduates, when we also take into consideration the fact that the explanatory power of firm size for wages increased especially for the younger age groups, the expansion of the wage gap due to firm size among college graduates in this period may be attributed to the rapid increase of the college graduate labor force. Prior to this period when college graduates were in short supply, the wages of college graduates were more or less the same regardless of the size of the company. However, a rapid increase of college graduates newly entering the labor market lowered the wages of small to mid-sized companies for younger college graduates relative to larger companies, resulting in the increase in the variance of wage levels and the wage gap due to firm size among college graduates.[14] The decrease of the wage ratio for college graduates to high school graduates, as confirmed above, may be also attributed to the relative wage drop of younger college graduates working in small to mid-size companies.

In the next chapter, which analyzes the school-to-work transition process in detail, we discuss how the increase of wage variance among younger college graduates and expansion of the wage gap among different firm sizes as a consequence of the increased number of college graduates affected the job-matching process of new college graduates.

III. Private Rate of Return on Investment in Higher Education

Is it true that the monetary benefits of advancing to higher education as investment in South Korean society are so great as to explain people's strong desire to go to college? How have the benefits been altered by the change in the wage structure

---

[14] We will analyze the mechanism more in detail in the next chapter.

since the 1980s? To investigate these issues, we analyze the private rate of return on investment in education.

Concept of Return on Educational Investment and Demand for Education

Return on educational investment, a key concept in economic explanations of the demand for educational attainments, is, as the term implies, monetary return on education that has been regarded as an investment. It is calculated from the total cost needed to obtain the desired academic credentials, including school fees and forgone income as well as the total benefits, namely anticipated increase in income as a result of advanced education (Becker 1964). More specifically, the rate of return on educational investment is a level of the temporal discount rate that equalizes the total cost of education with its total benefits, and as the rate is higher, additional monetary benefits expand more with advanced education.

There are two major types of rate of return on educational investment: one is the private rate of return calculated from the expenditures versus the benefits to the person who receives the education and the other is the social rate of return calculated from the cost and the benefits to society as a whole. Private rate of return is more important for understanding individual behavior vis-à-vis education. As mentioned in chapter 1, the context of human capital theory that regards advancement of education as investment presumes that each individual compares the private rate of return on investment in a specific stage of education with the interest rate or the return rate in the other capital markets to determine whether he/she will invest in that stage of education. If the private rate of return on educational investment is relatively high, people tend to invest in education more, and consequently there will be greater demand for advanced educational attainments.

Needless to say, such a presumption about individual action regarding advanced education may be overly simplified, discarding the non-economic aspects of actual decision making. However, considering that the drive for educational achievement in South Korean society is often explained by the degree of its socioeconomic benefits, the economic incentives for pursuit of educational achievement must be adequately observed. The private rate of return on educational investment is very useful as an index for measuring levels of incentive.

In this section, we discuss the monetary benefits of going to college in South Korea based on the private rate of return on educational investment in higher education and by comparing it longitudinally and internationally. As noted, the wage gap between college graduates and high school graduates in South Korea rapidly decreased from the 1980s on. What is the degree of decrease when measured as the private rate of return on higher education? Have the monetary benefits of advancing to higher education remained large when compared with other countries even after the wage gap was reduced by the increased number of college graduates?

Rate of Return and International Comparison

Kong Eun-Bae and his colleagues carefully measured the costs and benefits in order to calculate the private rate of return on educational investment using the data of not only school fees and foregone income, but also all the educational costs including course materials and school supplies.[15]

Their analysis reveals that the private rate of return on higher education in 1985 was: 14.8 percent and 11.6 percent for four-year college among males and females, and 14.1 percent and 16.2 percent for junior college among males and females, respectively (Kong Eun-Bae et al. 1985). On the other hand, the private rate of return in 1994 substantially decreases: 7.0 percent and 6.9 percent for four-year college among males and females, and 5.1 percent and 9.4 percent for junior college among males and females, respectively (Kong Eun-Bae et al. 1994). A similar tendency of decline in the return on educational investment is also shown from our estimation where we apply Mincer's simple-calculation method to wage data,[16] indicating that the change in the wage structure during the period significantly reduces the return on investment in college education.

How high was the rate of return on college education after the wage structure change shown above when it is compared with investment in other sectors? For this question, Kong and his colleagues estimated the real interest rate in the range of −2.5 to +6.5 percent for the individual's small financial capital, by subtracting the annual mean inflation rate (6.78 percent) and the taxation rate on interest (10 to 25 percent) from 1991 to 1994 from the interest rates of time deposits (8.5 to 15.0 percent) and national and corporate bonds (13.5 to 14.4 percent) during the same period. Comparing with this real interest rate, they state, "Regarding personal return on investment, except for junior college among males, educational investments at all academic levels have higher returns than investment for any other sector" (Kong Eun-Bae et al. 1994: 168). Thus, they conclude that people's high aspiration to advance to higher education in South Korea has a firm economic basis.

However, focusing only on interest rates in the formal financial market as the subject of comparison, as shown in the study by Kong and his colleagues' is inadequate in discussing the relative advantage of rate of return on human capital investment. Investment in human capital involves a long incubation period,

---

[15] In addition, Ryoo Jai-Kyung also published several articles on changes in the rate of return to higher education in South Korea (Ryoo Jai-Kyung 1992, Ryoo Jai-Kyung et al. 1993).
[16] Mincer indicates that the estimated coefficient of the educational years in the wage function may be applied as an approximation of the annual rate of return to educational investment with several assumptions such as that the total amount of income from part time job while studying is nearly equal to the total amount of the educational expense such as school fees (Mincer 1974).

Chapter 4   The Monetary Benefits of Academic Credentials | 115

increasing its risks, so a higher risk investment target is necessary as a subject for comparing the return rates.

In South Korea, in addition to formal financial organizations such as banks that offer relatively lower interest rates, there are many informal credit markets, access to which is easy. Many private companies relied on these informal credit markets in fundraising at least until the 1990s, and many ordinary citizens, too, enjoyed the benefit of high interest rates in the informal credit market through "gye," which is a mutual financing service widely practiced in South Korea, real estate deposits, and the like. Of course, the interest rates in the informal credit market are much higher than those of the formal financial organizations.

In South Korea, a method of leasing real estate has been generally the *jeonse* system, by which a tenant makes a certain deposit to a landlord, who earns rental revenue by investing it on the financial market—often the informal credit market. In many cases, part of the *jeonse* deposit may be replaced with the *wolse*-payment, which is a monthly payment to the landlord. In the mid-1990s, the ratio of replacement of the *jeonse*-deposit with *wolse*-payments was approximately 2 percent.[17] Observing this social custom, we may suspect that the interest rate in the informal financial market in South Korean society at that time was at the level of at least 2 percent monthly or approximately 27 percent annually.

Considering that ordinary people have easy access to such high interest rates in the informal financial market, and that the savings in the formal financial organizations has not been preferred due to their low interest rates, the interest rate in the informal financial market should be included as a comparative subject when we discuss the relative advantages of rate of return on educational investment. What is more, the interest rate in the informal financial market reaches at least 10-plus to nearly 20 percent even when taking into account the aforementioned inflation rate. This real interest rate in the informal financial market is much higher than the private rate of return on a college education in 1994, as estimated by Kong and his colleagues. Therefore, we may conclude that in South Korea in the 1990s, when the rate of return had significantly lowered due to the increase in college graduates, investment in higher education was not as attractive as a financial investment.

Furthermore, the rate of return on educational investment estimated by Kong and his colleagues is possibly even higher than the actual return rate, due to improper assumptions in their calculations. They consider after-school educational expenditures of students at the elementary school, middle school, and high school

---

[17] The author confirmed such a substitution rate between deposit and monthly payment through free information magazines including *Gyocharo* (Crossroads) and *Byeoruk shijang* (Flea Market) and real estate information bulletin boards in universities and other places in the mid-1990s.

level to be required educational costs for calculating the private rate of return at each school level. However, as shown in our discussion in section 2 of chapter 3 (pp. 77–79), as a result of the entrance examination reform for secondary schools, selection for entry to higher education became the most important selection process, and hence not only high school students but also elementary and middle school students take after-school lessons in preparation for the college entrance competitions. That being the case, the cost of after-school lessons prior to college advancement should be included in the educational expenses for college entrance. Therefore, in South Korea, it is quite possible that costs of advancement to higher education are much higher than that estimated by Kong and his colleagues. If this is true, the actual rate of return on higher education is even further reduced.

International Comparison of Rate of Return
How high is the private rate of return on higher education in South Korea as compared with other countries? George Psacharopoulos collected data on return rates by educational level in several dozen countries worldwide and compared them (Psacharopoulos 1985; 1994). According to his study, the return rates in advanced countries, where higher education is universalized to a certain degree, are generally lower than those in developing countries. However, in many countries, the private rate of return on higher education is at a level of at least 10 percent. The average rates of return in developing countries by region are 27.8 percent in sub-Saharan Africa, 19.7 percent in Latin America, 19.9 percent in non-OECD member countries of Asia, and 21.7 percent in non-OECD member countries of Europe, the Middle East, and North Africa. Compared with these, the rates of return in OECD member countries are very low, but their average is 12.3 percent, which is substantially higher than that of South Korea in 1994 (Psacharopoulos 1994).[18]

Judging from these results, we may conclude that the private rate of return on investment in higher education in South Korea was significantly reduced due to the substantial change in the wage structure from the late 1980s onward, and its return as a financial investment is not as high as for other investment sectors. Even when compared with other countries, the private rate of return on higher education in South Korea is not as high as the desire for achieving education.

---

[18] Although this paper cites the rate of return data in South Korea from Ryoo Jai-Kyung (1988), it is based on the data prior to a substantial change in the wage structure (1986), where the private rate of return on higher education is at a very high level of 17.9 percent.

IV. TIME-SERIES ANALYSIS ON DEMAND FOR ADVANCING TO HIGHER EDUCATION

The monetary benefits to be obtained by going to college were significantly reduced with the rapid increase in the number of college graduates. Did that decrease affect demand for advanced education? If obtaining monetary benefits is the objective of pursuing higher education for some people, demand for advancement to higher education would be somewhat reduced should the private rate of return significantly drop. In the previous sections of this chapter, we observed that the South Korean labor market responded to the rapid increase of college graduates in an equilibrium-achieving manner. Is there such a feedback mechanism for attaining equilibrium at work even in the market for opportunities for higher education?

It is anticipated that, in addition to the monetary benefits of higher education, various economic and non-economic factors affect demand for advanced education, and therefore, in investigating this issue, we need to control both factors to reveal the relationship between the monetary benefits and the demand for advanced education. In this section, in order to study the intense aspiration for educational achievement in South Korea, we examine the factors that determine demand for advancement to higher education from a broad point of view through a time-series analysis.

Selection of Variables

First of all, let us discuss how to measure demand for higher education. Previously conducted analyses of demand for higher education conducted in different countries take either of the following two approaches: measurement of the annual demand in terms of number of students who actually *enter* higher education, and in terms of number of students who *apply* for higher education. However, as we confirmed in chapter 3, in South Korea the annual number of students who advance to higher education is determined by the government, and its decision is basically not affected by demand for higher education in that year. Therefore, demand for advancement to higher education in South Korea should not be measured by the number of advancing students for the year, but rather by the number of applicants.

Here we use the "number of applicants to higher education among new high school graduates" as listed in the *Statistical Yearbook of Education* published annually by the Korean Ministry of Education. The data based on the complete surveys conducted at all Korean high schools, show the number of students who apply to one or more colleges among new high school graduates. While it has the limitation of not citing figures for applicants to four-year colleges vs. junior colleges, it is the only reliable data that is not affected by the change of the admission

Figure 4–8. College Application Rates among New High School Graduates

(%)

[Line graph showing female and male college application rates from 1971 to 1996, with values ranging from approximately 35% to 75%. Female line reaches about 67% by 1996, Male line reaches about 75% by 1996.]

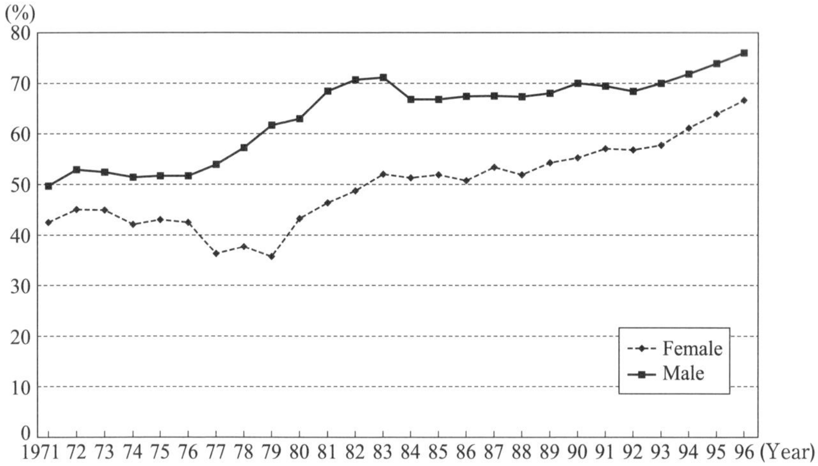

Source: Based on the annual editions of *Statistical Yearbook of Education* (Korean Ministry of Education).

system, and therefore we use "application rate" which is the rate obtained by dividing the number of new high school graduates who apply to go on for higher education by the total number of new high school graduates. Figure 4–8 shows this application rate during the analysis period.

Among the independent variables to explain the fluctuations in the application rate, we use a very simple index of the average wage ratio of college graduates to high school graduates to show a level of the monetary benefit obtained by advancing to higher education. The reason for this is that the calculation of the private rate of return on higher education for every year is difficult because of the limitations of information, and the analysis in the previous section confirms that the index adequately indicates the degree of wage gap between college graduates and high school graduates. In this section, we calculate the wage ratio for every year using the annual data listed for the Wage Structure Surveys.

For the cost of advancing to higher education, we first examined the effect of tuition and other school fees. We created a variable that expresses the direct costs of advancing to higher education for every year by summing up annual mean values (average of the highest and the lowest) of entrance fees to four-year colleges, tuition, and facility fees[19] adjusted by the consumer price index. As a variable that expresses the ability to pay these expenses, we add real household income to the

---
[19] This is the infrastructure maintenance fee for college facilities, payment of which was required at many colleges during the period.

model. This variable is expected to affect demand for advancement to college considerably even if education is regarded not as investment but consumption. Although income foregone in order to undergo advanced education ought in principle to be taken into account, we do not include this variable in the model because of limited data.[20]

In addition, in order to analyze the case of South Korea where institutional factors have a strong impact on the market of educational opportunity, we must also consider the effects of non-economic variables.

One of the foremost non-economic variables that may affect demand for higher education in South Korea is the college admission quotas determined by the government. Chapter 3 described how college admission quotas for all institutions of higher education including private colleges came to be strictly controlled by the government from the 1960s to the mid-1990s. College student quotas have been determined by economic factors such as demand for human resources and political factors, but the number of students among each year's new high school graduates wishing to advance to higher education has never been reflected in the admissions quotas. That being the case, we will need to examine the possibility that the opportunity to advance to higher education determined by the government affects the high school students' demand for advancement to higher education. In other words, the relative quota fluctuations may affect the self-judgment of potential applicants to colleges. For example, a student who wishes to go to a college, but whose academic performance is poor, might give up applying for higher education if the announced admissions quotas for the year suggest that the possibility of admittance is slim. Conversely, if the possibility of admittance is fairly high, a student who had given up the idea of applying might reverse the decision and apply. In order to examine the validity of such a hypothetical mechanism, we incorporate the higher education admissions quota in relative terms for each year—calculated by dividing the college admissions quota by the total number of new high school graduates—into the model.[21]

Yet another variable needs to be considered as an effect of educational policies on demand for advancement to higher education: the effect of the leveling of the academic high schools. As discussed in chapter 3 (p. 78), there is a possibility that the weakening of selectivity at the high school entrance stage increased high school students' desire to go on to college, resulting in the expansion of the demand for higher education in society. Because the leveling of high schools had been implemented since 1974, a dummy variable was introduced to differentiate

---

[20] In many studies, the forgone income is not included in the model because it has a very strong correlation with household income. See for example, Campbell and Siegel (1967).
[21] This treatment is also seen in Kim Young-Hwa and Ryu Han-Koo (1994) and Kim Yeong-Cheol (1979).

the periods before and after the leveling of the academic high schools by setting the value of 1 in and after 1977, when the students who entered high school in 1974 had graduated.

Since applications for college are submitted one year prior to actual admittance, we set a one-year time lag for the household income and wage gap variables. For the student admission quotas and school fees, we do not set any time lag, as the guidelines for the following year have been announced by the time of application. The period of analysis starts in 1972 due to data limitations. Because the government gradually transferred to colleges the right to determine student quotas from around 1997, we set the end of the target period at 1996. Since previous research revealed that there is a large gender difference in factors determining demand for advancement to higher education in South Korea, we separately conduct the analysis for male and female students.

Outcomes of the Analysis

The left half of figure 4–9 shows the result of regression analysis of the application rate to higher education among new male school graduates. As we check the results of regression for Model 1, which includes college admissions quota, household income, school fees, wage gap between college graduates and high school graduates, and dummy variable for leveling of the academic high schools as independent variables, we find that, except for the wage gap variable, the plus or minus sign of the estimated coefficient of each variable agrees with our pre-analysis expectation, showing its statistically significant effect. In other words, as college admissions quotas increase, and as household income increases, the application rate for higher education increases; as the school fees become higher, the application rate decreases.

We should note that the leveling of the academic high school dummy variable has a significant positive effect. Chapter 3 discussed how the leveling policy was implemented as part of the policy to open up and universalize high school education, and at the same time, the high school student quotas themselves substantially increased. In fact, from 1977 onward, the number of new high school graduates substantially increased. The noticeable increase had the intrinsic effect of lowering the application rate of new high school graduates, because the increasing number of new high school graduates means a larger denominator of the application rate to higher education among them. Nevertheless, the dummy variable had a positive significant effect. In other words, the increase of desire to advance to higher education after the leveling of the high schools is more than the lowering effect of the increasing number of new high school graduates. This observation supports the validity of the hypothesis, as proposed in chapter 3 (p. 78), that the

Figure 4–9. Results of the Regression Analysis of the College Application Rate among New High School Graduates

	Male		Female	
	Model 1	Model 2	Model 1	Model 2
Constant	.512**	.368**	−.111	−.035
College admission quota	.380**		.324**	
Four-year college admission quota		.645**		.576**
Household income	.004†	.010**	.031**	.027**
School fees	−.051†	−.029	−.037	−.021
College/High school wage gap	−.006	−.003	.176**	.127**
Leveling of academic high school dummy variable	.076**	.061**	−.142**	−.122**
R^2	.944	.968	.917	.947
D.W. ratio	1.288	1.964	1.499	2.030

Source: Based on analysis of the data from the annual editions of *Statistical Yearbook of Education* (Korean Ministry of Education), *Korea Statistical Yearbook* (Korean National Statistical Office), and annual reports of the Wage Structure Survey (Korean Ministry of Labor).
Notes: † $p < .10$, * $p < .05$, ** $p < .01$.

weakening of selectivity at the secondary education entry stage increases the desire to go on to college, intensifying the competition.

The results of the analysis reveal that the admissions quotas politically determined by the government, including for both junior and four-year colleges, have a significant effect on the higher education application rate among new high school graduates. However, considering that the admissions quotas for junior colleges and that for four-year colleges display different trends and that the latter is much preferred to the former by students, what affects the desire of new high school graduates for advancement to higher education may be the volume of opportunity for advancement not to higher education as a whole, but to four year colleges. To verify this possibility, Model 2 has the variable of admissions quota for four-year colleges instead of for all colleges. The results show that Model 2 has larger determination coefficients than Model 1, indicating that Model 2 fits better.[22] Moreover, the coefficient of the variable of the admissions quotas for four-year colleges turned out to be larger than that for all colleges. These results indicate that what affects the desire of new high school graduates for advancement to higher education is not the quotas for all colleges, but specifically the quotas for four-year colleges.

[22] In addition, the Durbin-Watson ratio of Model 2 is close to 2, indicating that there is essentially no serial correlation.

These results accurately represent the South Korean high school students' attitudes about advancement to higher education. The fact that the higher education application rate among new high school graduates sensitively reacts to the four-year college admissions quotas means that there is considerable latent desire for advancement to four-year college, and in this sense, the opportunity to enter a junior college would be the "next better career path" compared to entering a four-year college. In the 1970s, the Park Chung-Hee regime attempted to resolve the social frustration against the tight control of admissions quotas to higher education by increasing the quotas for vocational schools (the later junior colleges). We may conclude, however, that because of the strong latent desire to advance to a four-year college, the attempt was not successful.

On the other hand, the variable of wage gap between college graduates and high school graduates does not have significant effect. The estimated coefficient values of the variable are negative, thereby contradicting the prediction that reduction of the wage gap between college graduates and high school graduates would lower aspirations for higher education. We conclude that while the application rate to higher education shifts sensitively to the college admissions quotas or fluctuations in household income, it is not so sensitive to changes in the monetary benefits.[23]

The similar analysis for the application rate to higher education for new female high school graduates shows a somewhat different result from male students (the right half of figure 4–9). We obtained the same result on the effects of household income and the college admissions quotas: the female students' college application rate increases as household income and college admissions quotas increase; what affects the rate more is not the quotas for all colleges, but the quotas for four-year colleges. However, there is one significant difference from the results for male students: the dummy variable for the leveling of the academic high schools indicates a significant negative effect, and the wage gap between college graduates and high school graduates has a significant positive effect. As described before, the negative effect of the leveling of the academic high school dummy variable on the application rate may be explained by the increase in the number of high school graduates during that period. After the mid-70s, while the policy of expanding high schools greatly increased the number of new high school graduates, in the case of female students, the number of female applicants to colleges did not increase to the extent of canceling out the rapid increase of the denominator that is the total number of new high school graduates.

On the other hand, we should carefully interpret the positive effect of the wage gap between college graduates and high school graduates for female students. It is

---

[23] Although we also analyzed the effect of the wage gap variable by changing the time lag of the variable with the range of from 0 to 3 years, the outcome from the analysis was the same.

possible to interpret the positive effect based on the economic theory that the monetary benefits accompanied by advancement to higher education affects desire to go to college. However, in South Korea, there was a continued period when "women work only when they had no choice but to go to work to help out with family finances. The tendency decreases in the upper ranks of society, and hence women tend not to approach employment proactively" (Sechiyama 1990: 28). In fact, for women until the 1990s, the higher the academic credentials the lower the labor force participation rate of females. Therefore, in circumstances in which acquiring a college degree does not necessarily increase the rate of entering the labor market but rather decreases it, it would be unreasonable to consider that new female high school graduates would make decisions about whether to advance to college or not while sensitively reacting to the wage gap between college graduates and high school graduates. Interpretation of the positive effect of the wage gap for females remains unresolved and we need to find another opportunity to investigate in detail the mechanism of female student decision-making about whether or not to advance to higher education.

The above analysis of the college application rate for new high school students leads to the following conclusions. Demand for advancement to higher education in South Korea is very susceptible to household income—that is the capacity to pay the costs of higher education. Therefore, we assume that the strata of society that had been unable to fulfill a latent desire for higher education due to financial constraints, the continuous increase of household income in the South Korean economy gradually made the costs of advancing to higher education affordable, thereby contributing to the increase in the number of applicants to colleges.

Another important non-economic factor on demand for higher education is the college admissions quotas determined by the government. Students to be admitted to colleges are rigorously selected based on their academic ability, and those who wish to apply for higher education incur great non-economic costs including preparatory study for the entrance examinations. It is presumed that, among eligible applicants, some decide whether or not to advance to higher education according to their relative probability of passing the college entrance examination depending upon the admissions quotas. For this reason, in South Korea, the strict governmental control over the admission quotas has the effect of suppressing demand for higher education. In addition, in the case of male students alone, it is revealed that the weakening of selectivity in high school admissions worked to expand the demand for advancement to higher education.

Nevertheless, demand for advancement to higher education in South Korea does not react to the monetary benefits obtained by attending college, at least in case of male students, most of whom later enter the labor market. From the second half of the 1980s onward, although the wage gap decreased significantly, we find no evidence of decreased demand for advancement to higher education. Thus, despite reduction of the wage gap between college graduates and high school graduates, the college application rate for new high school graduates has remained high.

Conclusion

This chapter conducted an empirical analysis of changes in the wage structure from the 1980s to first half of the 1990s in order to study the effects of the rapid increase of college graduates in the 1980s on the monetary benefits obtained by advancing to higher education. The results of the analysis may be summarized as follows.

First, while the average wage ratio between college graduates and high school graduates stood at a fairly high level until beginning of the 1980s, it rapidly decreased from the mid-1980s. The lowered wage ratio is partly attributed to the change in the age distribution of high school graduates and college graduates, or the reduction of the wage gap among occupations triggered by the labor movement disputes of 1987. However, even though these effects are controlled, the wage gap between college and high school graduates was considerably reduced. Observing the wage gap by age bracket, the younger generations that newly entered the labor market particularly experienced a significant reduction of the gap.

Such changes in the wage structure, it may be pointed out, are very close to the prediction of the labor market model of neo-classical economics. While the relative wages of college graduates for the younger generations were lowered as the new labor force of college graduates increased, the relative wage level of high school graduates did not show an obvious decreasing tendency, contrary to the prediction of Thurow's job competition model.

In the past, the wage gaps among workers with different academic credentials were often attributed to cultural and historical effects such as the influence of Confucian traditions. The findings of the study, however, lead to the conclusion that the wage structure in South Korea from at least second half of the 1980s to the first half of the 1990s did not show rigidity but that the labor market responded sensitively to the shifts in the educational composition of the new labor force. Therefore, we consider that the basis for the wage gap among different academic credentials was to a large extent economic.

Second, such changes in the wage structure do not affect demand for advancement to higher education. The aforementioned response of the labor market greatly decreased the monetary benefits obtained from higher education. In fact, the private rate of return on investment in higher education in South Korea in the

1990s was not high at all when compared with investment in other sectors and the rates of return on higher education in other countries. Thus, the rapid increase of college graduates from the 1980s, which was supported by the society's high demand for higher education and was directly triggered by the political policy change in the college admissions quotas, resulted in a reduction of the monetary-benefit incentives for higher education.

However, the demand for advancement to higher education does not decrease in response to such a change in economic incentives. As our time-series analysis for demand for advancement to higher education finds that while the college application rate for new high school graduates sensitively reacts to changes in constraint factors including household income and the college admissions quotas, it does not react to the monetary benefits from advancement to higher education in such a way. We cannot find clear evidence that indicates that wage gap reduction from the second half of the 1980s lowered the college application rate.

Chapter 1 describe the model of neo-classical economics, according to which the educational opportunity market and the labor market reach equilibrium of demand and supply in each market through change in the wage disparities by different educational level and through the change in the educational composition of the newly graduated labor force. For example, a high demand for advancement to higher education increases the supply in the college graduate labor force in several years. It lowers their wages, which reduces demand for advancement to higher education. Hence the supply-demand equilibrium is achieved.

However, while the results of our analysis confirm an equilibrium-inducing mechanism for the labor market as these models predict, for the market of educational opportunity, we do not confirm such a mechanism. In other words, when a rapid increase in the supply of college graduates takes place, while the labor market lowers their relative wage levels, thereby reducing the economic incentive for advancement to higher education, demand in the market of opportunity for advancing to higher education does not decrease in response to the reduced incentive.

The above results imply that demand for higher education in South Korea may not be fully explainable by the human capital theory approach. In order to understand the demand or the background motivation of desire for academic achievement, we need to pay attention to the non-economic factors that the human capital approach did not take into account. In the next chapter, we will analyze another effect of educational credentials, namely the effect on promotion of occupational status, which is presumed to have a close relationship with people's desire for educational accomplishment in South Korea.

CHAPTER 5

Academic Credentials and Occupation Acquired

Previous research has primarily focused on occupation in order to understand people's status in society. The reason for this approach is that occupation is the most important factor that in most cases determines the individual's economic resources and interests (Blau and Duncan 1967: 6). However, occupation is important in a social stratification study for other reasons as well. It is generally accepted that social status is significantly affected not only by degree of possession of economic resources but also by non-economic resources such as prestige and power. The chance to gain access to these various social resources that determine social status differs greatly according to a person's occupation (Blau and Duncan 1967).

That being the case, when we consider the benefits of acquiring educational credentials in South Korean society, we should also pay careful attention to how educational credentials determine occupational status. South Korean's strong aspiration for educational attainments is aimed not only at obtaining increased income but also for the effect of enhanced occupational status that includes prestige and power.

Keeping these points in mind, this chapter presents an empirical analysis of the relationship between educational credentials and occupational status. It focuses in particular on the differences between college graduates and non-graduates as far as opportunities for acquiring the commonly preferred occupational statuses. In addition, similar to chapter 4, it also examines in detail how the rapid increase of college graduates since the 1980s affected the occupational opportunities they obtained and the nature of the relationship between educational credentials and occupational status in South Korean society.

Chapter 5 also considers unemployment among highly educated people, a phenomenon that appeared after the 1980s following the rapid increase in the number of college graduates. It looks at the importance to people, from their own perspec-

127

128 | Part II   Economic Rewards, Occupational Status, and Social Mobility

tive, of occupational status promotion obtained by virtue of a college degree. In short, the purpose of this chapter is to identify the effects of the rapid increase of college graduates on the labor market and on demand for higher education from the viewpoint of disparities in opportunities to engage in "preferred" occupations.[1]

I. OCCUPATIONAL OPPORTUNITY AND ACADEMIC CREDENTIALS:
THE MACRO STATISTICAL VIEW

This section analyzes the disparities in occupational opportunity according to level of academic attainment and how they have changed, relying on macro statistical data. Due to the nature of the aggregate data found in the governmental statistics reports on which the analysis relies, the occupational disparities are primarily limited to major groups in the standard classification of occupations. Nevertheless, as confirmed in chapter 2, there are large gaps in income and prestige among the major occupations in South Korea, so analysis based on the major groups can be assumed to be reasonably sufficient.[2]

The Census Perspective
Using data from the "Population and Housing Census" conducted by the Korean National Statistical Office, let us look at occupational composition by level of ed-

---

[1] There are two groups of existing studies on these issues: one group analyzes macro statistics to examine the relationship between academic credentials and job opportunity and its changes over the years (e.g., Jung Jin-Hwa 1996, etc.); the other group analyzes micro statistics to inquire into how the relationship between academic credentials and occupation was formed, focusing on institutional conditions (e.g., Lee Hyo-Soo 1984; 1991; Sato 1997). These studies provide interesting findings, and in particular the latter offers insights into the institutional characteristics of the South Korean labor market. However, they do have some limitations: (1) little attempt is made to integrate the outcomes of macroscopic analysis with that for microscopic analysis, (2) there is no detailed discussion of the characteristics of the South Korean educational system that produces "academic credentials," and (3) there is not sufficient dynamic analysis of the institutional aspects of the South Korean labor market.

Similar to the present book, Hattori (1998) attempts to discuss employment opportunities for new college graduates in relation to the rapidly increasing number of college graduates, focusing on the structural characteristics of the South Korean labor market (see chapter 5, section 3 of his book). However, the period of his analysis stops in the mid-1980s when the full-scale increase had not yet taken place. Here, while referring to these prior studies, I attempt to overcome these limitations.

[2] The period of analysis is limited here to the time prior to the year of 1992, when the standard classification of occupations was amended. The analysis in chapter 4, however, found that the rapid increase of college graduates significantly affected the labor market prior to 1992, so despite the limitation, we will be able to grasp the nature of the change in occupational opportunities for college and high school graduates caused by rapid increase of college graduates.

ucation and how it has changed. As observed in chapter 2, rapid progress in industrialization as well as significant change in the occupational structure has taken place in South Korea since the 1960s, and the number of white-collar and non-white-collar workers in the urban industrial sector has increased dramatically. How has the relationship between academic credentials and occupational status changed with shifts in the occupational structure?

Figure 5–1, showing the occupations of the employed by educational background in 1970, 1980, and 1990, indicates the rapid shift to workers with higher levels of education. While the ratio of workers who received secondary education and higher was only a little over 30 percent in 1970, it increased to 75 percent in 1990. The ratio of college-graduate workers also noticeably increased from 6.0 percent to 18.6 percent. The figures vividly illustrate how rapidly educational opportunities expanded in South Korea. Examining the expansion by period, people who completed secondary education expanded significantly in the 1970s and those who had completed higher education grew rapidly in the 1980s. Needless to say, as verified in chapter 3, these rapid expansions were triggered by changes in government policies on secondary and higher education: the open policy on secondary education from the second half of the 1960s to the first half of the 1970s, and the expansion of admissions quotas to higher education around 1980.

In spite of the rapid shift to workers with higher levels of education and changes in the educational composition of workers as a whole, the occupational distribution of each academic credential group remained essentially unchanged. While we indeed observe that, among working people who had completed higher education, jobs in the professions increased rapidly (by 9.8 percentage points) in the 1970s when the supply of new college graduates was smaller than the scale of economic expansion and decreased again (by 7.0 percentage points) as supply markedly increased in the 1980s, there was little noticeable change in the ratios for other occupations. Comparing the ratio of workers in white-collar occupations, i.e., professional, administrative and managerial, and clerical,[3] we observe that while workers with academic credentials of a college degree and higher increased five-fold, the ratio of white-collar workers among those with college and higher education did not change much: 67.6 percent in 1970, 75.7 percent in 1980, and 70.7 percent in 1990.

As for other academic credentials, except for the consistent decrease in workers engaged in agriculture, forestry, and fisheries and the consistent increase of manufacturing workers, the ratio of workers for individual occupations is nearly at the

---

[3] Partially because there were not many large-scale corporations in the retail business by the 1990s in South Korea, working conditions were poorer and compensation was much lower for sales jobs than for professional, managerial, and clerical jobs. Thus, researchers in South Korea did not necessarily regard sales jobs as white-collar.

Part II Economic Rewards, Occupational Status, and Social Mobility

Figure 5–1. Occupational Distribution by Educational Background

1970 (%)

	Uneducated	Elementary education	Secondary education	Higher education	Total	No. of people (thousand)
Professional	0.2	0.4	4.6	29.9	3.2	323
Administrative and managerial	0.0	0.3	1.6	6.4	1.0	96
Clerical	0.1	1.2	13.2	31.3	5.9	593
Sales	5.6	9.2	15.6	12.4	10.2	1,028
Service	2.8	7.8	9.2	4.3	6.7	678
Agriculture / forestry / fisheries	83.0	55.1	22.4	4.8	51.1	5,146
Manufacturing	8.2	23.9	33.3	10.9	21.8	2,197
Total	100.0	100.0	100.0	100.0	100.0	10,062
No. of people (thousand)	2,411	4,418	2,634	599	10,062	
Composition Ratio	24.0	43.9	26.2	6.0	100.0	

1980 (%)

	Uneducated	Elementary education	Secondary education	Higher education	Total	No. of people (thousand)
Professional	0.2	0.3	3.1	39.7	4.6	581
Administrative and managerial	0.0	0.1	1.0	7.5	1.1	134
Clerical	0.2	1.1	15.9	28.5	9.5	1,203
Sales	5.8	10.5	15.7	10.6	12.1	1,531
Service	3.5	7.4	8.7	3.3	7.1	895
Agriculture / forestry / fisheries	83.0	52.2	16.8	2.5	37.6	4,768
Manufacturing	7.3	28.4	38.8	8.0	28.1	3,570
Total	100.0	100.0	100.0	100.0	100.0	12,681
No. of people (thousand)	1,871	4,354	5,460	996	12,681	
Composition Ratio	14.8	34.3	43.1	7.9	100.0	

1990 (%)

	Uneducated	Elementary education	Secondary education	Higher education	Total	No. of people (thousand)
Professional	0.3	0.3	2.3	32.7	7.5	1,172
Administrative and managerial	0.1	0.4	1.6	5.9	2.1	328
Clerical	0.3	1.2	16.3	32.1	15.4	2,412
Sales	5.1	9.6	16.6	13.4	14.0	2,187
Service	5.5	10.2	10.2	4.3	8.8	1,373
Agriculture / forestry / fisheries	78.5	51.0	10.3	1.9	20.7	3,248
Manufacturing	10.2	27.3	42.7	9.7	31.6	4,955
Total	100.0	100.0	100.0	100.0	100.0	15,673
No. of people (thousand)	1,010	2,920	8,827	2,916	15,673	
Composition Ratio	6.4	18.6	56.3	18.6	100.0	

Source: Based on the annual editions of *Report on Population and Housing Census* (Korean National Statistical Office).

same level. For example, the ratio of white-collar workers among those who completed secondary education was steady: 19.4 percent in 1970, 20.0 percent in 1980, and 20.2 percent in 1990. Thus, although workers' academic credentials changed rapidly during these periods, there was a stable gap in the ratios of white-collar workers between those with and without higher education. As confirmed in chapter 2, between the white-collar occupations and other occupations in South Korea, aside from the income difference, there are considerable disparities in occupational prestige. For this reason, the large gap in the probability of obtaining a job in a white-collar occupation between college graduates and those with less education may cause people to seriously recognize the importance of college credentials in the pursuit of more prestigious occupational status.

On the other hand, the reason that the occupational composition of people for each level of educational attainment basically remained unchanged, despite the rapid increase of advancement to higher education, can be attributed to the fact that the occupational structure itself substantially changed due to the dramatic process of industrialization during this period. For instance, the number of workers engaged in white-collar jobs increased from one million in 1970 to four million in 1990 (figure 5–1). Similarly, both expansion of the number of workers in manufacturing jobs and reduction of the number of workers in agriculture, forestry and fisheries are rapid. Change in the occupational structure accompanying industrialization was very rapid, as was expansion of education.

Unlike the wage gap, therefore, disparities in occupational opportunity among people with different academic credentials probably changed little, even though the number of college graduates increased quickly. The above analysis, however, might be rough in that it focuses only on changes by decade; the target sample included people of all ages. Hence, in order to precisely examine what occupational opportunities were obtained by the rapidly increased number of college graduates since the 1980s, we need to conduct more detailed analysis using other data sets.

Occupational Opportunities for Younger Generations
Other than the population census, among government statistical resources that enable us to study occupational opportunity for the younger generations since the 1980s by academic qualification are the annual reports of the Wage Structure Survey and the *Statistical Yearbook of Education*, used in the previous chapter. The Wage Structure Surveys have been conducted with the primary objective of tracking the wages of workers, and thus they are not surveys of workers by occupation. However, because random sampling is performed in extracting the samples, with certain reservations[4] it is possible to make some observations about the occupa-

---
[4] Note that the Wage Structure Surveys have a somewhat higher sampling rate for large corporation workers.

tional opportunities of college and high school graduates based on the number of the sample by level of academic attainment, occupation, and age group listed in the survey reports.

The *Statistical Yearbook of Education* has data on new graduate career paths after graduation and the occupations of graduates who found jobs within one month after graduation. Because Korea's Ministry of Education collects data through each school, the information on career paths after graduation is limited to what is provided by each school. This is the reason for the large ratios of "career undetermined" and "unemployed" in the career paths of new graduates listed in the report. However, it is highly possible that these categories include graduates with jobs, the data about which the schools are not aware, or graduates who found jobs more than one month after graduation. For this reason, it should be noted that the occupational configuration listed in the *Statistical Yearbook of Education* is somewhat biased.

Now let us look at the relationship between academic credentials and occupational opportunity for the younger generations since the 1980s when the number of college graduates increased dramatically. There is a significant gender difference in the South Korean labor market, and the rate of employment for female students was very low until the 1980s. So here again, the analysis treats only male students, leaving the study of female students for future analysis.

Figure 5–2 shows the rate of those engaged in white-collar jobs among males in their 20s by level of education, using the sample of the annual wage structure survey. From this graph, we observe that the rate of four-year college graduates engaged in white-collar jobs is nearly 100 percent over the years, despite the rapid increase in the number of college graduates during that time. The rate of high school graduates with white-collar jobs gradually decreased from around 1983, and as a result, 40 percent of high school graduates who worked in white-collar occupations in the early 1980s decreased to a little over 20 percent in the second half of the 1980s. The rate of junior college graduates with white-collar jobs also started decreasing with a few years of delay. Furthermore, although not shown in the figure, the ratio of those engaging in professional jobs among white-collar jobs shows a similar pattern of changes.

It would be possible to interpret the decrease in the rates of high school and junior college graduates with white-collar jobs as a result of the increased labor force with higher education having pushed members of the labor force with lower educational credentials out of the white-collar occupations. The period when the rate of high school graduates engaged in white-collar jobs started decreasing coincided with the time when the number of junior college graduates significantly increased. Furthermore, the period when the ratio of junior college graduates engag-

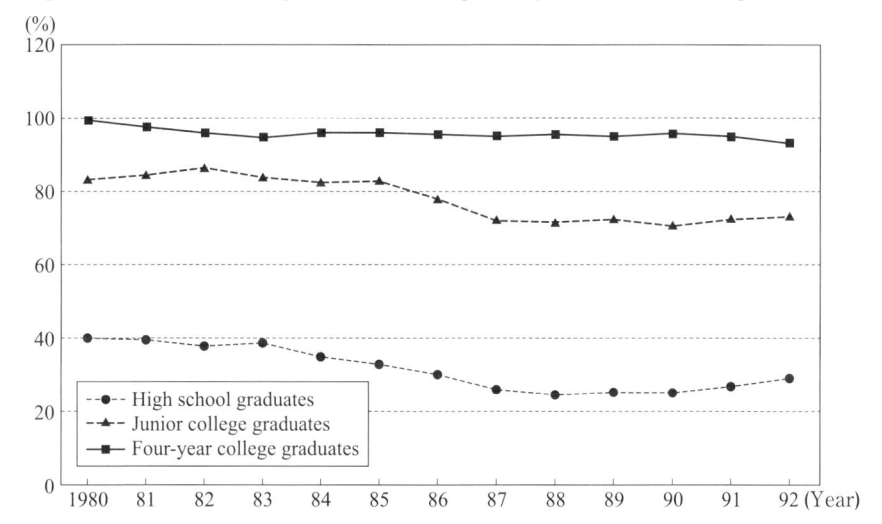

Figure 5–2. Rate of Entering White-Collar Occupation by Educational Level (Age 20s)

```
--●-- High school graduates
--▲-- Junior college graduates
--■-- Four-year college graduates
```

Source: Based on the annual editions of the Wage Structure Survey (Korean Ministry of Labor).

ing in white-collar occupations decreased coincided with the time when the number of four-year college graduates rapidly increased.

Next, let us analyze the occupations of new graduates based on the *Statistical Yearbook of Education*. Figure 5–3 shows the ratios of new male graduates engaged in white-collar jobs (graduates who were in the military service or could not be classified are excluded) and how they fluctuated.[5] The graph indicates that there is a very large gap between college graduates and high school graduates engaged in white-collar jobs. As for the shifts over the years, while the ratio for four-year college graduates essentially remained unchanged at around 80 percent, that for high school graduates decreased by more than 10 percentage points in the first half of the 1980s. The ratio for junior college graduates, too, decreased by more than 10 percentage points in the same period or slightly later, but the ratio began to show an upward tendency from 1988, and reached a level comparable with four-year college graduates in the early 1990s. Such recovery for junior college graduates is something we cannot discover through the Wage Structure Survey sample.

---

[5] *Statistical Yearbook of Education* greatly changed the report style from the 1982 edition onward, and around that time, some modifications were made in the classification standard of the occupation of new graduates (Jung Jin-Hwa 1996: 149). For this reason, this figure only shows the change from 1982 for high school and college graduates and from 1983 for junior college graduates to sufficiently assure the continuity of data.

134 | Part II   Economic Rewards, Occupational Status, and Social Mobility

Figure 5–3. Rate of Entering White-Collar Occupation among Newly Graduated Students

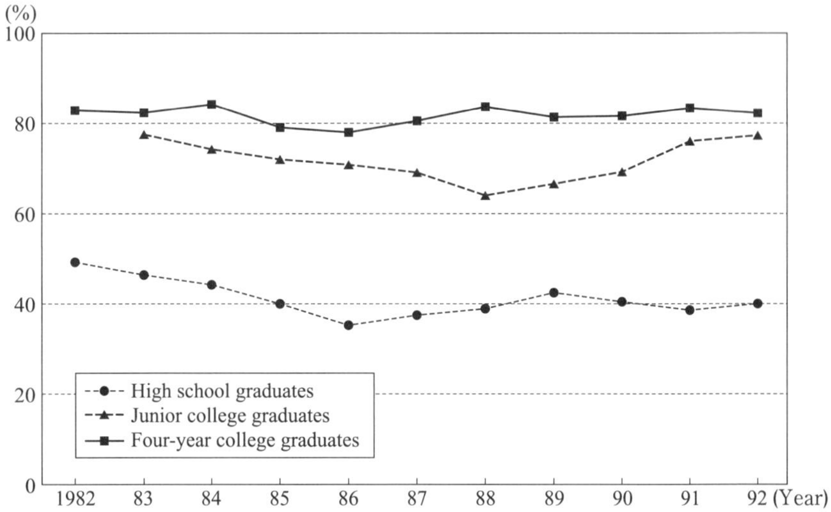

Source: Based on the annual editions of *Statistical Yearbook of Education* (Korean Ministry of Education).

The discrepancy in outcomes from the two data sources (Ministry of Labor and Ministry of Education) may be attributed to differences as follows: the Wage Structure Survey subjects are those working in business entities of 10 or more employees and hence the sample extraction rate is higher for large corporations, whereas the *Statistical Yearbook of Education* is a complete survey that covers graduates irrespective of the size of their companies. In other words, if the increase in the ratio of junior college graduates engaged in white-collar jobs since the late 1980s was caused by the increase in the number of graduates getting white-collar jobs in small companies, such a tendency might appear in educational statistical data, but would not appear clearly in wage structure survey samples. As for high school graduates, the ratio of white-collar jobs (about 20 to 30 percent), calculated from the wage structure survey samples whose subjects are all males in their 20s, is lower by about 10 percentage points than the ratio (about 30 to 40 percent) calculated from the new high-school-graduates subjects. This fact also implies that opportunities for white-collar jobs for high school graduates tended to be in small companies.

Be that as it may, according to the *Statistical Yearbook of Education*, there was a difference of 33.6 percentage points in the ratio of white-collar job finding between four-year graduates and high school graduates in 1982, and only 10 years later, it increased to 42.3 percentage points in 1992. The wage structure survey samples indicate a very similar tendency: despite the rapid increase in the number of college graduates, the ratio of four-year college graduates finding white-collar jobs did not markedly decrease, but rather, the ratio leveled off as they pushed high school graduates out of white-collar jobs. Simply based on these findings, we can say that the effect of increasing probability of finding white-collar jobs by advancing to college became relatively higher as the ratio of high school graduates getting white-collar jobs decreased.

Unemployment Rate of Younger Generations
However, if the rapid increase of college graduates since the 1980s substantially increased the unemployment rate of college graduates, we cannot directly interpret the aforementioned changes in occupational opportunities for college and high school graduates as the increased effect of college credentials on occupational position. Here, let us look briefly at the unemployment rate of the younger generations of college and high school graduates.

Figure 5–4 shows the unemployment rates of male graduates by educational level according to the *Annual Report on Economically Active Population* issued by the Korean National Statistical Office. The figure indicates the unemployment rate of high school and middle (and lower) school graduates largely decreased in the first half of the 1980s, while the rate for college graduates fluctuated at around 6 percent and became slightly higher than that for high school graduates in 1986. After the end of the economic boom around that time, however, the rate for college graduates gradually decreased, following the same pattern as in the case for high school graduates.[6]

Examining the configuration of unemployment by education level listed in the *Annual Report on Economically Active Population*, we find that the ratio of "new graduates who have never been employed" to the total number of unemployed graduates—this ratio became available from the 1989 edition onward—is about 40 percent for high school graduates and 50 to 60 percent for college graduates, indicating a high unemployment ratio for new college graduates. Although the *Report* does not list the unemployment rate by age group and level of education, Jung Jin-Hwa obtained the raw data from the survey to make that estimation. She shows that the male unemployment rate between the ages of 25 to 29 in 1994 has 4.5 percent for high school graduates and 4.0 percent for junior college graduates and as high as 7.8 percent for four-year college graduates. The difference is even more pronounced among men aged 20–24: 8.4 percent for high school graduates, 17.0 percent for junior college graduates, and 22.3 percent for four-year college

---

[6] After the economic crisis at the end of 1997, the unemployment rate of college graduates greatly increased along with the unemployment rate as a whole. We will consider the issue in a separate opportunity, and here we mainly present data up to 1997.

136 | Part II   Economic Rewards, Occupational Status, and Social Mobility

Figure 5–4. Unemployment Rate by Educational Level

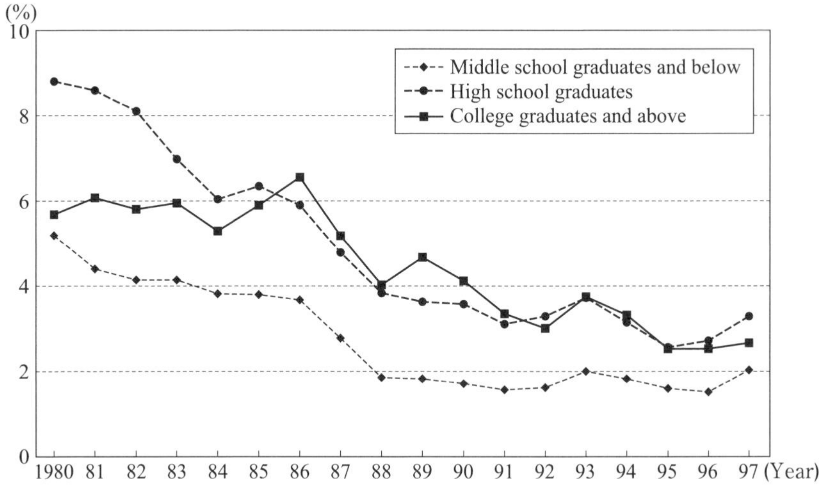

Source: Based on the annual editions of *Annual Report on Economically Active Population* (Korean National Statistical Office).

graduates[7] (Jung Jin-Hwa 1996). For these data, the unemployment rate of new college graduates is certainly at a much higher level when compared with new high school graduates.

We may also approach the employment opportunity of new graduates from the 1980s using "career paths of graduates" as listed in the *Statistical Yearbook of Education*. Figure 5–5 shows the employment rate of new graduates (males only) from each educational stage. The denominator is the number of graduates from each educational stage subtracted by the number of graduates either advancing to a higher-level school or fulfilling their military service obligations, and the numerator is the number of graduates who find employment.[8] From this figure, we notice

---

[7] However, we need to carefully interpret the high unemployment rate among college graduates in their early twenties. For male college graduates, many South Korean companies have as a condition of employment the completion of (or exemption from) compulsory military service. Because there are many males in their early twenties who have not completed military service, we conjecture that the unemployment rate is relatively high.

[8] Strictly speaking, the denominator includes graduates who do not want employment, although they are not going on to the next level of education nor fulfilling the military service. However, male college graduates should have a negligibly small ratio for these cases. As for high school graduates, students who, having failed the college entrance examination, are preparing for the next year's examination are included in the denominator. We believe that the relative expansion

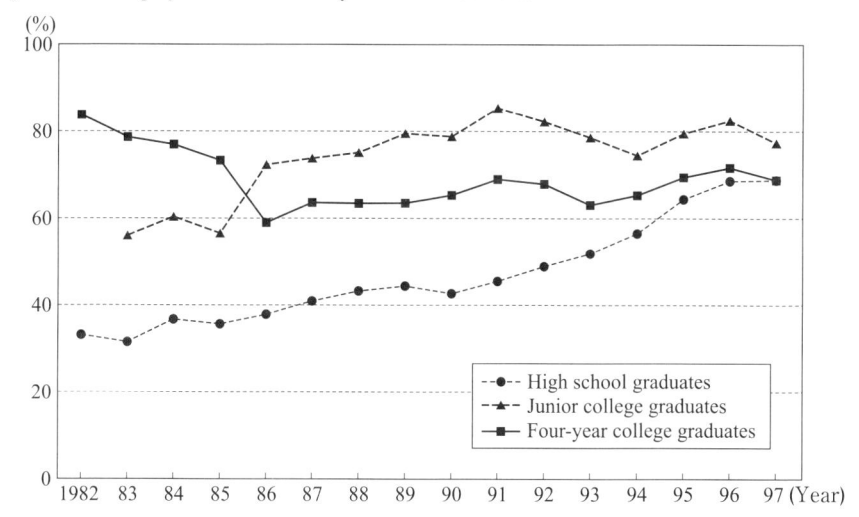

Figure 5–5. Employment Rate of Newly Graduated Students

```
(%)
100

 80

 60

 40

 20                          --●-- High school graduates
                             --▲-- Junior college graduates
                             --■-- Four-year college graduates
  0
    1982 83  84  85  86  87  88  89  90  91  92  93  94  95  96  97 (Year)
```

Source: Based on the annual editions of the *Statistical Yearbook of Education* (Korean Ministry of Education).

that the employment rate of new high school graduates and junior college graduates gradually increased from the 1980s while the employment rate of four-year college graduates suddenly dropped in the mid-80s when the number of college graduates rapidly increased. However, it soon increased again, although the increase was gradual. Given these findings, together with other findings, including that the unemployment rate of college graduates did not increase much even in the 1980s or rather decreased in the second half of the 1980s, we infer that most of the rapidly increased new college graduates eventually secured job opportunities despite the worsening of the job market due to the rapid increase of their numbers.

According to the *Statistical Yearbook of Education*, from the second half of the 1980s when the number of college graduates increased, at least 30,000 male graduates from four-year and junior colleges—the graduates who did not advance to a higher-level school or go into the military service—were unemployed each year. If these unemployed college graduates were unable to find jobs continuously, the number of unemployed college graduates would increase explosively as the years went by. The *Annual Report on Economically Active Population* indicates, how-

---

of college admission quotas increased the employment rate of high school graduates in the 1990s due to a decrease in the number of high school graduates who failed the entrance examination.

ever, that the actual number of unemployed college graduates with no employment experience stays at approximately 30,000 to 50,000, and the number gradually decreased from 1989 when data became available. Therefore, we presume that many of the college graduates considered (by the college authorities) unable to obtain jobs immediately after graduation somehow did obtain jobs later.

The newspapers, television, and other mass media reported the low employment rates or high unemployment rates for new college graduates based upon the *Statistical Yearbook of Education* as proof of the harsh job market for new college graduates. However, we must note that the low employment rate shown in the statistics does not lead immediately to the accumulation of unemployed college graduates. Rather than an increase and accumulation of unemployed college graduates, it should be considered an increase in the number of the graduates who found jobs outside the grasp of college authorities or as indicating the prolonged time required to obtain jobs after graduation. We will discuss this issue in detail in the next section.

Through the analysis described above, we may conclude that for college graduates, in particular four-year college graduates, employment opportunities for white-collar jobs are obtained at the same rate as in the previous period despite the rapid increase of college graduates in the 1980s. By contrast, many high school graduates are thought to have been pushed out of employment opportunities for white-collar jobs by the rapidly increasing number of college graduates. As a result, the benefits of gaining white-collar occupations by obtaining a college diploma has by no means been lowered despite the rapid increase.[9] Furthermore, the unemployment rate of college graduates is not significantly higher than that of high school graduates even though their unemployment rate did become relatively high as the number of college graduates rapidly increased. Therefore, the expected effect of college graduation above is not decreased much even after taking the unemployment rate into consideration.

Nevertheless, the above analysis of the disparity in occupational opportunities is relatively simple based on the major groups of occupations without considering the non-occupational conditions of employment opportunity. We also need to consider what processes make it possible for new college graduates to secure the white-collar jobs. In the next section, we discuss the job opportunity of college

---

[9] Cha Jong-Chun (1992), which conducted a path analysis on status achievement of males in Japan and South Korea using the data of equity survey in 1990 and SSM survey in 1975, indicates the influence of one's educational level on the status of one's first occupation is much stronger in South Korea (0.453) than in Japan (0.338). Such analysis outcome, too, may suggest a strong effect of the academic credential on occupational status in South Korea.

graduates and its change in detail through more concrete analysis for the actual employment process of college graduates.

II. NEW COLLEGE GRADUATE EMPLOYMENT PROCESSES AND HOW THEY CHANGED

How do newly graduated students obtain employment opportunities? Various prior studies have revealed that the processes by which new school graduates find employment are significantly affected not only by the pure market mechanism but also by non-market factors such as institutions and networks (Granovetter 1974; Kariya 1991). Given these factors, when we discuss the relationship between academic credentials and occupational status in South Korean society, it is necessary to consider in closer focus what processes newly graduated students go through to obtain jobs and what institutional conditions affect the processes.

This section takes up two themes relevant to the phase from the 1980s to the first half of the 1990s when college graduates rapidly increased. First, we explore the employment methods for "new graduates" in order to learn how the relationship between academic credentials and occupation came into being. We also study the employment opportunity preferences of new graduates, and how they relate to the characteristics of employment practices. Second, we investigate how employers and job seekers responded to the rapid increase of college graduates in the 1980s. Namely, how did employers modify their employment procedures in response to the rapid increase of college graduates, and how did the employment opportunity preferences of job seekers and their actual job-seeking activities change. Such micro-level analyses will complement our macro level discussion of the previous section.

In this section, in order to study the above issues, we use newspaper and journal articles along with the outcome of previous research. Regarding journal articles, we refer to articles of general-interest monthlies as well as job-hunting-related periodicals such as *Recruit*, which mainly targets new college graduates, and *Ipsa Saenghwal*[10] (Company Life) targeting new high school graduates. We believe these references will provide a clearer picture of the job-hunting situation for new graduates at the time.

Methods for Hiring New Graduates and Their Impact
The two main characteristics of methods for hiring new graduates in South Korea from the 1980s to the first half of the 1990s were "employment en masse by cor-

---
[10] This journal was formerly named *Chuijik* (Job Hunting).

porate groups" and "employment by education level."[11] During the rapid economic growth period in South Korea, major corporate groups (*chaebols*) grew dramatically, utilizing close ties with government-related personnel (Hattori 1994). These corporate groups—Samsung, Hyundai, and LG—are composed of subsidiaries in a wide variety of industrial fields including manufacturing, construction, finance, and distribution, and they have similar characteristics to pre-World War II Japanese financial conglomerate groups (zaibatsu).

En masse employment
During the rapid economic growth period, when college graduates and in some cases high school graduates were hired, normally they were not hired by individual subsidiaries but en masse by a corporate group.[12] The process of hiring new graduates en masse was managed by the personnel department that administered a whole corporate group, and the newly hired personnel were allocated to individual subsidiaries after overall training.

Owing to this employment method, the employment volume of each corporate group was very large. Mammoth corporate groups such as Samsung, Hyundai, Daewoo, and LG (then, Lucky Goldstar) each hired around 1,000 college graduates annually. These four corporate groups hired a total of over 6,000 new male four-year college graduates in 1985.[13] At that time, while the number of college graduates started gradually increasing, approximately 35,000 new male four-year college graduates were employed in South Korea, meaning that one out of six was hired by one of the four corporate groups. According to *Recruit* and other magazines, the annual total employment of new male four-year college graduates by 30 to 50 large corporate groups—regarded as *chaebols* in South Korea—was 10,000 to 20,000 in the mid-1980s, which indicates that one out of every two new male four-year college graduates was hired by these large corporate groups. Popular employment opportunities other than in these corporate groups included government employees, schoolteachers, and jobs in mass media, banks and government-sponsored enterprises. Therefore, until the first half of the 1980s, it was not very difficult for a male graduate of a four-year college to find a white-collar job with a large corporation in South Korea.

---

[11] After the 1990s, there were more cases where individual subsidiaries of corporate groups conducted their own hiring processes, and some announced the abolition of academic credentials as criteria for employment. In reality, though, academic credentials seem to carry great weight in the final stages of the hiring process, as previously.
[12] In case of hiring manufacturing workers, employment by individual subsidiary was rather common.
[13] *Recruit*, December 1985, p. 125; September 1984, pp. 26–27.

Employment by Education Level

Many South Korean companies, large companies in particular, specified the academic credential required as part of eligibility for hiring. The same was true in hiring just-graduated applicants. We must note that, while in some cases the minimum level of education required was indicated such as "high school and above," large corporations generally specified "high school graduate" or "college graduate."

The level of education required was strongly connected to occupation. Lee Hyo-Soo, who analyzed newspaper advertisements for hiring of new graduates from March 1982 to February 1983, shows that 93.9 percent of the 683 companies that placed the advertisements listed "academic credential" as a hiring requirement, a figure much higher than the percentage that listed "age" or "gender" (Lee Hyo-Soo 1984: 235). Similarly, according to an article of the April 1985 issue of *Ipsa Saenghwal* (Company Life), which analyzed academic credentials, occupations, and recruitment numbers by level of education appearing in the employment ads of 350 companies in the year of 1984, over 80 percent of the positions advertised for male college graduates were for professional, clerical, and administrative and managerial positions; a little over 10 percent were for sales. The same occupational positions for high school graduates accounted for only a little over 30 percent, and the remaining 60-plus percent were for manufacturing and sales.[14] Because of these employment activities by companies, academic credentials were closely tied to occupational status among new workers upon entering their companies.

According to the personnel regulations of a certain corporate group in the first half of the 1980s, the employment process for new graduates was conducted at three different job ranks: fourth-rank (non-manual) employee, fifth-rank (non-manual) employee, and technician; i.e., factory worker. In principle, a male four-year college graduate was hired as a fourth-rank employee, a high school graduate was hired as a fifth-grade employee, and one who had completed the mandatory education or above was hired as a technician (Lee Hyo-Soo 1984: 236).[15] Generally, an employee's job rank and type of occupation were primarily determined based on academic credentials, and many South Korean companies at

---
[14] *Ipsa Saenghwal* (Company Life), April 1985, p. 92. Incidentally, high school female graduates had ample hiring opportunities in clerical work in addition to manufacturing work and sales work. On the other hand, South Korean companies then were little motivated to hire female college graduates. In fact, the number of employed female college graduates was equivalent to only about 10 percent of male college graduates in each company (Lee Keun-Moo 1989).
[15] It was common practice in hiring junior college graduates until the late 1980s that they were hired within the same framework as high school graduates but were subsequently treated differently from high school graduates in terms of wages and promotion (*Recruit*, June 1986, p. 96).

142 | Part II   Economic Rewards, Occupational Status, and Social Mobility

Figure 5–6. Job-Ranking System of a South Korean Corporation (Case of Company L)

Job Rank	Non-Manual			Manual		
	Job position	Minimum years for promotion	Starting-salary grade name	Job position	Minimum years for promotion	Starting-salary grade name
First rank A	Department chief					
First rank B	Vice department chief	4 years				
Second rank	Section chief	4 years		Chief		
Second rank deputy	Acting section chief	2 years				
Third rank	Assistant section chief	3 years		Team leader	7 years	
Fourth rank	Subsection chief	1 year		Sub-team Leader	7 years	
	Worker	2 years	College graduate (male) 4–32 College graduate (female) 4–38	Worker	10 years	
Fifth rank (male) Fifth rank (female)	Worker	4 years	High school graduate (male) 5–42 High school graduate (female) 5–32			High school graduate (male) Manual 1

Source: Lee Chang-Wook and Kim Hyeon-Seok (1991: 249) as cited in Jeong Jea-Hoon (1998: 84).

the time established multi-track job-rank systems with totally different promotional paths between manual and non-manual occupations. It was extremely difficult for a person hired as a manual employee to be internally promoted to a non-manual position.[16] Figure 5–6 shows the job-ranking system of Company L, with the shortest number of years required to be promoted from a certain job rank to the next, as well as occupational differences. It illustrates the restricted promotions for

---

[16] Although there were many companies that offered promotions from a manual job (manufacturing work) track to a non-manual job (office work) track, actual cases were very few (Korean Council of Economic Organizations 1991). Hattori introduced an episode illustrating how South Korean skilled manual workers who received technical training in a plant of a Japanese company were surprised to hear that the deputy plant manager had once been a skilled worker of the plant. It was beyond their imagination that "even a skilled manual worker could be promoted to a managerial position" (Hattori 1988: 235).

manual employees compared with non-manual employees, and the disparity in promotional speed as well.[17] For example, the shortest number of years needed for a college graduate hired as a fourth-rank employee in the non-manual occupation to be promoted to a third-rank job was 3 years, whereas, for a high school graduate hired as a fifth-rank technician in a manual occupation it was as many as 17 years.

Thus, the difference in the job rank at the time of employment according to academic credentials would greatly affect a person's subsequent career. Academic credentials had such a powerful determining influence that the personnel system of South Korean companies was called the "academic-credential class system" (Hattori 1988: 178).

Hiring of new graduates
Now, let us review the actual methods used by South Korean companies in the 1980s and 1990s for hiring new graduates.[18] In hiring new college graduates, several methods were used, including open recruitment, school recommendation, and hiring by personal connection. For open recruitment, job advertisements were placed in newspapers and magazines calling for applicants irrespective of what institution they graduated from; hiring was determined based on application forms and other documents, written examinations, and interviews. Large corporations generally held open recruitment twice a year: the first recruitment (the first half of each year) for applicants discharged from the military service and August graduates, and the second from fall to winter each year for the large crop of upcoming new graduates. The employment examinations of many large corporations for the second recruitment concentrated around November. Those who failed had to find another job within the remaining three months before graduation in February.

For the school-recommendation hiring method, companies asked schools or teachers to recommend outstanding students. Similar to Japan, this is the method used mainly for recruiting engineers from among students majoring in science and engineering. Many smaller companies rely on employment through personal connections—links that may involve not only a relatively strong network such as kinship ties but often includes regional/communal and school ties (Ahn Hee-Tak 1993: 295). In addition, the internship system, which appeared during the 1990s and after, allowed for hiring of students who had served as interns for a certain pe-

---

[17] Some reforms were made in these personnel management systems in South Korea from the 1990s. For these "new personnel systems," see Kim Yong-Gi (1998) and Myung Tae-Sook (1998).
[18] Description of the employment system for new graduates in this section is based on Sato (1997), Lee Hyo-Soo (1984), and "Special Topic: How Can I Find a Job?" (*Chuijik* [Job Hunting], pp. 30–41, April 1986).

riod of time. Large corporations hold open-recruitment and school-recommendation hiring once or twice a year; they also hire people by other methods each time positions become available. Smaller companies hire new employees when necessity arises throughout the year.

The same hiring methods are used for high school and junior college graduates, but often with somewhat different weights. Junior college graduates are hired relatively rarely through open recruitment; in most cases they find jobs through school recommendations and personal connections.[19] This is partly because in the open recruitment of large corporations the number of positions available to junior college graduates is very low if any, and partly because junior college graduates find many of their jobs in smaller companies. High school graduates, too, are relatively rarely hired through open recruitment. Many find jobs through school recommendations and introductions from acquaintances. Technical high school graduates find their jobs through "practical training" (Lee Hyo-Soo 1984). In addition, in many cases of hiring manual workers, an employer informs his/her employees of the employment announcement through a bulletin board within the factory, utilizing the employees' personal connections to locate applicants from whom new workers are selected (Hattori 1988).

For government employee possitions, academic credentials are not specified in recruitment. However, as in Japan, new workers are selected according to the job rank originally corresponding to their academic credential: fifth rank for four-year college graduates, seventh rank for junior college graduates, and ninth rank for high school graduates.

Job preferences of college students
South Korean company methods of employing new graduates impart a distinctive characteristic to employment opportunities for college students, influencing the job preferences of college students.

Employment opportunities open to job seekers may be diversified and mutually differentiated by occupation and various additional conditions including industry, company size, company culture, business policy, location, and wage. Naturally, job preferences vary among job seekers according to their orientations and aptitudes for these conditions. In South Korea, however, "horizontal" differentiation of employment opportunities according to conditions such as industry had not yet been fully developed at least until the 2000s, and as a result, "vertical" variation based on company size was the primary factor of differentiation of employment opportunities in the period under study here.

The custom of en masse employment by the big corporate groups affects this

---

[19] *Recruit*, June 1986, p. 94.

phenomenon. Because a corporate group with links to various industrial sectors hires large numbers of new graduates, it is very difficult to differentiate the employment opportunities by industry, except for some, such as mass media and banking, that are not included in corporate groups. In addition, collective employment generally has very broad job frameworks for new four-year college graduates, e.g., natural science and engineering majors for engineering jobs and humanities and social science majors for office (general) jobs. For this reason, employment opportunities by occupation are not much diversified. The same can be said of job location. Even a company that is located in a provincial area as a subsidiary of a corporate group may hire new graduates through an en masse employment process conducted in Seoul, and therefore, many large corporate groups do not differentiate employment opportunities by location.

For these reasons, the size of the corporate group is the critical variable that differentiates employment opportunities for college students who want to work for private companies.[20] Furthermore, as the South Korean economic structure pivots around the large corporations, i.e., as large corporate groups have significant economic presence, capacity to pay high wages, and stable business management, the differentiation of employment opportunities by corporate size becomes even more vertical. College students tend to have a strong desire to work for a large corporation, believing that "the larger the corporation, the better the job opportunity," and this is manifested as their job preference. We also presume that the ranking of corporate groups by total sales (as frequently reported in the South Korean mass media) also promotes strong job-selection preferences according to corporate size among college students.

Let us confirm our argument using the outcome of a survey on the preferred career path of college students. In 1984, Korea Recruit Company conducted a survey of male college students to learn about their attitudes toward career paths and employment. Asked about their preferred career paths after graduation, 50.3 percent of respondents preferred private corporations, a figure much higher than that for government organizations/employees (13.3 percent), finance (8.4 percent), graduate schools (8.0 percent), mass media (5.3 percent).[21] The survey also asked those who preferred private corporations to specify a preferred corporation from a list of 30 large corporate groups along with an "other" option. Figure 5–7 shows the results, indicating the large differences in preference rates among corporate

---

[20] In addition, the "corporate culture" of an individual corporate group may influence them to a certain degree. But its importance is not very great compared with the corporate size.

[21] *Recruit*, December 1984, pp. 26–30. Incidentally, for female college graduates, because corporate groups' hiring volume of female college graduates was so small at that time, only 29.8 percent indicated private corporations while teaching (20.0 percent) and mass media (16.2 percent) had relatively high ratios.

146 | Part II   Economic Rewards, Occupational Status, and Social Mobility

Figure 5–7. Rank of Companies Preferred by College Students

Rank	Corporate Group Name	Ratio (%)
1	Samsung	13.6
2	Lucky Goldstar	12.9
3	Hyundai	10.7
4	Deawoo	7.7
5	Hanjin (KAL)	6.9
6	Ssangyong	5.0
7	Sunkyong	4.4
8	Doosan	3.7
9	Lotte	3.2
10	Hanwha Group	3.0
11	Kia Industry	2.6
12	Hyosung	1.7
13	Miwon	1.4
14	Kookche	1.2
15	Kolon	1.1
16	Haitai	1.1
17	Dong-A Construction	0.9
18	Daelim Construction	0.8
19	Sammi	0.7
20	New Dong-A	0.6
	Others/ NA	16.5
	Total	100.0

Source: Based on data from *Recruit* magazine, November 1984, p. 30.
Note: Company names as of the time of publication of the data.

groups. The top five groups accounted for over half the responses. What is notable here is that the ranking is strongly correlated with the size of the corporate group, indicating that South Korean college students' employment preferences are closely tied to corporate size. Furthermore, asking respondents to choose from a list of 30 large corporations to indicate their job preference is itself an indication that significant differences among employment opportunities of college students were regarded as identical with differences among corporate groups.[22]

However, the importance of corporate size is limited to white-collar jobs "suitable" to college graduates. When the number of college graduates was very small, which continued up to the early 1980s, it was almost unthinkable that new college

---

[22] Job-hunting-related magazines such as *Recruit* had many articles on the criteria for the hiring process of individual large-scale corporations such as Samsung, Hyundai, and Daewoo, including specific hiring methods used and the important points to keep in mind for employment examinations, indicating that such things were of great concern to many job hunters.

graduates would take anything other than a white-collar job.

Changes in Methods of Employment and Their Consequences

In the previous section, based on cases mainly in the first half of the 1980s, we discussed the methods of hiring new graduates, the structures of employment opportunity for college students, and student employment preferences. In South Korea, job matching for college graduates was conducted within the institutional framework explained above. However, as confirmed in chapter 3, from the second half of the 1980s, the number of college graduates newly entering the labor market dramatically increased. How did the rapid increase of college graduates affect the job matching process and how did their employment opportunities change as a result? Here, we discuss these issues by focusing on employers' responses to the drastic increase.

Change in the number of recruited college graduates
The number of college graduates employed by the South Korean big corporate groups was relatively large, and at the same time, college graduates viewed these companies as "attractive" workplaces. In this section, we will examine the shifts in the scale of employment by these corporate groups compared with the increase in the number of recruitable new college graduates.

To state the conclusion first, while the large corporate groups expanded the scale of their recruitment of college graduates to some extent, particularly during the "three-low boom"[23] from 1986 to 1988, the increase was not great enough to absorb the rapid rise in the number of college graduates. In the case of the four-major corporate groups, recruitment did increase; in the second recruitment of 1984, Samsung, Hyundai, Daewoo, and Lucky Goldstar each employed between 1,000 college graduates and several hundreds more, whereas in the second recruitment of 1988, Samsung hired 3,150, Hyundai 2,950, Lucky Goldstar 2,306, and Daewoo 2,000.[24] However, after 1988, as the economy slowed down, these employment figures gradually decreased. The total quantity of annual employment by 50 large corporate groups as a whole was a little over 10,000 at the beginning of the 1980s, and while it increased to 26,000 in 1988, it decreased to 20,000 in 1992.[25] Expansion of employment was not large, however, compared with the in-

---

[23] The economic boom that occured due to the low Korean won exchange rate (relative to the Japanese yen), low oil prices, and low interest rates.
[24] *Recruit*, October 1989, p. 56.
[25] Korean Ministry of Labor, "'88 Survey Report on College Graduate Employment by Large Corporations" (Recited from *Recruit*, May 1989, pp. 110–13), and Korean Ministry of Labor, "'92 Survey Report on College Graduate Employment by 50 Large Group Corporations" (Recited from *Recruit*, August 1993, pp. 105–09).

crease in the number of college graduates. For a decade from 1982 to 1992, the number of (four-year) college graduates jumped from 60,000 to 180,000; even male graduates alone dramatically increased from 45,000 to over 110,000.

Finding employment at a large corporate group was not difficult for a new college graduate in the first half of the 1980s, but it became gradually harder as the number of college graduates increased. The competition was even greater at the end of the 1980s when the economy slowed. In fact, according to *Recruit*, from the second half of the 1980s each year, the competition rate of the examinations held for open recruitment by corporate groups rose at least 4 to 5 times, and in some cases, more than ten times.

Changes in the recruitment system
Most notably, the recruitment practices of large corporate groups significantly changed against the backdrop of the increase of college graduates and the growing difficulty of entering major corporations. Most of the large corporate groups hired four-year college graduates through open recruitment and school recommendations, as discussed earlier. In the case of open recruitment, applicants were first screened based on documents submitted and then the narrowed number of candidates took a written examination and were interviewed to finalize employment. However, while the rapidly increased number of college graduates from the second half of the 1980s intensified the competition for employment with large corporate groups, there arose situations where many graduates of colleges outside the metropolitan area, which were regarded as "lower in rank" than those in Seoul, were excluded at the stage of document screening or were unable to receive school recommendations. Amid the dramatic increase in the number of college graduates, each company gave even more importance than ever to the institution applicants had attended.

As complaints from regional college graduates about their disadvantaged status in the job recruitment process grew louder, however, the South Korean government took action to remedy the problem. In June 1986, the Ministry of Labor recommended to 21 government-supported institutions, 54 financial organizations and 29 large corporate groups that they adopt more open recruitment methods in order to achieve greater fairness and select applicants using written examinations without prior document screening. The Ministry of Labor also advised them to limit the number of applicants who would pass the written examination from the range of 130 percent to 150 percent of the number of final successful applicants in order to minimize the use of personal connections or other such interventions in the consequent selection process based on interviews.[26]

---
[26] *Recruit*, July 1986, p. 130. As described in Chapter 3, the South Korean government then had a policy of decentralizing higher education institutions by rejecting the establishment of new

These government recommendations are themselves a clear indication of the importance South Korean society placed on employment with a large corporate enterprise. The government intervention in private company employment practices was meant to ensure as fair competition as possible, and, as in the case of the prohibition of after-school lessons in 1980, its recommendations were an expression of its efforts to eliminate unfair opportunities that might damage the optimistic social image of South Korea as a place of equal opportunity in achieving higher social status.

In response to the government's recommendation, from the time of the second recruitment of 1986, government-supported institutions, commercial banks, and large corporate groups adopted new selection systems in which written examinations were offered to all applicants and interviews then held with those who had passed the written examinations.[27] The subjects of written examinations were English, general knowledge, and questions related to the applicants' majors. Because the number of applicants was between several thousand and some tens of thousands, computer-scored, multiple-choice examinations were adopted to evaluate applicants' scholastic abilities. In the case of one corporate group, it first narrowed the number of candidates through written examinations to 1.5 to 2.0 times the number of those to be employed, and then interviewed the selected candidates to determine acceptance (Lee Keun-Moo 1989). Considering that, during this period, the competition to gain employment in a large corporate group was high, reaching two digits in some cases, the role of the written examination in selecting applicants was significant.

Furthermore, the Ministry of Labor recommended that the written examinations be given on the same day in order to avoid undercutting actual employment due to examinees being successful in more than one company's examination. In response to this request, many of the large corporate groups, financial organizations, and the government-supported institutions began around 1986 to conduct written examinations on one of the two specific days in November. In the second recruitment of 1986, for example, corporate groups such as Hyundai, Daewoo, Samsung, and Lucky Goldstar and many commercial banks, known to recruit large numbers each year, gave written examinations on the first Sunday, November 2, while some corporate groups, such national public enterprises as Korean Railroad Corporation

---

colleges in Seoul in order to suppress the population concentrated in the capital city. The fear that poor employment of regional college graduates might discourage students from attending regional colleges was responsible for the government's prompt action to improve the employment situation (*Recruit*, January 1986, p. 50).
[27] *Recruit*, October 1986, p. 126 and November 1986, p. 132. While document screening prior to paper examinations reemerged from the early 1990s, many corporations continued to conduct written scholastic ability examinations (Korea Employer's Federation 1994).

and the Korean Broadcasting System, conducted written examinations and interviews on the second Sunday, November 9.[28]

As explained above, after the recommendations of the Ministry of Labor in 1986, the weight of written examinations for employment became much heavier—so much so that the job-seeking process of new college graduates began to be called the "second college entrance examination."

Consequence of changes in the recruitment system
The changes in the recruitment system considerably affected the attitudes of new job-seeking college graduates and their actual job-seeking activities. Although large corporate groups, financial institutions, and government-affiliated organizations were very "attractive," there were at most only two opportunities to apply for such employment because their examinations were held simultaneously. Consequently, passing/failing was decisive in job-hunting activities. Establishment of this recruitment system made a visible distinction between large organizations, which conducted examinations on one of the two specific days, and smaller companies that continued recruiting after the examinations of the large corporations were over. A similar situation prevailed in the college entrance selection system at that time. Entrance examinations conducted by individual four-year colleges, regardless of national, public or private colleges, were held on one of the two specific days. After those examinations were over, the junior college examinations were held targeting those who had failed in or did not take the four-year college examinations. The similarity made the distinction between the larger, and more favorable, companies/organizations and the smaller, and less favorable, ones all the more visible.

Some additional characteristics of the recruitment system for new college graduates in South Korea should be mentioned. Eligibility to apply for employment was not restricted strictly to "new graduates," or to those who had graduated from college immediately before employment. As long as the employment conditions, such as age, determined by each organization were fulfilled, even older graduates could be employed without being discriminated from the new graduates passing through the same recruiting process.

Such practices are partly related to the compulsory military service for young South Korean men. Companies mostly limited male applicants to those who had either completed their military service or were exempted from it. Some college graduates performed their military service while at school and others after graduation.

In the case of Japan, businesses strongly believe that "school graduation" and

---

[28] *Recruit*, November 1986, pp. 68–81.

"employment" (should) occur simultaneously, and various systems for hiring new employees are designed on that assumption. Although the circumstances of employment are somewhat different these days, most job-seeking graduates are still employed immediately after graduation, and the time lag between these two life-events is very short in Japan. In South Korea, due to the institutional conditions mentioned above, the time lag is significant both normatively and empirically.

Under these circumstances, because of the intensified competition for jobs due to the rapid increase of college graduates from the second half of the 1980s and the consequent changes in the new employee recruiting system (including the simultaneous holding of the written examinations of large organizations and the increasing weight of the examinations), there inevitably emerged a large body of jobless college graduates preparing for employment examinations in the following year.

The rapid increase of college graduates and the intensified competition for employment meant that there were new college graduates who no longer found it easy to find employment in the large corporations. The written examinations of the large organizations held on the same specific dates reduced the opportunities for job hunting. Even more important, large corporate groups began to place greater weight on written examinations in the process of employing new graduates. Because it was believed that the scholastic ability tested by the written examinations was something that could be improved through effort, many prospective college graduates who were unable to obtain satisfactory employment opportunities decided to graduate without finding employment so that they could prepare fully and then take the employment examinations for a large corporation the following year. In October 1992, when the number of college graduates further increased, the "Pacific Insurance Company" conducted a survey of 550 new employees with a college degree. A surprisingly large 39 percent reported experiencing this period of preparation for examinations after graduation from college.[29]

The lowered employment rate of new four-year college graduates we mentioned in the previous section reflects the increase of college graduates remaining jobless in order to prepare for employment examinations. As we have observed, large companies, banks, and governmental organizations adopted new recruiting practices from around 1986, when the employment rate of new four-year college graduates suddenly dropped to about 60 percent from over 70 percent (see figure 5–5). As pointed out previously, the reduction of the employment rate of new four-year college graduates that appeared in the *Statistical Yearbook of Education* was understood as an indication of the worsening of employment conditions and an increase of unemployed new college graduates. However, the information on

---

[29] *Recruit*, November 1992, p. 158.

employment of graduates listed in the *Statistical Yearbook of Education* was limited to those who were employed within one month after graduation. That being the case, the lowered employment figures shown in the statistical yearbook were indeed caused by new college graduates who had postponed job hunting in order to prepare for employment examinations and secure better employment opportunities the following year.

The changes in the employment system for new college graduates, which significantly affected their job-searching behavior, might be said to have weakened the effect of college graduation on occupational status. The abolishing of document screening based mainly on the ranking of admission difficulty among colleges allowed all applicants to take the written examinations. At first glance, that change seems to have decreased the effect of academic credentials in the employment selection process. From a broader point of view, however, the changes in the employment system during the period—the increased weight of written examinations—helped to plant belief in academic credentials even more firmly in the employment selection process. That is to say, government guidance led to the spread of the employment selection process based on written examinations to test abilities in English, general knowledge, and applicants' majors, and that process served to legitimize employment selection based on scholastic ability. Inasmuch as the college entrance examination and examinations for promotion and graduation may adequately discriminate among people in terms of scholastic ability, the selection for employment based on written examination of scholastic ability was in principle the same as selection for employment based on institution attended.

Employment Opportunities for Four-year College Graduates
What was the job-hunting situation like for new college graduates and how did their job-searching behavior and employment preferences change as the number of new college graduates dramatically increased and recruitment practices changed? Let us discuss these issues, referring to actual examples based on newspaper and journal articles.

Increase of unemployed college graduates
What we first notice in reading articles in job-hunting-related periodicals during this period is the increase of unemployed college graduates. Many of these had not passed employment examinations, but a closer look shows that there were many cases where they were not yet employed because they were determined to seek a better job opportunity and chose to prepare for another round of applications.

The March 1990 issue of *Recruit* had a feature article on unemployed college graduates, titled, "Unemployed Graduates, What Are They Doing?" In this article, a Mr. Choi (a prospective graduate of the English department of a college in

Seoul, age 25) tells of applying to two companies[30] where he hoped to utilize knowledge of his major, English. However, because the competition rate was unexpectedly high, he did not pass the examination of either company. Although he also applied to several second-best companies, he did not pass the examinations or final interviews. Just around that time, the job-placement department of his college contacted him and asked if he was interested in a recommendation to a small trading company that was looking for a candidate. He was unable to convince himself he should accept the recommendation offered by the college, and declined it, deciding to prepare to retake the employment examination for the company of his first choice the following year.[31] Such a decision was presumably influenced by the increased weight of written examinations in the recruitment process.

There was of course another choice, i.e., temporarily working at a less desirable company while preparing to apply by open recruitment to a large corporation the following year. Mr. K (age 27), who did not pass the employment examination for a large company, found a job at a small trading company through an introduction by an older friend who had graduated from the same college. However, he preferred to retake the examination for employment at a large corporation to maintain his parents' pride. He commented: "Working as I am now for a nameless company, whenever I mention the company at a formal marriage interview, the prospective marriage partner seems to be disappointed."[32] These examples suggest that, for college graduates to find a job, the size of company and recognition by society were parameters that would influence their social status. Therefore, when not satisfied with smaller companies they often re-applied through the open recruitment campaigns of large corporations.

A graduate preparing for the employment examination may not always be able to find a job at a preferred company the following year. There were also many graduates who were left unemployed because they could not find any job at all. The aforementioned article, "Unemployed Graduates, What Are They Doing?," also introduced a Mr. Lee (graduate of the management department of a regional college, age 26). He failed to find a job in the year he graduated, and prepared for the employment examinations for one year. He applied to over 20 companies including large corporations, smaller companies, and banks, regardless of his personal preference, and still was unable to find a job. He finally decided he would apply for government employment the following year.[33] Another article reported

---

[30] We conjecture that these "two companies" were large corporate groups that offered the employment examinations on the two specific days.
[31] *Recruit*, March 1990, pp. 86–87.
[32] "Various Cases of College Graduates Employment," *Monthly Joong-Ang*, November 1990, pp. 400–407.
[33] *Recruit*, March 1990, p. 87.

that a Mr. Kim (graduate of a regional college, age 28) entered a second year of preparation to retake employment examinations. His words suggest that the employment circumstance surrounding college graduates became significantly worse:

> I think those who can afford to choose a company are graduates from top-notch universities. A graduate from a regional college like me, and especially a graduate in an unpopular major, does not have such chance at all. ... None of my friends of the same major who graduated together have found jobs at any company except when run by an acquaintance or an external sales company. I sent over 100 letters of self-introduction and resumés to smaller companies, but they had already decided informally who they would employ. I was very patient in waiting for success. Many of my friends gave up and chose another career, settling down in some form of self-employment or a job meant for high school graduates.[34]

Expansion of the disparities among colleges
The significant disparities that appeared since the 1980s in the job-seeking process between graduates of colleges in Seoul and those from regional colleges, as described by Mr. Kim, should be noted here. From even before that, South Koreans had tended to think that colleges in Seoul were "higher in quality" than those in other parts of the country. The rapid increase in the number of students advancing to higher education further widened the gap, as discussed in chapter 3. Because the government's policies for reducing the capital population only increased the student quotas of regional colleges and rural campuses, the chances of attending colleges in Seoul were relatively lowered and the value of those colleges rose even higher than before.

In fact, from the 1980s when the number of college graduates rapidly increased, graduates of regional colleges experienced increasing difficulties in finding jobs, resulting in a widening gap in the employment rates between graduates of colleges in Seoul and elsewhere. According to a survey of college graduates in February 1992 conducted by *Recruit* magazine in April that year, the employment rate for those from colleges in Seoul, excluding single-department colleges, was 67.5 percent (excluding from the denominator those who entered graduate school or military service) whereas for regional colleges the rate was only 53.4 percent. The difference was even greater for male graduates: the employment rate of college graduates in Seoul was 80.5 percent and that of regional college graduates was 62.5 percent, a disparity of 18 percentage points.[35] According to the same survey,

---

[34] "The Second Examination, College Graduates Employment War," *Monthly Joong-Ang*, November 1989, pp. 312–21 (p. 314).
[35] *Recruit*, May 1992, pp. 122–129. The reasons for the low employment rate for regional college graduates include that few large corporations had their headquarters in cities other than Seoul, and that new employees of regional companies affiliated with large corporate groups

the difference had been at most a few percentage points in the mid-1980s, indicating that the gap widened from the second half of the 1980s. Why?

Although the most widespread method for employing new college graduates in South Korea was open recruitment, many positions were also filled through school recommendations, accounting for 20 to 30 percent of the total number of those employed from the 1980s to the mid-1990s. In the case of employment by school recommendations, companies were likely to select candidates from specific colleges, and as a result, requests for school recommendations were concentrated at a handful of top-notch colleges. In fact, some job-seeking students expressed strong objections to this situation, protesting that the practice of companies requesting recommendations for a limited number of popular majors of famous universities narrowed the application opportunities for other students.[36]

Moreover, when selecting finalists from among recommended students, individual companies did not directly use the raw scores of student academic records but scores that had been adjusted by taking into account the ranking of difficulty of admission among colleges and departments (Lee Keun-Moo 1989: 45). Judging from these cases, the employment rate gap between colleges in Seoul and other parts of the country was likely caused primarily by the discriminatory practices of employers based on perceived disparities among colleges.

It should be noted that the Seoul-vs.-regional college disparity became pronounced with the reform of the entrance examination system. As pointed out in chapter 3, the "Preliminary College Entrance Examination," originally offered as a qualifying examination for college admission, changed in 1982 to a simple unified scholastic ability examination whose scores were used for selecting candidates for individual colleges. The previous qualification examination had functioned as a guarantee by the government of a base line of the scholastic ability of college applicants, but it completely lost that function due to the changes in the examination system. Such changes, as well as the rapid expansion of higher education, contributed to a greater range of admissions difficulty among colleges. The new unified scholastic examination (Scholastic Ability Test for College Entrance) made clearly visible the differences in degree of difficulty among colleges by exhibiting the different scores necessary for entering them (Sorensen 1994; Sato 1997). In fact, Sato had an interview with a manager of the personnel department of a company within the *chaebol* group, and the manager told her, "For our employment process, we obtain threshold scores for each university through the Scholastic Ability Test for College Entrance (which is available from magazines for college advancement and reference materials of preparatory schools), and refer to them in order to know the level of each university for us to determine whether

were recruited through their central headquarters in Seoul (Sato 1997: 119).
[36] *Recruit*, December 1990, p. 41.

to accept or reject each applicant" (Sato 1997: 119). The visualization of university rankings brought about by the change of entrance examination system enabled employers to discriminate among applicants based on the institution from which they graduated. Needless to say, the ranking of colleges overlapped with their locations, namely, whether or not they were located in Seoul.

Changes in employment opportunities for college graduates
Along with the relatively narrowing employment opportunities for college graduates, the increase of cases of "downward shift of employment" were significant. Since the mid-1980s, *Recruit* noted, "many college graduates rush to jobs considered sufficiently attainable by high school graduates, such as low-ranking civil service, marketing/sales at smaller companies, and book direct sales."[37] Let us briefly discuss the case of civil service employment, the data for which is easily accessible.

In South Korea, three civil service examinations are conducted for different ranks of officers, originally corresponding to the different academic qualifications required of applicants: the "advanced examination (fifth grade examination)" was aimed mainly at college graduates, the "seventh grade examination" was targeted at junior college graduates, and the "ninth grade examination" was oriented to high school graduates. In the second half of the 1980s when the number of college graduates started increasing, articles in *Recruit* magazine frequently introduced the seventh grade examination to college graduate readers. One 1984 article stated, "The employment shortage due to increasing manpower with higher academic credentials has directed prospective college graduates' attention to the seventh grade official examination, unlike the period when college graduates never thought about the civil service examinations other than the advanced examination (fifth grade)."[38] The increase in the number of applicants to the seventh-grade examination among college graduates was a recent phenomenon at the time the article was written.

Let us examine the distribution of academic credentials of those who passed the seventh grade civil service examination (figure 5–8). In the early 1980s, well over half of the successful candidates were high school graduates, and only a little more than 20 percent were graduates of four-year colleges or higher institutions. However, the rapid increase of four-year college graduates altered the situation completely. The increasing number of college graduates rushing to take the seventh grade examination raised the ratio of successful four-year college graduate candidates to nearly 90 percent in only a few years. As a result, the ratio of gradu-

---

[37] *Recruit*, December 1985, p. 80.
[38] *Recruit*, March 1984, p. 25.

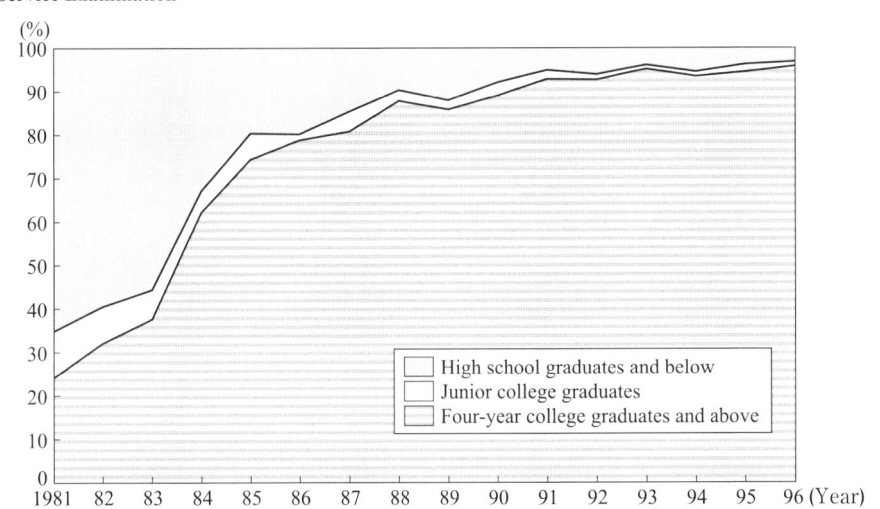

Figure 5-8. Distribution by Academic Credentials of Those Who Passed Seventh Grade Civil Service Examination

```
(%)
100
 90
 80
 70
 60
 50
 40
 30
 20
 10
  0
   1981 82  83  84  85  86  87  88  89  90  91  92  93  94  95  96 (Year)
```

☐ High school graduates and below
☐ Junior college graduates
☐ Four-year college graduates and above

Source: Based on the 1992 and 1997 editions of *Government Affairs Yearbook* (Korean Ministry of Government).
Note: Each category of education level includes prospective graduates.

ates from high school or lower grades, which had been 65.0 percent in 1981, dropped to 9.5 percent in 1988 in a short seven years.

Furthermore, college graduates who did not find jobs rushed to the ninth grade examination, which was offered primarily to high school graduates. Figure 5-9 shows the distribution of the academic credentials of successful candidates of the ninth grade officials examination. In 1981, a large majority of successful candidates were graduates of high school or lower grades. However, the ratio of four-year college graduates gradually increased, and by the mid-1990s, graduates of four-year colleges or higher made up the large majority. Consequently, the ratio of high school graduates, the original main target, dropped to a few percent. These radical changes occurred over the space of only ten years.

The tendency toward a "downward shift of employment" among college graduates was also observed in the private sector. Many college graduates rushed not only to large corporations but to smaller companies. The acceptance rate for positions in one medium-sized company, which recruited only a few dozen employees, was greater than one in 100 applicants.[39] From this and the above-described cases,

---

[39] *Recruit*, November 1992, p. 86.

Figure 5–9. Distribution by Academic Credentials of Those Who Passed Ninth Grade Civil Service Examination

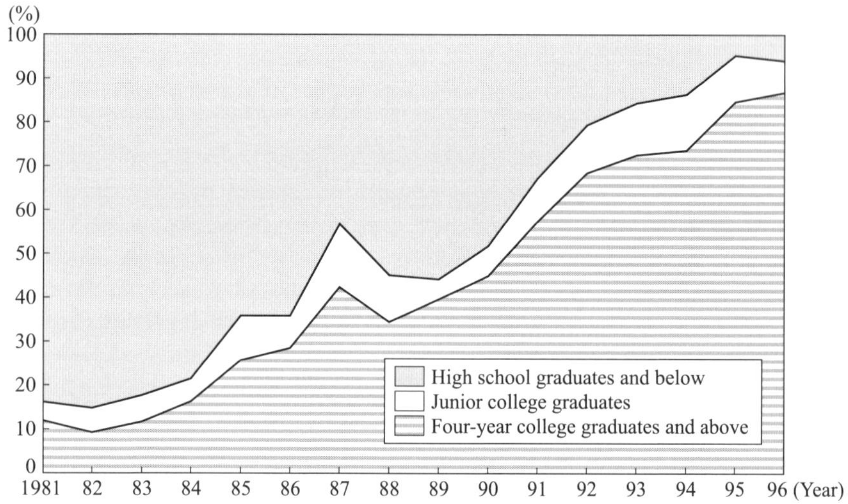

Source: Based on the 1992 and 1997 editions of *Government Affairs Yearbook* (Korean Ministry of Government).
Note: Each category of education level includes prospective graduates.

we can see that new college graduates were determined to gain employment, regardless of company size.

During this period, moreover, many college graduates applied for customer-service jobs in sales (*yeongeop-jik*). From the 1980s to the 1990s, the sales departments of such companies as those in pharmaceuticals and automobiles recruited for customer-service positions separately from the professional and clerical career track, and since those positions had less stable income and fewer opportunities for promotion than other white-collar workers, these jobs were not considered "attractive" to college graduates. In fact, until the early 1980s, the ratio of college graduates engaged in the sales business was extremely low. With the rapid increase of college graduates, however, many college graduates applied for customer-service jobs in sales, creating severe competition there as well.[40] The changing employment situation was reflected in the appearance during this period of many articles in *Recruit* magazine recommending such customer-service sales jobs, with titles like "Try Sales Jobs that Guarantee Freedom and High Incomes."[41]

---

[40] *Recruit*, January 1990, p. 37.
[41] *Recruit*, March 1992, pp. 90–93.

Based on these observations, the change in the job search behavior of new college graduates can be summarized as follows. Because many South Korean companies recruited new graduates separately according to their educational credentials, job-seeking college graduates were aware of employment opportunities for college graduates as clearly distinct from employment opportunities for others, namely high school graduates. The significant vertical differentiation of employment opportunities along the axis of company size in South Korea meant that college graduates generally considered professional and clerical jobs at large companies (as well as mass media, banks, and government-affiliated organizations), and fifth-grade level national civil service as popular employment opportunities when seeking jobs.

Perceptions of employment opportunities, however, collapsed amid the dramatic increase of college graduates. The fact that the college graduate unemployment rate did not increase much despite the decrease in the employment rate of new college graduates from the second half of the 1980s indicates that while new college graduates had a strong desire to find a job suitable to their educational attainments, those unable to find an appropriate job opportunity often turned to smaller companies or customer-service sales jobs. The rapid increase of college graduates thus brought a significant change in the attitudes of job-seeking college graduates. Of course, there were many cases where a college graduate with a strong desire to work for a large company needed a few years after graduation to give up the desire and end up with a job at a small company.

Despite the change in the focus of their job search from a large company to a smaller company or from professional/clerical work to customer-service sales, college graduates clung to the desire for a white-collar job.[42] As Hattori points out, they had a strong tendency to avoid non-white-collar occupations; for them "sales jobs in retail stores and other service jobs were not appropriate" for college graduates, and manufacturing was out of the question (Hattori 1988: 191). In fact, among job-related articles in *Recruit* magazine, few articles reported on case studies of service industries and manufacturing jobs in which college graduates were engaged or providing information on such occupations. Thus, the rate of white-collar employment among new college graduates changed little from the 1980s even though they were faced with severe difficulties in finding employment after the rapid increase in the supply of college graduates.

The employment situation for new college graduates and the changes in their job hunting behavior explained above, therefore, could be described as responsible for the relative decrease in the wages of college graduates of the younger generations from the second half of the 1980s, and for the expanded wage gap among

---

[42] Part of the "customer-service sales" jobs described above is statistically categorized as clerical work.

different sizes of corporations, as explained in chapter 4. This section argues that, while the employment situation worsened due to the rapid increase in college graduates, when new graduates were forced to give up their desire to work for a large company, many of them sought employment in smaller companies. Even though these smaller companies had been unable to hire them when the labor force of college graduates was small, they could afford to do so in this period without paying as high salaries as in large companies. During this transition, the wage gap between large and smaller companies widened among college graduates, and at the same time, the relative wage level of new college graduates decreased. From the job-seeking college graduates' viewpoint, white-collar jobs could still be found despite the dramatic increase of college graduates by accepting a position regardless of company size and the relatively lower wages offered.

Employment Opportunities for Junior College and High School Graduates
In order to determine how the effect of the four-year college degree on occupational status changed, it is also necessary to examine the employment opportunities of those who do not have four-year college credentials. The occupational premium value of a four-year college degree will be fully understood only when the occupational opportunities for four-year college graduates are compared with junior college or high school graduates.

New junior college graduates
For junior college graduates, we notice that the employment rate for new graduates listed in the *Statistical Yearbook of Education* shows no decline from the 1980s, unlike for four-year college graduates. As shown in figure 5–5, their employment rate, which was less than 60 percent in the early 1980s, gradually increased and rose over 80 percent in the first half of the 1990s, exceeding the rate for four-year college graduates by 10-plus percentage points.

The contrast of employment opportunities between four-year and junior college graduates also appears in the employment rate for new graduates who found employment related to their specialty in college. Figure 5–10 shows the ratio of new college graduates who obtained jobs related to their college specialty based on data from the *Statistical Yearbook of Education*. The ratio of four-year college graduates gradually decreased from the early 1980s, indicating that finding jobs suited to the knowledge and skills acquired in higher education became harder as finding jobs in general became difficult. On the other hand, the ratio of junior college students was around 80 percent, showing no distinct change even from the early 1980s, which indicates that junior college graduates may find their jobs suited to their majors relatively easy compared with four-year college graduates. Similarly to four-year college graduates, junior college graduates substantially in-

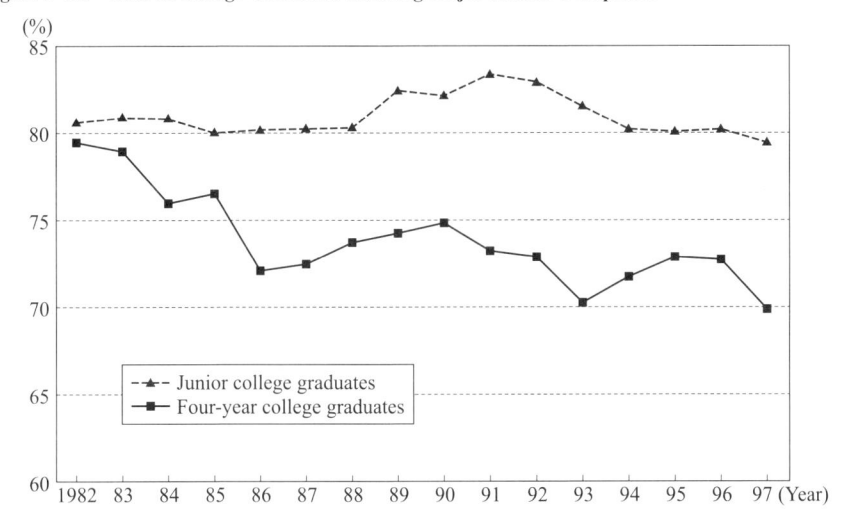

Figure 5–10. Rate of College Graduates Entering Major-related Occupation

Source: Based on the annual editions of *Statistical Yearbook of Education* (Korean Ministry of Education).

creased in the 1980s and after. However, the job-finding success of junior college graduates was much better than that of average four-year college graduates.

The better prospects for employment of junior college graduates (relative to four-year college graduates) is often attributed to the fact that vocational education in junior colleges matched the skills required by companies (Jung Jin-Hwa 1996). It should be noted, however, that the process of employment and the opportunities available for junior college graduates were quite different from those of four-year college graduates. Unlike four-year college graduates, over half of cases of employment of junior college graduates were through school recommendations, and the ratio continued to increase from the early 1980s to the early 1990s. By contrast, "employment through (open recruitment) examinations" for junior college graduates made up only about 20 percent, approximately half that of four-year college graduates.[43] Another notable feature was the high rate of employment by smaller companies. According to a survey of junior college graduates conducted by *Recruit* magazine in February 1990, 80.7 percent were hired by smaller companies.[44]

Needless to say, these two characteristics were very closely interrelated. Smaller companies in South Korea often hired new employees through school recom-

---

[43] Annual editions of the *Statistical Yearbook of Education*, Korean Ministry of Education.
[44] *Recruit*, June 1990, p. 75.

mendations and personal connections, rather than through open recruitment. Large companies, on the other hand, had a higher ratio of open recruitment. In open recruitment there was no separate employment category for junior college graduates during this period; when there was, the size of the category was rather small. For this reason, junior colleges had close relationships with smaller local companies aimed at obtaining jobs for their graduates. According to *Recruit* magazine, in the case of junior college graduates, unlike four-year college graduates, there was no distinct gap in employment rates between those in Seoul and in other parts of the country, reflecting the localized employment strategy of junior colleges.[45]

In this way, while four-year college graduates who desired to work for large companies confronted severe employment difficulties and their rate of employment decreased substantially, junior colleges utilized the network with local companies and school recommendations to secure jobs at smaller companies for their graduates. By type of occupation, junior college graduates had many "professional" and "clerical" jobs as well as jobs related to the specialty they had studied; however, in many cases, the actual job descriptions for them were similar to those for high school graduates.[46] Let us cite the words of a personnel department staff member of a company quoted in an article in *Recruit* magazine:

> Our company feels there is no particular difference between graduates of engineering departments of junior colleges and graduates of technical high schools. Jobs requiring high technology and professional knowledge are allocated to four-year college graduates and graduate school graduates whereas [jobs in] manufacturing and maintenance and after-sales services are allocated to junior college graduates. However, technical school graduates can also perform such work, which requires simple skills.[47]

As employment of junior college graduates had the above characteristics, in South Korea, a country with a particularly strong preference for large corporations and white-collar jobs, many students wanting to go on for higher education did not consider junior colleges as an attractive career path even though junior college graduates enjoyed high employment rates. In fact, many four-year college graduates went jobless because they declined jobs not much different from those for

---

[45] In fact, junior colleges established collaborative research projects with local small and medium-sized companies, and college faculty would visit local industrial parks to advertise their institutions and making overtures for hiring of their graduates. With such strategies for employment, three-quarters of the employed graduates from Kyungnam Junior College in Pusan, for example, were employed by local companies (*Recruit*, September 1986, pp. 87–89).
[46] Such low evaluation of junior college graduates at their companies was probably behind the fact, as confirmed in chapter 4, that the wages of junior college graduates were higher by only a few percent than those of high school graduates.
[47] *Recruit*, December 1994, p. 109.

high school graduates or because they refused to work at smaller companies. Judging from the above, we may conclude that employment opportunities for junior college graduates are quite different from those for four-year college graduates. Hence even if the employment rate for new junior college graduates was much higher than that of new four-year college graduates, the advantage of graduating from a four-year college to obtain a more desirable job hardly changed.

New high school graduates
Figures 5–2 and 5–3 in the previous section show that the rate of employment in white-collar jobs for high school graduates was much lower than that for college graduates already in the first half of the 1980s, and that it was gradually decreasing from the mid-1980s when the number of college graduates started rapidly increasing. In terms of absolute numbers, however, because the number of college graduates was small in the first half of the 1980s, high school graduates accounted for a fairly high proportion of white-collar employees. For example, as the numbers of the wage structure survey samples, which were used for figure 5–2 show, among male workers between the ages of 25 to 29 in 1980, more than 73,000 white-collar employees were high school graduates whereas some 55,000 white-collar employees were graduates of four-year colleges and above. Not only in smaller companies but in large corporations, there were a large number of male high school graduates hired for professional and clerical jobs.[48]

In fact, at least prior to the mid-1980s, several large corporate groups hired a certain number of male high school graduates—primarily commercial high school graduates—in addition to four-year college graduates when they recruited white-collar workers on a corporate group basis.[49] For example, the Samsung group, which hired more male high school graduates for clerical work than other corporate groups, recruited several hundred male commercial high school graduates annually through school recommendations and written examinations. The same job grade system was applied to white-collar workers employed from high school graduates and college graduates, and new high school graduates started their career path from the job grade one-step lower than new college graduates. Although their promotional speed and their salary growth were slower than those of college graduates (Hattori 1988: 181–82), much wider opportunities for internal promotion and wage increase were open to them compared to high school gradu-

---

[48] Detailed observation shows that professional jobs were taken much more by college graduates than high school graduates whereas clerical jobs were taken by more high school graduates.
[49] In the case of large corporate groups that did not conduct group-basis recruitment, each subsidiary company individually hired high school graduates (male and female) as clerical workers. Employment by individual companies was in many cases through students' high school recommendations as well (Lee Keun-Moo 1989).

ates hired in manufacturing. White-collar jobs offered by large corporations provided a valuable opportunity for high school graduates to be treated similarly to college graduates in South Korea.

Until the mid-1980s, it was the financial world that hired many male high school graduates as white-collar workers. Traditionally, finance had a higher rate of workers who were male, commercial-high-school graduates. Insurance, securities, and short-loan companies in particular had new-employment ratios of 30 percent for college graduates and 70 percent for high school graduates.[50] The high school graduates hired as white-collar workers could be promoted to relatively high positions, although the promotional speed might be somewhat slower than for college graduates. Also, the financial world offered relatively high and stable salary levels. For these reasons, commercial high school male graduates saw jobs in finance as very attractive. This is clearly shown in the results of a survey conducted by the magazine *Chuijik* (Job Hunting) about employment preferences among 1,000 commercial high school students in 1986. According to the survey, the employment opportunity most preferred by male students was finance (44.2 percent, nearly double compared with national civil service and state-run companies at 26.2 percent, and general (non-financial) corporations at 21.3 percent).[51]

As described above, at least prior to the mid-1980s, relatively "good" jobs—white-collar jobs of large companies and financial organizations—were widely available to high school graduates. How did this employment situation change as the number of college graduates rapidly increased?

A case in point are the financial organizations that were the most popular job choices of commercial high school graduates. Figure 5–11 shows the changes in the number of new high school graduates and new college graduates who entered the world of finance based on data in the *Statistical Yearbook of Education*. This graph indicates that the number of new high school graduates employed in finance was 2 to 3 times more than that of four-year college graduates in the early 1980s. After that time, however, the number of new high school graduates gradually decreased while new four-year college graduates gradually increased. As a result, the latter overtook the former in 1985. There was an exceptional few years from 1988, during which both four-year college graduates and high school graduates drastically increased as financial organizations established many branches due to the financial deregulation policy enforced at that time. After this sudden, temporary

---

[50] *Chuijik* (Job Hunting), July 1986, p. 60.
[51] *Chuijik* (Job Hunting), October 1986, p. 73. Incidentally, in the case of female students, "general corporations" occupied 47.5 percent and the financial industry only 26.2 percent. Large corporate groups hired many female high school graduates for office assistant work during this period, which was reflected in job-seekers' preferences.

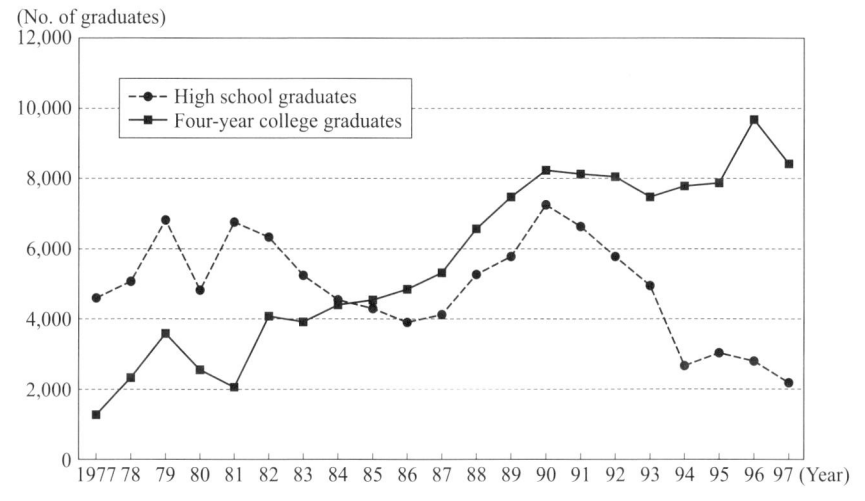

Figure 5–11. Number of New Graduates Employed in Finance

(No. of graduates)

- - ● - - High school graduates
—■— Four-year college graduates

Source: Based on the annual editions of *Statistical Yearbook of Education* (Korean Ministry of Education).

change, while the employment of four-year college graduates remained almost the same, the employment of high school graduates rapidly decreased, resulting in a wide difference between them.

As described above, the ratio by education level of new graduates employed in the financial industry rapidly changed in only a little more than a decade. During this period the total number of employed new high school graduates did not decrease at all because of the increase of students advancing to high schools and the increase of their percentage of population. However, the number of those employed in the financial industry, an "attractive" employment opportunity to them, rapidly dropped.

This phenomenon was a consequence of each company hiring more new college graduates and fewer new high school graduates as the number of college graduates increased rapidly. The companies that customarily hired new graduates at a certain ratio by education level, we might add, started reducing white-collar jobs for new high school graduates while expanding those for new college graduates.

Survey data reveals the fact that companies intentionally changed the number of white-collar jobs for new high school and college graduates during this period. Since 1979, the Korea Employer's Federation has been conducting surveys on the prospective employment size of companies with 100 or more employees (50 and

166 | Part II Economic Rewards, Occupational Status, and Social Mobility

Figure 5–12. Increasing Rate of Prospective New Hires by Level of Education (compared with previous year)

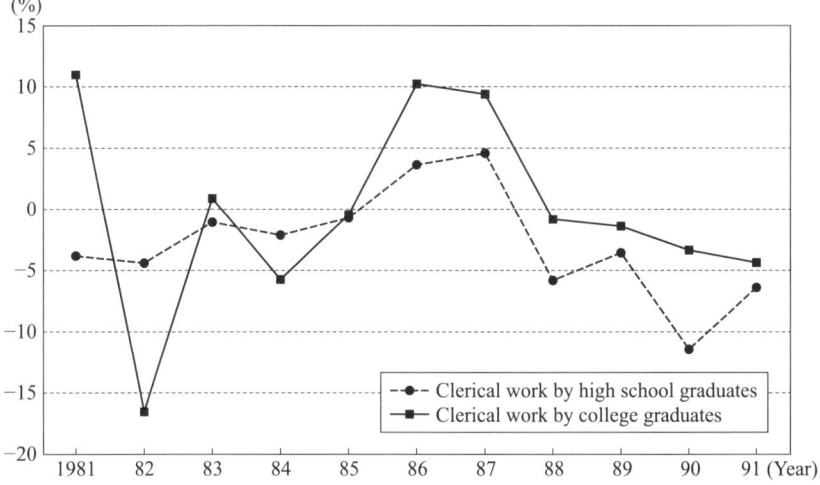

Source: Based on the annual editions of Survey on *Current Status and Prospect of Hiring New Graduate* (Korea Employer's Federation).

more since 1986). The survey outcome of each year up to (and including) 1991[52] shows the scale of planned employment of clerical workers from among college and high school graduates. Figure 5–12, which charts the annual increase rate of scale of planned employment compared with the previous year, indicates that while the relationship between the increase rates for college and high school graduates changed each year in the first half of the 1980s, the college graduate rate was continuously greater than that for high school graduates after 1986. In other words, companies clearly chose to hire more college graduates and fewer high school graduates for clerical work after the number of college graduates began to rapidly increase. Even if the difference in increase rates between high school and college graduates was only a few percentage points, the gap in the scale of actual employment by level of education significantly widened as an accumulation of different annual increase rates. If we suppose each company actually hired high school and college graduates according to the "planned" figures for each year and posit the scale of employment in 1985 at 100, college graduate employment for clerical work was up to 108.6 six years later in 1991, while high school graduate employment was down to 81.1, a decrease by 20 percent.

---

[52] Based on annual editions of the *Survey on Current Status and Prospect of Hiring New Graduates* published by the Korea Employer's Federation.

The first section of this chapter confirms that while the white-collar employment rate for new college graduates was stable despite the rapid increase of new college graduates, the white-collar employment rate for new high school graduates gradually decreased. This change in employment opportunities was certainly in part a consequence of competition between high school graduates and college graduates for the same job opportunities, as we saw for those who passed the employment examinations for the seventh grade and ninth grade civil service positions by education level. However, considering the above results, the change may also be attributed to South Korean companies' expansion of the employment opportunities customarily reserved for college graduates and their reduction of that for high school graduates. In other words, changes in the composition of employment quotas by educational level of each company institutionally pushed high school graduates out of opportunities for white-collar jobs.[53]

Employer Perspective on Applicant Academic Credentials
From the above discussion, we may observe that South Korean companies raised the educational requirements for hiring in response to the rapid increase of college graduates. One example was their expansion of clerical work opportunities for college graduates at the expense of such opportunities for high school graduates. The increased preference for graduates of colleges in Seoul was another example. The reactions of employers were close to Thurow's job competition model or Dore's assumption of the academic credential inflation model summarized in chapter 1.

From the above analyses, we see the strong tendency of South Korean companies to emphasize academic credentials in the employment process. Why did they give such great weight to academic credentials (as opposed to other indices)? What view of academic credentials was behind the corporate behavior that established institutional links between the academic credentials and occupational opportunity? Lee Jung-Pyo (1995) conducted a survey of academic credentials as viewed by employers, personnel managers, and college students. Let us discuss the issues, referring to the outcome of the survey.

In Chapter 1 we discussed the two major reasons for employers to prefer a work force with higher academic credentials: the first reason was that the higher level of academic credentials would pave the way for a high level of productivity through the advanced knowledge and skills acquired and the second reason was the possession of potential ability as proven by having passed through the competitive

---
[53] Nevertheless, the decreasing speed in the ratio of white-collar employment among high school graduates was not so significant, and that was because white-collar jobs increased to a certain degree thanks to the economic expansion of that time.

process. Among the questions Lee Jung-Pyo asked employers and personnel managers was: "Do you agree with the view that colleges do not offer the kind of education required at actual workplaces?" The affirmative answer would deny the first reason. A look at the answers to that question by more than 300 employers and personnel managers nationwide shows the affirmative answer of either "strongly agree" or "agree" were 51.5 percent, a proportion much higher than 21.6 percent for the negative answer, either "strongly disagree" or "disagree." Most employers, in other words, did not think that the learning experience in higher education was directly linked to the cultivation of the knowledge and skills required for activities in business.

On the other hand, some employers were more likely to consider "level of academic credentials" as proof of potential ability or level of general intellectual ability. This employer tendency is notable because such recognition by employers was opposite to that of most college students. For example, regarding the question, "Does the level of a college a student graduated from represent the level of potential ability of the student?," only 17.2 percent of college students were affirmative whereas 44.9 percent of the employers were affirmative, a figure much higher than the negative responses (30.4 percent). Only 16.0 percent of college students thought "a person with advanced academic credentials has advanced abilities in planning, decision making, and creativity," whereas 35.0 percent of employers agreed with the statement, exceeding the negative responses (25.0 percent). Judging from the outcomes, the companies' emphasis on academic credentials in hiring was possibly not so much because of the actual content of education offered by colleges, but rather because of the intellectual ability needed to pass entrance examinations and subsequent tests of various sorts, taking into consideration the difference in the difficulty of admission among colleges.[54] This possibility is endorsed by the earlier-mentioned personnel manager's remark that the scores on Scholastic Ability Test for College Entrance were used as a reference for determining employment.

Needless to say, test scores on the college entrance examinations were believed to indicate a certain level of intellectual ability, and this belief was based on a high degree of trust in the college entrance examination system. Introduction of the nationwide scholastic ability test administered by the government significantly improved people's trust in the power of the college entrance examinations to determine aptitude and ability.[55]

---

[54] South Korean companies during this period tended to prefer generalists with broad knowledge and ability rather than specialists in specific fields. That tendency was closely related to their preference for applicants with a general intellectual ability at the time of employment.

[55] The tradition of the old Confucian-style civil service examinations (*gwageo*) was another contributing factor behind people's trust in the capability of written examinations to judge academic ability. As Amano studies Japanese cases (Amano 1983), studying the "social history of

Furthermore, the increased number of applicants to the college entrance examinations also enforced the rationale of utilizing the results as a criterion in selecting recruits. As the national standard of living rose, there were fewer students who had sufficient academic skills but were prevented by economic circumstances from advancing to higher education. People came to think that what made one advance to higher education or not was not family financial situation but one's effort and ability. From the screening theory, as discussed in chapter 3, that tendency meant that the college entrance examination functioned more thoroughly to screen people in the same birth cohort as the number of those to be screened expanded. By expanding the range of those who were screened, of course, the value of the information on the outcome of the screening further increased.

Given the employer views of academic credentials described above, the raising of educational requirements in hiring was probably a logical response to the rapid increase in the number of college graduates. According to their view of the screening theory, the phenomenon of rapid increase of college graduates implies a situation in which students who might have previously had insufficient scholastic ability to pass the college entrance examinations would now be able to move on to college and obtain a college diploma. Under these circumstances, in order to secure a labor force with a level of ability similar to the previous level, it was necessary to raise the educational requirements for employment.

As long as employers followed this pattern of behavior, the educational requirements for hiring new graduates would continue to increase following the increase in people's level of educational attainment. The entrance examination competition for acquiring better, harder-to-seize educational opportunities, too, would continue to intensify in the situation.

III. The "Higher Occupational Status" Effect: Comparative Analysis of High School Student Job Preferences

Acquisition of a college degree increased the probability of finding a white collar job, and that probability was not in the least reduced despite the increase in the number of college graduates. Various institutional conditions worked to tie academic credentials and occupational positions even more closely together. However, unlike in the case of studying the effects of academic credentials on wage increase, we cannot precisely estimate how the effect of the academic credentials in raising occupational status affected people's desire for, and actual cases of, their advance to the next stage of education. The subject of analysis in human capital theory is limited to the advantage and cost of advancing to the next stage of edu-

examinations" in the Korean Peninsula would be critical in understanding the unique existence of the written examinations for assessing academic ability in the modern South Korean society.

cation that may be measured in monetary terms. Therefore, for these models, it is possible to determine which one is larger, cost or advantage, on a one-dimensional scale of monetary amount, and to assume that people will advance to the next stage of education when the advantages are greater than the cost. Needless to say, however, the advantages of raising occupational status cannot be directly measured through comparison with monetary cost, which makes it difficult to determine which is greater.[56]

Of course, there are differences among individuals in assessment of the effects of increasing occupational status through more advanced education, but conditions unique to a society such as the structure of occupational prestige can bring about certain commonalities in the society as well. In this section, we compare the occupational preferences of South Korean high school students with those of Japanese high school students in order to understand what "raising occupational status" means to people in South Korea by analyzing the data from our comparative survey.

Occupational Preferences and Occupational Aspiration
As discussed in chapter 2, the South Korean occupational prestige structure features large prestige gaps among occupations, especially between white-collar occupations and non-white-collar occupations. The gap of occupational prestige may stimulate people's overall desire for promotion of occupational status, which in turn may heat up aspirations to advance to higher education.

What we should note here, however, is that the logic behind the perspective that disparities in prestige among occupations increase people's aspiration for white-collar jobs, thereby stimulating their desire to advance to higher education, is based on the assumption that people's occupational preferences are primarily determined by occupational status. Little attention has been paid to the effect of other occupational conditions on individual occupational preferences. In order to validate the above assumption, it is necessary to empirically study several issues including whether South Korean people's desire for white-collar occupations is really that strong compared to other societies, and whether their occupational preferences are significantly influenced by occupational status ranking.

Prior research on the occupational preferences of young people in many cases views them as an issue of occupational aspiration. A typical instance is the so-called Wisconsin model. It understands individual occupational preferences as the aspiration for achieving higher occupational status. Various studies based on this model have demonstrated that individual occupational aspirations are determined

---

[56] To approach this issue from the economics point of view, it may be necessary to look at advancing to higher education not as "investment" but as "consumption" aimed to increase the effect of higher occupational positions.

by socio-economic background, and at the same time, such aspirations significantly affect the actual achievement of social status (e.g., Sewell et al. 1969).

Some point out, however, that the occupational preferences of young people should not be argued only in terms of occupational status. Aramaki questions the perspective dominant in traditional research on occupational preferences, which attempts to "understand the social status of preferred occupation as the degree of aspirations and desires" (Aramaki 2001: 82). He proposes the necessity of discussing the occupational preferences of high school students from a perspective different from social status. By analyzing data from the survey on Japanese high school students, he reveals that in their criteria for selecting occupations, there are orientations such as "desire for selffulfillment through occupation," apart from "desire for socio-economic status derived from occupation." He argues that the difference in occupational preferences depends on what aspect of occupation— self-fulfillment, socioeconomic status, etc.—is more important to students (Aramaki 2001).

If the above argument is true, there is a totally different standard, distinct from the occupational status, that determines high school students' preferred occupations in Japan. The premise that people's aspiration to an occupation is largely determined by that occupation's status may not always apply in the case of Japan. When compared with the Japanese case, what are the characteristics of occupational preferences among South Korean high school students? And, what is the effect of those preferences on aspirations for educational achievement?

Let us begin with a brief overview of the Japan-South Korea comparative survey used in the analysis. The survey was conducted in 2000 by the Research Society for Comparative Sociology of Education (Hikaku Kyoiku Shakaigaku Kenkyukai) of which the author is a member. The subjects of the survey were third-year students of high schools and of middle schools in Tokyo Metropolis and Tottori Prefecture (high school students only) and Gunma Prefecture (middle school students only) in Japan, and in Seoul and Gangwon Provinces in South Korea.[57] The samples of high school students used were 1,439 students (733 male and 706 female) of 12 Japanese high schools (7 general schools and 5 specialized schools), and 1,354 students (835 male and 519 female) of 12 South Korean high schools (9 general schools and 3 specialized schools).

---

[57] This students survey was conducted through schools. Although random sampling of the subjects was not performed completely, several conditions including the school location, the ratio of male to female students, the school characteristics, and the degree of difficulty in entering were evenly considered to choose the subject schools. For the detailed information on this survey, see Nakamura et al. eds. (2002).

172 | Part II Economic Rewards, Occupational Status, and Social Mobility

Preferred Occupations, Family Background, and Academic Achievements
First of all, we compare the distribution of preferred occupations of Japanese and South Korean high school students. Figure 5–13 shows the rates of response to the question, "What kind of job do you want to do?" The students were asked to choose from among occupations in the major group and the other options "housework and child care," "undecided," and "other."[58] This table indicates that the ratio of preference for professional occupations is overwhelmingly higher than other occupations: 50.1 percent in Japan and 67.2 percent in South Korea. The next higher preference is clerical work, around 10 percent in both Japan and South Korea. Assuming that these are white-collar occupations, the ratio of high school students preferring white-collar occupations is 61.1 percent in Japan and 76.7 percent in South Korea—the rate is much higher in South Korea. As for non-white-collar occupations including sales, service, transportation, and skilled work, although the ratio of South Korean students preferring self-employment is slightly higher, the ratio of Japanese students preferring non-white-collar occupations is much higher than that of South Korean students: 14.0 percent of Japanese students and only 5.3 percent of South Korean students.

From the above simple comparison we may conclude that South Korean students prefer white-collar jobs more than do Japanese students. In particular, the ratio of South Korean students preferring non-white-collar jobs is much smaller than that of Japanese students.

Second, we consider factors that differentiate the occupation preference. Here, we examine the influence of the socioeconomic conditions of students' families, in particular the parents' occupations. Figure 5–14 is a cross table that shows the relationship between preferred occupations (excluding "housework" and "undecided") of students and the parents' occupations, categorized into "white-collar occupations (professional, managerial, and clerical work)" and other "non-white-collar occupations." The influence of parents' occupations on their children's preferred occupations differ considerably between Japan and South Korea. The difference in ratios of students preferring white-collar jobs between white-collar and non-white-collar parents is nearly 10 percentage points in Japan, whereas the difference is very small in South Korea. The chi-squared test applied to this cross table indicates that independence of Japanese students' preferred occupations is rejected at the 0.1 percent level, i.e., students' preferred occupations are significantly influ-

[58] In both Japan and South Korea, it is general to appoint a managing post in a corporation or a government organization after accumulating experience in other types of jobs, and hence we exclude the "management" from the preferred occupations in our survey. Instead, to judge students' interest in independence and self-support, we offered an option "self-employment" that "manages a shop, a plant, or a company." But our categories of preferred occupations are somewhat rough, leaving some room for improvement in a later survey.

Figure 5–13. Occupations Preferred by High School Students in Japan and South Korea

(%)

	Professional	Clerical	Self-employed	Sales	Service	Transportation	Skilled work	Housework and child care	Other	Undecided/ unanswered	Total
Japan											
Male	45.8	11.7	4.4	1.4	4.8	2.5	6.3	0.1	5.5	17.6	100.0
Female	54.5	10.3	1.6	4.1	8.2	0.3	0.4	4.8	4.1	11.6	100.0
Total	50.1	11.0	3.0	2.7	6.5	1.4	3.4	2.4	4.8	14.7	100.0
South Korea											
Male	66.9	8.9	10.4	0.6	2.5	0.4	0.2	0.1	1.4	8.5	100.0
Female	67.6	10.6	2.5	1.0	6.7	0.0	0.4	2.1	2.1	6.9	100.0
Total	67.2	9.5	7.4	0.7	4.1	0.2	0.3	0.9	1.7	7.9	100.0

Source: Based on the data of the *2000 Survey on High School Students in Japan and South Korea*.

enced by their parents' occupations whereas the hypothesis of independence for South Korean students is not rejected even at the 5 percent level.

Although the figure does not show all the details, we have investigated the relationship between high school students' preferred occupations and their parents' occupations using more detailed occupational categories. In Japan, there is a certain tendency of high school students preferring the same occupations—mainly clerical and skilled work—as their parents: 23.3 percent prefer clerical work if their parents are also engaged in clerical work, and 12.0 percent prefer skilled jobs if their parents have skilled jobs, the proportions being higher than the overall average by several to 10 percentage points. In South Korea, except for professional occupations, the tendency to prefer parents' occupations is not particularly strong. Compared with Japan, in South Korea the tendency to prefer parents' occupations (non-white-collar jobs in particular) is weak,[59] and hence the influence of parents' occupations on students' preferred occupations is relatively small, which is partly responsible for a higher overall preference of white-collar occupations in South Korea.

We also need to study the influence of student's academic performance as another important factor for differentiation of occupational preferences. Previous

---

[59] From the cultural anthropological point of view, Ito points out the thin concept of succeeding family businesses in commerce and industry in South Korea: "As commerce and manufacturing are considered as humble occupations, succeeding these occupations has not been evaluated positively at all in terms of social status" (Ito 2001: 98).

Figure 5-14. Relationship between Preferred Occupation and Parent's Occupation

Japan

Parent's occupation	Preferred occupation		Total
	White-collar job	Non-white-collar job	
White-collar job	386	77	463
	(83.4%)	(16.6%)	(100.0%)
Non-white-collar job	357	130	487
	(73.3%)	(26.7%)	(100.0%)

$\chi^2 = 14.1$, d.f. $= 1$, $p = .000$

South Korea

Parent's occupation	Preferred occupation		Total
	White-collar job	Non-white-collar job	
White-collar job	459	66	525
	(87.4%)	(12.6%)	(100.0%)
Non-white-collar job	499	94	593
	(84.1%)	(15.9%)	(100.0%)

$\chi^2 = 2.4$, d.f. $= 1$, $p = .118$

Source: Based on the data of the *2000 Survey on High School Students in Japan and South Korea*.

research often points out that the preferred occupation of Japanese high school students is affected by their subjective assessment of their own academic performance. In Japan, "through experiencing selection processes from the early grades, young people tend to select 'appropriate' careers and have 'appropriate' occupational aspirations based on their own school records" (Mimizuka 1988: 35). Considering these facts, the correlation between Japanese students' occupational preferences and their parents' occupation is caused not only by the aforementioned tendency to prefer their parents' occupation, but through the mediation of student academic performance.

In order to study the effect of student academic performance and the influence of social class origin after controlling for academic performance, we conducted a logistic regression analysis where the dependent variable is the student's occupational preference (1 for white-collar jobs, and 0 for non-white-collar jobs). The model has independent variables concerning the student's academic performance such as high school type[60] and school record, in addition to the father's educational background and the parent's occupation.

---

[60] After classifying high schools in Japan and South Korea into specialized schools (vocational course) and general schools (academic course), we further divide the latter into three groups according to the degree of difficulty in admission: "General school A" for the most difficult

Figure 5-15 shows the results. It indicates that Japanese and South Korean high school students greatly differ with regard to the factors determining their preference of occupation. Compared with South Korean students, the school type and school record have less influence on job preference in the case of Japanese high school students. In Japan, among these variables, only the "general school A" dummy variable is significant, while the other variables show no significant influence. Furthermore, even after controlling for these academic-performance-related variables, students' preferences for occupation are significantly affected by their parents' occupations. In other words, even if school type is the same and school records are similar, students whose parents are engaged in white-collar occupations significantly prefer white-collar jobs compared with those whose parents are engaged in non-white-collar occupations in Japan.

By contrast, once the academic-performance-related variables are controlled, neither their fathers' academic credentials nor parents' occupations directly affect the preferred jobs of South Korean high school students at all. Instead, all of the school type variables and school records show an important influence on South Korean students' job preference. Namely, the higher their school record scores and the greater admission difficulty of their schools, the more likely South Korean students are to prefer white-collar occupations.

Although the above analysis uses a rough occupational classification, we may infer that these outcomes clearly show the difference of what determines job preference between Japanese and South Korean high school students. While job preferences of South Korean students are primarily determined by their academic performance, their parents' occupations hardly influence them. Japanese high school students are more likely to be influenced by their parents' jobs, as they tend to prefer the same types of work as their parents, but differentiation of job preferences according to their academic performance is not as noticeable.[61] If we assume a

---

school, "General school C" for the least difficult school group, and "General school B" for the others. Because of the high school leveling policy implemented in large and middle size cities in South Korea, there are few high schools that correspond to the "General school C," and this survey does not include it for South Korea.

[61] Although preferred occupations of South Korean high school students are not much influenced by their parents' occupations, later, after passing though the rigorous selection process for admittance to colleges, it is possible to generate a correlation between a student's preferred or actual occupation and his/her parent's occupation mediated by the difference in academic performance. In fact, the outcome of the analysis described in chapter 6 supports this conjecture. If that is true, we may assume the reason for the absence of a significant relationship between the preferred occupations of South Korean high school students and their parents' occupations is that their "final selections"—selections that force students to choose realistic career paths—are deferred to the time of advancing to higher education, and the tracking effect in high school is relatively weak.

Figure 5-15. Logistic Regression Analysis of White-collar Job Preference of High School Students

	Japan	South Korea
Constant	.379	.784
Female dummy	.589**	.329
Father's education	-.001	-.002
White-collar father dummy	.521**	-.010
General school A dummy	.869**	.894*
General school C dummy	-.451	–
Specialized school dummy	-.269	-.793***
School record	.147	.347***
Cox and Snell R^2	.065	.043
$-2 \log L$	768.0	834.7
N	812	1,072

Note: $*p < .05$, $**p < .01$, $***p < .001$
Source: Based on the data of the *2000 Survey on High School Students in Japan and South Korea.*

differentiation of job preferences according to academic performance as a consequence of student selection of career path befitting their school record, as Mimizuka points out, the initial ratio of preferring white-collar jobs in South Korea would have been much higher. The impression that "although everyone wishes to obtain a job of higher occupational position, actual job preference becomes differentiated as a consequence of student selection of career path according to their academic performance" is more applicable to South Korea than to Japan.

Occupational Value Orientation and Occupational Preference

Next, we will study the effect of students' value orientations regarding occupation on their occupational preferences, a topic treated by Aramaki (2001). What conditions do South Korean and Japanese students attach more importance to when they choose occupations, and how do value orientations affect their occupational preferences?

Our survey asked the participants whether they value (or not) each of nine factors ranging from "salary" to "preference by family" when choosing jobs. Figure 5-16 shows the ratios of Japanese and South Korean high school students who responded affirmatively regarding the nine items. This figure indicates that there were similar response patterns for high school students in both countries. The item of the highest affirmative ratio was "job interest": 84.9 percent for Japanese students and 90.7 percent for South Korean students. In addition, more than half affirmatively responded to "salary," "stability," and "knowledge utilization." As for

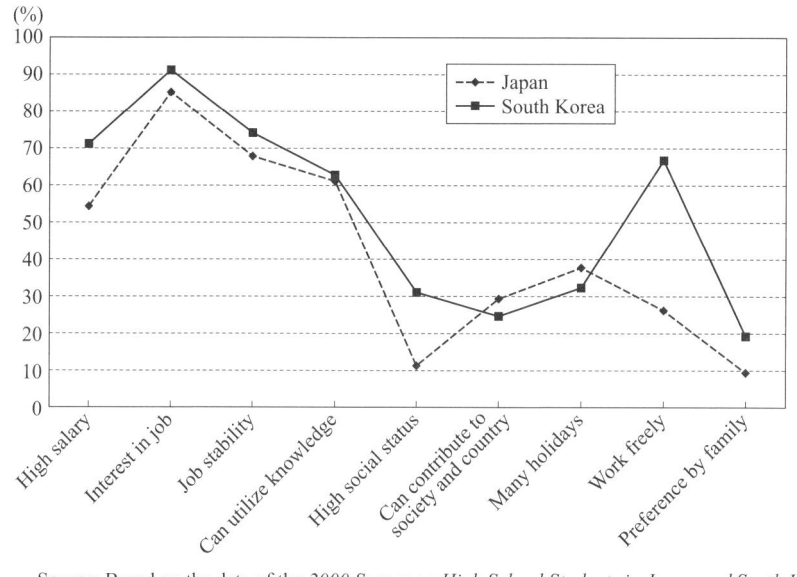

Figure 5–16. Comparison of Job Selection Factors in Japan and South Korea

Source: Based on the data of the *2000 Survey on High School Students in Japan and South Korea*.

the item, "work freely [without being given orders from above]," however, 66.5 percent responded affirmatively in South Korea as compared with only 26.3 percent in Japan, showing a very large gap between the two countries.

There are similar descriptions among these nine items. For example, "salary" and "status" are similar in that they both are socioeconomic conditions of occupation. Based on such similarities, it would be possible to extract from the answers to items potential patterns concerning the conditions to which the students give more importance in selecting jobs and reveal their occupational value orientation. To that end, below we will apply Hayashi's quantification method III analysis[62]—which is equivalent to correspondence analysis—to the answers to these nine items.

Figures 5–17 and 5–18 show the category weight of each item on X-Y plane with the horizontal I axis (the eigen values are 0.219 for Japan and 0.228 for South Korea) and the vertical II axis (Japan: 0.146 and South Korea: 0.140), which are obtained by the analysis.

First, let us examine the outcome for Japanese high school students (figure

---

[62] Hayashi's quantification method III is a method for classifying patterns of responses (qualitative data) to various questions, which allows us to classify people with similar response patterns, and also to determine if responses to questions are similar to each other.

178 | Part II Economic Rewards, Occupational Status, and Social Mobility

Figure 5–17. Category Weight of Job Selection Criteria (Japan)

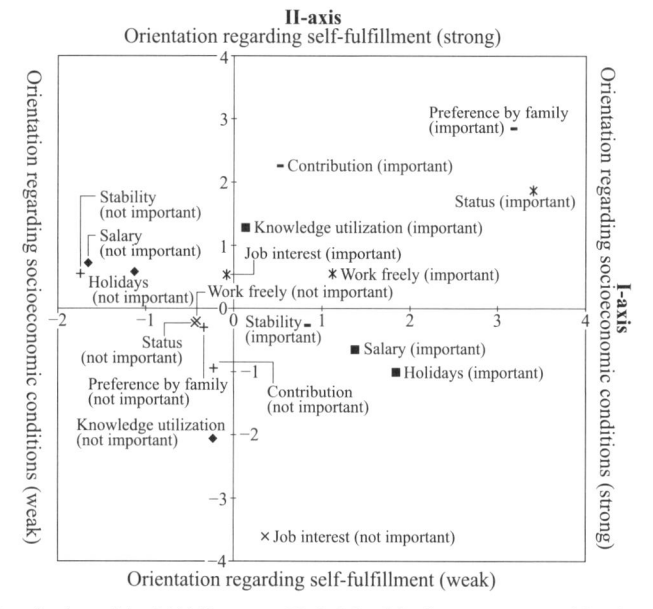

```
                        II-axis
          Orientation regarding self-fulfillment (strong)
                           4
                           |
                         3 |        Preference by family
                           |        (important) ▪
                           |     ▪ Contribution (important)
                         2 |                          *
              ┌ Stability |              Status (important)
              │ (not important)
              │ Salary    | ▪ Knowledge utilization (important)
              │ (not important) 1
              ♦           | Job interest (important)
              + Holidays  |♦ * Work freely (important)
              (not important) ┌ Work freely (not important)
        ─2 ────────── ─1 ─*+──0───── 1 ───── 2 ───── 3 ───── 4
                           | Stability ▪
                 Status    | (important)
                 (not important)
                         + | ▪ Salary (important)
              Preference by family ─1  ▪ Holidays (important)
              (not important)   Contribution
              Knowledge utilization (not important)
              (not important)  ♦
                          ─2
                           |
                          ─3
                           | × Job interest (not important)
                          ─4
          Orientation regarding self-fulfillment (weak)
```

Source: Based on the data of the *2000 Survey on High School Students in Japan and South Korea*.

5–17). Examining this scatter diagram, we notice there are three items that have large scores on the I axis (and only on this axis): "holidays," "salary," and "stability." There are also responses to "status" and "preference by family" that show a large score difference on the I axis. From these facts, we may consider that the I axis indicates "orientation regarding socioeconomic conditions of occupation." On the other hand, on the II axis, there are large score differences among responses to three other items: "can contribute to society and country," "knowledge utilization," and "job interest." Thus, we may consider that the II axis indicates "orientation regarding self-fulfillment through occupation."[63]

The figure for South Korean high school students (figure 5–18) reveals a very similar pattern to that of Japanese high school students. The II axis shows large score differences for "contribution to society and country," "knowledge utilization," and "job interest." Therefore, we may interpret that this axis also indicates "orientation regarding self-fulfillment through occupation." Similarly, we may also interpret that the I axis indicates "orientation regarding socioeconomic conditions of occupation." Although the figures from Japan and South Korea show

---

[63] The occupational value orientations extracted here are very similar to those by Aramaki (2001).

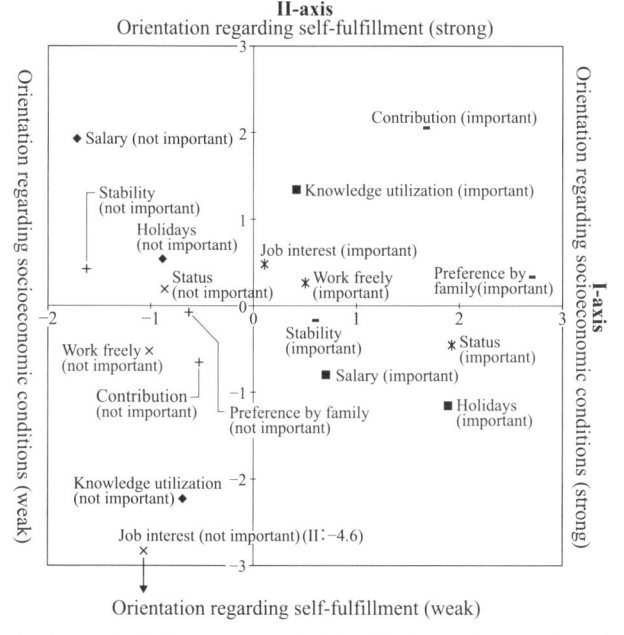

Chapter 5 Academic Credentials and Occupation Acquired | 179

Figure 5–18. Category Weight of Job Selection Criteria (South Korea)

II-axis
Orientation regarding self-fulfillment (strong)

[Scatter plot with axes: horizontal I-axis labeled "Orientation regarding socioeconomic conditions (weak)" on left and "Orientation regarding socioeconomic conditions (strong)" on right; vertical II-axis with "Orientation regarding self-fulfillment (strong)" at top and "Orientation regarding self-fulfillment (weak)" at bottom. Data points include: Salary (not important), Contribution (important), Stability (not important), Holidays (not important), Knowledge utilization (important), Status (not important), Job interest (important), Work freely (important), Preference by family (important), Work freely (not important), Stability (important), Status (important), Contribution (not important), Salary (important), Preference by family (not important), Holidays (important), Knowledge utilization (not important), Job interest (not important)(II: −4.6)]

Source: Based on the data of the *2000 Survey on High School Students in Japan and South Korea*.

some difference in positions of "preference by family" and "status," the overall response pattern is very similar between Japanese and South Korean students. In these responses we can extract almost the same axes of occupational value orientation for the two countries.

That being the case, merging the Japanese and South Korean data and analyzing them together would extract a similar orientation of occupational values. In order to understand the preferred occupations and their determining factors of Japanese and South Korean high school students in the same framework, it would be convenient if the extracted occupational value orientations were identical between the two countries.

Figure 5–19 shows the result when Hayashi's quantification method III was applied to the combined Japanese and South Korean data. Similar to previous results, the I axis (whose eigen value is 0.226) represents orientation regarding the socioeconomic conditions of occupations, whereas the II axis (whose eigen value is 0.143) represents orientation regarding self-fulfillment through occupation. The mean values of case scores of these two axes by country are: for the I axis −0.114 for Japan and 0.121 for South Korea; for the II axis −0.016 for Japan and 0.017

180 | Part II   Economic Rewards, Occupational Status, and Social Mobility

Figure 5–19. Category Weight of Job Selection Criteria (combining Japan and South Korea)

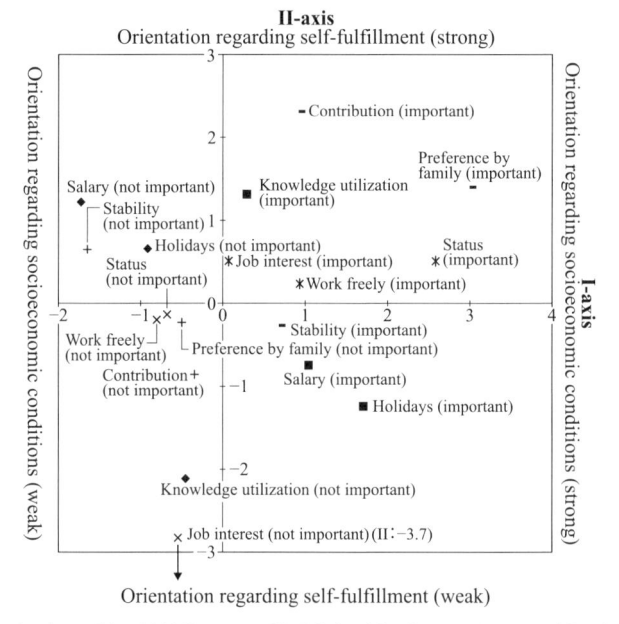

II-axis
Orientation regarding self-fulfillment (strong)

- Contribution (important)
- Preference by family (important)
- Salary (not important)
- Knowledge utilization (important)
- Stability (not important)
- Holidays (not important)
- Status (not important)
- Job interest (important)
- Status (important)
- Work freely (important)
- Work freely (not important)
- Stability (important)
- Preference by family (not important)
- Contribution (not important)
- Salary (important)
- Holidays (important)
- Knowledge utilization (not important)
- Job interest (not important) (II : −3.7)

Orientation regarding self-fulfillment (weak)

Source: Based on the data of the *2000 Survey on High School Students in Japan and South Korea*.

for South Korea.[64] While the differences in mean values on the II axis are negligible, there is some difference for the I axis between Japan and South Korea. As seen in figure 5–16, when selecting jobs, South Korean high school students are likely to consider salary, status, and "work freely" to be more important than do Japanese high school students. This is the reason for the score differences in orientation to socioeconomic conditions.

Next, let us discuss how occupational value orientation affects the actual occupational preferences of high school students, comparing Japan and South Korea. First, in order to assess the strength of the orientation regarding socioeconomic conditions and the orientation regarding self-fulfillment of Japanese and South Korean high school students preferring each occupation, we calculate the mean value of case scores on the I axis (representing the orientation regarding socioeconomic conditions) and on the II axis (representing the orientation regarding

---

[64] Because the South Korean sample has the somewhat smaller size of 1,354 than the Japanese sample of 1,439, a simple arithmetic average of Japan and South Korea does not become zero. It should be noticed that the difference in sample size is not that large, so we did not weight the data for merging the Japanese and South Korean data.

self-fulfillment) for each preferred occupation. Figure 5-20 plots the mean values by their preferred occupation on a plane of both axes.[65]

For Japanese high school students, there are relatively many occupations in the lower right and the upper left regions on the graph. In other words, the occupational value orientation of students preferring each occupation exhibits a clear contrast here: high along the one axis and low along the other axis. It should be noticed that students preferring professional jobs and clerical jobs are located at two opposite extremes in occupational value orientation. The students preferring a professional occupation have a lower orientation regarding socioeconomic conditions and a higher orientation regarding self-fulfillment, while those preferring clerical jobs have a higher orientation to socioeconomic conditions and a lower orientation to self-fulfillment.

These two occupations are both white-collar jobs, but students' motivations for preferring the jobs are completely different. That is, those who have a strong orientation regarding self-fulfillment through occupation prefer professional jobs while those who have stronger orientation towards socioeconomic conditions prefer clerical jobs. As for other occupations, students preferring service jobs are close to those preferring professional jobs. On the other hand, the students preferring sales jobs and full-time housewives (or househusbands) are very close to those preferring clerical jobs, indicating their occupational orientations are similar to each other. Students preferring self-employed have a somewhat higher orientation of socioeconomic conditions, and for students preferring skilled jobs neither of the orientations is very high.

These results show that the difference in occupational preferences among Japanese students is strongly tied to differences in their expectations of occupations. The result agrees with Aramaki (2001), which states that students prefer professional jobs and service and skilled jobs have stronger orientations of self-fulfillment while those preferring clerical and managerial jobs and sales and non-skilled jobs have a stronger orientation regarding socioeconomic conditions.

Can we find the same relationship between the occupational value orientation and occupational preference among South Korean high school students? Figure 5-20 shows that the constellation of preferred occupations of South Korean high school students is quite different from that of Japanese students. First of all, the mutual distance among occupations is relatively small and there is no clear contrast among them, unlike in the Japanese case. In particular, the South Korean students who prefer professional jobs and those who prefer clerical jobs are plotted very close to each other, indicating that there is not much difference in their occu-

---

[65] In order to guarantee the robustness of the results, only preferred occupations that have sample sizes of more than 30 students in each country are shown.

182 | Part II   Economic Rewards, Occupational Status, and Social Mobility

Figure 5–20. Occupational Value Orientation by Preferred Occupation

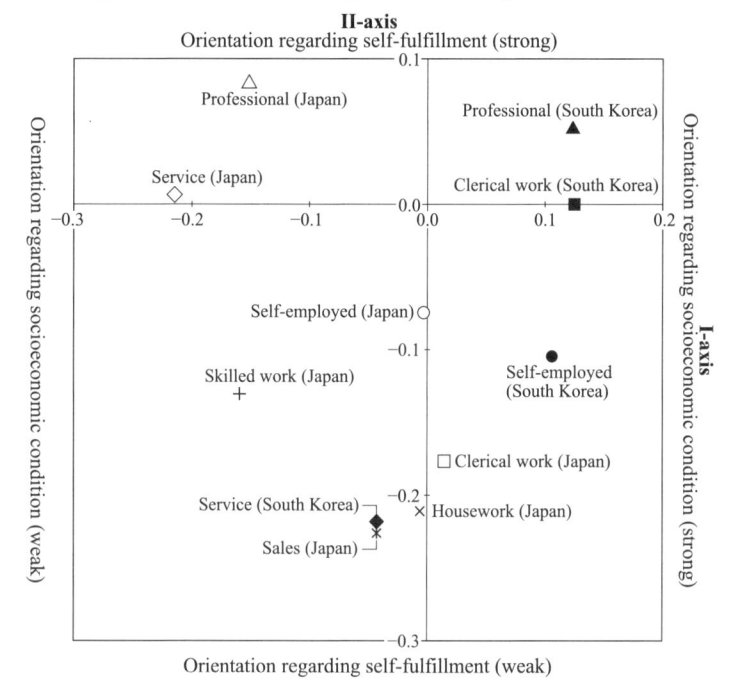

II-axis
Orientation regarding self-fulfillment (strong)

[Scatter plot with I-axis (horizontal, from -0.3 to 0.2) labeled "Orientation regarding socioeconomic condition (weak)" on left and "Orientation regarding socioeconomic condition (strong)" on right; II-axis (vertical, from -0.3 to 0.1) labeled "Orientation regarding self-fulfillment (strong)" on top and "Orientation regarding self-fulfillment (weak)" on bottom.

Data points:
- Professional (Japan) △
- Professional (South Korea) ▲
- Service (Japan) ◇
- Clerical work (South Korea) ■
- Self-employed (Japan) ○
- Self-employed (South Korea) ●
- Skilled work (Japan) +
- Clerical work (Japan) □
- Service (South Korea)
- Housework (Japan) ×
- Sales (Japan)]

Source: Based on the data of the *2000 Survey on High School Students in Japan and South Korea*.

pational value orientation. This situation is significantly different from the case of Japanese students, which shows the clear contrast in occupational value orientations between the two white-collar categories of occupation.

Compared with these two white-collar occupations, which occupy about 80 percent of the preferred occupations, the scores for service jobs and self-employment are low on both axes (although the lower degree of orientation is somewhat different for each occupation). This suggests that, in contrast to the white-collar occupations, the possibility is low that those students who prefer non-white-collar occupations do so with positive reasons. Needless to say, the same may be said of those who prefer clerical work vis-à-vis professional occupations.

After all, the occupational value orientation of South Korean high school students indicates the single dimensional ranking, in the order of professional, clerical, and service/self-employment, according to the scale of overall strength in orientation. South Korean students do not show the pattern that we observe in the case of Japanese high school students, the pattern in which the difference in their expectations of occupations corresponds to their occupational preference differentiation. Of course, the aforementioned ranking of occupations in occupational value orientations of South Korean students is clearly matched with that in occupational status as confirmed in chapter 2.

The above analyses reveal that in Japan the difference between the two occupational value orientations—"orientation regarding socioeconomic conditions" and "orientation regarding self-fulfillment"—which is not reducible to a one-dimensional high-low relationship, strongly relates to preferences for a particular occupation. From the outcome, we may conclude that the occupational preference of Japanese high school students has a strong tendency to differentiate horizontally according to what is wanted from a job. In the case of South Korean high school students, in contrast, there is no such tendency, but they only have the kind of vertical differentiation in which a student who wants more from a job is more likely to have a strong desire to find a job with higher socioeconomic status. From this analytical result, we can say that the aforementioned impression that although everyone wishes to obtain a job of higher occupational position, actual job preference becomes differentiated as a consequence of students' selection of career path according to their academic performance may be more applicable to South Korea than Japan.

Conclusion

According to macro-statistical data, the probability for new college graduates to engage in white-collar occupations did not decrease much even when the number of college graduates rapidly increased in the 1980s and after. Rather, we may conclude that the effect of college graduate credential on occupational status does not decrease at all, considering that the probability for new high school graduates to engage in white-collar occupations gradually decreased. Meanwhile, as often cited as proof of the "job shortage" due to the rapid increase of college graduates, the rate of finding jobs immediately after graduating from college began gradually decreasing in the mid-1980s.

In order to understand the mechanism that caused the above tendency, we conducted an analysis of the job-finding process of new graduates from the 1980s to the first half of the 1990s, focusing on the reactions of employers and job seekers to the rapid increase of college graduates. From this analysis, we confirmed the fact that many South Korean corporate groups have policies of "employment by academic credential" and "en masse employment." Due to this institutional condition, employment opportunities for South Korean college students are not differentiated so much by industry or working locations as by corporate size, which is almost the sole factor for differentiation of employment opportunities. The strong desire to work for large corporations prevalent among college students reflects the large-corporation-centered economic structure of South Korea. At the same time, that institutional condition also shapes the desire.

From the mid-1980s, as a rapidly increasing number of college graduates entered the labor market, two major changes occurred in the system of employment of new college graduates. One was that the employment process became a "second college entrance examination" with a heavy emphasis on written examinations. Accepting the advice of the Ministry of Labor, most large corporate groups filtered employment candidates with written examinations. The examinations, furthermore, were concentrated on specific days. Many college graduates who had a strong desire to work for large corporations but were unable to obtain such a job, often chose the status of jobless college graduate, while preparing for the next opportunity. This caused a decrease in college graduates who found employment immediately after graduation from the mid-1980s.

Second, the scale of employment by academic credentials changed. While the number of new college graduate recruits by large companies increased to a certain degree in the second half of the 1980s, it did not match the increase of new college graduates at all. Consequently, many new college graduates gave up seeking employment at large corporations and were absorbed into white-collar jobs at smaller companies. At the same time, from the mid-1980s to at least the early 1990s, corporations reduced white-collar job opportunities for new high school graduates, increasing those for new college graduates instead. The change of the scale of hiring by academic credential caused a decline among younger, high school graduates able to obtain white-collar occupations. In short, in response to the rapid increase of college graduates, companies raised the educational requirements for new employment. The increased number of college graduates gained opportunities for white-collar employment, driving high school graduates away.

The reason that corporations raised the educational requirements for new employment was not because the academic credentials of job seekers were regarded as the level of knowledge and skills they had acquired, but because academic credentials were regarded as proxy indicators of their general intellectual ability required to pass entrance examinations and engage in the subsequent academic work. In this "screening theoretic view" of academic credentials, raising the educational requirements for recruitment was a reasonable response to the increasing academic level of the new supply of the labor force.

For these reasons, in South Korean society, the effect of the college diploma on the rise of occupational status did not decline. Rather, we may conclude that the recruitment circumstance came to such a pass that finding a white-collar occupation required at least a college diploma.

How important is the effect of a college diploma on raising occupational status to the South Korean people? According to the Japan-South Korea comparative study on high school students' occupational preference and its determinants, there is a much weaker relationship between the preferred occupations of South Korean high school students and their parents' occupation compared with Japanese high school students. The horizontal differentiation of their preferred occupations corresponding to differences in occupational value orientation, i.e., "what to expect from a job," was also confirmed to be extremely small. In sum, in South Korea, academic performance is the crucial factor that differentiates the preferred occupations of high school students, and such vertical differentiation strongly reflects the ranking of occupational status. Considering the occupational preference and its determinants of high school students, we may conclude that the effect of a college diploma on raising occupational status is far more important to far more people in South Korea than in Japan. Due to these characteristics of occupational preference, South Korea displays strong aspirations for occupational achievement across all classes of society, and the desire for educational achievement for the purpose of enhancing occupational status is also high throughout society.

In fact, the outcome of the "Survey on Korean Attitudes Toward Education" conducted by the Korean Educational Development Institute in 1994 supports the validity of this conclusion. Figure 5–21 lists the distribution of responses (single choice) to a question on the "purpose of advancing to college" from parents with children of high school age or younger, from middle and high school students (limited to those who want to go to junior college or above), and from college students. The most frequently selected by all groups of parents, middle to high school students, and college students is the option "advantage in finding a socially recognized occupation."[66] By contrast, the rate of selecting the option, "advantage in gaining high income" was negligible. The survey asked another question, "what is the greatest disadvantage suffered by people who are not college graduates in South Korean society?" In response to this question, too, the rate of selecting "difficulty in finding a socially recognized occupation" (46.0 percent of the parents, 35.3 percent of the middle and high school students, and 43.8 percent of the college students) was much higher than that of "low income" (only a few percent for each group).

Based on the survey outcome, we may conclude that, regarding the purpose of advancing to college, South Koreans give more importance to the effect of raising occupational status than to the effect of increasing income and therefore, it is necessary to understand South Korean people's strong desire for educational achievement not only in terms of higher income but also in terms of the effect of academ-

[66] The fact that the expression, "a socially recognized occupation," is included in the survey questionnaire conducted by a government think-tank may itself indicate the presence of occupational prestige gap and discriminatory treatment of less prestigious occupations.

Figure 5-21. Reasons for Attending College

(%)

	Parents	Middle and high school students	College students
To become a mature person	32.7	13.7	16.2
To pursue learning	17.1	14.4	16.8
Advantage in finding a socially recognized occupation	40.5	51.0	44.4
Advantage in gaining high income	2.3	3.4	4.8
Not to be neglected by others	6.1	10.8	4.8
Advantage for meeting a good spouse	1.4	2.2	1.6
Parents want me to	–	2.9	2.8
As others do so	–	1.6	8.7
Total	100.0	100.0	100.0
N	879	1,103	505

Source: Korean Educational Development Institute (1994: 187).

ic credentials on raising occupational status. The reason that the desire to advance to college in South Korea did not clearly decline is because the effect of raising occupational status was not in the least lowered although the rapid increase of college graduates significantly reduced the effect of academic credentials on increasing income.

CHAPTER 6

Academic Achievement, Social Class Origin, and Social Mobility

This chapter examines the effects of social class origin on educational achievement and socioeconomic status. If a person's educational achievements are significantly influenced by social class origin, the difference in rewards according to educational credentials, which were explored in chapters 4 and 5, will lead to the reproduction of the social class structure.

In order to determine if people's optimistic perceptions of upward social mobility through academic achievement correctly reflect the South Korean social structure or, on the contrary, play a role in concealing the inequities of actual society, we must reveal how the two major issues—correlation between academic credentials and socioeconomic status and reproduction of the social class structure—are intertwined. In particular, we should examine the following questions: First, is the opportunity to achieve higher socioeconomic status through the acquisition of academic credentials open to each member of society equally? Second, does the close relationship between educational level and socioeconomic status in South Korean society contribute to the increasing fluidity or stability of the social class structure?

Section I of this chapter presents a scheme for accurately grasping the South Korean social class structure in preparation for addressing these issues. The scheme helps to clarify the socioeconomic profiles of each class.

Section II, we examine the direct effect of social class origin on socioeconomic status not mediated by education (see Introduction, figure 1, arrow [c]). If the direct effect on socioeconomic status is large, it means that even among people with the same academic credential, there will be a large difference in achieved status according to family background. Moreover, if academic achievement itself is significantly influenced by social class origin, then it is even possible that the correlation between academic credentials and socioeconomic status in reality is not one of cause and effect, but merely one of appearances. If that is the case, even onerous efforts to gain high educational achievements may not be rewarded by significant change in socioeconomic status.

Section III analyzes the actual effect of social class origin on educational achievement (see Introduction, figure 1, arrow [a]). The degree to which the relationship between level of educational achievement and socioeconomic status contributes to reproduction of the social class structure differs greatly depending upon the degree of disparity in educational achievement due to family background. Considering our discussion in previous chapters, we should also pay due attention to changes in the effect of social class origin over time. Opportunities to gain secondary and higher education in post-Liberation South Korea expanded very rapidly. For secondary education (and for studying in after-school classes), the formal equalization of the educational opportunity has been fervently pursued, even to the point of the sacrifice of educational freedom. Have the institutional reforms made along the way truly contributed to the elimination of disparities in educational achievement stemming from family background?

As depicted in Introduction figure 1, the degree of intergenerational social mobility is determined by the three factors: (a) the effect of social class origin on educational achievement, (b) the effect of educational level on socioeconomic status, and (c) the effect of social class origin on socioeconomic status not mediated by educational achievement. Needless to say, as long as there exists a correlation between educational level and socioeconomic status, intergenerational social mobility becomes easier as the influence of social class origin on educational achievement or the direct influence of social class origin on socioeconomic status diminishes. Section IV of this chapter considers how opportunities for intergenerational mobility in South Korean society were made possible by the above three effects and how those opportunities changed over the years.

One further issue to be considered in this chapter concerns the degree to which opportunities exist in South Korean society for attaining higher socioeconomic status *without* acquiring higher education. This book adopts the perspective of understanding people's strong desire for educational achievement as a means for achieving socioeconomic status, and the analysis of the effect of college graduate credentials was conducted for that purpose. What we need to deal with at the same time, however, is how exclusive educational accomplishment is to the attainment of desired socioeconomic status.

For this purpose, we analyzed intragenerational mobility in the urban self-employment sector. What is the effectiveness of becoming self-employed—which Hong Doo-Seung (1980) points out as an important path for achieving occupational status in South Korean society—in enhancing socioeconomic status? Is becoming self-employed an attractive career path for achieving occupational

Chapter 6   Academic Achievement, Social Class Origin, and Social Mobility | 189

Figure 6–1. Classification of Social Classes in This Book

			Employment Status		
			Employer	Self-employed (including unpaid family worker)	Employee
Occupation	Professional				
	Management	Corporate owner	Business owner class (38) [2.4%]		New middle class (324) [20.6%]
		Other			
	Clerk				
	Sales		Old middle class (425) [27.0%]		
	Service				Working class (355) [22.5%]
	Skilled work/labor				
	Agriculture, forestry, and fisheries		Farmer class (433) [27.5%]		

Source: Based on 1990 Equity Survey data.
Notes: Figures in parentheses indicate the numbers of samples and those in square brackets indicate composition ratios.

status not requiring academic credentials? Section V of this chapter discusses these issues, considering the socioeconomic benefits of academic credentials from the flipside.

I. Structure and Classification of South Korean Social Classes

In order to study the aforementioned issues in detail, it is necessary to construct a classification scheme for South Korean social classes that can be used for adequately understanding people's class origin and achieved class. In this section, according to the outcome of previous analyses, we classify the social classes based on people's occupation and status of employment, which well represent their socioeconomic status.

Classification of South Korean Social Classes

The social classes of South Korea shown in figure 6–1 consider the unique characteristics of the South Korean social class structure.[1] The primary criteria of the classification are: whether white-collar occupation or not, whether employed or

---
[1] This classification draws on prior works by Hong Doo-Seung (1983a; 1983b), Kim Yeong-Mo (1982; 1997), and Seo Gwan-Mo (1987).

190 | Part II Economic Rewards, Occupational Status, and Social Mobility

employer/self-employed, and whether engaged in agriculture and fisheries or not. The manager of a company with five or more employees is defined as a "business owner (employer)," which is separately categorized from the "old middle class".[2]

A note should be added regarding the criteria for the new middle class and the working class. The sales occupation is placed not in the new middle class, but rather in the working class because in South Korea there are large gaps in wages, occupational prestige, and job characteristics between sales and the occupations of professional, managerial, and clerical workers.

The following discussion applies this "five-class model" to the analysis of the classes. The samples used in this book consist of males only because the employment rate of women was not very high in the period covered compared with men, and female social mobility has to be treated with a different scheme from that for males.

Socioeconomic Profiles of the Social Classes

Let us start with a brief review of the socioeconomic characteristics of each class in order to understand the features of South Korean social stratification. Figure 6–2 shows the mean values of age, income, years of education, the amount of assets, and the rate of home owning by social class based on the 1990 Equity Survey data referred to in chapter 2.

Observations obtained from this table may be summarized as follows: (1) The business owner class had a much higher income and larger asset than other classes; (2) both the new and old middle classes were in favorable positions in terms of income (flow); (3) the amount of assets (stock) of the old middle class was much smaller than that of the new middle class; (4) the educational level of the old middle class was much lower than that of the new middle class, and was almost at the same level as for the working class; and (5) the economic levels of the working class and the farmer class were much lower compared with the business owner class and new/old middle classes.

Looking at figure 6–3, which shows the ratio of ownership of durable consumer goods by social class, we can observe noticeable gaps in the level of consumption between the business owner class and new/old middle classes on one hand and the working/farmer classes on the other. These observations suggest that not only the new middle class but also a large part of the old middle class, as befittingly called "middle classes," enjoyed high standards of living.[3]

---

[2] Here, the "old middle class" includes self-employed and employers engaged in clerical jobs and managerial jobs other than "business owners." However, the samples for these occupations are extremely small in size.

[3] With the above overview, the classification of social classes in this book based on the occupation and employment status is reasonable enough to capture significant inequality of life chanc-

Chapter 6 Academic Achievement, Social Class Origin, and Social Mobility | 191

Figure 6–2. Socioeconomic Profile of Social Classes

	Age (Year)	Individual income (thousand won)	Household income (thousand won)	Years in education (Year)	Assets amount (million won)	Rate of owning a house (%)
Business owner class (38)	44.1 (8.1)	1487 (993)	1725 (1115)	14.3 (2.2)	284.3 (307.6)	75.0 —
New middle class (324)	38.2 (9.4)	799 (463)	1076 (827)	14.1 (2.5)	92.4 (123.9)	63.1 —
Old middle class (425)	41.6 (9.8)	861 (615)	1021 (663)	11.0 (3.0)	71.1 (102.7)	54.2 —
Working class (355)	38.3 (10.1)	539 (216)	647 (265)	10.2 (3.0)	27.9 (48.8)	40.8 —
Farmer class (433)	49.6 (12.2)	377 (327)	475 (407)	7.6 (3.9)	50.3 (72.8)	95.7 —
Total (1,575)	42.4 (11.5)	658 (515)	814 (658)	10.6 (3.9)	65.1 (109.0)	65.4 —

Source: Based on 1990 Equity Survey data.
Notes: Figures in parentheses indicate standard deviation, except for the figures in parentheses following each class category that indicate numbers of the samples. "Assets amount" and "Rate of owning a house" are limited to householders only, their sample numbers being 36, 260, 389, 294, 392, and 1,371 (total), respectively from above.

Figure 6–3. Ratio of Ownership of Durable Consumer Goods by Social Class

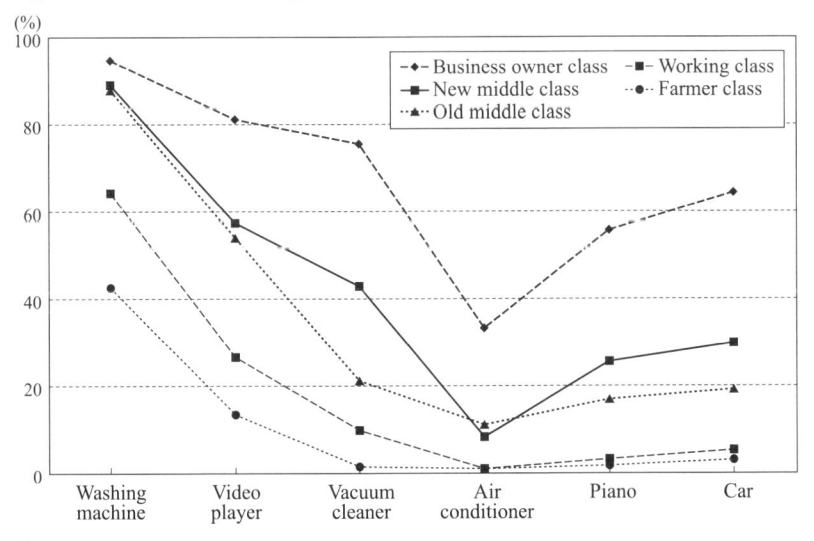

Source: Based on 1990 Equity Survey data.

Part II   Economic Rewards, Occupational Status, and Social Mobility

Figure 6–4.   Intra-generational Mobility Table

Social class at first occupation	Current social class					
	Business owner	New middle	Old middle	Working	Farmer	Total
Business owner	14 (70.0) [36.8]	1 (5.0) [0.3]	3 (15.0) [0.7]	1 (5.0) [0.3]	1 (5.0) [0.2]	20 (100.0) [1.3]
New middle	16 (3.8) [42.1]	279 (66.6) [86.1]	70 (16.7) [16.6]	24 (5.7) [6.9]	30 (7.2) [6.9]	419 (100.0) [26.8]
Old middle	3 (1.4) [7.9]	7 (3.3) [2.2]	162 (76.8) [38.4]	27 (12.8) [7.7]	12 (5.7) [2.8]	211 (100.0) [13.5]
Working	4 (0.8) [10.5]	32 (6.6) [9.9]	149 (30.6) [35.3]	261 (53.6) [74.6]	41 (8.4) [9.5]	487 (100.0) [31.1]
Farmer	1 (0.2) [2.6]	5 (1.2) [1.5]	38 (8.9) [9.0]	37 (8.6) [10.6]	348 (81.1) [80.6]	429 (100.0) [27.4]
Total	38 (2.4) [100.0]	324 (20.7) [100.0]	422 (26.9) [100.0]	350 (22.3) [100.0]	432 (27.6) [100.0]	1,566 (100.0) [100.0]

Source: Based on 1990 Equity Survey data.
Note: Figures in parentheses indicate outflow rates and figures in square brackets inflow rates.

What paths have these people followed to reach their current class position? Let us look at the characteristics of the social classes by examining the relationship between the social classes of first occupation and current occupation (intragenerational social mobility).[4]

Figure 6–4 is a cross table of social class at the point of first occupation (the class of first occupation) and the current class. Of course, even if the initial and the current classes are the same, there must be some who belonged to other classes between the two points. Even without counting such cases, we can observe from the figure that at least one-third of the total sample experienced intragenerational class mobility. Considering that we apply a relatively rough "five-class" model here and that the sample used includes many members of younger generations, we may conclude that the rate of intragenerational mobility is quite high in South Korean society.

es in South Korean society.
[4] In section IV, we analyze intergenerational social mobility, namely the relationship between own class and father's class.

Among the five classes, the old middle class in particular includes many who have experienced intragenerational mobility. The South Korean old middle class is a "high inflow class" into which many people intragenerationally flow from other classes. In fact, the ratio of people in the current old middle class who belonged to the same class at the time of the initial occupation is only 38.4 percent. In contrast, the inflow rates from the new middle class and the working class are 16.6 percent and 35.3 percent, respectively, indicating that more than half the current old middle class once belonged to either of these two other social classes. These facts show that the obstacles to entry into the urban self-employment sector are relatively low. Nevertheless, as we confirmed before, on average, the old middle class in South Korea enjoys relatively high income and living standards.

Compared to the old middle class, the new middle class is overwhelmingly a "high outflow class." Although the rates of outflow to other classes such as the old middle class were certainly high, the rates of inflow from others were extremely small, and as a result, 86.1 percent of the current new middle class is people who were already in the new middle class at their first occupation. The inflow rate from the working class was 9.9 percent, but a closer look shows that almost all of these people became clerical workers, most of them governmental workers in particular. In addition, there are a few who took professional or managerial positions, but their ratio is negligible. In chapter 5, we confirmed the fact that in general there were very limited opportunities for promotion to a managerial post for persons in non-white-collar occupations in South Korean companies. This is reflected in the low intragenerational mobility from the working class to the new middle class.

Next, let us examine in more detail the pattern of occupational mobility in the new middle class. A look at the job distribution, at the time of initial occupation, of people currently engaged in managerial or professional jobs, which earn relatively high remuneration among white-collar jobs, shows that, in the case of professionals, nearly 80 percent were initially professionals as well, 11.7 percent initially clerical workers and 7.4 percent skilled workers. As for people currently engaged in managerial jobs, over half were initially clerical workers, followed by managers (about 30 percent), skilled workers (about 10 percent), and professionals (less than 10 percent). Most of the managers were recruited from white-collar workers, many of them from among clerical workers. This is presumably because, similar to Japan, managers are often not engaged in the positions from the beginning, but are promoted to the management positions after gaining experience in clerical work. On the basis of the above analysis we may conclude that engaging in a white-collar job would be required for a worker to attain a management position in his organization, as South Korea has very limited promotional paths from non-white-collar jobs to management positions.

Examining the patterns of intragenerational mobility in the farmer class, working class, and business owner class, we first find that both the intragenerational inflow and outflow rates are low in the farmer class. Similar to the new middle class, the working class is a "high outflow class." This is not because inflow from other classes is difficult but because voluntary flow into the working class is considered to be small. On the other hand, the outflow rate from the working class is very high, and in particular, the rate of outflow to the old middle class is as high as 30.6 percent. As for the business owner class, it is notable that the number of people moving from the new middle class is comparable to the number of people who were in the business owner class initially as well, although it is difficult to generalize due to the small size of the sample for this class.

As described above, although intragenerational class mobility is relatively high in South Korea, we may conclude that initial class positions largely affect class status and the opportunity for intragenerational mobility at later times. In chapter 5, we showed that at the time of entering the labor market there were extremely large gaps in occupational opportunity according to the academic credentials of new graduates. Such gaps have a major effect on people's later working careers.

II. Effects of Social Class Origin and Academic Credential on Socioeconomic Status

In chapters 4 and 5, we considered the effect of educational level on wage and occupational status mainly using government statistics. In this section, the analysis relies on data from the 1990 Equity Survey, a comprehensive social survey that allows us to consider the effects on socioeconomic status of various variables that the governmental data were unable to capture.

In particular, we focus on the effect of social class origin on income and occupational status in order to quantitatively evaluate the direct effect of class origin on current status not mediated by educational level. By comparing the direct effect of social class origin (arrow [c] of Introduction figure 1) with the effect of achieved educational level on social status (arrow [b] in Introduction figure 1), it is possible to determine how large the effect of academic credentials are on social status, and how "meritocratic" the status-achievement process is in South Korea.

Analysis of Determining Factors of Income
Income analysis of employed males
Figure 6–5 shows the result of regression analysis on the monthly income of employed males. The regression equation used here is almost identical to the wage function we estimated in chapter 4, and the dependent variable is the natural logarithm of monthly income (excluding those with no income from the analysis). The academic credential has four dummy variables using high schools as the refer-

Chapter 6   Academic Achievement, Social Class Origin, and Social Mobility | 195

Figure 6–5. Regression Analysis of Income (Employed Males)

	Model 1	Model 2	Model 2'	Model 3
(Constant)	11.368***	11.324***	11.293***	11.343***
Age	.096***	.096***	.096***	.094***
Age squared (×100)	−.113***	−.112***	−.112***	−.120***
Education (ref. high school)				
Uneducated/elementary school	−.559***	−.529***	−.506***	
Middle school	−.293***	−.266***	−.257***	
Junior college	.142*	.104	.098	
Four-year college or higher	.396***	.339***	.332***	
Father's social class (ref. small/poor/tenant farmer class)				
Business owner class		.330**	.370**	.680***
New middle class		.163**	.202***	.484***
Old middle class		.166***	.203***	.401***
Working class		.013	.043	.079
Rich/middle farmer class			.095*	.230***
R^2	.308	.317	.320	.222
N	1,537	1,457	1,457	1,457

Source: Based on 1990 Equity Survey data.
Notes: *$p < .05$, **$p < .01$, ***$p < .001$

ence: elementary schools (including the uneducated), middle schools, junior colleges, and four-year colleges or higher. Each category of the academic credential includes both graduated students and dropouts, but the latter is very small in number.

As in the case of the analysis of employee wages in chapter 4, we can assume academic credentials and age to be the main factors that determine income level. Model 1 of figure 6–5 is a simple analysis model consisting of age and dummy variables for educational level. Our estimation using this model indicates a very similar result from the wage estimation for employees carried out in chapter 4 even if the self-employed and employers are counted in. Because age exhibits a positive effect and the squared age exhibits a negative effect, while income increases as people grow older, the increment grows gradually smaller, and even decreases after a certain age.[5] The estimated coefficient of each academic credential is also similar to that obtained in chapter 4: a graduate of a four-year college (or higher) earns an income about 1.5 ($\fallingdotseq e^{0.396}$) times higher than a high school graduate/

dropout. In 1990, when this survey was conducted, although it was after the wage gap according to academic credentials was significantly reduced due to the rapid increase of college graduates, the effect of advancement to a four-year college was an income higher by nearly 50 percent.

Does social class origin affect income even if the variables of age and academic credentials are controlled? If there is such a class origin effect, is it larger than the educational credential effect? Models 2 and 2' incorporate dummy variables for class origin into the regression equation[6] for the purpose of studying these issues. Based on the aforementioned five-class model, Model 2 incorporates four dummy variables for the father's social class using the farmer class as reference. The estimated outcome indicates that among dummy variables for father's social class, there will be positive significant effects for the business owner class, the new middle class, and the old middle class, and that even when age and academic credentials are controlled, several origin classes directly affect his income. We estimate that even if subjects are exactly the same in terms of age and academic credentials, those from the business owner class earn 39 percent more than those from the farmer class, and those from the new and the old middle classes earn 18 percent more.

However, we must remember that the farmer class, which serves as the reference for the father's social class, is internally very diverse. While the ratio of the survey sample of persons whose fathers belong to the farmer class is nearly 70 percent, considering their ages, we presume many of them were in the farmer class prior to the agricultural reform around 1950. This was a time of wide gaps in the scale of farmland ownership within the farmer class, suggesting large differences in life opportunities.

In order to understand the disparities within the farmer class, we divide the class for the father's side into two subclasses: "rich/middle farmers" whose farm holdings were one hectare or more and "small/poor/tenant farmers" whose farm holdings were less than one hectare. Five dummy variables for the father's social class (including a dummy variable for rich/middle farmers) are added with reference to "small/poor/tenant farmers" in order to conduct a similar regression analysis. Model 2' of figure 6–5 shows the results, which indicate that by dividing the farmer class in two we more clearly see the effect of social class origin on income. With the newly added father's class dummy variable for rich/middle farmer we see a positive significant effect at the 5 percent level. We can estimate that even

---

[5] The peak age for income estimated by the results is 42.7.
[6] The 1990 Equity Survey includes a question related to the occupation, employment status, etc. of the respondent's father (or householder if the father is dead) during the time when the respondent was growing up. Here, based on the responses to this question we classify father's social class.

when two people whose fathers were farmers are equal in age and academic credentials, one whose father had farmland of 1 hectare or larger earns income approximately 10 percent higher than the other whose father had farmland of less than 1 hectare. When we examine other dummy variables for father's social class, the effects become even larger with reference to the small/poor/tenant farmers. As long as we examine the estimated values of coefficients, we can say that the direct effect on income of social class origin is not small compared to the effect of academic credentials. We may conclude that, in South Korea, even if age and academic credentials are controlled, social class origin may affect a person's income to a certain degree.

As a primary path through which social class origin directly affects income, we may consider inheritance of the means of production. A person who inherits means of production including shops, plants, and farmland from a parent belonging to the business owner class, the old middle class, or the rich/middle farmer class, can increase current income significantly. Even if one's parent belongs to the new middle class, a similar effect would be obtained by converting inherited assets to means of production. Compared with self-employed and employers, for whom the scale of means of production greatly affects their economic situation, we can assume that the effect of social class origin is smaller among employees, who do not possess their own means of production. Here, we will ascertain whether our above hypotheses are valid by examining the determining factors of employee income.[7]

Analysis of employee income
With employees as the only subject of the analysis, figure 6–6 shows the results of a regression analysis using the same model. Comparing the estimated results for Models 1 and 2' of this table with the same models in figure 6–5, we observe, on the one hand, that the estimated coefficients of each educational credential dummy variable and age variable do not change appreciably.[8] On the other hand, the coefficient of one's social class origin is smaller than that in figure 6–5, and the dummy variables of the business owner class and the rich/middle farmer classes of the father's side are no longer significant although they are significant in figure 6–5. We may conclude that the direct effect of social class origin on economic activity as an employee is relatively small.

---

[7] The incomes of the self-employed and employers will be analyzed in section V.
[8] The estimated coefficient of "four-year college or higher" (0.367) in Model 1 of figure 6–6 is somewhat smaller than that in Model 1 (0.473) of figure 4–5 in chapter 4. We believe this difference is caused by the fact that the 1990 Equity Survey contains more samples of small/middle-scale company workers than the wage structure survey used in chapter 4.

Figure 6–6. Regression Analysis of Income (Male employees)

	Male employees		Male employees with higher education degrees
	Model 1	Model 2'	Model 2'
(Constant)	11.051***	10.982***	11.447***
Age	.106***	.106***	.074**
Age squared (×100)	−.120***	−.120***	−.064*
Education (ref. high school)			
Uneducated/elementary school	−.413***	−.392***	
Middle school	−.187***	−.167***	
Junior college	.136*	.126*	
Four-year college or higher	.367***	.354***	.265***
Father's social class (ref. small/poor/tenant farmer class)			
Business owner class		.122	−.063
New middle class		.113*	.059
Old middle class		.140**	.049
Working class		.075	.045
Rich/middle farmer class		.065	.100
R^2	.310	.329	.337
N	667	618	242

Source: Based on 1990 Equity Survey data.
Notes: $*p < .05$, $**p < .01$, $***p < .001$

Nevertheless, some of the variables related to father's social class have somewhat significant effects on individual income. Such effects of social class origin on employee income may be caused by differences regarding opportunities for employment with higher income or opportunities of obtaining non-labor income (such as inheritance of monetary assets) according to the father's social class. It should be noted that all analyses described above are estimates of the effect of social class origin regardless of academic credentials. In other words, the analyses do not take into account the possibility that the effect of social class origin on income might differ by educational level.

Whether a highly educated person's social class origin affects his income is particularly critical to the widely held social image in South Korea that anyone who obtains a higher education degree has equal access to higher socioeconomic status. The right column of figure 6–6 shows the result of regression analysis for employees with higher education to validate this image. From the results, we may conclude that no dummy variable for social class origin significantly influences income. In other words, as far as employees with higher education are concerned, there is little direct effect of social class origin on income.[9] Hence, whoever achieves higher education might equally obtain higher income regardless of social class origin, although the monetary benefits of higher education diminished after the number of college graduates rapidly increased.

Determining Factors of Occupational Status
Occupational status of employed males
Let us examine the effects of educational credentials and social class origin on occupational status.[10] Figure 6–7 shows the outcome of the regression analysis of occupational status using a model similar to the income analysis. Although the regression analysis of income includes age and age squared in the model, the analysis of occupational status includes only the former. In addition, the father's occupation is expressed by the occupational prestige score so that it may be treated as a single quantitative variable.

From the left columns for all male workers, we observe that the effect of educational level on occupational status is extremely large, both in Model 1, which has only age and academic credentials, and Model 2, which has father's occupation in addition to the two factors. In particular, higher education substantially raises occupational status: compared with high school graduates, four-year college graduates may obtain high occupational status, showing nearly 10 points higher in the occupational prestige score. The age factor, too, shows a positive significant effect, although the effect is not larger than those of the academic credentials.

We should note the effect of father's occupation included in Model 2 indicates that while the estimated coefficient is not very high, the father's occupation certainly exhibits a positive significant effect. In other words, even among people equal in age and educational level, the higher the father's occupational status, the higher their occupational status will be.

However, such a direct effect of father's occupation may be due to inheritance of the means of production. An analysis of the same model applied only to em-

---

[9] We also examined the direct effect of the father's academic credentials and mother's academic credentials on their child's income and found no direct effect on income of employees with higher education.
[10] Here, the international standard occupational prestige score is applied for analyzing determining factors of occupational status. Specifically, the international standard occupational prestige score shown in Appendix A of Treiman (1977) is allocated to 57 categories of occupation in the 1990 Equity Survey data. The reason for using Treiman (1977) is that the occupational classification used in the 1990 Equity Survey data is closer to ISCO68 than ISCO88.

Figure 6–7. Regression Analysis of Occupational Status

	All male workers			Male employees		
	Model 1	Model 2	Model 3	Model 1	Model 2	Model 3
(Constant)	39.767***	33.622***	17.926***	37.990***	36.379***	34.576***
Age	.092***	.081**	.056	.101*	.097*	−.155**
Education (ref. high school)						
Uneducated /elementary school	−8.114***	−6.760***		−14.705***	−14.398***	
Middle school	−4.411***	−3.633***		−7.730***	−7.009***	
Junior college	5.911***	5.587***		7.912***	8.535***	
Four-year college or higher	10.789***	9.724***		13.255***	13.421***	
Father's occupation		.153***	.375***		.034	.345***
R^2	.243	.257	.065	.374	.384	.099
N	1,557	1,484	1,484	666	619	619

Source: Based on 1990 Equity Survey data.
Notes: $*p < .05$, $**p < .01$, $***p < .001$

ployees (Model 2 in the right columns of figure 6–7) shows that there is no significant effect of the father's occupation. That is to say, the direct effect of father's occupation, as previously confirmed, is conspicuous in the self-employment sector[11] but hardly found among employees.

On the other hand, the dummy variable for each academic credential still has a significant effect, and the estimated value of its coefficient is even larger than that of the all-male worker sample. Although we do not clearly observe this trend in the regression analysis of income, by limiting the subject sample to employees, the coefficients of determination in both Models 1 and 2 are much higher than those or all male workers. This result indicates that the effect of academic credentials in determining occupational status is quite strong among the samples of employees in South Korea. This is attributed to personnel systems in organizations that amplify the relationship between academic credentials and occupational opportunity.

---

[11] We find that if we apply Model 2' of figures 6–5 and 6–6 (with father's social class dummy variables) to respondent's occupational status, the "rich/middle farmer class" category showed the strongest effect among father's social classes while other effects were generally not so strong. From this fact, we infer that the direct effect of social class origin on the self-employed person's occupational status is primarily due to succeeding to farm lands in the agricultural sector.

Reviewing the social image of the education meritocracy
South Korean people believe that "connections" (personal networks) are effective in finding jobs. In South Korea, the human networks utilized for finding jobs is not created by the job seeker, but by relatives, in particular, the father. If this is really the case, the occupation of an employee's father would significantly affect his occupational status. The outcome of the analysis in this section, however, denies such direct influence. Of course, there are certainly some cases where a father's personal connections help people secure employment opportunities, but they are very limited as far as the employee's occupational status is concerned. The ties between the individual's educational level and occupational status made by way of various institutions are much stronger than the ties between father's occupation and occupational status.

The conclusion from the above analyses is that the popular social image prevailing in South Korea that anyone who obtains a higher education degree has equal access to higher socioeconomic status somewhat reflects the reality of social resource distribution. As far as employees are concerned, regardless of their age and social class origin, they may equally earn high income and occupational status by achieving a high-level education. The outcome of the analysis confirms that the effect of educational level on income and occupational status is very large, and particularly so on occupational status.[12] The mechanism of social resource distribution in South Korea may be highly meritocratic insofar as educational level is considered to be what is achieved only through personal effort.

III. Effect of Social Class Origin on Educational Achievement

The analysis above revealed that educational level is the most important determining factor for income and occupational status in South Korea, and that the direct effect of social class origin is small, especially for an employee. If that is true, the openness of the social class structure in South Korea depends greatly upon how wide the gap in educational achievement is among people of different social class origins. If only some social classes monopolize educational opportunity, then there would be little intergenerational mobility through education no matter how much achieved educational level affected socioeconomic status.

In this section, we consider disparities in achieved educational level according

---

[12] The comparative analysis of Japanese and South Korean high school students' occupational preference discussed in section III of chapter 5 revealed the weak tendency to prefer a parents' occupation in South Korean society (p. 173). This is an important premise that makes it difficult for social class origin to directly affect a person's occupational status. The strong preference of white-collar jobs across the social classes works, needless to say, as the critical factor that increases the number of participants in the competition for higher level of education.

Figure 6–8. Regression Analysis of One's Years of Education

(Constant)	13.351***
Age	−.114***
Father's years of education	.243***
Father's Social Class (ref. small/poor/tenant farmer class)	
Business owner class	2.522***
New middle class	2.287***
Old middle class	1.613***
Working class	.161
Rich/middle farmer class	1.707***
R^2	.424
N	1,492

Source: Based on 1990 Equity Survey data.
Notes: *$p < .05$, **$p < .01$, ***$p < .001$

to the parents' social class and educational level and the factors that could cause such a gap. This section also pays attention to changes in such disparities. As discussed in chapter 3, South Korea achieved the repid expansion of educational opportunities after the Liberation in 1945, and the admission screening system at each educational stage (at the higher education level, in particular) was reformed in various ways to secure equal educational opportunities and fair college admission procedures. Have these measures for expanding educational opportunity and reforms of the system helped to eliminate the educational achievement gap due to family background? If not, what is the reason? To answer these questions we analyze below the determining factors of people's educational levels and compare them longitudinally.

Analysis of Determining Factors of Years of Education
Regression analysis of years of education
In order to grasp the outlines of the mechanisms of educational achievement in South Korean society, let us start with a relatively simple analysis of the determining factor of years of education. Figure 6–8 shows the results of regression analysis of years of education using all male samples. The analysis model includes several independent variables of age, father's years of education, and father's social class.

The outcome of the analysis indicates significant influences from the above independent variables: a negative influence of age, a positive influence from the father's years of education, and positive influences from all the social class dummy variables for fathers except for the working class. In other words, the younger a person is, the longer the father's years of education is, or if the father belongs to the business owner class, the new middle class, the rich/middle farmer class, or the old middle class, the more education he is likely to receive. While the strong negative effect of the age variable may be understood to be the consequence of the rapid expansion of the educational system after the Liberation, we see that the influence of the father's years of education variable is as strong as the age variable if we compare the magnitudes of standardized coefficients.[13]

Even if the father's years of education is controlled, the father's class variables show rather strong effects, and even when similar in terms of age and father's academic credentials, those from the business owner class and the new middle classes receive over two more years of education compared with those from the small/poor/tenant farmer class. Those from the old middle class and rich/middle farmer class also receive nearly 2 years longer education. It should be noted that even within those of farmer-class origin there is a large gap in educational achievement depending upon farmland scale. The determination coefficient of this model is 0.424, indicating that 42 percent of the differences in the years of education can be explained by only age, father's educational period, and father's social class.

As described above, educational achievement is affected by the father's years of education and social class, and the effects of these factors are not small, judging from the estimated coefficients of variables and the determination coefficient of this model. However, the above analysis is carried out using samples for all the age cohorts, and it is possible that the effect of father's social class and education may be quite different from one age cohort to another. Did the rapid expansion of educational opportunity and the various system-related reforms we observed in chapter 3 contribute to eliminating the educational opportunity gap among people of different social class origins? Let us look for an answer to this question by conducting an analysis for each age cohort. In the following analysis, the samples are limited to males aged 25 or older among the respondents of the 1990 Equity Survey, creating four age cohorts for those in their 20s (25 to 30), 30s (31 to 40), 40s (41 to 50), and 50s (51 to 60), and conduct an analysis by each cohort.[14]

The academic credential distribution for each age cohort as shown in figure 6–9 indicates that educational opportunity is very different from generation to genera-

---

[13] The standardized coefficient is 0.290 for the father's years of education, 0.178 for the rich/middle farmer class origin, 0.177 for the new middle-class origin, 0.140 for the old middle-class origin, and -0.332 for age.
[14] The 1990 Equity Survey, a nationwide survey of employed persons, has very few male college graduates in the sample who are under 25 years of age. This is because four-year college graduates find their first employment at around age 25 at the earliest, after fulfilling their compulsory military service.

Figure 6–9. Distribution of Educational Levels by Age Cohort

Year of birth	Age in 1990	Uneducated	Elementary school	Middle school	High school	Junior college	Four-year college	Graduate school or higher	N
1930–39	50s (51–60)	6.0	31.3	22.9	27.0	2.8	9.4	0.6	319
1940–49	40s (41–50)	1.2	19.4	24.6	37.1	2.5	13.5	1.7	407
1950–59	30s (31–40)	0.4	7.2	16.6	48.0	8.0	16.8	3.1	488
1960–65	20s (25–30)	0.0	0.9	14.0	42.8	18.0	22.1	2.3	222

Source: Based on 1990 Equity Survey data.

tion, reflecting the differences in educational policies and the social circumstances of each period. Such different distributions of academic credentials have a tendency similar to figure 3–2 in chapter 3 that was created based on the census data. Because some of those sampled who are in their 30s (born in 1950 to 59) and all those sampled in their 20s (born in 1960 to 65) in 1990 are the generations that took advantage of the open policies on secondary education such as middle school admissions without entrance examinations and leveling of the academic high schools. These groups thus show a larger ratio who have academic credentials of secondary education or higher. Furthermore, the rate of advancing to higher education for those in their 20s, who reached the age of entering college when the college admissions quotas were dramatically increased, is distinctly high, at 42.4 percent.

Considering the characteristics of academic credential distribution, let us analyze the determining factors of educational level achieved by age cohort. Figure 6–10 shows the result of regression analysis of years of education by age cohort similar to figure 6–8. It indicates a significant positive effect of the father's years of education at a level of 0.1 percent in all generations. Overall, dummy variables for father's social class have a significant positive effect except for the working class.

However, the effects of these variables are different from one generation to another. The later the birth year, the smaller are the estimated coefficients of father's education, which implies that the effect of a one-year difference on the father's years of education on his child's years of education diminishes the younger the generation. The effect of the dummy variable of father's social class has a similar tendency. While the dummy variables of the rich/middle farmer class and the old middle class have a significant effect for the generations born in the 1930s to the 1950s, the effect is no longer significant for those born in the 1960s.

The overall effect of these two variables of the father's academic credentials and social class is also quite different from one generation to another. Comparing the degrees to which the differences in the years of education received can be

Figure 6–10. Regression Analysis of One's Years of Education (by Age Cohort)

	1930–39 (age 50s)	1940–49 (age 40s)	1950–59 (age 30s)	1960–65 (age 20s)
(Constant)	6.638***	8.401***	9.675***	11.122***
Father's years of education	0.354***	0.265***	0.242***	0.161***
Father's social class (ref. small/poor/ tenant farmer class)				
Business owner class	.758	4.204**	1.394	2.466**
New middle class	3.896***	2.354***	1.593***	1.992***
Old middle class	2.628**	2.009***	1.461***	0.254
Working class	1.022	−0.070	−0.420	0.358
Rich/middle farmer class	2.836***	1.555***	0.978**	0.329
R^2	.305	.269	.268	.245
N	308	388	454	206

Source: Based on 1990 Equity Survey data.
Notes: *$p < .05$, **$p < .01$, ***$p < .001$

explained by these variables (i.e., the determination coefficient of the regression model), we find that the overall determination power of these variables gradually becomes weaker: from 30.5 percent for those born in the 1930s, to 26.9 percent for those born in the 1940s, to 26.8 percent for those born in the 1950s, and to 24.5 percent for those born in the 1960s. We may conclude that as the generation becomes younger, the degree to which social class origin and father's education determine years of education gradually diminishes.

Change of determining factors of educational level
What factors cause the change that could be recognized as "equalized distribution of educational opportunity"?

As briefly discussed in chapter 1, the primary effect of social class origin on achieved educational level is the economic impact caused by the different abilities to pay the expenses for advanced schooling. In fact, according to the longitudinal analysis of the demand for higher education, which we presented in section IV of chapter 4, the rate of new high school graduates wishing to advance to higher education in South Korea is largely influenced by average household income. From the result, we may conclude that the rapid increase in income levels during the rapid economic growth period substantially reduced the number of students unable to go to advanced schools due to economic reasons. Hence, the effect of family background of years in education grows smaller the younger the generation.

Figure 6–11. Reasons for Insufficient Education by Age Cohort

	Reason for insufficient education					Received sufficient education	Total	N
	Performance issue	Health issue	Economic condition	Dislike study	Other			
1930–39 (50s)	0.6	1.3	79.6	2.8	8.2	7.5	100.0	319
1940–49 (40s)	3.4	1.0	72.0	9.3	2.5	11.8	100.0	407
1950–59 (30s)	7.0	0.8	58.5	16.9	3.3	13.4	100.0	484
1960–65 (20s)	6.3	1.4	45.9	23.4	5.0	18.0	100.0	222

Source: Based on 1990 Equity Survey data.

In fact, the survey respondents' answers to the question, "Why were you unable to receive sufficient education?" (Figure 6–11) in the 1990 Equity Survey, confirms the conclusion. The ratio who answered, "I was unable to receive sufficient education due to the economic condition of my family" was nearly 80 percent for those born in the 1930s (age 50s) and became less than 50 percent for those born in the 1960s (age 20s).[15] Although these responses are subjective, the difference in responses across generations indicates the rapid decrease of students that gave up going on for advanced schooling due to lack of funds. That was the critical factor that weakened the influence of family background on years of education as the South Korean economy grew.

At the same time, we cannot neglect another background factor that weakened the influence of family background. That was the rapid increase of educational opportunities. Enforcement of the open and equal opportunity policies for secondary education and expansion of educational opportunities from the end of the 1960s onward greatly increased the rate of advancement to secondary education, reducing disparities in years of education. Consequently, the effect of family background on years of education may have become unnoticeable. In fact, disparities in the years of education steadily decreased despite the increase in average years of education itself: the standard deviations for years of education for each generation are 4.101 (born in the 1930s), 3.568 (the 1940s). 3.119 (the 1950s), and 2.445 (the 1960s).

---

[15] Because the overall educational levels increase, it is natural that the ratio of answering "educated adequately" increases as the generation gets younger. However, we should also notice that the ratios of "because of disliking studying" and "because of poor academic performance" also increase. The background factor of these increments may be: increase of the number of participants in the academic credential competitions along with the overall increase of household incomes makes the competition more severe, enlarging to a great extent the physiological cost such as excessive study for entrance examination.

Chapter 6   Academic Achievement, Social Class Origin, and Social Mobility | 207

Nevertheless, it may be too hasty to draw conclusions about progress in equalization of educational opportunity among the social classes in South Korea based on the above analysis. Considering the emphasis in the South Korean selection system on advancement to higher education encouraged by the government's secondary and higher education policies—especially the open secondary education policy—from the end of the 1960s onward, as discussed in chapter 3, the inequality in opportunities for higher education may remain even though opportunities for secondary education have been greatly equalized. If this is true, we need to examine determining factors of educational achievement in more detail for each educational stage. Only after such a detailed analysis can we evaluate the effect of social class origin on educational achievement.

Determining Factors of Advancement to a Higher Level of Education
Logistic regression analysis of educational advancement
Here, we focus on more specific educational advancement, and examine factors that affect it. The educational advancement we study here involves (1) completion of secondary education (i.e., whether a student can graduate from high school), and (2) whether a high school graduate can advance to higher education. Regarding (2), we analyze determining factors for the advancement to higher education of any school type (2–1) and for the advancement to four-year college (2–2).

Figure 6–12 shows the results of the logistic regression analysis of educational advancement using a model similar to the one applied in the previous section. Figure 6–12 (1), using all male samples, shows the result of analysis by generation of the effect of father's social class and years of education on the completion of secondary education, i.e., graduation from a high school.

This analysis outcome reveals that determining factors of the completion of secondary education are not much different from the previous analysis of years of education. That is, while father's years of education significantly influence the probability of completion for all generations, its degree seems to be smaller for those aged in their 20s and 30s than for those in their 40s and 50s. The same tendency is observed in the effect of father's social class: the effect of dummy variables for father's rich/middle farmer class is significant for people in their 40s and 50s, but is no longer so for those in their 20s and 30s.[16] When, following the classic method proposed by Hosmer and Lemeshow, we compare the values of likelihood ratio R-squared (R^2L), which indicates the degree of how the logistic regres-

---
[16] The effect of the new middle-class origin also seems to become smaller as the generation gets younger. The significant effect of the old middle-class origin appears only in their 30s and 40s while it does not in their 50s. This result may be a consequence of rapid income increase of the South Korean urban self-employed during its economic growth.

Figure 6–12. Logistic Regression Analysis of Educational Advancement

(1) Secondary education completion (for all samples)

	1930–39 (age 50s)	1940–49 (age 40s)	1950–59 (age 30s)	1960–65 (age 20s)
(Constant)	−1.728***	−1.125***	−0.368	0437
Father's years of education	0.175***	0.214***	0.168***	0.121**
Father's social class (ref. small/poor/tenant farmer class)				
Business owner class	20.666	1.663	−0.150	19.429
New middle class	2.464***	0.463	1.649*	1.673
Old middle class	1.018	1.058*	1.066**	0.122
Working class	0.305	−0.621	−0.029	0.568
Rich/middle farmer class	1.371***	0.880**	0.553	0.500
χ^2	78.94	92.42	87.62	18.08
R^2_L	.197	.183	.160	.097
N	308	385	454	203

(2–1) Advancement to higher education (for high school graduates)

	1930–39 (age 50s)	1940–49 (age 40s)	1950–59 (age 30s)	1960–65 (age 20s)
(Constant)	−1.518***	−1.557***	−2.015***	−1.018*
Father's years of education	0.020	−0.018	0.117***	0.078
Father's social class (ref. small/poor/tenant farmer class)				
Business owner class	−19.951	3.093**	22.161	1.933
New middle class	1.367	2.198***	0.921*	2.778***
Old middle class	1.789*	1.610	1.121**	0.417
Working class	−19.807	1.248	−0.572	0.335
Rich/middle farmer class	1.011	0.645	0.671	0.241
χ^2	12.68	29.08	56.99	35.76
R^2_L	.089	.119	.133	.154
N	110	193	322	168

(2–2) Advancement to four-year college (for high school graduates)

	1930–39 (age 50s)	1940–49 (age 40s)	1950–59 (age 30s)	1960–65 (age 20s)
(Constant)	−1.694***	−1.570***	−2.435***	−2.357***
Father's years of education	0.017	−0.043	0.109***	0.156**
Father's social class (ref. small/poor/tenant farmer class)				
Business owner class	−19.728	3.217**	2.834*	1.573
New middle class	1.318	2.063***	1.137*	1.115
Old middle class	1.177	1.493**	0.931*	0.280
Working class	−19.610	0.409	−19.610	−0.492
Rich/middle farmer class	0.677	0.567	0.783	−0.130
χ^2	7.87	24.12	54.30	32.00
R^2_L	.062	.105	.142	.152
N	110	193	322	168

Notes: *$p < .05$, **$p < .01$, ***$p < .001$

Chapter 6 Academic Achievement, Social Class Origin, and Social Mobility | 209

sion model fits,[17] they gradually decrease as the generations get younger. This result suggests that the overall effect of father's social class and years of education on the probability of completing secondary education tends to be smaller as the generation becomes younger.

The situation in the case of advancing to higher education, however, is very different. Figure 6–12 shows the results of the analysis of whether students who had completed secondary education were able to enter an institution of higher education or not (2–1), and whether students who had completed secondary education were able to enter a four-year college (2–2), using the same model. From these results, we notice that the effect of father's social class and education on advancement to higher education does not show any trend observable in the analysis of completion of secondary education. Rather, the effect appears to become larger for younger generations. For those in their 40s and 50s, the father's years of education did not have a significant influence on the advancement to higher education, but for those in their 20s and 30s, it did have a significant positive influence (four-year college only for those in their 20s). The father's social class did not have a clear tendency toward a lessened effect for younger generations.[18] Furthermore, the value of likelihood ratio R-squared becomes rather larger for younger generations. Based on these outcomes, we may conclude that the trend of the effects of father's social class and education on acquiring opportunity for higher education across the age cohorts is clearly different from the cases of years of education and completion of secondary education. For advancement to higher education, the effect of one's class origin on educational achievement never decreases.

Based on all results obtained from the study, whether one can advance to higher education, in particular, to a four-year college, has become a truly important disparity in academic achievement in South Korea.[19] If the effect of class origin on educational achievement, at this increasingly important stage, is not decreasing, then class origin can be assumed to continue to influence status achievement

---

[17] This $R^2{}_L$ value is the proportional reduction of the absolute value of the logarithmic likelihood, which is similar to the determination coefficient in OLS that is the proportional reduction of the residuals (Hosmer and Lemeshow 1989: 148).

[18] Because the number of samples of each category is inadequate, we need to perform an additional analysis based on sufficient data for discussing the changes in the effect of the father's social class.

[19] In fact, according to the data of the 1990 Equity Survey, the ratio of junior college graduates who evaluate their own educational levels as "quite unsatisfactory" or "somewhat unsatisfactory" was 43.6 percent, which is quite high and comparable to 49.3 percent of high school graduates, while four-year college graduates showed a very low value of 17.4 percent. These results suggest that in studying disparities in educational achievement in South Korea, we need to pay more attention to advancement to a *four-year college* than merely to advancement to higher education in general.

through a finer yet more important disparity in academic achievement. We will discuss this issue in detail in section IV.

Effect of Social Class Origin on Educational Achievement
Higher educational expansion and the opportunity gap
Opportunities for advancing to four-year college rapidly increase, especially from around 1980, as discussed in chapter 3. However, the outcome of analysis shows that the expansion of opportunities hardly changes the effect of family background variables on opportunity for advancing to four-year college.[20] Rather, as the importance of "institution graduated from" for four-year college graduates was increasing, family background variables continued to influence educational achievement in terms of whether or not students could advance to the highly selective four-year colleges.

Han Man-Gil conducted a comparative study on family background of freshmen at several universities in Seoul, large cities, and middle/small cities based on survey data from each university. His study reveals that the fathers of freshmen differ greatly in educational level and occupation among university locations as of the end of the 1980s, when the college admission (and graduation) quotes largely increased. But even in the same area they also differ significantly, depending on the level of difficulty of the entrance examination among universities. For example, for colleges in Seoul whose graduates are favored for employment opportunities, the mean ratio of freshmen whose fathers are college or higher-level graduates is 53.4 percent, whereas for colleges in small/medium cities the ratio is only 15.9. In the case of the university most difficult to enter in Seoul, nearly 80 percent of freshmen fathers are at least college graduates (Han Man-Gil 1991).

Another survey reveals that the influence of the family background of first-year students on opportunity to advance to the more selective four-year colleges is not decreasing, but rather increasing with time. The Center for Social Sciences, Seoul National University published a report (2004) on the family background of over 12,000 students who entered the College of Social Sciences, Seoul National University, between 1970 and 2003, based on student report cards, which include information such as students' hometown and their patents' academic credentials and occupations. This report, which drew a lot of attention when published, shows a considerably high ratio of freshmen at the most prestigious Seoul National University who had fathers with advanced academic credentials and high-income occupations such as professional and manager. Nearly 70 percent of the freshmen

---

[20] In addition, through an analysis using raw data from the population census, Kim Young-Hwa (1990 [2000]) also concludes that the effect of father's educational level and occupation on the opportunities for higher education do not fluctuate greatly despite the expansion of higher education around 1980.

in the 1990s had fathers engaged in professional and managerial jobs (and government civil service jobs).

What is of further interest is the analysis of time-series changes. Students' probability of college entrance by father's educational credential, calculated by controlling changes in academic credential distribution of the fathers' generation, shows that the probability for students whose fathers are at least college graduates was only about 1.4 times that of high school graduates in 1975. The probability gradually increased to approximately 3 times in 2000. Looking at changes in student college entrance by father's occupation over the years, the report indicates that the probability for students whose fathers are engaged in "high-income occupations," such as professional and managerial jobs, is several to ten or more times higher than that for other occupations. This shows that the probability gap did not change much during the period. The report concludes that "there is no evidence that the change in education policy over the last three decades has increased the possibility for low-income class children to enter Seoul National University" (Center for Social Sciences, Seoul National University 2004: 20).

Changes in the influence of social class origin on educational achievement
The above discussion leads us to conclude that when we focus simply on the difference in the years of education, or on educational achievement in terms of whether secondary education is completed or not, the effect of family background on educational achievement decreases the younger the generation. The reason for this tendency is that the overall increase of income and the expansion of secondary education opportunities greatly reduced the number of students who gave up going on for advanced education for financial reasons. On the other hand, if we look at opportunities for advancing to a four-year college—which has become the truly important disparity in academic credentials with the establishment of the "college-entrance-centered, government-controlled, and unified" admission system—the effect of fathers' academic credentials even showed an upward tendency; the overall effect of family background variables did not decrease at all Opportunities to enter four year colleges, especially the most prestigious colleges, were monopolized by students whose parents held advanced academic credentials and high-income occupations, and this tendency did not change much.

Judging from the above observations, although the disparities in educational opportunities among different social classes appear to have shrunk due to the prevalence of secondary education and the increase in income overall, the opportunities for advancing to a four-year college—a truly important disparity in academic credentials and an important factor in the process of employment—among different social classes hardly changed. Educational opportunity did continuously expand, it is true. However, what served as the medium between social class origin and achieved social status simply shifted from years of education to finer disparities in education at specific stages of education. The relationship between social class origin and achieved social status itself hardly changed. Therefore, the South Korean educational system may still play a major role in supporting reproduction of the social class structure.

It is extremely difficult to empirically reveal the mechanisms that result in disparities in educational opportunity among different social classes, and we do not have sufficient data to investigate this issue completely. Nevertheless, our analysis indicates that the mechanism of the effect of social class origin on educational achievement changed from something that was relatively visible to one that is difficult to assess. In earlier times the difference in the ability to bear educational advancement expenses among diverse social classes was the critical factor behind disparities in educational level achieved by their children. Such a direct and visible inequality decreased gradually as household income levels increased across the social classes. Meanwhile, as the selection process for college entrance became refined and the entrance competition more severe, non-economic conditions including students' academic performance and drive to advance to higher levels of education began to be the most important factors determining who could gain entrance to a four-year college. Students' family background variables including their parents' academic credentials may relate to these non-economic conditions in ways that are much more difficult to perceive.[21]

Non-economic influence of social class origin
Parents' attitudes toward their children's education, such as encouragement and care/concern, are often pointed out as part of the non-economic mechanism of the effect of social class origin or family background on educational achievement. Parents' attitudes can influence their children's academic performance and educational achievement (Kim Young-Hwa 2000; Kim Mee-Ran 2000).

Nakamura and Watanabe (2002) use data from the comparative survey of Japanese and South Korean middle and high school students, referred to in Chapter 5, to discuss the correlation between parents' attitudes toward education and their children's academic performance, and the differences in parents' attitudes among different social classes. Their study indicates that there are greater disparities among South Korean parents of different social classes in their commitment to children's education—on such points as "taking care to facilitate children's study" and "preventing children from watching too much TV"—as compared to Japanese

---

[21] Evidence of this from the prior analysis of the factor of advancing to four-year colleges is that the father's educational level, which is more related to cultural capital and the like, gradually has become more important than the father's social class variable that primarily indicates the economic condition of family origin.

parents. The results of their path analysis on the relationship of family background (father's academic level), family environment (parents' attitudes toward education), and student's academic performance indicate that in the case of Japanese middle school students the parents' attitudes toward education do not have any significant influence on their children's academic performance, whereas they do in the case of South Korean middle school students. The academic performance of South Korean middle school students significantly differs according to parents' attitudes toward education.

Fujita and Watanabe (2002) use the same survey data to study the relationship between social class and study time. They find that the difference in study time at home of middle school students according to differences in social class (especially difference in fathers' academic level) is larger in South Korea than in Japan, although the tendency is reversed for high school students. As we have observed, because South Korea does not have a severe selection process for middle school students advancing to high school, "study pressure" on them is not very strong. This being the case, the disparity in study time among the different social classes is likely generated by the parents' attitudes toward education at home. In other words, parents who have higher academic level are concerned about the college entrance examination from an early stage of their children's education, and are enthusiastic about their children's education, which influences children's study time at home, and ultimately their academic performance and educational achievement.

What deserves our renewed attention is that these phenomena unfold under circumstances where there is not a large gap among the different social classes in the educational level that parents expect for their children. Although most parents expect their children to acquire higher education at a four-year college or above, there is a large social class gap in actual strategy for fulfilling this educational expectation.[22]

Robinson conducted fieldwork and interviews in a South Korean elementary school and argued that the gap in children's academic performance among different social classes may be caused partly by biased attitudes of teachers toward students (Robinson 1994). According to Robinson's fieldwork, homeroom teachers obtain information on the occupations and academic level of their students' par-

---

[22] At an interview with the author, a teacher, Mr. G, of K-middle school in the southwest district of Seoul attended by many children of the working class states, "many students go to cram schools, and that is because both of their parents work and are not at home for a long time with their children. Many parents are satisfied by letting their children go to cram school without other involvement in their education" (interview on March 8, 2000). These different attitudes may explain the fact that significant differences are observed in actual educational achievement among social classes even though there is not a large difference in the educational level that parents expect for their children or the ratio of those attending after-school classes.

ents through "home survey sheets" which are distributed and collected annually and from which they judge the socioeconomic status of the students' family. The interesting aspect that Robinson's study revealed is that there were clear correlations between the teacher's assessment of the social class of the student and their attitudes toward students. He reports the following example. When a student makes a mistake, if a teacher believes the student is from a family of high social class and the parents are enthusiastic about education, the teacher encourages the student while pointing out the mistake. On the other hand, if the teacher believes a student's family is of low social class and economic position, the teacher gives the student a stiff scolding. How often a student is called on in class also greatly differs depending on the teacher's judgment of the socioeconomic position of the student's family. Through a multivariate analysis using a sample taken from students he observed in Korean schools, Robinson shows that there is a significant difference in students' academic performance due to their teachers' differing attitudes (Robinson 1994).

Of course, the gap in educational opportunity that arises from difficult-to-see factors of that kind may not be called "unfair" in a classical sense. However, as long as such a gap exists, the educational system obviously contributes to the reproduction of the social class structure. At the same time, because this kind of gap is produced in a situation where, on the surface, the educational opportunity appears open to everyone and student selection appears to be fairly conducted, such a gap hardly becomes a social issue.

In fact, the inequality of educational opportunity that has been regarded as a social issue in South Korea has remained a more direct and visible inequality, such as the inequality due to the household's capacity to afford tuition fees. However, the number of students unable to move on to a higher level of education for economic reasons diminished as income levels increased. Then, the inequality of extracurricular work attracted attention as the "new" educational inequality due to the differences in the capacity to afford it. The perspective from which to criticize unequal opportunity of education is still within a traditional framework of thought that "economic inability to bear educational expenses causes the gap in educational achievement." Hence, South Korean society has hardly considered the gap in educational opportunity from the perspective of non-economic factors. This may have something to do with the optimistic impression that (aside from other socioeconomic resources) at least educational opportunity is equally distributed, an impression maintained as a result of the Korean government's policy efforts. But this impression might collapse if the existence of hard-to-solve inequality caused by complex and invisible non-economic factors came to the surface. This might be one reason that criticism of the inequalities in education led to focus on the economic rather than the non-economic factors.

IV. EDUCATIONAL ACHIEVEMENT AND INTERGENERATIONAL SOCIAL MOBILITY

Chapter 1 noted the assumption of theorists of industrial society that, as industrialization progresses, social stratification becomes more open and opportunities for intergenerational mobility increase. The factors causing such changes are considered to be expansion of educational opportunity and increasing equalization of educational opportunity. Industrial progress is thought to ensure that socioeconomic position is determined not by personal attributes but by achievement and performance, and achievement and performance, in turn, are largely affected by level of education. The industrial society theorists believe opportunities for advanced education gradually become open to more people and disparities in the distribution of educational opportunities become smaller, thereby weakening the correlation between social class origin and achieved social status.

In South Korean society, expansion of education does seem to have led to a gradual diminishing of the disparities in educational opportunity according to social class origin. Nevertheless, social class origin is still strongly connected to finer distinctions of educational achievement at specific stages of education, namely, in higher education. Furthermore, with the overall expansion of education these "finer distinctions" become more critical in determining the occupation and wages of those who newly enter the labor market. If that is true, no matter how educational opportunity expands, the variable connecting social class origin and achieved social status merely shifts from "length of education" to "finer distinctions of educational achievement" and the degree to which social class origin determines attained social status may not change significantly.

The introduction showed that South Korean society appears to have been optimistic about the possibility of intergenerational mobility across the social classes (at least until the 1990s). However, if the mechanisms of educational and social status achievement have the characteristics described in the pages above, intergenerational social mobility may not be easy in South Korea as compared to other countries.

Below, we examine these problems by quantitatively analyzing the relationship between people's social class origin and their achieved social class. We also consider the role of education in intergenerational class mobility.

Analysis of Intergenerational Mobility Table
Figure 6–13 shows the intergenerational social mobility between current social class and father's social class for the male samples of the 1990 Equity Survey. In this figure, we first notice that the ratio of current social status, being the same as the father's class shown in square brackets, is generally low. While the ratio exceeds 90 percent in the farmer class, it is around 20 percent in the new and old

Figure 6–13. Intergenerational Mobility Table

Father's social class	Current social class					
	Business owner	New middle class	Old middle class	Working class	Farmer class	Total
Business owner	3 (12.5) [8.8]	10 (41.7) [3.4]	7 (29.2) [1.7]	4 (16.7) [1.2]	0 (0.0) [0.0]	24 (100.0) [1.6]
New middle class	8 (5.2) [23.5]	70 (45.2) [23.6]	38 (24.5) [9.4]	25 (16.1) [7.6]	14 (9.0) [3.3]	155 (100.0) [10.4]
Old middle class	9 (4.4) [26.5]	50 (24.6) [16.9]	93 (45.8) [23.0]	48 (23.6) [14.5]	3 (1.5) [0.7]	203 (100.0) [13.6]
Working class	1 (1.2) [2.9]	22 (25.9) [7.4]	15 (17.6) [3.7]	40 (47.1) [12.1]	7 (8.2) [1.6]	85 (100.0) [5.7]
Farmer class	13 (1.3) [38.2]	144 (14.0) [48.6]	251 (24.4) [62.1]	214 (20.8) [64.7]	406 (39.5) [94.4]	1,028 (100.0) [68.8]
Total	34 (2.3) [100.0]	296 (19.8) [100.0]	404 (27.0) [100.0]	331 (22.1) [100.0]	430 (28.8) [100.0]	1,495 (100.0) [100.0]

Source: Based on 1990 Equity Survey data.
Notes: Figures in parentheses indicate outflow rates (or self-retention rates) and figures in square brackets inflow rates (or self-reproduction rates).

middle classes, and only 10-some percent in the working class. These ratios are the consequence of rapid change in the social class structure that occurred during the transition from the father's generation to the current generation; in particular, we note the substantial shrinkage of the farmer class and expansion of various urban classes. In fact, nearly 70 percent of the father's generation belongs to the farmer class while the rate is less than 30 percent for the child's generation.

Due to the rapid change in its social class structure, South Korea has experienced numerous cases of intergenerational mobility across social classes. According to the mobility table, out of 1,495 persons, 883 experienced intergenerational mobility, and the ratio (i.e., the actual mobility ratio) is 59.1 percent. Of the remaining 612 non-mobile persons (40.9%), nearly two-thirds are in the farmer class, indicating that the ratio of intergenerational social mobility among urban residents is extremely high.

The high ratio of the actual mobility may suggest the openness of the social class structure in South Korean society. However, other indexes exhibit rather opposite results. Prior social mobility studies created indices that are useful for measuring the openness of the social class structure. In order to use such indices, we need to understand the distinction between structural mobility and exchange mobility. Structural mobility (or forced mobility) is caused by external conditions such as change in the industrial structure. Inevitable mobility from the farmer class to various urban classes due to the shrinkage of the agricultural sector is an example of this type. Exchange mobility (or pure mobility), which is the mobility left after subtracting structural mobility from actual mobility, is in contrast caused by equal opportunity given to each person for attaining social status regardless of social class origin.[23] Thus, actual mobility of society as a whole may be divided into structural mobility and exchange mobility; but it is not the former but the latter that best indicates the openness of the social class structure, that is, the low barriers to social class mobility (Yasuda 1971: 59–60).

Based on the above, the actual mobility rate (59.1%) calculated from figure 6–13 may also be divided into structural mobility rate and exchange mobility rate. The number of the cases of structural mobility caused by change in the social class structure during the transition from the father's generation to the current generation is as large as 598 among all the 883 people who experienced intergenerational mobility. The remaining 285 are assumed to have experienced exchange mobility. Similarly, the actual mobility rate of 59.1 percent (= 883/1,495) may be divided into a structural mobility rate of 40.0 percent (= 598/1,495) and an exchange mobility rate of 19.1 percent (= 285/1,495).[24] In short, approximately two-thirds of all instances of mobility that occurred from the father's generation to the current generation may be interpreted as the "forced" mobility caused by changes in the social class structure prompted by changes in the industrial structure.

One other basic index, called the Yasuda index of social mobility (hereinafter "Yasuda index"), compares actual exchange mobility with the ideal exchange mobility that is calculated by assuming that the father's social class and the son's social class are completely independent of each other. The Yasuda index indicates how large the actual exchange mobility rate is compared with the ideal exchange mobility rate; it is null if there is no actual exchange mobility at all, and its value is 1 if mobility is completely free. Using the intergenerational mobility table (figure 6–13), the Yasuda index is calculated at 0.574 for South Korean society. Although we note that the index value differs somewhat depending on the method of classi-

---

[23] Pure mobility (or exchange mobility) is a mobility in which positions of mutual social classes appear to have been exchanged, as in the case where children of the working class move to the new middle class and children of the new middle class move to the working class.
[24] For details on the method for calculating these indices, see Yasuda (1971).

fying social classes, the Yasuda index for each country shown in Yasuda (1971) is in the range of 0.5 to 0.8. The value for South Korea, 0.574, is not high at all compared with the values for other countries.

In fact, several prior studies indicate that the degree of openness of the social class structure in South Korea is not very high compared with other countries. Yun Young-Min (1994) analyzes the social class composition and mobility of Japan, Taiwan, and South Korea based on the log-linear analysis of mobility tables with a four-class model, concluding that social class mobility is greatest in Taiwan among the three countries. Furthermore, in South Korea the "service classes," consisting of high-level professionals and managers, showed the highest degree of closedness among these three countries. Phang Ha-Nam and Lee Sung-Kyun (1996) also examine the ratio of intergenerational exchange mobility and conclude that social mobility is more difficult in South Korea than in Taiwan. Kagoya (2002), too, indicates that the Yasuda index is lower in South Korea than in Hong Kong and Japan.

Rapid change in the South Korean industrial structure certainly provided people with many opportunities for social mobility. However, considering the above analysis outcomes and results of prior research, we may observe that "pure" chances for social mobility, independent of structural change, are not very high compared with other East Asian industrial societies that have experienced similar structural changes. If that tendency does not change, intergenerational social mobility will become very difficult in South Korean society after the rapid structural change brought about by industrialization comes to an end.

Whether this pessimistic scenario becomes real or not entirely depends on changes in exchange mobility opportunities. As theorists of industrial society predict, if the exchange mobility rate increases with time, ample opportunities for intergenerational mobility will continue. If not, the social class structure will soon become solidified. How are opportunities for exchange mobility changing as time passes in South Korea?

Opportunity for Intergenerational Mobility by Age Cohort

The most appropriate method for discussing this issue would be to construct mobility tables for social survey data from past to present, and compare the results. We cannot do so, however, because South Korea did not continuously conduct social surveys equivalent to the Japanese national Social Stratification and Social Mobility (SSM) survey until the 1990s. Therefore, as an alternative method, we analyze intergenerational mobility for each age cohort using the 1990 Equity Survey data as a basis for discussing time-series change in the openness of social class structure. Because we need to control the effect of aging on the

Chapter 6   Academic Achievement, Social Class Origin, and Social Mobility | 219

Figure 6–14.   Intergenerational Mobility Index by Age Cohort

	1930–39 (age 50s)	1940–49 (age 40s)	1950–59 (age 30s)	1960–65 (age 20s)
Actual mobility rate (whole)	0.455	0.586	0.687	0.654
Structural mobility rate (whole)	0.364	0.440	0.484	0.498
Exchange mobility rate (whole)	0.091	0.147	0.202	0.156
Yasuda index (whole)	0.464	0.535	0.616	0.508
Yasuda index (business owner + new middle class)	0.356	0.552	0.611	0.450
Yasuda index (old middle class)	0787	0.917	0.848	0.625
Yasuda index (working class)	0.853	0.439	0579	0.856
Yasuda index (farmer class)	0.223	0.165	0.153	0.081
Odds ratio (business owner + new middle class)	13.10	5.44	3.79	5.55
Odds ratio (old middle class)	3.04	1.69	2.26	4.84
Odds ratio (working class)	2.11	5.92	3.13	1.50
Odds ratio (farmer class)	10.16	12.15	13.11	30.00
N	308	389	450	205

Source: Based on 1990 Equity Survey data.

achieved social class, we use social class at the time of first occupation instead of current social class and discuss the relationship with father's social class.[25]

In addition, we should keep in mind the following point in analyzing intergenerational mobility by age cohort: dividing data considerably reduces the counts in each cell of the mobility table. In order to avoid resultant instability, we combine the business owner class and the new middle class, which are similar to each other in class characteristics. Furthermore, for our analysis, instead of an elaborate technique like the log-linear model, we use more robust indices such as the Yasuda index and the odds ratio for achieving entry into a particular class from the same class and from other classes.

Figure 6–14 shows the mobility indices calculated based on the intergeneration-

---

[25] Chang Sang-Soo (2001), a valuable work on this issue, discusses the trends in intergenerational mobility, analyzing the relationship between current social class and father's social class by age cohort. It limits the subject to males of age 30 and older because "males enter into the occupationally mature stage at age around 30–35" (Chang Sang-Soo 2001: 153), based on other works including Goldthrope (1987) and Erikson and Goldthrope (1992). However, we all too often see occupational mobility across social class boundaries even after their 40s in South Korea.

al mobility table for each age cohort: 1930–1939 (age 50s), 1940–1949 (age 40s), 1950–1959 (age 30s), and 1960–1965 (age 20s).

A look at actual mobility, counting all mobility cases, shows that the mobility rate for those born in the 1940s (0.586) is higher than that for those born in the 1930s (0.455), while the mobility rates for those born in the 1950s (0.687) and in the 1960s (0.654) are even higher than that for those born in the 1940s. Among those born in the 1950s and the 1960s, two-thirds have social class positions different from their fathers' at the time of their first occupation. These changes in actual mobility indicate that total opportunity for intergenerational mobility greatly increases the younger the generation. A substantial part of those born in the 1940s and all of those born in the 1950s and the 1960s assumed their first occupations after rapid economic expansion started in South Korea. Therefore, we consider that increases in the actual mobility of these cohorts are due to the structural change that accompanies industrialization.

In fact, looking at the rate of structural mobility generated by change of the social class structure itself, we observe that the rate gradually increases the younger the generation. Structural mobility occupies 70 to 80 percent of actual mobility, indicating that structural change during the period of the rapid industrialization provided people with many opportunities for intergenerational mobility. However, the rate of exchange mobility shows a somewhat different pattern of change from that of structural mobility. The rate of exchange mobility gradually increases from 0.091 for those born in the 1930s to 0.147 for those born in the 1940s, and to 0.202 for those born in the 1950s; it then decreases to 0.156 for those born in the 1960s, indicating that openness of the social class structure did not consistently increase.

Let us investigate the openness of each social class in more detail, looking at the Yasuda index for each social class as shown in figure 6–14. The index values for the farmer class are extremely small compared with the other classes. This is because there are extremely few newcomers to the farmer class; this social class shows an overwhelming outgoing trend.[26] On the other hand, the index values for the old middle class are extremely high. The South Korean old middle class had high mobility, i.e., flowing into the old middle class from other social classes is relatively easy, and at the same time, flowing out of the old middle class to other social classes was also frequent. When we look at the time trend, it is notable that, while the Yasuda index for the new middle (and the business owner) classes gradually increased from those born in the 1930s to the 1950s, it greatly decreased for those born in the 1960s. A similar tendency is also observed in the old middle class.

[26] This can be attributed partly to the institutional factor that non-farmers were restricted from purchasing farmland after the farmland reform implemented just after the Liberation in South Korea.

The odds ratio, which is a measure of actual barriers for entry into each social class, shows a similar trend. The odds ratio is the ratio of the odds of a person entering the same social class as the original, to the odds of one entering the social class from a different social class. For example, for the new middle class, the ratio indicates the degree of ease for one from the new middle class to enter the same class compared with one entering from a different social class. A look at the new middle (and business owner) classes, which enjoy the best socioeconomic conditions among the four classes, indicates that the ratio does decrease between those born in the 1930s and in the 1950s but increases from 3.79 for those born in the 1950s to 5.55 for those born in the 1960s. One from the new middle class born in the 1960s may enter the same new middle class five to six times easier than those from the other classes.

Changes in Intergenerational Mobility and the Role of Education
The above analysis of outcomes can be summarized as follows. In South Korea in the period from the 1960s to 1990s, intergenerational mobility increased for each younger generation. However, that is largely because the structural mobility rate increased due to changes in the industrial structure while openness of exchange mobility did not show a consistently increasing trend. In particular, moving into the new middle class (and the business owner class), which forms the wealthiest strata in South Korean society, became even more difficult than before for people born in the 1950s to the 1960s. As we confirmed earlier, the generation born in the 1960s fully enjoyed the benefits of the equalization of secondary education and the explosive increase of higher education opportunities from around 1980. In terms of years of education alone, the effect of family background on disparities in educational level diminished for this generation compared with that for older generations. However, we find no evidence that the generation born in the 1960s enjoyed more open intergenerational social mobility than do previous generations.

Limited opportunities for social mobility for the youngest generation in the study may be attributed to the following: regarding the advantages of advancing to a four-year college or not, the effect of social class origin is still large, and, as their economic situation improves, new middle-class parents of members of the younger generations are able to invest more effort in assuring their children remain in the same social class.

Therefore, the explosive expansion of opportunities for secondary and higher education in South Korea has by no means increased the openness of the social class structure. Amid the overall educational expansion and shrinkage of disparities in education, social class origin still had a significant effect on achieved social class through the "finer distinctions of educational achievement." In South Korean society, the tendency for openness of the social class structure to gradually increase with progress of industrialization is not clearly observed. All this is attributed to the fact, as described in section III of this chapter, that the effect of social class origins on the truly important differences in academic achievement that occur at the stage of higher education does not decrease at all.

According to the determining factors of achieved socioeconomic status analyzed in section II, the direct effect of social class origin on income and occupational status is certainly smaller than that of academic credentials. That being the case, the popular image among South Koreans that their society is meritocratic and in which "anyone with higher education may equally acquire high socioeconomic status," does in its own way adequately reflect reality.

However, in terms of the feasibility of fulfilling the precondition of acquiring higher education, there is still a large gap across the social classes. Despite the overall expansion of educational opportunities, the influence of social class origins on the opportunity of advancing to a four-year college has not decreased. Thus, social class origins continue to indirectly affect income and occupational status through educational achievement.[27]

V. Characteristics and Mobility of the Old Middle Class: Achievement of Socioeconomic Status without Advanced Education

According to the screening theory, people's educational levels influence the distribution of status and rewards because employers cannot acquire full information on the productivity of job seekers due to the incompleteness of information in the labor market. If this is true, level of education strongly determines a person's socioeconomic status primarily as an employee of an organization.

In this book, we have regarded engagement in white-collar occupations mainly in firms and government offices as the important status achievement, and explored the determining factors for achieving that status. The reason for this approach is that, in South Korea, white-collar workers have advantageous positions in terms of income and prestige compared with non-white-collar workers, and people's desire to engage in white-collar jobs is extremely strong. At the same time, we need to notice that members of the old middle class, which is primarily composed of urban self-employed workers, earn high incomes comparable to those of the new middle class on average. The South Korean old middle class is a considerably open social class where intergenerational and intragenerational inflow rates are both high. Hong Doo-Seung points out that becoming self-employed is as import-

---

[27] In fact, observing the estimations in Model 3 shown in figures 6–5 and 6–7, we find the gross effect of social class origin, including the indirect effect through educational achievement, is considerable, while the coefficient of determination of Model 3 is much smaller than those for Models 1 and 2.

Chapter 6   Academic Achievement, Social Class Origin, and Social Mobility | 223

ant a channel for achieving social status in South Korea as becoming a white-collar worker in an organization by acquiring academic credentials (Hong Doo-Seung 1980). Given that high income and extremely low barriers to inflow mobility are features of the South Korean old middle class, moving into that class may be an important path for South Koreans seeking to raise their socioeconomic status.

Since this book seeks to investigate the factors behind South Korean's strong desire to acquire high academic credentials for the purpose of enhancing their socioeconomic status, we also need to carefully consider the nature of "status achievement through self-employment." If we expand on the premise of the screening theory, we can say that while in the case of employees academic credentials do have a significant effect upon acquisition of socioeconomic status, the effect is likely much smaller for those who are self-employed, whose labor is directly invested in economic activity without the medium of the labor market. If that is the case, self-employment may become an important path for achieving socioeconomic status without academic credentials. In order to determine whether acquiring a high level of education is the exclusive means of achieving socioeconomic status or not in South Korea, we need to study the extent to which self-employment raises socioeconomic status, and whether self-employment can really become an alternative path to high socioeconomic status without advanced academic credentials. In this section, too, we use the 1990 Equity Survey data in order to reveal the characteristics of the old middle class, which has not received sufficient scholarly attention even in South Korea.[28]

Intragenerational Mobility and Its Determinants
Intragenerational mobility to the old middle class and income increase
Our analysis so far has revealed that a substantial part of the South Korean old middle class shed its marginal character during the process of rapid economic growth (see p. 47), and as of 1990, people of this class earned high average incomes comparable to that of the new middle class. Their length of education is shorter than that of the new middle class and almost the same as that of the worker class, but they own the means of production and manage their own economic activity, allowing them to enjoy relatively favorable economic conditions.

At the same time, the analysis of intragenerational mobility described in section I of this chapter indicates that the old middle class in South Korea consisted of many people who experienced intragenerational mobility from the working class and the new middle class. In addition, the analysis of the intergenerational mobility described in section IV of this chapter reveals that the South Korean old

---
[28] Although empirical research on the subject has been increasing little by little, until 1990s studies on South Korean urban self-employment had seldom been conducted.

Figure 6–15. Socioeconomic Profile of Old Middle Class by Social Class at First Occupation

Social class at first occupation	Age (year)	Individual income (thousand won)	Household income (thousand won)	Length of education (year)	Assets amount (million won)
New middle class (70)	42.2 (10.9)	965 (748)	1259 (924)	13.1 (2.3)	95.4 (107.1)
Old middle class (162)	41.4 (9.6)	880 (634)	1034 (591)	11.0 (2.8)	79.6 (107.3)
Working class (149)	40.3 (9.6)	820 (558)	940 (621)	10.3 (2.9)	53.0 (102.1)
Farmer class (238)	45.8 (7.7)	767 (479)	898 (465)	9.3 (2.7)	65.3 (66.8)
Total (422)	41.6 (9.8)	862 (616)	1023 (664)	11.0 (3.0)	71.3 (103.0)

Source: Based on 1990 Equity Survey data.
Notes: In the above table, figures in parentheses indicate standard deviations, except for those following each category that indicate numbers of the samples. "Total" also includes the samples of business owner class not shown in the table. "Family income" and "Asset amount" are limited to householders only, their sample numbers being 64, 146, 137, 37, and 387 (total), respectively from above.

middle class is very open for intergenerational mobility. Based on these findings, although the South Korean old middle class had low entrance barriers and required only a moderate level of education, once entering that social class, people benefited from a relatively high level of rewards.

However, we should be careful that our discussion so far is based on the "mean values" of variables such as income and asset amount. Considering the substantially broad internal diversity of the South Korean old middle class, we should investigate whether all people entering that social class enjoy high income, or whether there are significant income disparities according to mobility experience and educational level.

Because so many in the South Korean old middle class entered that class through intragenerational mobility, we first need to study the influence of their social class at the time of their first occupation. Figure 6–15 shows the income and the asset amount of the old middle class (here we use only male samples and the same samples are used for the subsequent figures) by social class at the first occupation, along with the mean age and length of education.[29]

This table indicates disparities in individual income, household income, and assets amount within the old middle class, depending upon their social class at the time of their first occupation. In particular, we note that people who entered the

---
[29] Given that social class at first occupation is not much different by average age, differences in income, assets, and years of education due to differences in age can be considered negligible.

old middle class from the new middle class through intragenerational mobility have individual income and household income somewhat higher than those who already belonged to the old middle class at the time of first occupation. We may interpret this observation as follows: the occupational experience in the high-income new middle class helps to increase the initial capital, which in turn generates a large increase in income. The mean income of those who entered the old middle class from the new middle class is higher than that of those currently in the new middle class by over 100,000 won, as shown in figure 6–2. Therefore, on average, becoming self-employed from the new middle class may bring a certain level of increased income.

Those who entered from the working class, meanwhile, have a lower monthly income by several thousand to over 100,000 won than those from the old middle class or the new middle class at the time of first occupation, indicating that the different first occupation correlates with the economic position inside the old middle class. Nevertheless, the income they earn is significantly higher than that of the current working class. From these facts, we may conclude that intragenerational mobility into the old middle class by becoming independent is an important path to high economic status for members of the South Korean working class, who have limited opportunities for promotion inside organizations.

Intragenerational mobility from new to old middle class
As we pointed out, becoming self-employed increases income to a certain degree on average, for both from the new middle class and from the working class at the time of first occupation. Among employed workers in an organization, then, who would obtain the opportunity to become self-employed and enjoy higher income? Would social class origins, especially having a father who is also self-employed, have a strong effect on such intragenerational mobility? In this section, we examine the determining factors of intragenerational mobility from the new middle class to the old middle class and thereby provide a more detailed description of becoming self-employed in South Korea.

First, we analyze intragenerational mobility from the new middle class to the old middle class. Using samples of persons who belonged to the new middle class at the time of their first occupations, a logistic regression analysis (left side columns of figure 6–16) was conducted to examine who moved to the old middle class and who remained in the new middle class (or moved to social classes other than the old middle class). Model 1 includes age, years of education, and the dummy variable for whether the father also belongs to the old middle class or not as independent variables.

The analysis outcome of this model shows that the father in the old middle-class dummy variable has a positive significant effect. In other words, those in the new middle class at the time of first occupation who have a father in the old middle class easily move to the old middle class within the generation. Years of education indicates a significant negative effect. That is, among people in the new middle class at first occupation, those whose length of education is shorter are more likely to choose self-employment.

We consider that the effect of years of education is not caused by the conditions of the old middle class (to which one moves), but by the conditions of the new middle class (from which one moves). That is, as confirmed in chapter 5, because the possibility of internal promotion in a South Korean company is closely related to academic credentials, people engaged in white-collar jobs with a relatively low level of education face limited promotional opportunities and tend to leave organizations and seek possibilities for achieving higher status outside them. In this regard, although intragenerational mobility from the new middle class to the old middle class certainly increases income, it might be their "second-best choice."

A similar outcome is observed in Model 2, which adds company size variables to Model 1. Therefore, we should interpret the negative effect of the years of education on becoming self-employed not as a spurious correlation created by the company size of the first occupation, but as the aforementioned direct effect.[30]

Intragenerational mobility from working class to old middle class
Next, let us analyze intragenerational mobility from the working class to the old middle class. The results of Model 1 shown at the right side of figure 6–16 indicate that the age has a positive significant effect on mobility, while years of education and the old middle-class origin dummy variable do not have significant effects. Thus, the older you are, the more likely you are to become self-employed from the working class; but educational level and old middle-class origin do not have clear correlations with the tendency to become self-employed. The positive effect of age is that the longer the number of working years, the more the start-up capital and skills are accumulated that are required for self-employment. Unlike mobility from the new middle class, mobility from the working class is not affected by length of education. This is because the possibility for blue-collar workers of raising their occupational status within a companiy is extremely restricted, regardless of their educational level.

On the other hand, the variables for company size at the time of first occupation in Model 2 indicate significant positive effects. In other words, those who work for small to midium-size companies rather than large corporations are more likely

---

[30] It is a very interesting result that corporate size at the time of first occupation has no significant effect. In other words, the probability of large-corporation white-collar workers (who enjoy better working conditions) becoming self-employed is not that much different from that of white-collar workers at small/mid-sized-companies.

Chapter 6 Academic Achievement, Social Class Origin, and Social Mobility | 227

Figure 6–16. Logistic Regression Analysis of Intra-generational Mobility into Old Middle Class

	From new middle class (first occupation) into old middle class (current occupation)		From working class (first occupation) into old middle class (current occupation)	
	Model 1	Model 2	Model 1	Model 2
(Constant)	−.606	−.678	−2.532***	−3.253***
Age	.020	.021	.030**	.035**
Years of education	−.147*	−.154*	.051	.052
Father of old middle class	.806*	.833*	.455	.407
Company size at first occupation (ref. Large company [300+ employees])				
Small company (–19 employees)		.090		.787**
Medium-size company (20–299 employees)		.350		.631*
χ^2	15.0	16.2	9.5	19.2
Cox & Snell R^2	0.038	0.041	0.021	0.042
N	391	391	448	448

Source: Based on 1990 Equity Survey data.
Notes: *$p < .05$, **$p < .01$, ***$p < .001$

to choose self-employment. As Hiroshi Ishida, who studies the factors for entering into the urban self-employment sector in Japan, points out, this phenomenon is caused by a combination of the negative factor of working conditions in small to mid-sized companies are unfavorable and a positive factor of working for small to midium-sized companies nurture various skills required for self-employment (Ishida 2004: 379).

Intragenerational mobility to old middle class and education
We have studied the factors behind intragenerational mobility from the new middle class and the working class into the old middle class, which constitutes a large portion of the mobility into the old middle class in South Korea. In this study, we observe no tendency for people with a high level of education to become self-employed. Rather, among employees in the white-collar sector, where importance is attached to academic credentials, those with lower educational levels tend to choose self-employment.[31]

From this observation, we conclude that independence as a member of the urban

---
[31] We suspect that factors other than length of education and social class origin, such as strong entrepreneurial spirit and human networks required for self-employment, greatly contribute to intragenerational mobility into the old middle class.

self-employed certainly functions as an alternative path to achieving status that does not require a high level of education. In particular, for the working class, which has very limited opportunities for internal promotion, self-employment is an attractive path to achieving status as it does not require a high level of education and may also bring much higher average income than could be earned as a company employee. The same can be said of the farmer class. The reason why the old middle class does not decrease, or rather expands in South Korea, is due to the presence of people who newly move to the class in considerable numbers, motivated by the above reasons.

Mobility to the Old Middle Class and Change in Socioeconomic Status
Determining factors of income in the old middle class
Even though such variables as educational level and social class origin do not have a significant effect on mobility into the old middle class, we cannot deny the possibility that those variables may have a considerable effect on business after entering self-employment by way of different start-up capital and other conditions. In other words, the determining factors behind success in this class may be different from those behind the mobility into the class. In order to investigate this issue, we carried out an OLS regression analysis of (logged) income of those in the old middle class, as shown in figure 6–17.

The results from Model 1 indicate significant effects of age, age squared, and dummy variables for educational levels except the middle school dummy variable.[32] In other words, among the urban self-employed there is a significant difference in income according to academic credentials. For example, all other conditions being equal, college graduates earn more than high school graduates by almost 1.3 times. Based on the results from Model 2', which adds dummy variables for father's social class to Model 1, there is no significant influence of father's social class on income. When the age and educational level variables are controlled, social class origin does not generate a clear difference in income.

Although the income of those in the old middle class is affected by educational level, the effects of these academic credential dummy variables on the income of the self-employed are considerably weaker than those on the income of employees. Comparing figure 6–17 with figure 6–6, the latter targeting only employees, we find that the estimated coefficient of each academic credential dummy variable for the old middle class is generally smaller than that for employees. Namely, the disparity in income according to academic credentials among the self-employed is

---
[32] We consider that the positive effect of age on income is probably because more skill and capital are accumulated the older a person gets and the longer the number of years working. However, the effect can hardly be considered strong because the age variable is not significant in the following Model 2'.

Chapter 6 Academic Achievement, Social Class Origin, and Social Mobility | 229

Figure 6–17. Regression Analysis of Old Middle Class Income

	Model 1	Model 2'
(Constant)	12.758***	12.949***
Age	.039*	.032
Age squared (×100)	−.047*	−.040
Education (ref. high school)		
Uneducated/elementary school	−.290**	−.273**
Middle school	−.106	−.106
Junior college	.259*	.218
Four-year college or higher	.275**	.247**
Father's social class (ref. small/poor/tenant farmer class)		
Business owner class		.269
New middle class		.146
Old middle class		−.083
Working class		−.263
Rich/middle farmer class		.023
R^2	.088	.106
N	409	388

Source: Based on 1990 Equity Survey data.
Notes: *$p < .05$, **$p < .01$, ***$p < .001$

smaller than that among employees, and in this regard, our hypothetical interpretation proposed at the beginning of this section—"while in the case of employees academic credentials do have a significant effect upon acquisition of socioeconomic status, the effect is likely much smaller for those who are self-employed, whose labor is directly invested in economic activity without the medium of the labor market"—is reasonable.[33] The determination coefficient of this model is

---

[33] That one's education level affects the income in self-employment is likely due partly to the benefits of education in improving skills conducive to better management. At the same time, different educational levels cause differences in wages and retirement allowances, and that likely causes differences in start-up capital.

In the franchise shops and restaurants system, which is an increasingly popular way to become self-employed, we see cases in which the franchise headquarters would examine an applicant's academic credentials as one of the criteria for judging whether to accept applications. The author conducted an interview with a person of a major convenience store chain who was in charge of examining franchise applicants. According to him, in screening applications, the items he checks, along with the health of the applicant and the spouse and the like, include academic credentials. The fact that the screening based partly on academic credentials is conducted even in the urban self-employment sector is an institutional factor of the correlation between academic credentials and income level in this sector.

considerably small, indicating that in the urban self-employment sector, economic status is affected by various conditions other than age and academic credentials.

From the above results, we may infer that one's educational achievement contributes little to either entry into the self-employment sector or success in the sector, unlike in the case of company employees.[34] At least in terms of economic rewards, intragenerational mobility into the old middle class may be a meaningful alternative path to achieving socioeconomic status that does not necessarily require a high level of education.

Subjective evaluation of social status of old middle class
Although focus on economic rewards alone may lead to affirmative interpretation of the intragenerational mobility into the old middle class, if we also consider subjective evaluations of the social status of self-employment, such an interpretation is rather optimistic.

In chapter 2, we mentioned that the 1990 Equity Survey includes a question that asks respondent's subjective status identification, or status consciousness, on a scale of seven. Responses to this question may be considered as survey respondents' evaluation of their status in the society. Figure 6–18 shows the distribution of subjective status identification from each of the four classes (excluding the business owner class, which has a small sample size). This figure indicates that the status identification of the new middle class is considerably high among the four classes; nearly 50 percent of those in the new middle class answer that their status is of the middle category (4). If we consider the "middle class" is the middle category plus both adjacent categories (3 and 5), nearly 90 percent of the new middle class think of themselves as belonging to the middle class. The old middle class's status identification is somewhat lower. The category that receives the highest response rate is the category (3), one category rank lower than the middle, and only 75 percent consider themselves to belong to the middle class (3 to 5). Of course, this percentage is higher than the 56 percent of the working class and the 52 percent of the farmer class. However, we may conclude that the old middle class has a somewhat lower status identification compared with the new middle class.

Is this tendency observed even if other variables that affect the status identification are controlled? Figure 6–19 shows the results of regression of status identification. The model includes the logarithmic value of one's income and the dummy variable of each social class as independent variables. This table shows the posi-

---

[34] However, the self-employment sector in South Korea shows an extremely high rate for leaving the sector, similar to cases of newly entering it. We should carefully examine the bias in the results because the sample does not include newcomers to the sector who have already left without earning sufficient income there.

Chapter 6   Academic Achievement, Social Class Origin, and Social Mobility | 231

Figure 6–18.   Subjective Status Identification by Social Class

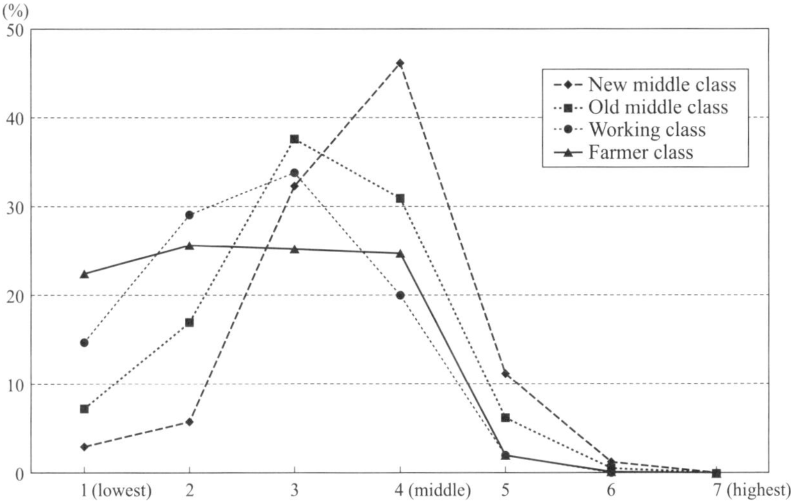

(%)

- New middle class
- Old middle class
- Working class
- Farmer class

x-axis: 1 (lowest), 2, 3, 4 (middle), 5, 6, 7 (highest)

Source: Based on 1990 Equity Survey data.

Figure 6–19.   Regression Analysis of Subjective Status Identification

(Constant)	−5.441***
Individual income (logged)	0.672***
Social class (ref. new middle class)	
Business owner class	−0.163
Old middle class	−0.514***
Working class	−0.429***
Farmer class	−0.722***
R^2	.257
N	1,534

Source: Based on 1990 Equity Survey data.
Notes: *$p < .05$, **$p < .01$, ***$p < .001$

tive significant effect of individual income, confirming that subjective status identification is greatly determined by one's income. Interestingly enough, the dummy variables of all the classes, including the old middle class, have negative significant effects. Status identification of those in the old middle class is significantly lower than those in the new middle class even when the two are similar in individual incomes.[35] Given that the self-deprecation of the old middle class is comparable to that of people belonging to the working class, indicated by the similar magnitude of negative coefficients of both classes, we conclude that the tendency may be attributed to the disparity in prestige between white-collar and non-white-collar occupations, a gap that has hardly changed in spite of rapid industrialization.

Self-evaluation of success by people who experienced intragenerational mobility into the old middle class also indicates that mobility into the old middle class does not necessarily mean the ideal opportunity for status achievement. The 1990 Equity Survey includes the question "What do you think is the degree of your socioeconomic success?" to be answered on a scale of five from "very successful" (5 points) to "very unsuccessful" (1 point). When we compared the mean scores of this subjective evaluation for those who experienced mobility into the old middle class from the new middle class and the working class, and those who did not experience mobility, we obtain the following outcome: the mean score is 2.97 for non-mobility in the new middle class (i.e., those who are in the new middle class at the time of first occupations as well as their current occupations), whereas it is 2.77 (lower by 0.2), for those who were in the new middle class for their first occupation but are currently in the old middle class. A t-test indicates that the difference is significant at the 1 percent level. That is, those who moved to the old middle class from the new middle class are more likely to evaluate their socioeconomic achievement as less successful than those who remain in the new middle class.

By contrast, the mean score of people who went from the working class to the old middle class is 2.82, which is higher than the 2.66 of those who remain in the working class. A significant difference is also found at the 1 percent level. People who moved from the working class are more likely to affirmatively evaluate their own current socioeconomic status than those who did not.

These results suggest that the barriers to the urban self-employment sector are low in South Korea. Once entering to this sector, one may earn a higher income on average regardless of educational level and social class origin. However, self-employment in South Korea is an ambiguous path to socioeconomic status. For the working class, which has limited promotional opportunities in corporations, becoming self-employed is certainly an attractive path to higher status and income. In terms of economic conditions alone, the same can be said for the new middle class. However, if we take into consideration subjective status identification and self-evaluation of success, we observe that entering into the self-employment sector is not a sufficiently alternative path to socioeconomic status to replace

---

[35] Incidentally, another model that includes length of education in addition to individual income and social class also indicates the significant negative effect of the old middle-class dummy variable at the 0.1% level.

the "orthodox" path taken by white-collar workers through educational credentials.

South Korean people's subjective status identification or their self-evaluations of socioeconomic success are influenced, we may conclude, not only by economic conditions, but also by the social condition of occupational prestige. In South Korean society, where there are large gaps in prestige among occupations, intragenerational mobility into the old middle class from the new middle class could reduce prestige significantly, although it increases income. Intragenerational mobility into the old middle class may be a "second best choice" for South Koreans.[36]

Conclusion

This chapter presents a comprehensive analysis of the relationships between social class origin and educational level, and between social class origin and socioeconomic status achievement, to see if South Koreans' widespread image of their country as a meritocratic society—"anyone with a high level of education may achieve high socioeconomic status equally"—correctly reflects the reality of the society. The findings of the analysis may be summarized as follows.

First, regarding the relationship between social class origin and socioeconomic status, we verified the direct effect of the former on the latter without being mediated by educational achievement is quite small. If we control for educational level, the effect of social class origin on individual income and occupational status is relatively small, and this is even more the case with employees, especially employees with a college degree. From these observations, we conclude that anyone with a high level of education may obtain high socioeconomic status regardless of social class origin in South Korean society.

However, our analysis of this chapter has revealed that there is a large gap among the original social classes in terms of level of education achieved, which significantly influences the social status achieved, and that the gap does not show a clear downward tendency. Certainly, due to overall increase in income level and the egalitarian educational policy, the overall effect of the social class origin on length of education and completion of secondary education has been decreasing as the generations get younger. This result agrees with the theories of industrial society,

---

[36] Numazaki points out that there is an intense occupational preference for independent business in Taiwan: "Even if you are in a position of section chief or departmental chief in a large corporation, or even if your remuneration is very high, being hired by others is not a desirable situation" (Numazaki 1996: 298). Although it is emphasized that South Korea and Taiwan share much in common as East Asian countries newly industrialized in the second half of the twentieth century, as for the preference for employment opportunity, there is a vast difference between these countries.

and furthermore, it may lead us to predict that the trend toward equal educational opportunities will expand opportunities for intergenerational exchange mobility.

The reality is different from the optimistic prediction described above, however. While it is true that the effect of the social class origin on the simple length of education decreases the younger the generation; if we focus on the opportunity to advance to a four-year college, which is becoming the "truly meaningful difference in educational achievement" when new college graduates find jobs, the effect of social class origin on this stage of educational achievement never shows a clear tendency of decrease. Furthermore, the cause of the effect of social class origin on educational achievement is changing from economic factors, such as the capacity to pay educational expenses, to non-economic factors that are harder to measure and capture.

Reflecting this circumstance, the openness of intergenerational mobility has not changed much even though educational opportunities have expanded and equalized. Particularly, the new middle class, which is at quite an advantageous position in terms of income and prestige, becomes more exclusive, and mobility into this class becomes harder.

Needless to say, South Korea has had numerous opportunities for social mobility. In this regard, the social perception that "achieving social status through education is easy" is not that wrong. However, most of the opportunities have been brought about by the changes in the social stratification structure itself due to change in the industrial structure. Opportunities for mobility due to equal opportunity for status achievement are not many. Overall, the openness of the South Korean social class structure is not at all high compared with other Asian societies.

For this reason, we cannot deny the possibility that, as changes in the social class structure slow down, the total chances of mobility substantially decrease and the social class structure becomes more rigid. The South Korean educational system may contribute to the rigidity of the social class structure through the persistent effect of social class origin on educational achievement.

Lastly, we discussed the possibility of achieving social status without a high level of education by studying the socioeconomic status of the old middle class and the intragenerational mobility into this class. Entering the self-employment sector in South Korea is easy, and even though a high level of education is not required to enter this sector, entrants may enjoy a relatively high income on average. Particularly for the working class, which has limited promotional opportunities, entry into the self-employment sector is a very important path to higher social status. However, with the large gap in prestige between white-collar jobs and non-white-collar jobs, people of the old middle class have a much lower subjective status identification compared with the new middle class. This is also the case with the subjective evaluation of "degree of success" for those who moved into the old middle class. Thus, considering both economic and social conditions, there are many cases where becoming self-employed is the second-best means of achieving social status overall. Based on these observations, you understand that "acquisition of a higher academic credential" is almost the exclusive way to higher social status in South Korean society.

CHAPTER 7

Images and Impact of the Academic Credential Society

This chapter summarizes the responses of this study to the questions raised in the introduction to this book regarding the characteristics of South Korean aspirations for educational achievement in relation to the socioeconomic benefits of academic credentials. It examines how people's expectation and anticipation of status achievement through education are intertwined with issues of distribution and its fairness, and how those issues define the education system in South Korea.

I. REVIEW OF IMAGES OF THE ACADEMIC CREDENTIAL SOCIETY

The introduction discussed the special aspiration for educational achievement that may be considered a phenomenon distinctive to South Korean society and how it is driven by the expectation of upward social mobility and status achievement. In order to better understand such aspirations in relation to the actual social benefits of academic credentials, we need to review the following three questions corresponding to "intensity," "persistence," and "universality" of aspirations for educational achievement. The answers presented in the chapters above may be summarized as follows.

Three Questions
Question 1
"Are the socioeconomic benefits of attaining academic credentials so great that they can explain the *intensity* of the popular aspiration for education in South Korea? If that is true, why?"

First, we considered monetary benefits as part of the socioeconomic benefits of academic credentials. The outcome of the wage analysis performed in chapter 4 indicated that, until the 1970s when college graduates were small in number, the increase of wage levels as a result of advancing to college was fairly high. However, after the expansion of higher education in the mid-1980s, the increase rapidly declined. This tendency diminished the private rate of return on a college degree to only a few percent, rather low compared with other countries in the world. Furthermore, the private rate of return on a college degree in South Korea was not particularly higher than the rate of return on an investment in other sectors. Thus, it is difficult to explain the distinctly intense desire for educational achievement in South Korea only by looking at the monetary benefits.

Advancement of occupational status is another important benefit of academic credentials. The discussion in chapter 5 found that the degree to which academic credentials determines occupational status is quite high due to personnel management practices emphasizing academic credentials in South Korean companies.

Moreover, there are very pronounced disparities in prestige among occupations, especially between white-collar and non-white-collar jobs, and this drives people's aspirations to enhance their occupational status in South Korea. Under such circumstances, neither a tendency to prefer the occupations of their parents, nor the horizontal differentiation of preferred occupations corresponding to differences in occupational value orientation were observed. Consequently, most students prefer white-collar jobs of high occupational status, provided they can achieve the high level of education required to obtain them.

Given these occupational opportunity preferences, we conclude that South Koreans have become strongly conscious of the effect of academic credentials on achieving occupational status. Because of the tendency of corporate personnel management practices to rely on academic credentials in screening applicants, in order to obtain the white-collar jobs that hold much preferred occupational status, there is no other way but to achieve a high level of education. If we understand the "effect of academic credentials" as discussed above considering an inherent aspect of society, the effect of college graduation is significantly large in South Korea.

The conclusions of our analyses are that the essence of South Korean aspirations for high occupational status lay in acquisition of the social prestige associated with an occupation. Social prestige is a value that continues to be reproduced in a society only when its members internalize the system of prestige and evaluate one another according to it. Through fieldwork on the South Korean urban middle class, Lett showed how South Koreans struggled to attain higher social status in various realms of their lives such as business, consumption, education, and marriage. According to her, people's efforts were rooted in the drive to show their high social status to others and to obtain recognition of it (Lett 1998). Drawing on her research results, we may conclude that the South Korean people's aspiration for high occupational status is essentially to receive the high appraisal of others—at least to avoid discriminative treatment from others.

People's sensitivity to "the evaluations of others" can be considered a notable characteristic of South Korean society. The basic premise of this book is that South Korean enthusiasm for educational achievement is related to the economic rewards and occupational status obtained through academic credentials. However, given the nature of Korean attitudes, we cannot exclude the possibility that their aspirations are driven by the high evaluation per se that advanced education elicits from others in a society where learning is highly valued due to historical background. If that is true, the intense competition for educational advancement in South Korea may continue indefinitely as long as people are able to bear the costs.

Question 2
"Have the socioeconomic benefits of academic credentials remained high in South Korea despite the rapid expansion of education?"

As discussed in chapter 1, predictions of how the expansion of educational opportunities changed the monetary rewards obtained by receiving a certain level of education differ considerably from one another depending upon the theoretical standpoint on which they rely. According to orthodox neo-classical economics, expansion of educational opportunities reduces the monetary rewards obtained, and consequently, people's demand for ever-higher levels of education is predicted to eventually diminish. Thurow's job-competition model, diverging from such conclusions, predicts that expansion of education could even *increase* monetary rewards and demand for higher levels of education. In addition, even when institutional conditions strongly affect the wage structure, it is likely that educational expansion does not have a clear influence on monetary rewards and demand for education.

According to the outcome of the analysis in chapter 4, the rapid increase of college graduates greatly reduced the wage levels of college graduates in relative terms. This conclusion is very close to that of neo-classical economics, and the South Korean labor market very flexibly reacted—through the wage-adjustment mechanism—to changes in the academic configuration of the labor supplied to the market. Lowered wages could reduce the economic incentives for going to college, and it was predicted that such a trend would reduce the demand for advancement to college.

However, in promoting occupational status, the effect of academic credentials has had a different consequence. In chapter 5, we revealed that the personnel management practices heavily relying on academic credentials continued to keep the connection between academic credentials and occupation quite strong, and the rapid increase of college graduates in fact raised the bar for academic-credential requirements for obtaining jobs. As new college graduates increased in number, they began to take away the opportunities for white-collar jobs that had been available to high school graduates. Thus, the effect of a college degree in increasing occupational status, especially in increasing the probability of securing a white-collar job in a large corporation, did not necessarily decrease, but rather even relatively increased. Unlike wages, the prestige ranking and disparities among occupations are quite stable and they were not significantly altered by changes in the occupational structure. Under these circumstances, people's demand for advancement to college to acquire higher occupational status did not decrease at all.

Depending on which of the above two effects of academic credentials—income increase or raising of occupational status—is given more importance, the feedback effect of rapid expansion of higher education on demand for advancement to college will be totally different. As pointed out earlier, in South Korean society people are keenly aware of the social prestige of individual occupations. In fact, between the above two objectives of advancing to college, pursuit of higher occupational status is likely considered more important than income increase. Considering the purpose of advancing to college in South Korea discussed above, the academic-credential effect continued to function despite the rapid increase in the supply of college graduates. Naturally, people's enthusiasm for educational achievement also shows a similar trend.

People's demand for advancement to college may not decrease as long as there is a strong link between academic credentials and occupational opportunity. The link prevails, as shown by the analysis in this book, because employers and corporate personnel managers regard academic credentials as proxy indicators of job applicants' general and potential ability. The academic credential information utilized in the process of hiring is meaningful not in an absolute sense but relative to the applicant pool. In other words, whether one's academic credential is "better" than those of other applicants, even slightly, is important.

We should not forget that the utilization of academic credentials in hiring is made possible because of people's confidence in the effectiveness of education and the selection system in gauging students' abilities. The Korean government's aggressive reforms and control of the selection system since the 1960s played an important role in that regard. As confirmed in chapter 3, since the Park Chung-Hee regime, the South Korean selection system has been characterized as being "college-entrance-centered, government-controlled, and highly unified," which prompted more students to participate in the college entrance examination competition and thereby increased the reliability of academic credentials—the result of the selection system—as proxy indicators of individual intellectual abilities.

Although theoretical studies have seldom examined this issue, the empirical analyses in this book suggest that the following requirements must be fulfilled in order for job seekers' academic credentials to be used as indicators of their ability at the time of hiring as the screening theory assumes. First, the selection system has to have improved enough to be able to screen students' intellectual abilities, as discussed above. Second, the academic credential information resulting from the selection has to be easily accessible and comparable among different applicants. In South Korea, the government's aggressive reforms of the entrance examination system unintentionally fulfilled these requirements and thereby increased the effectiveness of academic credentials.

Question 3
"In South Korea, can anyone, regardless of their social class origin, obtain high socioeconomic status once having acquired advanced academic credentials? Are there not considerable disparities in educational opportunities from one social class to another, and is it a society where intergenerational mobility is easy?"

According to the analysis in chapter 6, people who are similar to each other in academic credentials will find that their social class origin have only small effects on the social class and income they achieve. Particularly, the effects are negligible among employees with higher education. These results certainly suggest a "yes" answer to the question above: in South Korea, anyone, regardless of their social-class origin, can obtain high socioeconomic status once having acquired advanced academic credentials.

We must note, however, that there are still large disparities in the level of educational achievement that critically affects socioeconomic status according to social class origin. As the times progress, the simple disparities in years of education gradually decrease, and equalization of educational opportunity seems to progress. However, the effect of social class origins on whether one could advance to four-year colleges or not, which became the "truly meaningful difference in educational achievement" due to the high school leveling policy, did not decrease even for the younger generations who supposedly received various benefits from the government's egalitarian educational policies.

Needless to say, with the dramatic changes that took place in the industrial structure of South Korea since the 1960s, there were many opportunities for social mobility. However, except for the opportunities for mobility inevitably resulting from structural changes, intergenerational pure mobility (exchange mobility) across the social classes afforded by equal opportunities to achieve socioeconomic status was not that plentiful when compared with other Asian countries. Exchange mobility did not show a clear upward tendency. Rather mobility into the new middle class became more difficult. Therefore, if the speed of structural change slowed, it was likely that the social structure might quickly become rigid.

High Educational Aspirations in Comparative Perspective
So far we have discussed how the close connection between academic credentials and socioeconomic status and rewards affects people's aspirations for educational achievement. When we reconsider the results of the discussion in this book from a comparative point of view, however, there are several other characteristics of South Korean society that serve as factors that heighten people's aspirations for education across all social classes.

First of all, South Korea achieved industrialization rapidly in a matter of several decades and its history of social stratification based on industrialization is short. Its people are highly homogenous in terms of culture and preferences. As substantial parts of the new middle class, the old middle class, and the working class consist of members who moved from other social classes, the "class culture"—with certain aspects of counter culture in some cases—which we see generally in Western society, has not yet clearly formed. Willis vividly describes the British working-class culture and the process by which children of the working class who accepted the anti-school student culture choose manual labor jobs of their own free will (Willis 1977). In modern South Korean society, where there was no rigid class culture, people were unlikely to choose jobs against the tide based on the working-class culture. Thus, as shown in chapter 5, many students, regardless of their social class origin, want to find white-collar jobs and achieve the high level of education required for white-collar jobs.

However, South Korea is not the only country that, even though full-scale industrialization progressed, has not formed a clear class culture that might lead to the reproduction of the social class structure. In East Asia, Japan and Taiwan exhibit similar circumstances.

Comparison with Japan brings out the characteristics of South Korea more clearly. As the analysis of the occupational preferences of high school students showed in chapter 5, while parents' occupations do not directly influence the occupational preferences of South Korean high school students, Japanese high school students tend to prefer the same occupations as their parents, reflecting a more positive evaluation in Japan of succeeding to the family business than in South Korea. The tendency to prefer the same occupations as their parents may consequently contribute to the reproduction of the social class structure in Japan, but because of that tendency Japan does not have a strong preference for white-collar jobs across the social classes as is the case in South Korea.

More importantly, perceptions of social inequality in the two countries are different. Although the situation has been rapidly changing since the 2000s, in Japan there has not been a strong perception of social inequality, as since its rapid economic growth period around the 1960s most people think of themselves as belonging to the "middle class."[1] Japanese society displays relatively high regard for manual skills and occupational preferences are diverse, so Japanese have not been very conscious of the disparities in prestige among occupations. By contrast, in South Korea the social classes and the inequality among them have been far more visible, reflecting the significantly different consumption styles due to the income gap. The fact that only some members of the rich benefitted from the government-led economic development through their connections with the government also raised Korean's awareness about the unfair distribution of social resources. The keen awareness of social inequality created in this way appears to have heightened people's impulse to "overcome" it by climbing the social ladder. Japanese people's interest in and awareness of their position in the social status hierarchy, by contrast, has been rather weak—at least so far—and there are diverse paths available to status achievement in Japan, which may explain why the extremely intense desire for upward mobility through education has not emerged in Japan.

Although we did not make a detailed comparison of Taiwan and South Korea in this book, the critical difference may be seen in how self-employment is recognized as an attractive career path. In Taiwan, the presence of large corporations in the economy is relatively weak and the business environment is favorable to small and medium-sized enterprises. Under these circumstances, people attempt to achieve higher status by becoming business owners (*laoban*) even if the scale of the business is small (Numazaki 1996). That being the case, people's aspiration for academic credentials as a requirement of employment within an organization is not as strong as in South Korea. Compared with Taiwan, self-employment is not as attractive a career path to status achievement in South Korea, and consequently acquiring higher academic credentials is a fairly exclusive path to higher status.

II. PERCEPTIONS OF ACADEMIC MERITOCRACY AND THE ISSUE OF DISTRIBUTION

As discussed in this book, South Korean's perception of their society as being based on academic meritocracy does not correctly reflect the reality of the society. Nevertheless, in South Korean society, the optimistic perception of "upward social mobility through education" prevailed and sustained people's aspirations for higher education—at least until 1990s. What is the reason for this optimism?

---

[1] For example, Kariya points out that in Japan, the viewpoint of social inequality in discussing education issues quickly declined after the rapid economic growth period (Kariya 1995: 54–56).

Perspective on the Inequality of Educational Opportunity

The expansion of education in South Korea appears to have contributed to that optimistic image of society and its reproduction. As observed in chapter 3, the expansion that took place after the Liberation was explosive. The post-Liberation generations received higher levels of education than their parents' generation ever imagined. Kaneko points out that the "quantitative expansion of educational opportunity is perceived as the popularization of education, which often is considered the same thing as equal opportunity" (Kaneko 1987: 38). The rapidity with which the expansion was achieved in South Korea can be presumed to be the critical factor behind people's optimism regarding the distribution of educational opportunity. Similarly, the fact that industrial structural change created many opportunities for intergenerational mobility likely helped impress people with the ease of social mobility.

In addition, we need to note the considerable distance in South Korean society between the actual mechanisms that generate inequality of educational opportunity and the perspective that turns that inequality into a social issue. Our analytical results suggest that, among the various disparities originating in family background, the "less visible" gap in non-economic conditions (such as cultural capital and parent's attitudes toward children's education) comes to exert greater effect on children's educational achievement than the more visible disparities in economic conditions (such as ability to pay educational expenses).

As the cases when students had to give up advancing to a higher level of education for financial reasons gradually decreased thanks to rapid economic growth, what newly emerged as educational inequality was the opportunity gap in receiving after-school lessons due to the financial situation of a student's family. Despite the absence of any empirical research on the extent to which after-school lessons really influenced students' academic performance and educational achievement, the traditional perspective, which focuses on the disparity in the ability to pay educational expenses, was applied in the critique of educational inequality. Meanwhile, the inequities in education stemming from non-economic factors, such as cultural capital and parental attitudes, did not receive due attention.[2]

Fishkin points out the difficulty in simultaneously fulfilling the following three conditions: "the principle of merit: there should be widespread procedural fairness in the evaluation of qualifications for positions" (Fishkin 1983: 22), "equality of life chances: the prospects of children for eventual positions in society should not vary in any systematic and significant manner with their arbitrary native characteristics" (Fishkin 1983: 32), and "Autonomy of the family: consensual relations

---

[2] A similar tendency was observed in Japan (Kariya 1995: 149), but it was even more noticeable in South Korea.

within a given family governing the development of its children should not be coercively interfered with except to ensure for the children the essential prerequisites for adult participation in the society" (Fishkin 1983: 35–36). These conditions become a trilemma on the assumption that the difference in performance (merit) is inevitably generated through the transmission of family's cultural capital to children as long as there is no intervention in the family autonomy and raising children is left as a family matter (Kariya 1995). However, these mechanisms generating disparities in performance received inadequate recognition in South Korean society; they were seen only in terms of the disparity in educational opportunities due to differences in the economic capacity to bear the cost.

Government Policy and "Equal Opportunity of Education"
Here, let us focus on the government stance. As long as the South Korean government, because of the confrontation with the communist regime in North Korea, needed to sustain the liberal capitalist system and develop its economy, it could not possibly deny the performance-based principle of distribution. Implementing drastic reforms to the extent of undermining family autonomy against deeply rooted Confucian norms would also have been difficult. Nevertheless, the South Korean government must have wanted to avoid Fishkin's trilemma and prevent unequal educational opportunity from becoming a serious social issue.

As explained in the pages of this book, the South Korean government's educational reforms often reflected its commitment to solving the distribution issue in society by amending the method for distribution of educational opportunity. The repeatedly implemented measures for equalization of secondary education were based on the government's determination to achieve equal opportunity for higher status and rewards by improving the educational and selection systems. At the same time, these measures represented the government's attempts to utilize the school education system to solve the issue of unequal distribution without doing anything in other fields. However, the perception that differences in student performance stem from the educational attitudes or cultural capital of each family could directly undermine the effectiveness of the government's efforts to solve the inequality issue through educational reforms.

Under these circumstances, it was important, from the government's point of view, that people *not* widely recognize the effect of non-economic conditions of the educational achievement of children. This is because the educational inequalities stemming from non-economic factors are extremely difficult to resolve, and if they were to become serious social issues, the government's attempt to solve the distribution issue through education would suffer, triggering fundamental skepticism among the people about the distribution system. For this reason, the South Korean government presumably had no intention of officially admitting the effect of non-economic conditions on children's educational achievement or of attempting to resolve the matter. Rather, we may even suspect that the government deliberately drew people's attention to the "new" dimension of traditional inequality—the unequal educational opportunities due to the economic factors, such as the inequality of after-school lessons—thereby concealing the difficult-to-solve educational inequality.

If we consider the issue this way, we can understand that the strong adherence of the South Korean government to the equalization of educational opportunity may have been motivated in a similar manner: by implementing drastic education policies, the government diverted people's attention, focusing it on equal educational opportunity in the direction of formal equalization, namely the provision of the same education to all, and successfully trivialized the other issues. The elimination of the selection process and thorough formal equalization at the secondary education stage were seen in a positive light by many parents who feared that their children might fall behind in the college entrance competition. With these radical attempts at the formal equalization of educational opportunity, the unique view emerged in South Korea that regarded "providing exactly the same education to all" represented the equalization of educational opportunity. As this view spread, it became difficult to criticize inequality at the "equalized" secondary education stage (such as the disparities in academic performance stemming from the differences in the non-economic conditions of students' families) inasmuch as education of the same quality was supposedly provided to all. The aggressive attempt at formal equalization in secondary education may be considered partly responsible for the optimistic perception of equal distribution of educational opportunity in South Korea.

From the standpoint of the South Korean government, the image of the "academic credential society" has been quite convenient. That image played a part in diverting people's attention from the structural factors of inequality by attributing it to individual circumstances (Bowles and Gintis 1976; Kariya 1995). As a typical example, people with low income in urban areas of South Korea tended to explain their poverty as a consequence of individual circumstances such as "lack of education" (Bae Sook-Hee 1991). The image of the academic credential society shared in South Korea does have the ideological aspect of justifying inequality. This may be one reason the government has sought to sustain that image through aggressive educational reforms.

However, it is unlikely that such an image can be maintained indefinitely. The era of rapid industrialization ended and the speed of change in the South Korean industrial structure has gradually been slowing. In addition, the expansion of educational opportunity has leveled off. The effect of quantitative expansion of opportunity in sustaining the image of the equal opportunity of education has also gradually been fading. In fact, optimistic perceptions of equal distribution of educational opportunity and of status achievement through education have been losing traction. South Korean society may be facing the necessity to reconsider how to solve the distribution issue at its very root.

III. Diagnosis of the Education System in South Korea

The South Korean education system has many serious problems. With the gradual removal of the ban on after-school lessons, middle and high school education has been further neglected. In recent years, in order to avoid the problematic educational environment and the intensely competitive college entrance examination in their own country, many students even have begun choosing to study abroad.[3] The South Korean public education system might be "hollowing out." Why does the system have such serious problems?

Trust in Selection through the Scholastic Achievement Examination
This book revealed that South Koreans recognize the distribution of status and rewards based on academic credentials as effective and reasonable. The firm confidence in scholastic achievement examinations as a means for selection—a confidence that was based on the traditional higher civil-service examination system—has contributed greatly to the popular acceptance of academic-credential-based distribution.

In fact, written examinations to measure scholastic achievement are frequently used in the process of selection. Although many criticisms have been voiced about the difficulty of the College Scholastic Ability Test (CSAT) conducted by the government and its capacity to measure academic ability, for example, the criticism generally is not directed at the concept of selection based on written examinations; the concept itself seems to be widely accepted.

Scholastic achievement examinations have enjoyed full confidence in South Korea because they are believed to be an objective and fair selection method. After the Liberation, South Korea frequently witnessed incidents in which persons in power attempted to bestow privileged positions on their own children, each

---

[3] Because the South Korean government has had strict control over the education system, there has been no way out of the "college-entrance-centered" system, in which no differentiation among students is made at the elementary and secondary education levels but those wishing to advance to college must compete in rigorous entrance examinations. This is significantly different from Japan where private schools are authorized to have their own admission systems. Due to the absence of any alternatives, parents who hope to give better education to their children to have an advantage in the severe college entrance examinations or to avoid the severe competition entirely, have no choice but seek educational opportunities abroad.

time drawing intense ire from the public. Under such circumstances, the selection method using scholastic achievement examinations has been trusted as an objective and fair means to prevent wrongdoing by the privileged.[4]

The strong confidence in selection through scholastic achievement examinations, as well as the prevalence of the view that educational level is determined by effort rather than economic capacity to bear the cost, has contributed significantly to legitimation of distribution based on academic credentials. As a result, in the distribution of status and rewards, academic credentials have further increased in importance.

The Function of Selection
It would be easy to attribute the causes of the serious problems of the South Korean education system to personal traits including people's excessive enthusiasm for education. However, the results of this study indicate that what we really need to focus on is the fact that the South Korean education system is excessively burdened by its function as the tool of selection for society.

Education systems perform two major social functions: socialization—transmitting knowledge, technology, and values necessary for citizens to lead life in society, and selection and social placement—allocating members of society to various social positions according to the results of selection. The South Korean education system is far more heavily burdened by the function of selection and social placement, and society places high expectations on it to carry out that function appropriately and fairly. Any attempt at educational reform, if it does not conform to the requirements of that function, tends to fail.

In fact, the school education system in South Korea plays a greater role in students' career diversification than it does in Japan. In Japan, occupational preferences are diversified by various factors other than academic performance, such as differences in occupational value orientation and a tendency to prefer parents' occupations. In South Korea, by contrast, everyone initially aims for what society considers "high status"; only later do preferred occupations diversify according to academic performance as young people go through the selection processes of school education. Needless to say, the diversification of preferred occupations generated in this manner brings about the diversification of the actual occupations in which graduates are engaged. Thus, the South Korean education system assumes a much greater role in selection and social placement than does its counterpart in Japan.

---

[4] On the other hand, the public demand for objective selection is so strong that multiple-choice tests, with which correct answers can be more objectively scored, are often preferred to subjective essay type examinations where the grader's subjective opinion is likely to reflect the score. In this way, the function imposed on the South Korean selection system strongly determines the actual conditions of selection.

Role of the Government

As Ronald Dore pointed out, the later industrialization starts, the more strongly academic credentials determine social status and the more school education becomes focused on the preparation for the entrance examinations (Dore 1976). His explanation regarding the "diploma disease" generally applies to the South Korean case. The various characteristics of the South Korean education system may be attributed to the late development of the country.

However, the case of South Korea, where the "diploma disease" is more advanced than other late-developing countries, cannot be explained only by the late-development effect. Other factors include the particular role that the government has played in education as well as the unique fabric of social conditions.

Dore explains how a society burdens the educational system with the functions of selection, primarily through economic and social factors, while regarding the role of the government as less important. Certainly, he suggests the possibility that the government may expand educational opportunities in order to solve the distribution issue, stating "to provide schooling and the hope, however fallacious, of escape into the modern sector, is often easier than, say, carrying out a land reform or otherwise redistributing resources in ways that might make life in rural areas more productive and more tolerable" (Dore 1976: 76–77). Nevertheless, what Dore mostly assumes is an academic credential inflation mechanism led by private demand, in which the government implements educational expansion in response to people's demands.

Of course, South Korea's educational opportunity equalization policies were implemented under a social pressure for educational expansion. However, those policies were sometimes so radical that they far exceeded society's expectations, because the government attempted to solve the distribution issue through these policies. Its excessive intervention in the distribution of educational opportunities had the effect of persuading South Koreans that educational accomplishment is the only way to achieve socioeconomic status and that the opportunity for such achievement is open widely and equally. It thus has encouraged people of all social classes to participate in the competition for acquiring academic credentials.[5] We suspect that the intense competition for acquiring academic credentials in South Korea is not only because South Korea was a late-developing country but also because the government utilized the education system to solve the distribution issues in general. It is for the same reason that the weight of the selection function imposed on the South Korean education system has become excessive.

[5] Kim Dong-Chun considers the government's full-scale expansion of educational opportunities to be a strategy to transform social class conflict into educational competition (Kim Dong-Chun 2000). Similarly, the popularization of competition for academic credentials has the aspect of national mobilization in a state-led system of development.

In order to solve the various educational issues South Korea faces, it is most important to ease the heavy burden of that selection function. Solutions to the social distribution issues need to be sought outside the school education. The school system should be reorganized based on its original purpose. Furthermore, the centralized and hierarchical character of the South Korean educational system needs to be reformed in order to deliberately reduce the availability of academic credentials as proxy indicators of intellectual ability.

Limitations of This Book and Future Tasks
This book has examined a wide range of issues, but like any study that attempts to examine a wide range of issues, it also has its limits. Three, in particular, should be mentioned.

First, the subjects of analysis in this book are mainly males, and females were insufficiently analyzed. In addition to restrictions on available data, the patterns of employment and status achievement during the period of the analysis for women are significantly different from those for men, requiring completely separate analyses. The opportunities for educational and status achievement for females need to be compared with the cases for males studied in this book.

Second, the primary objective of this book has been to present an overall sketch of South Korean education, social stratification, and social mobility, and therefore some specific issues were not discussed in detail. In particular, we should conduct a more detailed study on the mechanism of creation and reproduction of social prestige in South Korea from a micro perspective. This issue is deeply connected with the principle of social stratification in South Korean society.

Third, the scope of the study of the changes in South Korean society does not reach beyond the economic crisis at the end of the 1990s. The crisis triggered changes in people's optimistic perceptions of opportunities for educational achievement and upward mobility. Changes in the structure of employment, furthermore, are notable. Since the economic crisis, employment has become more flexible and the number of non-regular forms of employment has been increasing. In addition to the social status of an occupation, employment stability has also become an important criterion of job preference. Under these circumstances, the difficulty in finding decent jobs for four-year college graduates has grown serious. Amid rapid changes in the society and the prevalent mood of "reforming everything," the social structure of South Korea that we have described in this book seems to be undergoing significant changes.

Nevertheless, the distribution mechanism based on academic credentials is very likely to stay in place in South Korean society. In order to determine if our prediction is true, it is necessary to conduct a detailed study on the relation between academic credential on the one hand and status and rewards of employment opportunities, on the other, as well as on how people's aspirations for educational achievement will change from now on.

References

Note: Works with titles in characters in parentheses after the English title are in either Japanese or Korean.

1995 SSM Research Committee, 1997, *Basic Data Table of 1995 SSM Survey* (1995年 SSM 調査基礎集計表). Tokyo: 1995 SSM Research Committee.

2003 Social Stratification Survey Research Committee, 2004a, *Code Book and Basic Data Table of 2003 National Survey on Work and Life Style* (2003 年仕事と暮らしに関する全国調査コードブック・基礎集計表). Sendai: 2003 Social Stratification Survey Research Committee.

2003 Social Stratification Survey Research Committee, 2004b, *Code Book and Basic Data Table of 2004 Korean National Survey on Occupation* (2004 年韓国・職業に関する全国調査コードブック・基礎集計表). Sendai: 2003 Social Stratification Survey Research Committee.

Abe, Hiroshi, 1971, "South Korean Secondary Education Reform: Implementation of Admission to Middle School without an Entrance Examination" (韓国の中等教育改革: 中学無試験進学制の実施をめぐって), *Monthly Journal of Institute of Developing Economies* (アジア経済) 12:8, pp. 41–56.

Abe, Hiroshi, 1972, "South Korean Education after the Liberation" (「解放」後の韓国教育), in Munemitsu Abe and Hiroshi Abe eds., *Educational Development in South Korea and Taiwan* (韓国と台湾の教育開発), pp. 83–139. Tokyo: Institute of Developing Economies.

Abe, Makoto and Momoko Kawakami, 1996, "Transformation of Distribution of Corporate Size in South Korea and Taiwan: Does 'South Korea Have an Economy Led by Large Corporates and Does Taiwan Have an Economy Led by Small to Middle Size Companies'?" (韓国・台湾における企業規模構造の変容:「韓国は大企業, 台湾は中小企業中心の経済」か), in Tamio Hattori and Yukihito Sato eds., *Developing Mechanism of South Korea and Taiwan* (韓国・台湾の発展メカニズム), pp. 147–168. Tokyo: Institute of Developing Economies.

Abe, Munemitsu and Hiroshi Abe, eds., 1972, *Educational Development in South Korea and Taiwan* (韓国と台湾の教育開発). Tokyo: Institute of Developing Economies.

Ahn, Hee-Tak, 1993, "Korean Employment System" (한국의 고용제도), in Ui-Young Han and Takashi Sago eds., *Korea-Japan Comparison of Corporate Management and Labor-Management Relationship* (기업 경영과 노사 관계의 한·일 비교), pp. 291–319. Seoul: Seoul National University Press.

Amano, Ikuo, 1982, *Education and Selection* (教育と選抜). Tokyo: Daiichi Hoki.
Amano, Ikuo, 1983, *Social History of Examinations: Examinations, Education, and Society of Modern Japan* (試験の社会史: 近代日本の試験・教育・社会), Tokyo: University of Tokyo Press (English edition: *Education and Examination in Modern Japan*, trans. William K Cummings and Fumiko Cummings. University of Tokyo Press, 1990.)
Amsden, Alice H., 1989, *Asia's Next Giant: South Korea and Late Industrialization*. New York: Oxford University Press.
Arai, Kazuhiro, 1995, *Economics of Education* (教育の経済学). Tokyo: Yuhikaku.
Aramaki, Sohei, 2001, "Occupational Preference of High School Students" (高校生にとっての職業希望), in Fumiaki Ojima ed., *Quantitative Sociology of Current High School Students* (現代高校生の計量社会学), pp. 81–106. Kyoto: Minerva Shobo.
Arita, Shin, 1999, "Issue on Extra Curricula Activity in South Korea Society and '7.30 Educational Reform Act'" (韓国社会における課外授業問題と「7.30教育改革措置」), *Komaba Journal of Area Studies, University of Tokyo* (東京大学年報地域文化研究) 2, pp. 1–19.
Arita, Shin, 2000, "Phenomena of the Rapid Increase of College Graduates and Change in Wage Structure in the South Korean Society in 1980s" (1980年代韓国社会における大卒者急増現象と賃金構造の変動), *Komaba Journal of Area Studies, University of Tokyo* (東京大学年報地域文化研究) 3, pp. 43–61.
Arita, Shin, 2001, "Time-Series Analysis for Determining Factor of Demand for Advancing to College" (한국사회에서의 대학진학수요 결정요인에 관한 시계열 분석), *International Journal of Korean Studies* (국제고려학) 7, pp. 203–217.
Arita, Shin, 2002, "Emerging Process and Social Awareness of Middle Classes in South Korea" (韓国における中間層の生成過程と社会意識), in Tamio Hattori, Tsuruyo Funatsu, and Takashi Torii eds., *Emergence and Characteristics of the Asian Middle Classes* (アジア中間層の生成と特質), pp. 37–73. Chiba: Institute of Developing Economies.
Arrow, Kenneth J., 1973, "Higher Education as a Filter," *Journal of Public Economics* 2: 3, pp. 193–216.
Bae, Jong-Geun and Mi-Na Lee, 1988, *Reality of Korean Education: What Do Korean People Think?* (한국교육의 실체: 국민은 교육을 어떻게 생각하나). Seoul: Gyoyuk Gwahaksa.
Bae, Moo-Gi, 1982, "Structural Change in Korean Labor Economy" (한국 노동 경제의 구조 변화), *Korean Economic Journal* (경제논집) 21:4, pp. 571–621.
Bae, Sook-Hee, 1991, *Study on Korean Urban Poor Area* (한국의 도시 빈민 지역 연구), Ph.D. thesis, Department of Geography, Kyungpook National University.
Becker, Gary S., 1964, *Human Capital: A Theoretical and Empirical Analysis, with Special Reference to Education*. New York: Columbia University Press.
Bernstein, Basil B., 1990, *Class, Codes and Control, Volume 4*. London: Routledge.
Blau, Peter M. and Otis D. Duncan, 1967, *The American Occupational Structure*. New

York: Free Press.
Bourdieu, Pierre, 1979a, *La Distinction: Critique sociale du jugement*. Paris: Editions de Minuit.
Bourdieu, Pierre, 1979b, "Les Trois Etats du Capital Culturel," *Actes de la Recherche en Science Sociales* 30, pp. 3–6.
Bowles, Samuel, 1971, "Unequal Education and the Reproduction of the Social Division of Labor," *Review of Radical Political Economics* 3:4, pp. 1–30.
Bowles, Samuel and Herbert Gintis, 1975, "The Problem with Human Capital Theory: A Marxian Critique," *American Economic Review* 65:2, pp. 74–82.
Bowles, Samuel and Herbert Gintis, 1976, *Schooling in Capitalist America*. New York: Basic Books.
Bray, Mark, 1999, *The Shadow Education System: Private Tutoring and Its Implications for Planners*, Paris: UNESCO.
Byun, Soo-yong, 2014, "Shadow Education and Academic Success in Republic of Korea," in Hyunjoon Park and Kyung-keun Kim eds., *Korean Education in Changing Economic and Demographic Contexts*, pp. 39–58. Singapore: Springer.
Byun, Soo-yong and Kyung-keun Kim, 2010, "Educational Inequality in South Korea: The Widening Socioeconomic Gap in Student Achievement," in Emily Hannum, Hyunjoon Park, and Yuko Goto Butler eds., *Globalization, Changing Demographics, and Educational Challenges in East Asia*, pp. 155–182. Bingley, UK: Emerald Group Publishing Limited.
Campbell, Robert and Barry N. Siegel, 1967, "The Demand for Higher Education in the United States, 1919–1964," *American Economic Review* 57:3, pp. 482–494.
Center for Social Sciences, Seoul National University, 2004, *Change in Admission System: Who Will be Admitted to Seoul National University?* (입시제도의 변화: 누가 서울대학교에 들어오는가?), Mimeo.
Cha, Jong-Chun, 1992, "Structure and Process of Social Stratification" (사회계층의 구조와 과정), in Il-Chung Hwang ed., *Inequality and Equity of Korean Society* (한국사회의 불평등과 형평), pp. 71–140. Seoul: Nanam Publishing House.
Cha, Jong-Chun, 1997, "Occupational Structure and Distribution Inequality" (직업 구조와 분배의 불평등), in Hyun-Ho Seok ed., *Inequality and Fairness of Korean Society* (한국사회의 불평등과 공정성), pp. 95–126. Seoul: Nanam Publishing House.
Cha, Jong-Chun, 1998, "Occupational Prestige and Stratification Structure" (직업위세와 계층구조), *Korean Journal of Sociology* (한국사회학) 32:3, pp. 737–756.
Cha, Jong-Chun, 2002, "Recent Trend of Korean Social Mobility: 1990–2000" (최근 한국사회의 사회이동 추세: 1990–2000), *Korean Journal of Sociology* (한국사회학) 36:2, pp. 1–12.
Chang, Kyung-Sup, 2010, *South Korea under Compressed Modernity: Familial Political Economy in Transition*. London: Routledge.
Chang, Sang-Soo, 2001, *Social Mobility in Korea* (한국의 사회 이동), Seoul National University Press.

Cho, Gang-Hwan, 1979, "Collapsing Educational Field" (무너지는 교육현장), *Shin Dong-A* (신동아), May 1979 issue, pp. 214–223.

Choi, Bong-Young, 2000, "Historical Evolution and Characteristics of Educational Fever" (교육열의 역사적 전개와 성격), in Mahn-Seug Oh et al., ed., *Social and Cultural Structure of Educational Fever* (교육열의 사회문화적 구조), pp. 55–120. Seongnam: Academy of Korean Studies.

Choi, Young-Sup, 2003, "Analysis of Expected Wage Gap among College Graduates and Above by Major" (대학 이상 졸업자의 계열별 기대소득 격차에 대한 분석), *Korean Journal of Labor Economics* (노동경제논집) 26, pp. 97–127.

Chun, Taek-Won, 1978, "Extracurricular Tuition, up to 630 thousand Won per Person" (과외수업비, 두당 63 만원까지), *Monthly Joong-Ang* (월간중앙), January 1978 issue, pp. 268–279.

Clark, Burton R., 1962, *Educating the Expert Society*. San Francisco: Chandler.

Collins, Randall, 1971, "Functional and Conflict Theories of Educational Stratification," *American Sociological Review* 36:6, pp. 1002–1019.

Collins, Randall, 1979, *The Credential Society*. New York: Academic Press.

Davis, Kingsley and Wilbert E. Moore, 1945, "Some Principles of Stratification," *American Sociological Review* 10:2, pp. 242–249.

Dore, Ronald P., 1976, *The Diploma Disease*. London: George Allen & Unwin Ltd.

Editorial Department, *Shin Dong-A*, 1980, "Extracurricular Activity, Nothing we can?" (과외 공부, 속수무책인가?), *Shin Dong-A* (신동아), April 1980 issue, pp. 314–325.

Erikson, Robert and John H. Goldthorpe, 1992, *The Constant Flux: A Study of Class Mobility in Industrial Societies*. Oxford: Clarendon Press.

Fields, Gary S., 1975, "Rural-Urban Migration, Urban Unemployment and Underemployment, and Job-Search Activities in LDCs," *Journal of Economic Development* 2, pp. 165–187.

Fishkin, James S., 1983, *Justice, Equal Opportunity, and the Family*. New Haven: Yale University Press.

Fujita, Hidenori, 1979. "Role of Education in Social Position Achieving Process" (社会的地位形成過程における教育の役割), in Kenichi Tominaga, ed., *Japanese Stratification Structure* (日本の階層構造), pp. 329–361. Tokyo: University of Tokyo Press.

Fujita, Hidenori, 1998, "Consideration of the Structure of Occupational Image and Occupational Aspiration" (職業イメージと職業アスピレーションの構造に関する一考察), in Takehiko Kariya ed., *National Survey Study on Modern Japanese Social Stratification 11 Education and Occupation: Analysis of Structure and Awareness* (現代日本の社会階層に関する全国調査研究 11 教育と職業: 構造と意識の分析), pp. 119–147. Tokyo: 1995 SSM Research Committee.

Fujita, Takeshi and Tatsuo Watanabe, 2002, "Structure of Study Hour" (学習時間の構造), in Takayasu Nakamura, Takeshi Fujita, and Shin Arita eds., *Comparative Sociol-*

ogy of Academic Credential, Selection, and School: Japan and South Korea as Viewed through Education (学歴・選抜・学校の比較社会学: 教育からみる日本と韓国), pp. 91–112. Tokyo: Toyokan Publishing.
Goldthorpe, John H. 1987, *Social Mobility and Class Structure in Modern Britain,* 2nd ed. Oxford: Clarendon Press.
Granovetter, Mark S., 1974, *Getting a Job: A Study of Contacts and Careers.* Cambridge: Harvard University Press.
Han, Jun-Sang, 1990, "Disputes on 7.30 Educational Reform Action and Lee Gyu-Ho's Education Policy" (7.30 교육개혁조치와 이규호 교육정책 논쟁), *Disputes on Korean Society in 1980's* (80년대 한국사회 대논쟁집), Seoul: Joong-Ang Ilbo.
Han, Man-Gil, 1991, "Study on College Diversification and Unequal Educational Opportunity due to Higher Education Expansion" (대학 교육기회의 확대에 따른 대학의 분화와 교육기회의 불평등에 관한 연구), *Korean Journal of Educational Research* (교육학연구) 29:1, pp. 251–266.
Hara, Junsuke and Kazuo Seiyama, 1999, *Social Stratification: Inequality in an Affluent Society* (社会階層: 豊かさの中の不平等). Tokyo: University of Tokyo Press. (English edition: Junsuke Hara and Kazuo Seiyama, 2005, *Inequality Amid Affluence: Social Stratification in Japan,* trans. by Brad Williams. Trans Pacific Press.)
Hattori, Tamio, 1987, *South Korean Industrialization: Scheme of Development* (韓国の工業化: 発展の構図). Tokyo: Institute of Developing Economies.
Hattori, Tamio, 1988, *Management Development in South Korea* (韓国の経営発展). Tokyo: Bunshindo.
Hattori, Tamio, 1994, "Economic Growth and Formation of '*Chaebol*'" (経済成長と「財閥」の形成), in Katsuji Nakagane ed., *Lecture on Modern Asia 2 Modernization and Structural Change* (講座現代アジア 2 近代化と構造変動), pp. 239–266. Tokyo: University of Tokyo Press.
Hayashi, Chikio, ed., 2002, *Social Survey Handbook* (社会調査ハンドブック). Tokyo: Asakura Publishing.
Hong, Doo-Seung, 1980, "Two Channels of Social Mobility: Patterns of Social Mobility in Urban Korea," *Social Science Review* (사회과학논문집) 5, pp. 137–159.
Hong, Doo-Seung, 1983a, "Preliminary Consideration for Korean Social Stratification" (한국사회 계층연구를 위한 예비적 고찰), in Sociology Research Association of Seoul National University ed., *Tradition and Transition in Korean Society* (한국사회의 전통과 변화), pp. 169–213. Seoul: Bobmunsa.
Hong, Doo-Seung, 1983b, "Social Stratification Research through Occupation Analysis: Around the 'Korean Standard Classification of Occupations'" (직업분석을 통한 계층연구: <한국표준직업분류>를 중심으로), *Social Science and Policy Research* (사회과학과 정책연구) 5:3, pp. 69–87.
Hong, Doo-Seung, 1988, "Occupation and Social Class: Classification through Cluster Analysis" (직업과 계급: 집락 분석을 통한 계급 분류), *Korean Journal of Sociology* (한국사회학) 22:2, pp. 23–45.

Hong, Doo-Seung, 1992, "Distributive Justice and Equity Consciousness" (분배적 정의 와 형평의식), in Il-Chung Hwang ed., *Inequality and Equity of Korean Society* (한국사회의 불평등과 형평), pp. 141–170. Seoul: Nanam Publishing House.
Hong, Doo-Seung and Hagen Koo, 1992, *Social Stratification and Class* (사회계층·계급론). Seoul: Dasan Books.
Hong, Doo-Seung, Byeong-Jo Kim, and Dong-Gi Jo, 1999, *Occupational Structure of Korea* (한국의 직업구조). Seoul: Seoul National University Press.
Hopper, Earl I., 1968, "A Typology for the Classification of the Educational System," *Sociology* 2, pp. 29–46.
Hori, Kazuo, 1976, "Agricultural Policy in Korea under Japanese Imperialism: Formation of Colonial Landlord System in the 1920s" (日本帝国主義の朝鮮における農業政策: 1920年代植民地地主制の形成), *Journal of Japanese History* (日本史研究) 171, pp. 1–35.
Hosmer, David W. and Stanley Lemeshow, 1989, *Applied Logistic Regression*. New York: Wiley.
Hsiao, Hsin-Huang Michael ed., 1999, *East Asian Middle Classes in Comparative Perspective*. Taipei: Institute of Ethnology, Academia Sinica.
Hwang, Il-Chung ed., 1992, *Inequality and Equity of Korean Society* (한국사회의 불평등과 형평). Seoul: Nanam Publishing House.
Imada, Takatoshi, 1979, "Trend Analysis of Social Inequality and Opportunity Structure" (社会的不平等と機会構造の趨勢分析), in Kenichi Tominaga ed., *Japanese Social Stratification Structure* (日本の階層構造), pp. 88–132. Tokyo: University of Tokyo Press.
Inaba, Tsugio, 1993, "South Korean High School Reform: Focusing on Leveling Policy" (韓国の高校改革:「平準化」を中心として), *Education and Medicine* (教育と医学) 41:8, pp. 86–91.
Inkeles, Alex and Peter H. Rossi, 1956, "National Comparison of Occupational Prestige," *American Journal of Sociology* 61:4, pp. 329–339.
Ishida, Hiroshi, 1993, *Social Mobility in Contemporary Japan*. London: MacMillan.
Ishida, Hiroshi, 2004, "Entry into and Exit from Self-Employment in Japan," in Richard Arum and Walter Müller eds., *The Reemergence of Self-Employment: A Comparative Study of Self-Employment Dynamics and Social Inequality*, pp. 348–387. Princeton: Princeton University Press.
Ito, Abito, 2001, "Confucianism as a Restrictive Factor on Industrialization" (産業化の制約要因としての儒教), in Koji Matsumoto and Tamio Hattori eds., *Anatomy of the South Korean Economy: Was the Theory of Transition to Advanced Country Correct?* (韓国経済の解剖: 先進国移行論は正しかったのか). pp. 83–113. Tokyo: Bunshindo.
Jang, Soo-Myung, 2002, "Economics of College Education" (대학교육의 경제학), *Quarterly Journal of Labor Policy* (노동정책연구) 2:1, pp. 47–79.
Jeong, Jea-Hoon (translated by Tomohiko Kawaguchi), 1998, "Korean Human

Resource Management System at Transition Period" (転換期における韓国の人的資源管理制度), in Ohara Institute of Social Research, Hosei University ed., *Modern South Korean Labor-Management Relations* (現代の韓国労使関係), pp. 75–103. Tokyo: Ochanomizu Shobo.

Jeong, Jin-Ho et al., 2004, *Change in the Wage Gap among Academic Credential and Factor Analysis* (학력간 임금 격차의 변화와 요인 분석). Seoul: Korea Labor Institute.

Jung, Ee-Hwan, 1992, *Change in the Internal Labor Market in Manufacturing Industry and Labor-Management Relations* (제조업 내부노동시장의 변화와 노사관계), Ph.D. thesis, Department of Sociology, Seoul National University.

Jung, Jin-Hwa, 1996, *Popularization of Higher Education and Direction of Manpower Policy* (고학력화와 인력 정책의 방향). Seoul: Korea Institute for Industrial Economics and Trade.

Jung, Tae-Soo, 1991, *7.30 Educational Reform* (7.30 교육개혁). Seoul: Yejigak.

Kagoya, Kazuhiro, 2002, "Analysis of the Stratification Structure in Asian Countries Comparing Mobility Tables" (移動表比較によるアジア各国の階層構造分析), in Tamio Hattori, Tsuruyo Funatsu, and Takashi Torii eds., *Emergence and Characteristics of the Asian Middle Classes* (アジア中間層の生成と特質), pp. 235–259. Chiba: Institute of Developing Economies.

Kaneko, Motohisa, 1987, "Idea and Reality of Equal Educational Opportunity" (教育機会均等の理念と現実), *Studies of Educational Sociology* (教育社会学研究) 42, pp. 38–50.

Kaneko, Motohisa and Masayuki Kobayashi, 1996, *Education, Economy, and Society* (教育・経済・社会). Tokyo: Foundation for the Promotion of the Open University of Japan.

Kang, David C., 2002, *Crony Capitalism: Corruption and Development in South Korea and the Philippines*. New York: Cambridge University Press.

Kanomata, Nobuo, 2004, "Issue on Comparison in Social Science: Context vs. General Principle" (社会科学における比較の問題: コンテキスト vs. 一般原理), *Journal of Japan Society for Fuzzy Theory and Intelligent Informatics* (知能と情報) 16:3, pp. 208–214.

Kariya, Takehiko, 1991, *Sociology of School, Occupation, and Selection: Japanese Mechanism of Employment of High School Graduates* (学校・職業・選抜の社会学: 高卒就職の日本的メカニズム). Tokyo: University of Tokyo Press.

Kariya, Takehiko, 1995, *Future of Mass Education Society: Post War History of Diploma Society and the Equal Opportunity Myth* (大衆教育社会のゆくえ: 学歴主義と平等神話の戦後史). Tokyo: Chuo Koron Sha.

Kariya, Takehiko, 2001, *Stratified Japan and Education Crisis: From Inequality Reproduction to Incentive Divide Society* (階層化日本と教育危機: 不平等再生産から意欲格差社会へ). Tokyo: Yushindo.

Kerr, Clark, John T. Dunlop, Frederick H. Harbison, and Charles A. Myers, 1960, *In-*

dustrialism and Industrial Man. Cambridge: Harvard University Press.

Kim, Bu-Tae, 1995, *Academic Credential Society of South Korea* (한국학력사회론). Seoul: Naeileul Yeoneun Chaek.

Kim, Chae-Yoon, 1980, "Structure and Change in Korean Social Stratification" (한국 사회계층의 구조와 병동), in Korean Social Science Institute ed., *Study of Korean Society* (한국사회론), pp. 92–115. Seoul: Minum.

Kim, Dong-Chun, 2000, *Shadow of Modernity: Modernity and Nationalism in Korea* (근대의 그늘: 한국의 근대성과 민족주의). Seoul: Dangdae.

Kim, Gwang-Jo, 1995, "Expanding Opportunity of Higher Education and Change in Wage Gap Among Different Academic Credentials: 1980–1990" (고등교육의 기회 확대와 학력간 임금격차의 변화: 1980–1990), *Korean Journal of Economics and Finance of Education* (교육재정·경제연구) 4:2, pp. 313–334.

Kim, Kyong-Dong, 1970, "Managers' and Workers' Attitudes toward Work and Occupation" (관리자와 근로자의 근로관과 직업관), Kyong-Dong Kim et al., *Vocational Education and Occupation* (실업교육과 직업), Population and Development Studies Center, Seoul National University, Reprinted in Kyong-Dong Kim, 1992, *Korean's Sense of Values and Social Consciousness* (한국인의 가치관과 사회의식), pp. 109–197. Seoul: Pakyoungsa.

Kim, Kyong-Dong, 1979, "Managers' and Workers' Attitudes toward Work and Occupation" (관리자와 근로자의 근로관과 직업관), *Social Science and Policy Research* (사회과학과 정책연구) 1:3, Reprinted in Kyong-Dong Kim, 1992, *Korean's Sense of Values and Social Consciousness,* (한국인의 가치관과 사회의식), pp. 221–284. Seoul: Pakyoungsa.

Kim, Kyung-Keun, 2014, "Determinants of Academic Achievement in Republic of Korea," in Hyunjoon Park and Kyung-keun Kim eds., *Korean Education in Changing Economic and Demographic Contexts*, pp. 13–37. Singapore: Springer.

Kim, Mee-Ran, 2000, *Sociological Consideration for Structures of Higher Educational Opportunity and the Academic Meritocracy of South Korea: Around Social Stratification and Gender* (韓国における高等教育機会と学歴社会の構造に関する社会学的考察: 社会階層とジェンダーを中心に), Ph.D. Thesis, Graduate School of Education, University of Tokyo.

Kim, Nam-Sun, 1992, *Educational Finances and Educational Expenses* (교육재정과 교육비 연구). Seoul: Gyoyuk Gwahaksa.

Kim, Pil-Dong, 1991, "Preliminary Consideration for Establishing Social Status Theory" (신분이론구성을 위한 예비적 고찰), in Sociology Research Association of Seoul National University ed., *Social Stratification: Theory and Reality* (사회계층: 이론과 실제), pp. 447–465. Seoul: Dasan Books.

Kim, Yeong-Cheol, 1979, "Analysis of Students' Demand for Higher Education in Korea" (한국 고등교육에 대한 학생수요 분석), *Journal of Korean Education* (한국교육) 6:1, pp. 37–49.

Kim, Yeong-Mo, 1982, *Research on Korean Social Stratification* (한국 사회계층 연구).

Seoul: Iljogak.
Kim, Yeong-Mo, 1997, *Research on the Korean Middle Classes* (한국 중산층 연구). Seoul: Chung-ang University Press.
Kim, Yong-Gi, 1998, "Human Resource Reform in South Korean Heavy Chemical Plants" (韓国の重化学大工場における人事制度改革), in Ohara Institute of Social Research, Hosei University ed., *Modern South Korean Labor-Management Relations* (現代の韓国労使関係), pp. 125–144. Tokyo: Ochanomizushobo.
Kim, Yong-Suk, 1986, *Patients of Diploma Disease: Who are They?* (학력병환자: 그는 누구인가). Seoul: Minjok Munhwasa.
Kim, Young-Chun, 2016, *Shadow Education and the Curriculum and Culture of Schooling in South Korea*. New York: Palgrave Macmillan.
Kim, Young-Hwa, 1990, "Consequence of Higher Education Expansion" (고등교육 팽창의 결과), *Korean Journal of Educational Research* (교육학 연구) 28:3 Reprinted in Young-Hwa Kim, 2000, *Korean Education and Society* (한국의 교육과 사회), pp. 19–57. Seoul: Gyoyuk Gwahaksa.
Kim, Young-Hwa, 2000, *Korean Education and Society* (한국의 교육과 사회). Seoul: Gyoyuk Gwahaksa.
Kim, Young-Hwa and Han-Koo Ryu, 1994, "Time-Series Analysis of Factors Determining Demand for Advancing to Colleges: 1962–1992" (대학진학수요 결정요인의 시계열 분석: 1962–1992), *Korean Journal of Educational Research* (교육학연구) 32:1, pp. 79–101.
Kimiya, Tadashi, 1994, "Failure of the Inclusive Industrialization Strategy in South Korea: Structural Limit to National Autonomy of 5.16 Military Government" (韓国における内包的工業化戦略の挫折: 5.16軍事政府の国家自律性の構造的限界), *Review of Law and Political Sciences* (法学志林) 91:3, pp. 1–78.
Kimiya, Tadashi, 2003, *South Korea — Dynamism of Democratization and Economic Development* (韓国―民主化と経済発展のダイナミズム), Tokyo: Chikuma Shobo.
Kong, Eun-Bac ct al., 1985, *Scale and Return of Investment in Education* (교육투자규모와 수익률). Seoul: Korean Educational Development Institute.
Kong, Eun-Bae et al., 1994, *Study on Educational Investment and Return of Investment in Korea* (한국 교육투자의 실태와 수익률 분석에 관한 연구). Seoul: Korean Educational Development Institute.
Koo, Hagen and Doo-Seung Hong, 1980, "Class and Income Inequality in Korea," *American Sociological Review* 45:4, pp. 610–626.
Korea Consumer Agency, 1997, *Private Educational Expense and Mitigation Plan* (사교육비 지출 실태 및 경감 방안). Seoul: Korea Consumer Agency.
Korea Employer's Federation, 1994, *Korean Corporate Custom of Hiring New College Graduates* (한국기업의 대졸 신규인력 채용관행). Seoul: Korea Employer's Federation.
Korean Council of Economic Organizations, 1991, *Research on Korean Company's Promotional System and Salary Raising System: Around Issues on Wages and*

Employment Management (한국기업 승진·승급제도의 실태조사연구: 임금과 고용관리의 문제점을 중심으로). Seoul: Korean Council of Economic Organizations.

Korean Educational Development Institute, 1981, *Countermeasure for Mitigating Competitive Extracurricular Activities for Normalizing School Education* (학교 교육 정상화를 위한 과열 과외 해소 대책). Seoul: Korean Educational Development Institute.

Korean Educational Development Institute, 1993, *Study of Korean Educational Fever* (한국인의 교육열 연구). Seoul: Korean Educational Development Institute.

Korean Educational Development Institute, 1994, *Survey Study on the Korean Educational Attitude* (한국인의 교육의식 조사연구). Seoul: Korean Educational Development Institute.

Korean Educational Development Institute, 1997a, *Korean Education and National Development* (한국의 교육과 국가발전). Seoul: Korean Educational Development Institute.

Korean Educational Development Institute, 1997b, *Trace of Korean Education based on Statistics* (통계로 본 한국교육의 발자취). Seoul: Korean Educational Development Institute.

Korean Educational Development Institute, 2017, *A Window into Korean Education*. Jincheon: Korean Educational Development Institution.

Korean Education 30 Years History Compilation Committee, 1980, *Thirty Years of Korean Education* (한국교육 30 년). Seoul: Korean Ministry of Education.

Korean Education Decade History Compilation Committee, 1959, *Ten Years of Korean Education* (한국 교육 10 년사). Seoul: Pungmunsa.

Korean Ministry of Education, 1958, *Overview of Education* (문교개관). Seoul: Korean Ministry of Education.

Korean National Statistical Office, 1999, *Social Indicators in Korea* (한국의 사회지표). Daejeon: Korean National Statistical Office.

Korean National Statistical Office, 2018, *The 2017 Private Education Expenditures Survey Report*. Daejeon: Korean National Statistical Office.

Korea Rural Economic Institute, 1989, *Forty-year History of Korean Agricultural Administration (I)* (한국 농정 40 년사 (상)). Seoul: Korea Rural Economic Institute.

Kuramochi, Kazuo, 1994, *Changes in the Agricultural Structure in Modern South Korea* (現代韓国農業構造の変動). Tokyo: Ochanomizu Shobo.

Lee, Chang-Wook and Hyeon-Seok Kim, 1991, *Management Performance and Wage System* (경영 성과와 임금체계). Seoul: Korea Productivity Center.

Lee, Hyo-Soo, 1984, *Labor Market Structure Theory: Theory and Reality of the Korean Labor Market* (노동 시장 구조론: 한국 노동 시장의 이론과 실증). Seoul: Bobmunsa.

Lee, Hyo-Soo, 1991, *Popularization of Higher Education and Employment* (고학력화 현상과 고용). Seoul: Korea Labor Institute.

Lee, Jong-Gak, 2000, "Conceptual Reestablishment of Educational Fever" (교육열의

개념 재정립), in Mahn-Seug Oh et al., eds., *Social and Cultural Structure of Educational Fever* (교육열의 사회문화적 구조), pp. 7–52. Seongnam: Academy of Korean Studies.
Lee, Jong-Gak, 2003, *Proper Observation of Educational Fever* (교육열 올바로 보기). Seoul: Wonmisa.
Lee, Joon-Gu, 1993, *Study on Transition of Social Status and Occupational Position in Late Joseon Dynasty* (조선 후기 신분 직역 변동 연구). Seoul: Iljogak.
Lee, Jung-Pyo, 1995, "Study on Social Meaning of Academic Credential Appeared in View of Academic Credentials of Corporate Employers and College Students" (기업체 고용주와 대학생의 학력관에 나타난 학력의 사회적 함의에 관한 연구), *Korean Journal of Educational Research* (교육학연구) 33:1, pp. 163–179.
Lee, Keun-Moo, 1989, *Sociological Study on Employment Custom of Large Korean Corporations* (한국 대기업의 고용관행에 관한 사회학적 연구), Ph.D. thesis, Department of Sociology, Yonsei University.
Lee, Kwang-Ho, 1995, "Economic Approach to Educational Demand Analysis" (교육수요 분석의 경제학적 접근), *Journal of Korean Education* (한국교육) 22, pp. 105–128.
Lee, Man-Gap, 1957, "Occupational Image of Urban Students" (도시학생의 직업관념), *Social Science* (사회과학) 1, pp. 125–141.
Lee, Min-Jin, 2000, *Korea-Japan Comparison of Wage Determination System: The Different Situation of Negotiation System by Corporate* (賃金決定制度の韓日比較: 企業別交渉制度の異なる実態), Matsudo: Azusa Shuppan.
Lee, Sang-Beck and Chae-Yoon Kim, 1966, *Study on Korean Social Stratification* (한국사회계층연구). Seoul: Minjosa.
Lett, Denise P., 1998, *In Pursuit of Status*. Cambridge: Harvard University Press.
Lewis, W. Arthur, 1954, "Economic Development with Unlimited Supplies of Labor," *Manchester School of Economic and Social Studies* 22:2, pp. 139–191.
Lin, Nan and Wen Xie, 1988, "Occupational Prestige in Urban China," *American Journal of Sociology* 93:4, pp. 793–832.
Lipset, Seymour M. and Reinhard Bendix, 1959, *Social Mobility in Industrial Society*. Berkeley: University of California Press.
March, James G. and Herbert A. Simon, 1958, *Organizations*. New York: Wiley.
Mimizuka, Hiroaki, 1998, "Occupational Aspiration: Educational Selection and Aspiration Crisis" (職業アスピレーション: 教育選抜とアスピレーション・クライシス), *Youth Problem* (青年心理) 72, pp. 30–36.
Min, Kwan-Sik, 1975, *Revolution and Future of Korean Education* (한국교육의 개혁과 진로). Seoul: Kwang Myong Publishing.
Mincer, Jacob, 1974, *Schooling, Experience, and Earnings*. New York: Columbia University Press.
Miyajima, Hiroshi, 1995, *Yangban* (両班). Tokyo: Chuo Koron Sha.
Myung, Tae-Sook, 1998, "New Human Resource Management System and Female

Labor in South Korean Corporates" (韓国企業における新人事制度と女性労働), *The Journal of Business Studies: Ryukoku University* (経営学論集) 38:1, pp. 66–82.

Nakamura, Takayasu, 2003, "Educational Aspiration and the Warming-up/Cooling-down Process: A Comparative Study between Japan and South Korea," *Social Science Japan Journal* 6:2, pp. 199–220.

Nakamura, Takayasu, Takeshi Fujita, and Shin Arita eds., 2002, *Comparative Sociology of Academic Credential, Selection, and School: Japan and South Korea as Viewed through Education* (学歴・選抜・学校の比較社会学: 教育からみる日本と韓国). Tokyo: Toyokan Publishing.

Nakamura, Takayasu and Tatsuo Watanabe, 2002, "Family Structure, Family Environment, and Education" (家族構造・家族環境と教育), in Takayasu Nakamura, Takeshi Fujita, and Shin Arita eds., *Comparative Sociology of Academic Credential, Selection, and School: Japan and South Korea as Viewed through Education* (学歴・選抜・学校の比較社会学: 教育からみる日本と韓国), pp. 155–173. Tokyo: Toyokan Publishing.

Nam, Ki-Gon, 1999, "Cause of the Wage Gap by Firm Scale" (규모별 임금격차의 원인), in Moo-Gi Bae and Woo-Hyun Cho eds., *Korean Labor Economy: Issues and Prospects* (한국의 노동경제: 쟁점과 전망), pp. 183–201. Seoul: Kyung Moon Publishers.

Naoi, Atsushi, 1979, "Construction of Occupational Status Scale" (職業的地位尺度の構成), in Kenichi Tominaga ed., *Japanese Stratification Structure* (日本の階層構造), pp. 434–472. Tokyo: University of Tokyo Press.

Naoi, Atsushi and Tatsuzo Suzuki, 1977, "Social Evaluation of Occupations: Analysis of Occupational Prestige Score" (職業の社会的評価の分析: 職業威信スコアの検討), *Review of Contemporary Sociology* (現代社会学) 4:2, pp. 115–156.

Numazaki, Ichiro, 1996, "Laoban-Led Development of Business Enterprises in Taiwan" (台湾における「老板」的企業発展), in Tamio Hattori and Yukihito Sato eds., *Development Mechanism of South Korea and Taiwan* (韓国・台湾の発展メカニズム), pp. 295–318. Tokyo: Institute of Developing Economies.

OECD Education Research Group (translated by Junro Fukashiro), 1976, *Japanese Educational Policy* (日本の教育政策). Tokyo: Asahi Shimbun Company.

Oh, Mahn-Seug et al., 2000, *Social and Cultural Structure of Education Fever* (교육열의 사회문화적 구조). Seongnam: Academy of Korean Studies.

Oh, Ook-Whan, 2000, *Education Fever in Korean Society: Origin and Deepening* (한국 사회의 교육열: 기원과 심화). Seoul: Gyoyuk Gwahaksa.

Okada, Hiroki, 2001, *Yangban* (両班). Tokyo: Fukyosha.

Okamoto, Hideo, 1993, "Social Stratification" (社会階層), in Kiyomi Morioka, Tsutomu Shiobara, and Kohei Homma eds., *A New Dictionary of Sociology* (新社会学辞典), p. 751. Tokyo: Yuhikaku.

Paik, Il-Woo, 1990, "Research on Definitive Factors of Demand for Higher Education:

Around Graduates from Academic High School" (고등 교육 수요의 결정요인에 관한 연구: 일반계 고등학교 졸업생을 중심으로), *Korean Journal of Educational Administration* (교육 행정학 연구) 8:1, pp. 1–22.

Paik, Il-Woo, 1993a, "Demand for Higher Education (1)" (고등교육 수요에 관한 연구 (1)), *Korean Journal of Economics and Finance of Education* (교육재정·경제연구) 2:1, pp. 139–164.

Paik, Il-Woo, 1993b, "Demand for Higher Education (2)" (고등교육 수요에 관한 연구 (2)), *Korean Journal of Economics and Finance of Education* (교육재정·경제연구) 2:2, pp. 165–196.

Park, Hyunjoon, 2003, "Educational Expansion and Inequality in Korea," in David Baker, Bruce Fuller, Emily Hannum, and Regina Werum eds., *Inequality Across Societies: Families, Schools and Persisting Stratification*, pp. 33–58. Bingley, UK: Emerald Group Publishing Limited.

Park, Hyunjoon, 2013, *Re-Evaluating Education in Japan and Korea: De-mystifying Stereotypes*. New York: Routledge.

Park, Hyunjoon and Kyung-keun Kim eds., 2014, *Korean Education in Changing Economic and Demographic Contexts*. Singapore: Springer.

Park, Jin-Do, 1987, "Development of Landlord-Tenant Relation and its Structure in Post-War South Korea (I)" (戦後韓国における地主小作関係の展開とその構造 (I)), *Monthly Journal of Institute of Developing Economies* (アジア経済) 28:9, pp. 2–20.

Park, Jong-Min, 1997, "Reality and Ideal of Equality and Fairness" (평등 및 공정성의 현실과 이상), in Hyun-Ho Seok ed., *Inequality and Fairness of Korean Society* (한국사회의 불평등과 공정성), pp. 153–196. Seoul: Nanam Publishing House.

Park, Nam-Gi, 1994, "Alternative View for Understanding Korean's High Desire for Education: Education War Theory" (한국인의 높은 교육열 이해를 위한 대안적 관점: 교육전쟁론), *Korean Journal of Educational Research* (교육학연구) 32:5, pp. 185–205.

Park, Se-Il, 1982, "Effect of Higher Education Expansion on Labor Market (1)" (고등 교육 확대가 노동시장에 미치는 영향 (1)), *KDI Journal of Economic Policy* (한국개발연구) 4:4, pp. 149–170.

Park, Se-Il, 1983, "Effect of Higher Education Expansion on Labor Market (2)" (고등 교육 확대가 노동시장에 미치는 영향 (2)), *KDI Journal of Economic Policy* (한국개발연구) 5:1, pp. 26–52.

Park, Se-Il, 1984, "Cause and Changing Process of Wage Gap by Academic Credential" (학력별 임금격차의 발생요인과 변화과정), in Hwon-Gu Park and Se-Il Park eds., *Korean Wage Structure* (한국의 임금구조), pp. 123–178. Seoul: Korean Development Institute.

Phang, Ha-Nam and Sung-Kyun Lee, 1996, "Structural Change and Inter-generational Class Mobility in Developing Countries: In the Case of Korea and Taiwan" (신흥 개발국에서의 구조변동과 세대간 계급이동: 한국과 대만의 경우), *Korean Journal of*

Sociology (한국사회학) 30:3, pp. 575–604.
Psacharopoulos, George, 1985, "Returns to Education: A Further International Update and Implications," *Journal of Human Resources* 20:4, pp. 583–604.
Psacharopoulos, George, 1994, "Returns to Investment in Education: A Global Update," *World Development* 22:9, pp. 1325–1343.
Robinson, James, 1994, "Social Status and Academic Success in South Korea," *Comparative Education Review* 38:4, pp. 506–530.
Ryoo, Jai-Kyung, 1988, "Changes in Rates of Return to Education over Time: The Case Study of Korea," Stanford University, Ph.D. dissertation.
Ryoo, Jai-Kyung, 1992, "Time Variation of Return of Educational Investment" (교육 투자 수익률의 시간적 변화), *Korean Journal of Educational Administration* (교육 행정학 연구) 9:2, pp. 33–48.
Ryoo, Jai-Kyung, Young-Sook Nam, and Martin Camoy, 1993, "Changing Rates of Return to Education over Time: A Korean Case Study," *Economics of Education Review* 12:1, pp. 71–80.
Sandefur, Gary and Hyunjoon Park, 2007, "Educational Expansion and Changes in Occupational Returns to Education in Korea," *Research in Social Stratification and Mobility* 25, pp. 306–322.
Sato, Shizuka, 1997, "Unemployed with Higher Education in South Korea: '7.30 Education Reform, Act' and Labor Market for New College Graduates" (韓国における高学歴失業問題:「7.30 教育改革措置」と新規大卒労働市場), *Annual Report of the Economic Society, Tohoku University* (研究年報経済学) 59:3, pp. 109–128.
Schultz, Theodore W., 1963, *The Economic Value of Education*. New York: Columbia University Press.
Sechiyama, Kaku, 1990, "South Korean and Taiwanese House Wives and Female Labor: Prediction of Female's Future Labor Participation" (韓国・台湾の主婦と女子労働: 女性の社会進出の行方を占う), *Monthly Journal of Institute of Developing Economies* (アジア経済) 31:12, pp. 22–40.
Sechiyama, Kaku, 1996, *East Asian Patriarchy: Comparative Sociology of Gender* (東アジアの家父長制: ジェンダーの比較社会学). Tokyo: Keiso Shobo.
Seo, Gwan-Mo, 1987, *Study on the Class Composition in Korea* (한국 사회계급 구성의 연구), Ph.D. thesis, Department of Sociology, Seoul National University.
Seo, Gwan-Mo, 1990, "Korean Social Class Structure" (한국 사회계급 구조), in Peace Institute, Korea University ed., *Peace Lecture Volume 1: Conflict Structure of Korean Society* (평화강좌 1 집: 한국사회의 갈등구조), pp. 199–230. Seoul: Hangilsa.
Seok, Hyun-Ho, 1992, "Design of Research on Inequality and Equity" (불평등과 형평 연구의 설계), in Il-Chung Hwang ed., *Inequality and Equity of Korean Society* (한국사회의 불평등과 형평), pp. 49–69. Seoul: Nanam Publishing House.
Seoul City Board of Education, 1981, *History of Education in Seoul* (서울교육사). Seoul: Seoul City Board of Education.
Seth, Michael J., 2002, *Education Fever: Society, Politics, and the Pursuit of School-*

ing in South Korea. Honolulu: University of Hawai'i Press.
Sewell, William H., Archibald O. Haller, and Alejandro Portes, 1969, "The Educational and Early Occupational Attainment Process," *American Sociological Review* 34:1, pp. 88–92.
Shikata, Hiroshi, 1938, "Population by Social Status in Joseon Dynasty" (李朝人口に関する身分階級別的観察), in Association for Law and Letters, Keijo Imperial University ed., *Research on Korean Economy Vol. 3* (朝鮮経済の研究　第三部), Reprinted in Hiroshi Shikata, 1976, *Research on Korean Socioeconomic History* (朝鮮社会経済史研究), pp. 107–241. Tokyo: Kokusho Kankokai.
Shima, Kazunori, 1999, "Economic Analysis of Activity for Advancing to College" (大学進学行動の経済分析), *Studies of Educational Sociology* (教育社会学研究) 64, pp. 101–121.
Shin, Yong-Ha, 1991, "View of Social Status and Reform Ideas of Social Status System of Park Je-Ga" (박제가의 사회 신분관과 사회 신분 제도 개혁 사상), in Sociology Research Association of Seoul National University ed., *Social Stratification: Theory and Reality* (사회계층: 이론과실제), pp. 495–518. Seoul: Dasan Books.
Song, Jun-Ho, 1987, *Korean Social History: Study on Structure and Transition of Joseon Society* (조선 사회사 연구: 조선 사회의 구조와 성격 및 변천에 관한 연구). Seoul: Iljogak.
Song, Kwang-Yong, 1989, *Evaluation of Policy of College Student Quota* (대학정원 정책의 평가연구), Ph.D. thesis, Department of Education, Seoul National University.
Sonoda, Shigeto, 1998, "Japan-China Comparison on Occupational Evaluation: Findings from Contrasting SSM Data with Harbin Data" (職業評価の日中比較: SSMデータとハルピンデータの対比からの知見), in Shigeto Sonoda ed., *National Survey Study on Modern Japanese Social Stratification 19 Comparison of East Asian Social Stratification* (現代日本の社会階層に関する全国調査研究 19 東アジアの階層比較), pp. 21–40. Tokyo: 1995 SSM Research Committee.
Sorensen, Clark W., 1994, "Success and Education in South Korea," *Comparative Education Review* 38:1, pp. 10–35.
Spence, Michael, 1973, "Job Market Signaling," *Quarterly Journal of Economics* 87:3, pp. 355–374.
Spence, Michael, 1974, *Market Signaling: Informational Transfer in Hiring and Related Screening Processes*. Cambridge: Harvard University Press.
Stiglitz, Joseph E., 1975, "The Theory of 'Screening,' Education, and the Distribution of Income," *American Economic Review* 65:3, pp. 283–300.
Suenari, Michio, 1987, "Yangbanization in South Korean Society" (韓国社会の「両班」化), in Abito Ito et al., eds., *Modern Social Anthropology 1* (現代の社会人類学 1), pp. 45–79. Tokyo: University of Tokyo Press.
Suhr, Myong-Won, 1973, *Report on Renovating High School and College Entrance Examinations* (고등학교·대학교 입시제도 개선에 관한 연구보고서). Seoul: Council for the Reform of Entrance Examination System.

Takeuchi, Yo, 1995, *Meritocracy in Japan* (日本のメリトクラシー), Tokyo: University of Tokyo Press.
Taromaru, Hiroshi, 1998, "Occupational Prestige and Social Stratification: Social Stratification as a Semi-ordered Relationship" (職業威信と社会階層: 半順序関係としての社会階層), in Kazuharu Tsuzuki, ed., *National Survey Study on Modern Japanese Social Stratification 5 Structure of Occupational Evaluation and Occupational Prestige Score* (現代日本の社会階層に関する全国調査研究 5 職業評価の構造と職業威信スコア), pp. 1–14. Tokyo: 1995 SSM Research Committee.
Thurow, Lester C., 1975, *Generating Inequality*. New York: Basic Books.
Todaro, Michael P., 1969, "A Model of Labor Migration and Urban Unemployment in Less Developed Countries," *American Economic Review* 59, pp. 138–148.
Tominaga, Kenichi, 1979, "Approach to Social Stratification and Social Mobility" (社会階層と社会移動へのアプローチ), in Kenichi Tominaga ed., *Japanese Stratification Structure* (日本の階層構造), pp. 3–29. Tokyo: University of Tokyo Press.
Treiman, Donald J., 1977, *Occupational Prestige in Comparative Perspective*. New York: Academic Press.
TRI-KITA (Trade Research Institute, Korea International Trade Association), 2002, *Republic of Korea as Viewed with 202 Indices of Economy, Trade, and Society* (202개 경제·무역·사회지표로 본 대한민국). Seoul: Korea International Trade Association.
Tsuzuki, Kazuharu ed., 1998, *Structure of Occupational Evaluation and Occupational Prestige Score* (職業評価の構造と職業威信スコア). Tokyo: 1995 SSM Research Committee.
Turner, Ralph H., 1960, "Sponsored and Contest Mobility and the School System," *American Sociological Review* 25:6, pp. 855–867.
Umakoshi, Toru, 1981, *Study on Modern South Korean Education* (現代韓国教育研究). Tokyo: Koma Book.
Wade, Robert, 1990, *Governing the Market: Economic Theory and the Role of the Government in East Asia Industrialization*. Princeton: Princeton University Press.
Watanabe, Toshio, 1982, *Analysis of the Modern South Korean Economy: Development Economics and Modern Asia* (現代韓国経済分析: 開発経済学と現代アジア). Tokyo: Keiso Shobo.
Watanabe, Toshio, 1985, "Economic Development in Korea: Lessons and Challenge", in Toshio Shishido and Ryuzo Sato eds., *Economic Policy and Development: New Perspectives*, pp. 95–111. Dover: Auburn House.
Watanabe, Toshio ed., 1990, *Overview of the South Korean Economy* (概説韓国経済), Tokyo: Yuhikaku.
Welch, Finis, 1975, "Human Capital Theory: Education, Discrimination, and Life Cycles," *American Economic Review* 65:2, pp. 63–73.
Westphal, Larry E., 1978, "The Republic of Korea's Experience with Export-led Industrial Development," *World Development* 6:3, pp. 347–382.

Willis, Paul E., 1977, *Learning to Labour: How Working Class Kids Get Working Class Jobs*. Abingdon, Oxon: Ashgate Publishing Limited.
World Bank, 1993, *The East Asian Miracle*. New York: Oxford University Press.
Yamauchi, Koichi, 2000, "Establishment of Joseon Dynasty and System of Government by 'Yangban'" (朝鮮王朝の成立と両班支配体制), in Yukio Takeda ed., *Korean History* (朝鮮史), pp. 165–221. Tokyo: Yamakawa Shuppansha.
Yasuda, Saburo, 1971, *Study of Social Mobility* (社会移動の研究), Tokyo: University of Tokyo Press.
Yokota, Nobuko, 1994, "Change in the Labor Market Structure of South Korea in the 1980s: Around the Male Production Workers of Manufacturing Industry" (1980年代の韓国における労働市場構造の変化: 製造業生産職男子労働者を中心に), *Monthly Journal of Institute of Developing Economies* (アジア経済) 35:10, pp. 64–84.
Yoshida, Mitsuo, 1998, "Social Status and Social Group in Joseon" (朝鮮の身分と社会集団), in Mio Kishimoto ed., *Formation of Traditional Societies in East and Southeast Asia* (東アジア・東南アジア伝統社会の形成), pp. 215–234. Tokyo: Iwanami Shoten.
Youth Affairs Administration, Management and Coordination Agency, Prime Minister's Office, ed., 1996, *Study Report on International Comparison of Children and Family* (子供と家族に関する国際比較調査報告書). Tokyo: Printing Bureau, Ministry of Finance.
Yun, Young-Min, 1994, "Class Structure and Class Mobility in East Asia: A Comparison among South Korea, Japan and Taiwan," *Korea Journal of Population and Development* 23:2, pp. 257–282.
Yun, Jeong-Il, 1980, "Extracurricular Activity: What Is the Problem?" (과외 공부: 무엇이 문제인가?), *Educational Development* (교육개발) 5, pp. 18–20.
Yun, Jeong-Il, 1985, *Finance of Korean Education* (한국의 교육 재정). Seoul: Korean Educational Development Institute.
Yun, Jeong-Il et al., 1991, *Policy on Korean Education* (한국의 교육 정책). Seoul: Gyoyuk Gwahaksa.
Yun, Jeong-Il et al., 1996, *Investigation of Korean Education Policy* (한국 교육정책의 탐구). Seoul: Gyoyuk Gwahaksa.

Index

academic achievement iii, 8, 187, 209–10, 222; after-school classes and 87; aspirations to 1, 10, 79, 96, 125; belief in 5; resources for 3; social class origin 187; social mobility through 187; test 77 (*see also* educational achievement)
academic credential 124: distribution 203, 204; effect i; inflation model (Dore) 167; requirement 26, 141; employment by 184; hiring by 184
academic credential society 246
academic credentials 4, 9, 10, 20, 21, 124, 152, 169, 184; and age 230, 240; as proxies for general intellectual ability 185, 250; distribution of 156–57; effect of 7, 8, 200; in employment process 167; and internal promotion 226; nature of 81, 84; objective effects of 8; and occupation 139; and occupational opportunity 132, 167, 201; wage gap between persons 95; and wages 95; white-collar sector 227; of workers 131
academic high schools 64; leveling of 69, 71, 79, 84, 89, 119, 120, 204; original function 80
academic meritocracy 7, 243
academic performance 173, 185, 248; of children 212–13
academic selection systems 61
"academic-credential class system" 143
academic-credential-based distribution 247

academic-performance-related variables 175
achieved class 189
achieved social status 189, 212
administrative and managerial personnel 44, 141
admission system 202: change of 117; open 78; secondary schools 70; quotas 75, 88, 129; standards 90
admittance: possibility of 119
after-school classes 84–88, 89, 90; as not productive investment 87
after-school educational expenditures 115
after-school lessons 116, 149, 244
after-school private tutoring (*see also* tutoring; extracurricular study; supplementary study) 2
age 41, 61, 82, 84, 101, 103, 195, 197, 199, 228; as constant 195, 198, 200, 202, 227, 229; in recruitment advertisements 141; distribution 57, 58, 100–101, 124; economic status 230; effect 100; employment conditions 150, 201; intergenerational mobility 224, 225, 227; mean values of 190–91; school 63, 64, 65; and social class 224; as variables 196, 197, 202, 203
age bracket 105, 123, 124
age cohort 203, 204, 205, 206, 218, 219
age group 76, 100, 102, 112, 132; unemployment rate 135
aging, effect of: on social class 218
agricultural land reform 34, 39, 59, 72

271

agricultural sector 39, 40; population outflow 47–48
applicants ii, 27, 76–78, 80–81, 89, 91, 156, 158, 168–69, 241: to academic high schools 64; academic qualifications of 156; calls for 143; civil-service examinations 32; to colleges 123; female 122; to colleges 123; discharged from military service 143, 150; hiring just graduated 141; institution attended 148, 156; ability 91–92, 240; for middle school 67; number of 117; scholastic ability of 78, 155; screening of 238; utilizing personal connections 144; written examinations 148–49, 152
application rate 118, 120–22; fluctuations 118 (*see also* college application rate)
art high schools 69n
attitudes 145, 150, 159, 214; biased, of teachers 213–14; educational 245; Korean 239; parents' 212–13, 244; Survey on Korean Attitudes Toward Education 185; teachers 214

birthrate: of Korea 2–3
blue-collar workers i, 59, 226
blue-collar employment 59
business owner class 190, 192, 194–98, 202, 203, 205, 208, 216, 219, 221, 224, 229–31, 243

capital population: policies for reducing 149n, 154
capitalist class 22, 39, 47
career path 164, 176; college students 145; new graduate 132; subsequent 143
chaebol conglomerates 36, 40, 140, 155 (*see also* corporate groups)
cheonmin (underclass) 31
Chun Doo-Hwan regime 75, 84, 87
civil service 164: examinations 31, 32, 156; ninth-grade examination 157; positions 167
"class culture" 242
class origin 174, 189, 196, 217–21
class structure 24, 28, 39–41, 187–89, 212, 234, 242
classes, socioeconomic profiles of 187
clerical career track 158
clerical jobs 181
clerical positions 141
clerical work 41, 47, 56, 159, 193; by level of education 166; male high school graduates for 163; opportunities 141n, 166–67; preference for 172–73, 182; opportunities for females 141n
college admission: government intervention in 76; procedures 202; quotas 95, 119, 120, 121, 122, 125, 210; quota fluctuations 119; policy 99
college application rate 121–25
college diploma 19, 80, 138, 169; effect of 185
college enrollments: state control of 73
college entrance: "-centered" system 247; competition 79, 246; government control of 66; student's probability of 211
college graduates 5, 26, 95, 97, 111–12, 124, 132–33, 135–39, 153–67, 183–84, 196, 228, 239–40: "downward shift" 157; employment conditions 72; employment situation 154, 156, 159; finding white-collar jobs 135;

increase in number 25, 27, 99, 127–28n, 132; jobless 151; military service 150; new 143, 147, 150, 152, 184, 234; ratio by educational level 16; regional 149n, 154, 155n; unemployed 72, 152; unemployment 137–38, 151–52, 159; and wages 97–98, 100–108, 122–23
College Scholastic Ability Test (CSAT) 2, 77, 89, 248
colleges: disparities among 154; four-year academic courses 65; perceived disparities among 155; social issues 73
colonial rule 33, 34, 96
colonial period 22, 34, 35, 72
colonial-inheritance hypothesis (Park Se-Il) 96–97
commercial high school graduates 163–64
Committee on National Security 87
Company Life (*Ipsa Saenghwal*) 139, 141
company size 144, 153, 158–60, 226, 227
competition 10, 27, 69, 120, 247, 249; for acquiring academic credentials 249; between high school graduates and college graduates 167; for customer-service jobs 158; for employment; 148–49, 151, 153; entrance examination 169, 212; for gaining entrance to higher education 91; for higher education 201n, 239, 240, 246; social ills 67; compulsory education 67, 70
Confucian-style sellection 168n
Confucian traditions, influence of 4, 4n, 32, 97, 124, 245; values 97, 245; work ethic 52
conglomerates, family-based. See *chaebols*.
connections 201; advised to limit 148; for employment 143, 144, 162; personal networks 201; with the government 67n, 243;
constitution, of Korea 61–62, 63
corporate sector 39
corporate culture 145n
corporate groups 140, 147; large 151, 184, 226; college graduates rush to 157; and employment 145; employment examinations of 143; preferences for 162; white-collar jobs
corporate size 109, 145n, 146 (*see also* company size; firm size); explanatory power 111164
costs, educational 1, 23, 63, 66, 116, 123; of advancement to higher education 118; and benefits 114; after-school tuition 87; non-monetary 3; social 6; of training 20
Council on Reform of the Entrance Examination System 68
credit markets, informal 115
cultural capital 23, 24, 244
cultural reproduction theory 23
customer-service jobs 158–59

decision making: non-economic aspects of 113
Declaration of Democratization and Reform (1987) 107
demand: for advancement to higher education 123; for education 113; for higher education 11; and supply equilibrium of 125
democratization 36, 89, 107; movement 46
determination coefficient 203, 205,

229, 108–10
determining factors 194, 197, 201, 202, 204, 205, 207, 222, 228
developing countries 27
differential treatment of students 22
diploma disease 26
disparities among occupations 240
distribution industry 39
distribution: of academic credentials 156–58, 203–204, 211; age 124; issues 12n, 249–50; educational level, and labor force 84; educational opportunity 10, 205, 215; level of education 48; occupational 129–30; performance-based principle of 245; of preferred occupations 172; of productivity 19; sector 140; social resource 201; of social status according to academic credentials 22; of status and rewards 222; system 245; white-collar jobs 163
document screening 148, 149, 152
Dore, Ronald 26, 27, 96

economic conditions iii, 181, 232–33, 244; unequal 91
economic development 36, 70, 72, 73; Five-Year Economic Development Project 35; government-led 12n, 71, 243; link with educational policy 74, 90; measures 35; Park Chung-Hee regime 64; wages of manufacturing workers 108
economic disparities, in family of origin 23
economic factors 23, 233, 234, 246; college student quotas 119; and educational opportunities 246
economic rewards 50, 96, 230; higher education effect on 96;

intragenerational mobility 230; occupational prestige 56–57; relationship to academic credentials 96; relation to educational achievement 26, 239; for various occupations 44, 50, 59;
economic structure: dual 27; large-corporation-centered 145, 184; and labor mobility 35; South Korean 145
economy South Korean 33, 75, 123, 206, 245; as "crony capitalism" 36; during industrialization 39; labor-intensive industry 45; growth in 1970s 75; after 1988 147; Taiwan 243;
"education fever" 4n, 7, 7n, 8
Education Law (1949) 63
education policies 11, 66, 79, 207, 246
Education Reform Plan ("7.30"; 1980) 87–89
education system 237, 247–50: expansion 63; traditional 16; and unequal distribution 245
education, expansion of 1, 8–9, 15, 27–29, 63–66, 72, 81–82, 84, 102, 131, 155, 203, 206, 215, 222, 239, 244; consequences 10, 24–25; elementary schools 63; government role 249; higher education 210–11, 238; leveled off 246; Rhee Syngman regime 72; secondary education 79
education: age 226; effect on wages 103; length of 226; monetary benefits 103; years of 241
educational achievement 11, 24, 91, 202; aspiration for 237; and class origin 209; and farmland scale 203
educational advancement 207; expenses for 212
educational attainment 20; used as a

criteria for hiring 27
educational background 16
educational credentials 19, 34, 23, 108n, 127, 159, 233 (*see also* academic credentials) 125; and occupation
educational expenses 23, 63, 116, 214, 234, 244 (*see also* costs)
educational investment 112
educational level 3, 21, 198, 201; and social class origin 23
educational opportunities 23, 91–92, 206, 212, 214, 246; distribution of ii, 5–6, 17; cost 245; disparities in 7; equalization of 206, 241, 246, 249; expansion of 239; fairness in 84; formal equalization 246; market of 119; policies on ii; unequal distribution 91
educational system 8, 9, 11, 12n, 21–23, 66, 90, 128n, 202, 203: after Liberation 203
egalitarian educational policy 71, 79, 90, 233, 241
employers 197; and increase of college graduates 139
employment 4: advertising 141; competition for 149; downward shift 156; educational requirements 18; en masse by big corporate groups 144–45; examinations 148, 153; methods 139; non-occupational conditions of 13; school recommendations 161
employment opportunities 138–40, 144–46, 147, 151, 152, 156, 159–60, 184, 201, 251; of college students 146, 167, 184; colleges in Seoul 210; differentiation of 145; high-school graduates 167; horizontal differentiation 144; junior college graduates 160, 163; new college graduates 128; obtaining 42; preferences 139, 144–46 (*see also* job preferences); structures of 147; vertical differentiation 144, 159; women 98
employment practices: government intervention 149
employment rate 137; gap between colleges 154n, 155; low 138; new graduates 160
enrollment quota policy 73; control of 76
enrollment rate: elementary schools 63
entrance examination 67n, 137n, 169, 206n, 210, 213
entrance examination system 67, 155–56, 241; Council on Reform of the Entrance Examination System 68–70; reform of 155; trust in 168
entrance examinations i, ii, 75, 204, 270, 150, 247n, 249; competition 89; individual colleges 88, 89, 150; middle school 68; high school 69, 70; college 76, 79, 80
equal educational opportunities 202
equal opportunity ii, 6, 87, 149, 217, 234, 244, 246; "Equal Opportunity of Education" policy iv, 70, 245; for secondary education 206
exchange mobility 217, 241; openness of 221
extracurricular work 214; prohibition of 149

fairness ii–iv, 5n, 43, 85, 90, 91, 148–49, 244; distribution 237; social fairness 87
family background 172, 187–88, 202, 205, 206, 210–12, 213; effect of 211,

212, 221, 244
family: autonomy of 244–45; cultural capital 245; environment 213; origin, influence on educational achievement 23
farmer class 190, 196, 197, 212, 306; shrinkage of 216; few newcomers to 220; independent 40
farmland: ownership 33, 196; distribute 34
father's academic credentials 199, 200, 204; effect of 211
father's social class 196, 198, 203, 204, 207, 209; influence on income 228
feedback effect 95, 96, 97n
female applicants to colleges 122
female college graduates 141n, 145n
female high school graduates 122
female social mobility 190
finance: career path 145
financial burden 32, 63, 86 (*see also* costs)
financial conglomerate groups (*zaibatsu*) 140 (*see also* conglomerate groups; *chaebols*)
firm size 109, 110–111, 112 (*see also* company size; corporate size)
Fishkin's trilemma 244, 245
Five-Year Economic Development Project 35
formal egalitarianism 77–78
four-year college graduates: hiring of 101, 104, 107, 141

Gabo Reforms 33
general schools 175n
government (Republic of Korea) 1, 63, 90; budget 2
government control 123: college entrance examinations 80; college enrollment 73; educational system 66; higher education 71–84, 90, 92
government employee positions 144, 145
government policy, on education 66, 129, 214; on secondary education 77
government intervention: in selection 61, 66; in private employment practices 149
graduate school 1, 9, 82, 154, 204: career path 145
graduates, new college 143; 147, 152, 184; employment situation 159; ratio by educational level 165
graduation quotas 75
Gwangju Uprising 84, 87

Hayashi's quantification method analysis 177, 179
hierarchical division of labor 22
high school graduates 98, 99, 118, 135, 144, 163; employment rate 137–38; and white-collar jobs 132–34
high school students 11, 175n; attitudes 122; graduates of 104, 107; comparative study of Japanese and South Korean 175, 176, 178, 180, 181, 183, 185; Japanese 11, 170, 171, 178, 181; leveling policy 241
high schools: attendance rate 70
high schools: of Korea 64; leveling of 67
high schools: special professional (*teuksu mokjeok*) 64
high socioeconomic status 241
"high-income occupations" 211
higher education 11, 25, 84, 120: advancing to 170, 209; colonial Korea 72; completion ratio 81; cost of advancing to 118; demand for

117, 123, 125; equality opportunity for 245; expansion of 71, 72, 81, 238; gaining admission to 77; intervention policy in 72; investment in 125; investment in 115; monetary advantages of 95; monetary benefit 117, 118; non-economic variables 119; opportunity to advance to 119; policy 73; private rate of return 112–14, 238; rate of advancement to 73; ratio of enrollment 83; selection system 88; status without acquiring 188; students advancing to 65, 76; beneficiaries pay costs of 66; universal aspiration to 2
hiring process: large-scale corporations 146n; school recommendation 143–44; open recruitment 143; personal connection 143
Hopper's definition 78
household income 122, 123, 125, 205
housewives, full-time 181
human capital theory 17, 18, 95; approach 125
human capital, investment in 17
human resources 17; distribution of 16

income 4, 5, 42, 44, 44, 47, 52, 197, 199, 225, 232, 243; class origin effect 196; difference 46; disparities 224; distribution 52; educational credential effect 196; GNP per-capita 35, 63; levels 214, 233; increase of 211, 240;
independent farmers 34, 52, 54, 59
individual abilities: information on 91
individual, effort and ability of 4
individuals' occupation 31
industrial society 23, 215; theory 16, 218

industrial structure 221, 241; change 244; of South Korea 218
industrialization 15, 35, 41, 43, 50, 54, 97, 128–129, 220, 242, 249; speed of 35
industry 71, 72, 75, 145; demand for human resources 78; workforce 75
inequality: in education 214, 244; in educational opportunity 23; maintaining 23; in society 6; structure of 31; of status and rewards 71; structural factors 246
inflation of academic credentials 27
inflow mobility 223
information 18; in the labor market, complete 25; source 118; incomplete asymmetric 18–20, 222
inheritance 198; colonial-inheritance hypothesis 96; of cultural capital 23; means of production 197, 200
institution attended 152
institutional conditions 112, 169
institutional reforms 188
institutions: ranking 81; visibility 81
intellectual ability 22, 92, 168
intellectual occupations 52
intergenerational mobility 188, 192–94, 201, 215, 216, 217, 218–19, 220, 221, 234, 241, 244
intragenerational mobility 192, 193, 223–25, 227, 230, 232, 233
investment 17, 95, 112

Japan-Korea Annexation Treaty (1910) 33
jeonse (deposit) system 115
job competition model 19, 25, 101
job market: for new college graduates 138
job opportunities 139, 152

278 | Index

job preferences 144, 145, 175
job rank 141, 143
job-finding process 11, 150, 152, 161, 184
Joseon dynasty (1392–1897) 32, 33, 58, era 31
jung-in class 52n
junior college graduates 132, 144 163; employment rate 137; employment prospects 161
junior colleges (*jeonmun daehak*) 65, 75; PCEE required 77; graduates of 104; employment strategy 162

Keijo (Seoul) Imperial University 71
Kim Young-Sam administration 76
Kong Eun-Bae 114
Korea Employer's Federation 166
Korean Educational Development Institute 185
Korean Federation of Teachers' Associations 68
Korean industrial capitalists 33
Korean Ministry of Labor 44
Korean Standard Classification of Occupations 104
Korean War 34, 59, 72n
Kyungnam Junior College (Pusan) 162n

labor force 16, 45; college graduate 112; (new), educational composition of 124; participation rate 123
labor market 18, 25, 84, 91, 98, 103, 128, 184, 229; college graduates in 147; colonial rule 96; and education 96; model 95; as a "training (opportunity) market" 20; South Korean 97

labor movement 36, 46, 107, 108; disputes 111, 124; 1980s 109; manufacturing employees 112
labor-intensive industry 45
Land Survey Project (following the 1910 annexation) 33
landlord-tenant system 33
late development: effect 249
late-developing country, dual economic structure in 27
level of education 16, 23, 48–49, 70
Liberation (1945) 63, 71, 76, 81, 87, 96, 202
life-changing events 151
log-linear model 219
logistic regression analysis 174, 176, 207, 208, 225, 227

males 140, 154, 190; employed 195, 200
manufacturing 37, 164; industries 35, 38; positions 141; workers 46n, 109
Marxist theory 41
means of production, inheritance of 197
merit principle 17, 18, 70, 21, 23, 28; merit-based opportunities 23; social status achievement by 22
meritocracy 5, 201, 222, 233
middle school 67: admissions without entrance examinations 204; attendance 63; entrance examinations 67, 68; free education 62, 63; older established schools 63; running costs of 63; without examinations 67, 68
middle schools: no-entrance examination 69, 70; prestigious 71; policy barring entrance exams 71
military service 102, 133, 137, 143,

150; obligations 136
Mincer's method 103–04, 114
Ministry of Education 63, 68, 69, 79, 89; College Establishment Standards 72; enrollment quota system 73; qualification examination 77; education reforms 89; data collection 132, 134;
mobility 32, 226, 228, 232; structural 217, 220, 221; upward 6, 71
modern industries, in Korea 33
monetary benefits 100, 103, 113, 122–25, 237–38; of attending college 116;
monopsonistic discrimination model 96
multi-track job-rank systems 142

National Center Test (Japan) 77
neoclassical economics 18, 20, 25, 95, 103, 125, 239
Neo-Confucianism 32
networks, personal 201, 227n (*see also* connections)
new middle class 40, 47, 190, 193, 196, 219, 221, 234; income 225
non-economic conditions 97, 117, 125, 127, 212, 214, 234, 244, 245; on demand for higher education 123
non-labor income 198
non-manual occupations 142
non-market factors 139
non-white-collar occupations 55, 58, 159, 170, 172, 174, 175, 183, 193, 194, 238

occupation: agricultural and fisheries 190; business owner 190; discrimination on basis of 50; distribution 41; educational level 42; employed 189; manufacturing-related 38; self-employed 190; status identification 49
occupational opportunity: preferences 238; relationship to academic credentials 128–32, 167, 201, 240
occupational classification 57, 138, 172, 175
occupational mobility 193, 219n
occupational opportunity: disparities in 131, 135
occupational preferences i, ii, 170, 181; differentiate horizontally 183; vertical differentiation 183
occupational prestige 10, 50, 59, 233; structure of 54; in Japan 54; ranking 55–57; score 51, 199; structure 50, 170
occupational status 11, 170, 199, 238, 239; college graduate credential effect on 183; by educational level 19; effect of college graduation on 152; high 238: ladder 59; and individual's educational level 201
occupational structure 131, 240; change in 129
occupational value orientation 180, 181, 238, 248
odds ratio 220–21
old middle class 40, 190, 193, 196, 220, 223–24, 230
OLS regression analysis 228
open recruitment 143–44, 148, 161–62; by large corporations 153, 155
optimistic social perception iii, 214, 215, 230, 243–44

parents: engaged in the education of their children 2; economic status 23;

attitudes 212–13; occupations 172–73, 174, 242, 248; social class 201
Park Chung-Hee regime 35, 72, 122
personnel department 140, 155, 168
personnel management practices 143, 238, 239
personnel management systems 143
petite bourgeoisie class 47
post-Liberation generations 244
preferred occupations 172–73, 185, 248
Preliminary College Entrance Examination 77, 155
Prestige gaps 170
prestige ranking 240
prestige, educational 8
private schools 66, 68, 90, 247n
private tutoring 23
productivity 18, 26, 28; indicator of 19
professional career track 158
professional jobs 41, 141, 163n, 181; jobs in 41, 129
promotional speed 143, 164
public education system 2, 4, 86, 87, 88n, 91, 247
public schools 90

rapid economic growth 36, 56, 59, 140, 205, 220, 223, 243, 244
rapid industrialization 41, 232, 246
rate of return (*see also* higher education)
recruitment practices: by large corporate groups 147–48; change 150, 152; newspaper advertisements 141; process 153
regional college graduates 148, 154
regression analysis 108–10, 197, 199
reproduction of social classes 22–24, 187–88, 212, 214, 242
Republic of Korea, establishment of 34
resource distribution mechanism 250
rewards 10, 16, 18, 21, 224, 245
rote memorization 22, 67

salary growth 164
sales 39, 158; jobs 181, 141
sales workers 41–44, 45n
sangmin (commoners) 31
scholastic ability 70; employment selection based on 152, 247; examination 155, 168
Scholastic Ability Test for College Entrance 77, 80, 89, 155
scholastic achievement examinations 248; confidence in 247; test 81
school education, function of accumulating human capital 28; screening function of 28; system 11, 90, 245
school fees 120
"school pedigree" 9
school recommendations 155
science high schools 65, 69n
screening applicants 238
screening function 27
screening theory 18, 19, 27, 28, 80, 96, 184, 222–23
secondary education 130, 223: expanded enrollment quotas 71; open and equal opportunity 206–207; reforms to 71; selectivity 71; universalization of 70;
secondary industries 36, 37
selection ii, iv, 10, 78, 79, 91, 240, 247, 248; academic credentials 80; education as tool for 248; of employment 11; process 90; college entrance 96, 150; government-

controlled 78; United States 78–79
selectivity 71, 78–80, 91, 119, 120, 123
self-employed 48, 57, 96, 188, 197, 200, 222–23, 225, 226, 229, 235
self-employment 172, 182, 223, 227, 228, 234, 243
self-evaluation 232
self-fulfillment 179–81, 183
Seoul-vs.-regional college disparity 155
Seoul: colleges in 154
shipbuilding 35
skilled workers 41
small businesses 34
small to medium-sized companies 226
smaller companies 112, 157, 161–62, 184
social class origin 9n, 11, 22, 187, 188, 198, 241: effect 199, 201; and achieved class 221; and educational level 233; and educational achievement 234; father's education 205; influence on opportunity 222; reproduction of 187, 188, 242
social class structure, openness of 201, 217–18, 221; change of 220; reproduction of 214
social classes: profiles of 190 94
social image 199, 201
social inequality, perceptions of 242–43; reproduced through education 23
social issues: and expansion of higher education 82
social mobility 7, 9, 17, 34, 59, 78, 87, 241; studies 217; intergenerational 5, 6; intragenerational 6; upward 12, 187, 188; "pure" chances of 218; opportunities for 234
social prestige, reproduction of 250; gap i; reproduction of value of 238
social resources iv, 6, 12, 39, 43, 127, 243; distribution of 71
Social Statistics Survey 5
social status: achievement 22; identification 42–43; Joseon times 32; origin 11; perceptions 42; without high level of education 234
social stratification 5, 127, 190, 242, 250
social structure of South Korea 10; traditional 59
social-class origin 9, 9n, 22, 24
socioeconomic benefits 113, 237
socioeconomic conditions 172, 177, 181
socioeconomic position 4, 5, 7; primary determinant 9
socioeconomic rewards 16, 28; distribution of 24; relationship between level of education and 23, 24
socioeconomic status 15, 161, 87, 188, 228, 230; of individuals 24; and academic credentials 92; of employee 222; of student's family 214
special professional high schools 65, 69n
spccializcd schools 174n
standard of living 1, 169, 192
start-up capital 226, 228
state-run companies 164
status achievement 232, 243
status identification 230–32
status-achievement process 194
student quotas 83, 88, 90, 120; high school 120; policy changes 81, 84
study time 213
subjective assessment 174
subjective evaluation 230, 235
subsidiary companies 140, 145
supplementary study (*see also* after-

school classes); access to 8; ban on 85, 86; cost of 23; as social issue 85
supply-and-demand relationship 103
Survey on Inequality and Equity 43

technology transfer 35
tertiary industries 35, 37, 38
theoretical research 10
Thurow job competition model 26–28, 101–102, 124, 167, 239
time-series analysis 79n, 96, 117, 211
traditional Korean society 31–34
training 16, 20, 26; corporate group 140; elementary school teachers 65; middle-echelon technicians 70; "practical training" 144; vocational schools 75, 80
transition from manufacturing to service industries 40
tuition fees 214
tutors 69, 85–86, 90

unemployed 132; college graduates 72, 135, 137, 138, 152, 153
unemployment 35; among highly educated 127; among younger generations 135–36; college graduates 72, 138, 159; rate, in the 1950s 35
unified examination 80–81
unskilled labor 41, 46, 59
upward mobility 9, 50, 71, 91
urban industry 37, 129
urban population 34, 37, 39; social mobility of 216
urban self-employed 52, 57, 59, 188; class 40, 41; workers 46–48; path to achieving status 227; differences in income 228; sector 230

value orientation 176, 181, 183
vocational high schools 64, 70, 75
vocational schools (*jeonmun hakkyo*) 65

wage competition model 20, 25, 26
wage disparities 25, 97n, 104, 107
wage gap 59, 100, 102, 112, 120, 122, 123, 131, 196; college graduates 159; reduction of 106, 107
wage levels: dispersion of 110
wage ratio 108, 124; average 97–100, 104
wage structure 11, 45, 100, 116n; changes in 110, 114, 124; South Korean 9
Wage Structure Surveys 44, 103, 118, 131, 163
wage system 96
wage-adjustment mechanism 239
wage-increase effect 104
wages 6, 7, 20, 25, 26, 46; average 44; increase in 46; of manufacturing workers 107; relationship between academic credentials and 18
white-collar employment rate 159; high school graduates 167
white-collar jobs 131, 132, 138, 143, 169, 234, 242; desire for 159; high school graduates 164; preference for 163; rate of employment in 163; with a large corporation 140
white-collar occupations 108, 129, 170, 172, 182; preference for 174
white-collar workers i, 131, 164, 233
Wisconsin model 170
women 98, 123, 190, 250
working class 22, 40, 47, 190, 230, 234; income 225
working conditions 36, 38, 39, 227;

composition of 38
working-class culture 242
written examinations 32, 148, 149, 150, 152, 184; increased weight of 153

yangban class 31, 32 52n

yangbanization 33
Yasuda index of social mobility 217–20
years of education 104, 190, 202–12, 207
younger generations 109, 111, 124, 131, 135, 160, 193, 209, 221